THE PENGUIN DICTIONARY OF ARCHITECTURE

John Fleming was born in 1919 and was educated at Rugby School and Trinity College, Cambridge. His main interests are eighteenth-century art and architecture, especially British and Italian. In 1961 he published *Robert Adam and His Circle in Edinburgh and Rome*, which was awarded the Bannister Fletcher Prize and the Alice Davis Hitchcock Medal. He is completing a second volume on Robert Adam, and his account of the Rococo style is to be published in the Pelican *Style and Civilization* series.

Hugh Honour was born in 1927 and was educated at the King's School, Canterbury, and St Catherine's College, Cambridge. After working in the British Museum he became assistant director of the Leeds City Art Gallery. Since 1954 he has been working in Italy as a freelance journalist and writer. He published *Chinoiserie: The Vision of Cathay* in 1961 and *The Companion Guide to Venice* in 1965. He has specialized in later Italian sculpture and is writing a biography of Canova and a general book on Romanticism. His *Neo-Classicism* has already been published in the *Style and Civilization* series. He has collaborated with John Fleming in the forthcoming *Penguin Dictionary of Design and Decoration*.

Nikolaus Pevsner, who was born in 1902 and educated at Leipzig, is Emeritus Professor of the History of Art, University of London, and an Honorary Fellow of St John's College, Cambridge. He is an Honorary D.Litt. and has four other honorary degrees. He is a member of the Historic Buildings Council, the Royal Fine Art Commission and the Advisory Board on Redundant Churches. He was knighted in 1969.

Since its inception he has edited the *Pelican History of Art*. His numerous publications include over thirty volumes of *The Buildings of England*, *An Outline of European Architecture*, *Pioneers of Modern Design* and *The Englishness of English Art*.

THE PENGUIN DICTIONARY OF
ARCHITECTURE

JOHN FLEMING, HUGH HONOUR
NIKOLAUS PEVSNER

DRAWINGS BY DAVID ETHERTON

PENGUIN BOOKS

Penguin Books Ltd, Harmondsworth, Middlesex, England
Penguin Books Inc., 7110 Ambassador Road, Baltimore, Maryland 21207, U.S.A.
Penguin Books Australia Ltd, Ringwood, Victoria, Australia

—

First published in 1966
Reprinted 1967, 1969

—

Copyright © John Fleming, Hugh Honour, Nikolaus Pevsner, 1966

—

Made and printed in Great Britain
by Richard Clay (The Chaucer Press) Ltd,
Bungay, Suffolk
Set in Monotype Bembo

FOREWORD

This dictionary is the work of three authors. Nikolaus Pevsner wrote the entries about medieval and nineteenth- and twentieth-century architects, also the European and American national entries and most of the stylistic entries. He was assisted by Sabrina Longland in connexion with definitions of medieval terms, and by Enid Caldecott in connexion with modern technical terms. The rest of the volume was written jointly by John Fleming and Hugh Honour, who would like to acknowledge the help and advice they received from Ralph Pinder-Wilson of the British Museum (Middle Eastern and Indian entries) and from Peter Swann of the Ashmolean Museum (China and Japan).

The printed sources which have been used are too numerous to record in full, but the authors wish to acknowledge their debt to Thieme & Becker's *Künstler-Lexikon* and to the works of James Ackerman, Sir Anthony Blunt, Howard Colvin, John Harris, John Harvey, Henry Russell-Hitchcock, Sir John Summerson, and Rudolf Wittkower.

In addition to considering afresh the merits of the architects selected for biographical entries (and many more who were not), the authors have done their best to review all the various technical terms in order to provide closer definitions and a more consistent terminology.

The authors will be most grateful to readers who inform them of errors in the text.

A

AALTO, Alvar (b. 1898), among the most important living architects, and certainly pre-eminent in his native Finland, started neo-classically, in a typically Scandinavian idiom, c. 1923–5, and turned to the INTERNATIONAL MODERN with his excellent Library at Viipuri (1927–35), Convalescent Home at Paimio (1929–33), and factory with workers' housing at Sumila (1936–9, with large additions of 1951–7). He possesses a strong feeling for materials and their characters, which, Finland being a country of forests, inspired him to use timber widely. He also invented bent plywood furniture (1932). Timber figured prominently in his Finnish Pavilion at the Paris Exhibition of 1937 and in the Villa Mairea at Noormarkku (1938). Aalto's most original works date from after the Second World War. By then he had evolved a language entirely his own, quite unconcerned with current clichés, yet in its vigorous display of curved walls and single-pitched roofs, in its play with brick and timber, entirely in harmony with the international trend towards plastically more expressive *ensembles*. The principal works are a Hall of Residence at the Massachusetts Institute of Technology, Cambridge, Mass. (1947–9), with a curved front and staircases projecting out of the wall and climbing up diagonally; the Village Hall at Säynätsalo (1951); the Pensions Institute at Helsinki (1952–7), a more straightforward job; the church at Imatra (1952–8), on a completely free plan; and the Hall of Culture at Helsinki (1958).

ABACUS. The flat slab on the top of a CAPITAL. *See figure 64.*

ABADIE, Paul, *see* VAUDREMER.

ABBEY, *see* MONASTERY.

ABUTMENT. Solid masonry placed to counteract the lateral thrust of a VAULT or ARCH. *See figure 4.*

ACANTHUS. A plant with thick, fleshy, scalloped leaves used on carved ornament of Corinthian and Composite CAPITALS and on other mouldings. *See figure 1.*

Fig. 1. Acanthus

ACROPOLIS. The citadel of a Greek city, built at its highest point and containing the chief temples and public buildings, as at Athens.

ACROTERIA. Plinths for statues or ornaments placed at the apex and ends of a PEDIMENT; also, more loosely, both the plinths and what stands on them. *See figure 2.*

ADAM, Robert (1728–92), the greatest British architect of the later C18, was equally if not more brilliant as a decorator, furniture designer, etc., for which his name is still a household word. He is comparable in his chaste and rather epicene elegance with his French contemporary SOUFFLOT, but without Soufflot's chilly solemnity. He was a typically hard-headed Scot, canny and remorselessly ambitious, yet with a tender, romantic side to his character as well. Both facets were reflected in his work, which oscillates between a picturesque version of neo-classicism and a classicizing version of neo-Gothic. His work has an air of unceremonious good manners, unpedantic erudition, and unostentatious opulence which perfectly

Fig. 2. Acroterion, antifixa, and general view
Key:

1. Pediment   2. Acroterion   3. Antifixa

reflects the civilized world of his patrons. Appreciating that it would be bad manners, and bad business, to make any violent break with established traditions, he devised a neo-classical style lighter and more gaily elegant than that of the Palladians who preceded or the Greek Revivalists who succeeded him. He avoided startling innovations such as the Greek Doric for classical buildings or the pic-

turesquely asymmetrical for Gothic ones. He answered the current demand for a new classicism by enlarging the repertory of decorative motifs and by a more imaginative use of contrasting room plans derived largely from Imperial Roman Baths. In his cunning variation of room shapes and in his predilection for columned screens and apses to give a sense of spatial mystery, no less than in his neo-Gothic castles – so massively romantic outside and so comfortably classical within – he answered the taste for the picturesque. He became the architect *par excellence* to the Age of Sensibility, as BURLINGTON had been to the English Augustan period. His influence spread rapidly all over England and beyond, as far as Russia and America. His output was enormous, and only the unlucky Adelphi speculation robbed him of the fortune he would otherwise have made.

His father William Adam (1689–1748) was the leading architect of his day in Scotland and developed a robust, personal style based on VANBRUGH, GIBBS, and the English Palladians, e.g., Hopetoun House (1721 etc.) and Duff House (1730–9). His brothers John (1721–92) and James (1732–94) were also architects, and all three trained in their father's Edinburgh office: Robert and James attended Edinburgh University as well. Robert Adam's early work is no more than competent, e.g., Dumfries House (designed 1750–4). His genius emerged only after his Grand Tour (1754–8), most of which was spent in Rome studying Imperial Roman architecture under CLÉRISSEAU, with whom he also surveyed Diocletian's palace at Split in Dalmatia (later published by him as *Ruins of Spalatro*, 1764).

In 1758 he settled in London, where he was joined by his brother James after a similar Grand Tour with Clérisseau (1760–3). The columnar Admiralty Screen, London (1759–60), gave immediate proof of his ability and originality, but all his other early commissions were for the internal transformation of old houses or the completion of houses already begun by other architects. Nevertheless, his style rapidly matured, and the interiors of Harewood House (1758–71), Kedleston Hall (1759 etc.), Syon House (1760–9), Osterley Park (1761–80), Luton Hoo (1766–70), Newby Hall (1767–85), and Kenwood (1767–9) are perhaps his masterpieces of interior design. His meticulous attention to detail is revealed no less in the jewel-like finish of the painted decorations and very shallow stucco work than in the care he lavished on every part of each room from the carpets to the keyhole guards. No previous architect had attempted such comprehensive schemes of interior decoration. Although individual decorative motifs are often small in scale they are woven together with such skill that the general effect is rarely finicking, and although the same artistic personality is evident in each room the effect of a series is never monotonous. They perfectly illustrate those qualities for which he and James expressed their admiration in the introduction to their *Works in Architecture* (1773; 2nd vol. 1779; 3rd vol. 1822): movement or 'the rise and fall, the advance and recess and other diversity of forms' and 'a variety of light mouldings'. His neo-classicism is most evident in the planning of Syon with its varied geometric shapes (basilican hall, rotunda, projected central Pantheon, etc.), and on the south front of Kedleston, modelled on a Roman triumphal arch.

His originality and ingenuity in planning culminated in his London houses of the 1770s – e.g., 20 St James's Square, 20 Portman Square – in which, however, the decoration became increasingly shallow and linear, tending towards the flippancy and frippery for which he was much

criticized towards the end of his life.

Between 1768 and 1772 he and James embarked on their most ambitious enterprise, the Adelphi, a vast palatial group of houses on the banks of the Thames (now destroyed). Unfortunately the speculation failed and they were saved from bankruptcy only by the expedient of a lottery and by loans from their elder brother John in Edinburgh.

Partly as a result of the Adelphi fiasco the quality of Robert Adam's work declined sharply after 1775. But it recovered amazingly during the last decade of his life under the stimulus of large commissions in Edinburgh – the University (begun 1789, completed by W. H. Playfair to modified designs 1815–34) and Charlotte Square (designed 1791). The entrance front to the University is his most monumental building and perhaps his masterpiece as an architect. To the same period belong most of his sham castles, e.g., Culzean Castle (1777–90) and Seton Castle (1789–91), which were much in advance of their date. His earlier neo-Gothic style, e.g., the interiors of Alnwick Castle (*c.* 1770, now destroyed), had been similar in its sophisticated elegance to his neo-classical style. Now he developed a much bolder manner. At Culzean he took full advantage of a dramatic site on the Ayrshire coast for a martial display of round towers and battlements embracing rooms of feminine delicacy inside. The charm of the place lies in this contrast, which would have been greatly relished by the C18 Man of Sensibility, who could here enjoy the chilling horror of storms at sea from an eminently safe and civilized interior.

ADDORSED. An adjective applied to two figures, usually animals, placed symmetrically back to back; often found on CAPITALS.

ADOBE. Unburnt brick dried in the sun, commonly used for building in Spain and Latin America.

ADYTUM. The inner sanctuary of a Greek temple whence oracles were delivered; also, more loosely, any private chamber or sanctuary.

AEDICULE. Properly a shrine framed by two columns supporting an ENTABLATURE and PEDIMENT, set in a temple and containing a statue; but also, more loosely, the framing of a door, window, or other opening with two columns and an entablature and pediment.

AFFRONTED. An adjective applied to two figures, usually animals, placed symmetrically facing each other; often found on CAPITALS.

AGORA. The open space in a Greek or Roman town used as a market place or general meeting-place, usually surrounded by porticos as in a FORUM.

AICHEL, Giovanni Santini (1667–1723). A Bohemian architect of Italian extraction who worked sometimes in a Baroque (derived from BORROMINI and GUARINI) and sometimes in a neo-Gothic style. His speciality was the latter, a carpenter's Gothic, gay, naïve, and very personal, with a predilection for star-shaped forms (derived from Borromini) in his elegant and airy vaulting: e.g., Marienkirche, Kladrau (1712–26), and the churches at Seelau (begun 1712) and Saar (1719–22). But he was a freak, and had no influence or followers at all.

AISLE. Part of a church, parallel to, and divided by piers or columns – or in rare cases by a screen wall – from the nave, choir, or transept. See figure 10.

ALAN OF WALSINGHAM. Sacrist of Ely Cathedral at the time when the new Lady Chapel was begun (1321) and the tower over the Norman crossing collapsed (1322) and was replaced by the celebrated octagon. From the documents it is almost certain that the bold idea of replacing the square crossing tower by a larger octagon was his.

ÁLAVA, see JUAN DE ÁLAVA.

ALBERTI, Leone Battista (1404–72). Playwright, musician, painter, mathematician, scientist, and athlete as well as architect and architectural theorist, he came nearer than anyone to the Renaissance ideal of a 'complete man'. Aristocratic by temperament, he was the first great dilettante architect. He confined himself to designing, and had nothing to do with the actual building of his works. But his few buildings are all masterpieces, and his De re aedificatoria (1452, fully published 1485) is the first architectural treatise of the Renaissance. It crystallized current ideas on proportion, the orders, and ideal (symbolic) planning. But though he began with theory his buildings are surprisingly unpedantic and undogmatic. They progressed from the nostalgically archaeological to the boldly experimental. Perhaps his dilettante status allowed him greater freedom than his professional contemporaries. He designed only six buildings and saw only three of them completed. To some extent he was indebted to BRUNELLESCHI, whom he knew personally and to whom (among others) he dedicated his treatise Della pittura (1436), but whereas Brunelleschi's buildings were elegantly linear his were massively plastic. Architectural beauty he defined as 'the harmony and concord of all the parts achieved in such a manner that nothing could be added, or taken away, or altered except for the worse' and ornament as 'a kind of additional brightness and improvement of Beauty'. By ornament he meant the classical vocabulary of orders, columns, pilasters, and architraves which he always used correctly and grammatically but frequently out of context, e.g., his columns always support architraves (not arches), but are frequently merely decorative and without real structural purpose. His most notable and influential achievement was the adaptation of classical elements to the wall architecture of the Renaissance.

The illegitimate son of a Florentine exile, he was probably born in Genoa.

Educated in the humanist atmosphere of Padua, he later studied law at Bologna university and visited Florence for the first time in 1428. In 1431 he went to Rome, where he joined the Papal civil service which apparently allowed him ample time for both travel and the cultivation of his various talents. As Papal inspector of monuments (1447–55) he 'restored' and radically altered the C5 circular church of S. Stefano Rotondo, Rome. His first independent work was the façade of Palazzo Rucellai, Florence (1446–51, executed by Bernardo ROSSELLINO). With rusticated walls articulated by three superimposed orders of pilasters (Ionic and Corinthian very freely interpreted), it is indebted to Brunelleschi's Palazzo di Parte Guelfa. But it has certain novelties, e.g., square-headed door-cases, a vast cornice instead of eaves, and double windows with pilasters and a central column supporting an architrave beneath the rounded cap. The exquisite adjustment of the proportions distinguishes the palace from that designed and built in emulation of it at Pienza by Rossellino. In 1450 he was commissioned to transform the Gothic church of S. Francesco, Rimini, into a memorial to the local tyrant Sigismondo Malatesta, his wife, and courtiers. It was subsequently called the Tempio Malatestiano. He designed a marble shell to encase the old building, the front freely based on a Roman triumphal arch (symbolizing the triumph over death), the side walls pierced by deep arched niches each containing a sarcophagus. The front was never finished, and it is now difficult to visualize how he intended to mask the upper part of the old Gothic façade. As it stands it is a magnificent fragment, one of the noblest and most poignant evocations of the grandeur, *gravitas*, and decorum of Roman architecture. His next work was another addition to a Gothic church, the completion of the façade of S.

Maria Novella, Florence (1456–70). Entirely coated with an inlay of different coloured marbles, it owes as much to the C11–12 church of S. Miniato, Florence, as to any Roman building, though the central doorway is derived from the Pantheon. But the whole design is based on a complex geometrical arrangement of squares, and is thus the first instance of the use of HARMONIC PROPORTIONS in the Renaissance. The upper part of the façade is in the form of a pedimented temple front linked to the sides by great scrolls which were to be much copied in later periods. It was commissioned by Giovanni Rucellai whose name is inscribed across the top with typical Renaissance confidence. For the same patron he designed the exquisite, casket-like little marble-clad shrine of the Holy Sepulchre (1467) and perhaps also the Cappella Rucellai, Florence, in which it stands.

S. Sebastiano (1460) and S. Andrea (1470), both at Mantua, are the only buildings which he designed entire. For S. Sebastiano he chose a centralized Greek cross plan and designed the massively austere façade as a pilastered temple front approached up a wide flight of steps. But he broke the entablature with a round-headed window (derived from the Roman arch of Tiberius at Orange, *c.* 30 B.C.) and increased its severity by reducing the pilasters from six to four. This alteration and his complete rejection of columns marks his increasing tendency to stray from correct classical usage in the creation of a more logical wall architecture. The church was completed, with further alterations, after his death. At S. Andrea his plans were carried out more faithfully, though the dome he designed to cover the crossing was never executed. The façade is a combination of a pedimented temple front and a triumphal arch, with shallow pilasters in place of columns and a deep central recess framing the main door. Inside he abandoned the traditional aisle structure for a barrel-vaulted nave flanked by side chapels. Interior and exterior are carefully integrated. The sides of the nave, with pilastered solids and arched recesses alternating, repeat the rhythmical pattern and the Triumphal Arch of the façade on exactly the same scale. These two buildings herald a new and less archaeological attitude to antiquity. They reach forward from the Early to the High Renaissance and even beyond.

ALEIJADINHO (António Francisco Lisboa, 1738–1814). The greatest Brazilian sculptor and architect. A mulatto (illegitimate son of a Portuguese architect), he worked in the rich gold-mining province of Minas Gerais, and combined barbarically rich and contorted sculptural decoration with the more dignified architectural forms of traditional Lusitanian church design. His masterpieces are São Francisco, Ouro Preto (1766–94), and the monumental scenic staircase in front of Bom Jesus de Matozinhos, Congonhas do Campo (1800–5).

ALESSI, Galeazzo (1512–72). The leading High Renaissance architect in Genoa. Born in Perugia and trained in Rome where he was much influenced by MICHELANGELO, he settled in Genoa by 1548. He was adept at turning difficult sloping sites to advantage, and made great play with monumental staircases, colonnades, and courtyards on different levels. His several palaces, notably Villa Cambiaso (1548), Palazzo Cambiaso (1565, now Banco d'Italia), and Palazzo Parodi (1567), set the pattern for Genoese domestic architecture. He also built the imposing S. Maria di Carignano, Genoa (1552), based on BRAMANTE's design for St Peter's.

ALFIERI, Benedetto (1700–67), a Piedmontese nobleman (uncle of the poet), began as a lawyer, turned to architecture, and succeeded JUVARRA as royal architect in Turin (1739). He was largely employed in completing Juvarra's work in Palazzo Reale, Turin, and elsewhere. His main independent building is the vast parish church at Carignano (1757–64), with a severe façade and very rich interior on a peculiar kidney-shaped plan.

ALGARDI, Alessandro (1595–1654). Born in Bologna but settled in Rome, best known as a sculptor, representing the sobriety of Bolognese classicism in opposition to BERNINI. His reputation as an architect rests on the Villa Doria-Pamphili in Rome of which he had the general direction, though it seems to have been designed by G. F. Grimaldi.

ALMONRY. The room in a MONASTERY in which alms are distributed.

ALTAR. A table or slab on supports consecrated for celebration of the sacrament; usually of stone. In the Middle Ages portable altars could be of metal. After the Reformation communion tables of wood replaced altars in England.

ALTAR-TOMB. A post-medieval term for a tomb resembling an altar with solid sides but not used as one. See TOMB-CHEST.

AMADEO, Giovanni Antonio (1447–1522). Born in Pavia, and primarily a sculptor, he was working at the Certosa there by 1466; then he worked in Milan (MICHELOZZO's Portinari Chapel in S. Eustorgio), where he encountered the Early Renaissance style. The immediate result was the Colleoni Chapel (1472–6) attached to S. Maria Maggiore, Bergamo – based on the Portinari chapel but encrusted with Renaissance ornamentation in Gothic profusion. He designed the lower storey of the façade of the Certosa outside Pavia (1474) in a similar manner. From 1500 onwards he worked on Milan Cathedral (retardataire Gothic in style).

AMBO. A stand raised on two or more steps, for the reading of the Epistle and the Gospel; a prominent feature in medieval Italian churches. Sometimes two were built, one for the Epistle and one for the Gospel, on the south and north sides respectively. After the C14 the ambo was replaced by the PULPIT.

AMBULATORY. A semicircular or polygonal aisle enclosing an APSE or a straight-ended sanctuary; originally used for processional purposes.

AMMANATI, Bartolomeo (1511–92), was primarily a Mannerist sculptor. His architectural masterpiece is the very graceful Ponte S. Trinità, Florence (1567–70, destroyed 1944 but rebuilt). With VIGNOLA and VASARI he played some part in designing Villa Giulia, Rome (1552). He enlarged and altered Palazzo Pitti, Florence (1558–70), building the almost grotesquely over-rusticated garden façade. In Lucca he designed part of the Palazzo Provinciale (1578) with a handsome Serlian loggia.

AMPHIPROSTYLE. The adjective applied to a temple with porticos at each end, but without columns along the sides.

AMPHITHEATRE. An elliptical or circular space surrounded by rising tiers of seats, as used by the Romans for gladiatorial contests.

ANCONES. 1. Brackets or CONSOLES on either side of a doorway, supporting a CORNICE. 2. The projections left on blocks of stone, such as the drums of a column, to hoist them into position.

ANGLO-SAXON ARCHITECTURE. Most Anglo-Saxon architecture must have been of wood; but no secular buildings survive, and there exists only one, log-built, church – Greensted (c. 1013). The earliest Anglo-Saxon stone churches belong to the C7 and fall into two groups, one in the south-east, characterized by apses and a triple arcade dividing the choir from the nave, the other in the north, with long, tall, narrow nave and straight-ended chancel: the first group includes St Pancras and St Martin at Canterbury, Reculver, and Bradwell-on-Sea; the latter, Monkwearmouth, Jarrow, and Escomb. None of these

has aisles, but instead they have side chambers called *porticus*. Towers did not exist, but there were west porches. Between the two groups stand Brixworth in Northamptonshire, larger than the others and with aisles, and Bradford-on-Avon in Wiltshire. But the typically Anglo-Saxon decoration of Bradford, with its pilaster-strips, flat blank arches, triangles instead of arches – the whole applied like the timbering of timber-framed work – is as late as the C10 and is indeed the most prominent decorative feature of later Anglo-Saxon architecture. Towers seem to have made their appearance in the C10 too; they are either at the west end or placed centrally between nave and chancel. Highly decorated examples are to be found at Earls Barton and Barton-on-Humber. Transepts also appear, and aisles become a little more frequent. Many churches of the later C11 have Anglo-Saxon side by side with Norman motifs; the mixture is called the *Saxo-Norman overlap*.

ANNULET, *see* SHAFT-RING.

ANSE DE PANIER, *see* ARCH.

ANTA. A PILASTER of which the base and CAPITAL do not conform with the ORDER used elsewhere on the building; it is usually placed at a corner.

ANTECHURCH (or FORECHURCH). An appendix to the west end of a church, resembling a porch or a NARTHEX, but several bays deep and usually consisting of nave and aisles.

ANTEPENDIUM. A covering for the front of an altar, usually of metal or fabric.

ANTHEMION. Ornament based on the honeysuckle flower and leaves, common in Greek and Roman architecture. *See figure 3.*

Fig. 3. Anthemion and palmette

ANTHEMIUS OF TRALLES. Geometrician and theorist rather than architect, he is known for sure to have designed only one building, but that among the greatest in the world: Haghia Sophia, Constantinople (A.D. 532–7). The dates of his birth and death are unknown. Born at Tralles in Lydia, he came of a Greek professional middle-class family; his father was a physician. In 532 Justinian chose him to design the new church of Holy Wisdom (Haghia Sophia) to replace a predecessor which had been burnt in riots. This vast undertaking was completed in the incredibly brief period of five years, to the gratification of Justinian who claimed to have surpassed Solomon. Anthemius described architecture as 'the application of geometry to solid matter', and his great work with its dome 107 ft in diameter is remarkable as a feat of engineering. But it is also much more, for by the cunning use of screened aisles and galleries around the central area of the church he concealed the supports of the dome which thus seems to float above the building, creating an atmosphere of mystery emphasized by the contrast between the light central space and the dark aisles. He was assisted by ISIDORE OF MILETUS.

ANTIFIXAE. Ornamental blocks on the edge of a roof to conceal the ends of the tiles. *See figure 2.*

ANTOINE, Jacques-Denis (1733–1801). A leading architect in the reign of Louis XVI. His masterpiece is the Mint, Paris (designed 1768, begun 1771) – huge, solemn, and very Roman, though he did not visit Italy until 1777. He used Paestum Doric for the peristyle of the Charité Chapel, Paris (1778–81), but his other works are less sternly neo-classical.

ANTONELLI, Alessandro (1798–1888). Professor of Architecture at Turin from 1836 till 1857. His most famous works are the crazily high, externally classical and internally iron-supported towers of the so-called Mole Antonelliana at Turin (originally intended as a synagogue and about 550 ft high) and of the cathedral of Novara (about 420 ft high). The former was designed in 1863, the latter in 1840.

APEX STONE. The top stone in a GABLE end, sometimes called the *saddle stone.*

APOLLODORUS OF DAMASCUS (active A.D. 97–130). Born in Syria, he went to Rome and became official architect to Trajan (A.D. 97–117), accompanying him on his military campaigns and designing or inspiring almost all the buildings erected under him. His first recorded work is the stone-and-wood bridge over the Danube at Dobreta (A.D. 104). But his masterpieces were naturally in Rome itself: an odeon circular in plan (probably that built by Domitian in the Campus Martius), the Baths of Trajan, and Trajan's Forum. The latter, with its imposing axial planning and subtle play of symmetry, illustrates his style, a brilliant compromise between the Hellenistic and the pure Roman traditions. He also planned the markets at the extreme end of the Quirinal hill, and was probably involved in work at the port of Rome (Fiumicino) and at Civitavecchia. The triumphal arches at Ancona and Benevento have been attributed to him. Though he was on less happy terms with Hadrian, he collaborated with him on at least one project, and dedicated to him his treatise on the construction of engines of assault, *Poliorketa.* But, according to Dio Cassius, Hadrian banished him from Rome in about A.D. 130, and later condemned him to death because of his harsh criticism of the Temple of Venus and Rome.

APOPHYGE. The slight curve at the top and bottom of a column where the SHAFT joins the CAPITAL and FILLET.

APPLIED COLUMN, *see* ENGAGED COLUMN.

APSE. A vaulted semicircular or polygonal termination, usually to a chancel or chapel. *See figure 10.*

APTERAL. An adjective describing a classical-style building with columns at the end, but not along the sides.

AQUEDUCT. An artificial channel for carrying water, usually an elevated masonry or brick structure; invented by the Romans.

ARABESQUE. Intricate and fanciful surface decoration generally based on geometrical patterns and using combinations of flowing lines, tendrils, etc., and classical vases, sphinxes, etc.

ARAEOSTYLE. With an arrangement of columns spaced four diameters apart. *See also* DIASTYLE; EUSTYLE; PYCNOSTYLE; SYSTYLE.

ARCADE. A range of arches carried on PIERS or columns, either free-standing or blind, i.e. attached to a wall.

ARCH. *Anse de panier* is a French term for an arch whose curve resembles that of the handle of a basket; also called *basket arch*. It is formed by a segment of a large circle continued left and right by two segments of much smaller circles.

Basket arch, see above.

Discharging arch, see relieving arch.

Equilateral arch, see pointed arch.

A *four-centred or depressed arch* is a late medieval form – a pointed arch of four arcs, the two outer and lower ones springing from centres on the SPRINGING LINE, the two inner and upper arcs from centres below the springing line.

A *horseshoe arch* is often found in Islamic buildings; it can be either a pointed or a round horseshoe.

A *lancet arch* is pointed, with radii much larger than the span.

An *ogee arch* is pointed and usually of four arcs, the centres of two inside the arch, of the other two outside; this produces a compound curve of two parts, one convex and the other concave. Introduced *c.* 1300 this arch was popular throughout the late Middle Ages and in England especially in the early C14.

A *pointed arch* is produced by two curves, each with a radius equal to the span and meeting in a point at the top; also called an *equilateral arch*.

A *relieving arch* is usually of rough construction placed in a wall, above the true arch of an opening, to relieve it of much of the superincumbent weight; also called a *discharging arch*.

A *shouldered arch* consists of a lintel connected with the jambs of a doorway by corbels. The corbels start with a concave quadrant and continue vertically to meet the lintel.

A *stilted arch* has its springing line raised by vertical *piers* above the IMPOST level.

A *strainer arch* is one inserted, in most cases, across a nave or an aisle to prevent the walls from leaning.

A *Tudor arch* is a late medieval pointed arch whose shanks start with a curve near to a quarter circle and continue to the apex in a straight line. *See figure 4.*

ARCHER, Thomas (1668–1743). The only English Baroque architect to have studied continental Baroque at first hand. His buildings are unique in England in showing an intimate appreciation of BERNINI and BORROMINI. He came of good family and made a four-year Grand Tour after Oxford, returning home about 1693. A Whig, he was successful at Court and in 1703 obtained the lucrative post of Groom Porter. His buildings date between then and 1715, when he acquired the even more profitable post of Controller of Customs at Newcastle, whereupon he gave up architecture. The north front of Chatsworth (1704–5) and the garden pavilion at Wrest Park (1711–12) are his best surviving secular buildings, but his reputation rests mainly on his three churches – Birmingham Cathedral (1710–15); St Paul, Deptford, London (1712–30); and St John, Smith Square, London (1714–28), with its spectacular and much-maligned towers.

ARCHITECTS' CO-PARTNERSHIP. A group of English architects born about 1915–17. Their principal works in-

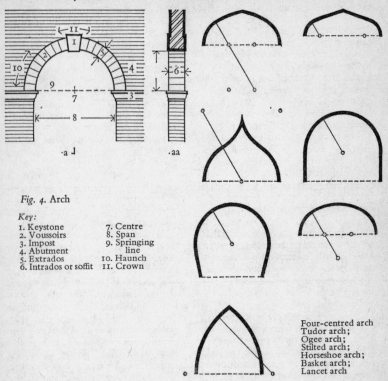

Fig. 4. Arch

Key:
1. Keystone
2. Voussoirs
3. Impost
4. Abutment
5. Extrados
6. Intrados or soffit
7. Centre
8. Span
9. Springing line
10. Haunch
11. Crown

Four-centred arch
Tudor arch;
Ogee arch;
Stilted arch;
Horseshoe arch;
Basket arch;
Lancet arch

clude: a factory at Bryn Mawr in Wales (1949); a range of students' sets for St John's College, Oxford (1956–9); a range of sets for King's College, Cambridge (1960–2); a school at Ripley, Derbyshire (1958–60) and other schools; housing at Ikoyi, Lagos (1957–9); and the Biochemistry Building, Imperial College, London (1961–4).

ARCHITRAVE. The lowest of the three main parts of an ENTABLATURE; also, more loosely, the moulded frame surrounding a door or window. *See figures 39, 42, and 64.*

ARCHITRAVE-CORNICE. An ENTABLATURE from which the FRIEZE is elided.

ARCHIVOLT. The continuous architrave moulding on the face of an arch, following its contour.

ARCUATED. A term applied to a building dependent structurally on the use of arches or the arch principle, in contrast to a TRABEATED building.

ARENA. The central open space of an AMPHITHEATRE; also, more loosely, any building for public contests or displays in the open air.

ARISS, John, the first professional architect in North America, emigrated from England in or shortly before 1751, when he advertised in the *Maryland Gazette* as being 'lately from Great Britain' and ready to undertake 'Buildings of all Sorts and Dimensions

... either of the Ancient or Modern Order of Gibbs, Architect'. Unfortunately his work is unrecorded, but some of the finer Virginian houses were probably designed by him, e.g., Mount Airey, Richmond County (1755–8); they are English Palladian, with Gibbsian overtones.

ARK, see ECHAL.

ARNOLFO DI CAMBIO. A Florentine sculptor and mason of the later C13 (d. 1302?). Assistant of Nicola PISANO in 1266, he is already called a *subtilissimus magister* in 1277. He signed works of decorative architecture and sculpture combined in 1282, 1285, and 1293. The architectural forms used are truly Gothic, aware of French precedent, and include trefoil-headed and trefoil-cusped arches. In 1296 the new cathedral of Florence was begun; Arnolfo was master mason. His design is recognizable in the nave and aisles, but the present centralizing east end with its three polygonal apses is Talenti's, though it only enlarged and pushed considerably farther east the east end as intended by Arnolfo, perhaps under the influence of Cologne. It is curious that Arnolfo, in the earliest source referring to him (though as late as *c.* 1520), is called a German. Several other buildings have been attributed to Arnolfo, among them, with convincing arguments, S. Croce (begun 1295).

ARRIS. A sharp edge produced by the meeting of two surfaces.

ARRUDA, Diogo (active 1508–31). The leading practitioner of the MANUELINE STYLE in Portugal. His main work is the nave and chapterhouse of the Cristo Church, Tomar (1510–14), with its almost surrealist sculptured decoration: sails and ropes around the circular windows, mouldings of cork floats threaded on cables, buttresses carved with patterns of coral and seaweed. His brother Francisco (active 1510–47) was mainly a military architect, but built the exotic, almost Hindu, tower at Belem (1515–20).

ART NOUVEAU. The name of a shop opened in Paris in 1895 to sell objects of modern, i.e. non-period-imitation, style. The movement away from imitation of the past had started in book production and textiles in England in the 1880s (see MACKMURDO), and had begun to invade furniture and other furnishings about 1890. Stylistically, the origins lay in the designs of William MORRIS and the English Arts and Crafts. One of the principal centres from 1892 onwards was Brussels (see HORTA, van de VELDE). In France the two centres were Nancy, where in Émile Gallé's glass Art Nouveau forms occurred as early as the 1880s, and Paris. Art Nouveau forms are characterized by the ubiquitous use of undulation like waves or flames or flower stalks or flowing hair. Some artists kept close to nature, others, especially van de Velde, preferred abstract forms as being a purer expression of the dynamics aimed at. The most important representative of Art Nouveau in America is Louis C. Tiffany (1848–1933), in Germany Hermann Obrist (1863–1927) and August Endell (1871–1925). In architecture by far the greatest is GAUDÍ. It has rightly been pointed out that Art Nouveau has a source and certainly a parallel in the paintings and graphic work of Gauguin, Munch, and some others. The climax in Britain, and at the same time the beginning of the end, is the work of Charles R. MACKINTOSH of Glasgow, in whose architecture and decoration the slender curves and the subtle opalescent colours of Art Nouveau blend with a new rectangular crispness and pure whiteness of framework. Vienna took this up at once, and found from it the way into the twentieth-century emphasis on the square and the cube (see LOOS *and* HOFFMANN).

ASAM, Cosmas Damian (1686–1739) and Egid Quirin (1692–1750), were brothers who always worked together as architects though sometimes separately as decorators (Cosmas Damian was a fresco-painter and Egid Quirin a sculptor). Sons of a Bavarian mason, they did not emerge from provincial obscurity until after visiting Rome (1711–14), where they studied under Carlo FONTANA. As a result of this Roman training they remained Baroque instead of becoming Rococo architects. They seem to have admired the juicier C17 Italians rather than their elegant and frivolous contemporaries. They decorated many important churches (e.g., Weingarten; Einsiedeln; St Jacobi, Innsbruck; Fürstenfeldbruck; Osterhofen; Freising Cathedral; St Maria Victoria, Ingolstadt; Aldersbach), but designed and built only four, in which, however, they carried to unprecedented lengths the melodramatic effects of concealed lighting, spatial illusionism, and other tricks which they had picked up in Rome. Their emotionalism is seen at its wildest in the fantastic *tableau vivant* altar-pieces at Rohr (1717–25) and Weltenburg (1717–21). They attempted something better in St John Nepomuk, Munich (1733–5), a church which is attached to their house and was entirely paid for by them. This is a tiny but sensational church, a masterpiece of German Baroque in which architecture and decoration are successfully combined to achieve an intense atmosphere of religious fervour. Their last work, the Ursulinenkirche, Straubing (1736–41), is almost equally good.

ASHLAR. Hewn blocks of masonry wrought to even facing, as opposed to rubble or unhewn stone straight from the quarry.

ASPLUND, Gunnar (1885–1940), the most important Swedish architect of the twentieth century, started in the Scandinavian classicism first developed by the Danes; his principal work in that style is the Stockholm City Library (1920–8) with its high circular reading room rising as a drum above the rest of the *ensemble*. With his work for the Stockholm Exhibi-

tion of 1930 he changed to the Central European Modern, but instead of treating it in the relatively massive manner then current, he lightened up his forms by means of thin metal members, much glass, and some freer forms of roof, etc., thereby endowing the style with a grace and translucency which had a great international impact. But Asplund was never demonstrative or aggressive. His buildings always observe a noble restraint. The finest of them are the extension of the Town Hall of Göteborg (1934–7), with its beautifully transparent courtyard, and the Stockholm Crematorium (1935–40), which may well be called the most perfect example of genuine C20 monumentality and religious architecture in existence.

ASPRUCCI, Antonio (1723–1808). A notable early neo-classical architect in Rome. His masterpiece is the interior of Villa Borghese, Rome (1777–84), and the elegant temples, sham ruins, and other follies in the park.

ASSYRIAN AND SUMERIAN ARCHITECTURE. As early as the fourth millennium the Sumerians in the Euphrates delta had evolved a complex architecture. The main material was brick: techniques included the arch, the dome, and the vault (though the latter appears to have been used only for underground burial chambers). Having solved these basic problems of construction, architects applied themselves to decoration. An astonishing proof of their ability is provided by the great ZIGGURAT temple of the Uruk period (late fourth millennium) at Warka (Biblical Erech), where the surface was decorated with a mosaic of red-, black-, and buff-coloured terracotta cones arranged in geometrical patterns. The façades were further articulated by a succession of decorative buttresses – a device that was to distinguish sacred buildings in Mesopotamia until Hellenistic times. The temple of Al 'Ubaid near Ur, built by King A-annipaddi, *c.* 2600 B.C., shows that by this date painted and relief decorations were used not merely as ornaments but to emphasize the structure. But perhaps the most remarkable of these early constructions is the vast ziggurat at Ur, built in the C22 B.C. – a remarkably sophisticated building with dramatic staircases ascending to the shrine on top and with every line subtly curved to correct optical illusions. The principles of this architecture were taken over by the Assyrians of northern Mesopotamia towards the end of the second millennium. So far as may be judged from the excavated sites (unfortunately their great cities at Nineveh and Nimrud yield little for the student of architecture), the Assyrians were unable to make any technical advances of importance on the Sumerians, but they demanded effects of greater grandeur with lavish use of brilliant colour and much sculpture in the round as well as in relief. The Palace of Sargon at Khorsabad reveals that they achieved their effects of splendour by the multiplication of units rather than by bold over-all designing.

ASTRAGAL. A small moulding circular in section, often decorated with a bead and reel enrichment. *See figures 5 and 42.*

Fig. 5. Astragal

ASTYLAR. A term applied to a façade without columns or pilasters.

ATLANTES. Supports in the form of carved male figures, used especially by German Baroque architects instead of columns to support an ENTABLATURE. The Roman term is *telamones.*

ATRIUM. 1. In Roman domestic architecture, an inner court open to the sky and surrounded by the roof. 2. In Early Christian and medieval architecture, an open court in front of a church; usually a colonnaded quadrangle.

ATTACHED COLUMN, *see* ENGAGED COLUMN.

ATTIC STOREY. 1. A storey above the main ENTABLATURE of a building and in strictly architectural relation to it, as, e.g., in Roman triumphal arches. 2. Also, more loosely, the space within the sloping roof of a house or the upper storey of a building if less high than the others.

AUMBRY (or AMBRY). A cupboard or recess used to keep sacred vessels in.

AUSTRIAN ARCHITECTURE. Austria originated in the Ostmark (Eastern Marches) established in 803 by Charlemagne after he had subdued the Bavarians in 788. When the Hungarian invasion had been halted (955), the Ostmark was renewed and remained in the hands of the Babenberg dynasty from 976 to 1246. After that Austria passed to the Habsburgs. The archbishopric of Salzburg was created in 789; additional bishoprics came much later: Gurk in 1070, Seckau in 1218, and Vienna only in 1480.

Of pre-Romanesque architecture in Austria little is known. Salzburg Cathedral (767–74) was, according to excavations, nearly 200 ft long and had a straightforward Early Christian basilica plan with one apse. The Romanesque style is an interesting mixture of elements from Bavaria and Lombardy, although West Germany (especially Hirsau, the centre of Cluniac architecture for Germany) and even France also play a part. Bavarian influence means basilican churches with pillars (Hirsau stood for columns – see St Paul im Lavanttal in Austria), no transepts, and three parallel apses, while Lombardy was the source of much of the best decoration; it is to be found at Klosterneuburg (1114–33), Gurk (1140s–*c.* 1200; crypt of a hundred marble columns), Millstatt, and even the portal of St Peter at Salzburg (*c.* 1240). Another source of ornament was Normandy (zigzag, etc.) via Worms, Bamberg, and Regensburg (see St Stephen, Vienna; St Pölten; and the Karner at Tulln). Karners are bone-houses with chapels, centrally planned, and they are an Austrian speciality. The largest church of the C12 was Salzburg Cathedral as rebuilt in 1181 etc. It was as long as Old St Peter's in Rome, and had double aisles, round towers over apses in the end walls of the transepts, two (older) west towers, and an octagonal crossing tower.

Cistercian colonization was actively pursued in Austria, and Viktring (built 1142–1202) is indeed an early and faithful follower of Fontenay, the earliest preserved house in France; it has, for example, the pointed tunnel vaults of Fontenay. On the other hand Heiligenkreuz (begun c. 1150–60) has rib vaults with heavy square ribs, a Lombard characteristic. Heiligenkreuz received a choir in 1295, of the hall type. This is of course fully Gothic, and hall churches are characteristic of the German Late Gothic. The hall choir was suggested by an earlier Cistercian hall choir in Austria: Lilienfeld (1202–30), also nearly entirely Gothic. This is an extremely early case of the hall elevation and one which establishes Austria as one of the sources of German hall churches. Zwettl, also Cistercian, received its splendid hall choir with ambulatory and low radiating chapels much later (1343–83). From here influences again reached out to South and South-west Germany. The friars, the most active order of the later C13 and the C14, went in for halls too.

The principal achievement of the C14 and C15 is of course St Stephen in Vienna, not a cathedral originally. The hall chancel is of 1304–40, the glorious south tower of 1359–1433. Connexions in the early C14 were principally with Bohemia (Vienna) and Bavaria (Franciscan Church, Salzburg, 1408 etc.; by Hans STET-HAIMER). Developments in architecture in the later C15 and early C16 were as great and important as they were in sculpture: intricate vaults, with star, net, and even rosette motifs, are characteristic, and culminate in the stucco ribs with vegetable details of Laas (c. 1515–20) and Kötschach (1518–27) in Carinthia. Supports may be twisted piers (Salzburg Castle, 1502) or even tree-trunk piers (Bechyre Castle, just across the Moravian border). The first secular buildings are also of these late years: the Bummerl-haus at Steyr (1497), the Goldenes Dachl at Innsbruck (completed 1500), and the Kornmesserhaus at Bruck on the Mur (1499–1505). The arcading here suggests Venetian influence.

But Italian influence was very soon to mean something quite different from the Gothic of the Kornmesser-haus. The portal of the Salvator Chapel in Vienna of just after 1515 is entirely Lombard Renaissance and must be the work of a sculptor from there. Similar works, especially funerary monuments, picked up the new forms at once. In architecture the next examples are the portal of the Arsenal at Wiener Neustadt (1524) and the elegant court-yard of the Portia Palace at Spital (c. 1540); a comparison of this with the much heavier courtyard of the Landhaus at Graz (1556–65; by Dome-nico dell'Allio) shows a characteristic development. The stage after this is represented by the courtyard of the Schallaburg near Melk (1572–1600) with caryatids, etc. – what would in Britain be called Elizabethan. On the whole, Austria is less rich in first-rate Renaissance buildings than Bohemia. The Hofkirche at Innsbruck (1553–63) is a Gothic hall, though with slender columns instead of piers. The only fully Italian building in the ecclesiastical field is Salzburg Cathedral, by Santino SOLARI, with two west towers and a crossing dome, and this is of 1614–34. The cathedral, the Archi-episcopal Palace, and the Franciscan church show a very complete development of Italianate C17 stucco decoration.

In Vienna a remarkable number of churches were built and rebuilt, but they appear minor when one measures them by the achievements of the Austrian Baroque of c. 1690–1730. The great names are first the theatrical designer and engineer Lorenzo Burnacini (1636–1707), who designed the wildly Baroque Trinity Monument on the Graben in 1687; then Domenico MARTINELLI (1650–1718) of the two Liechtenstein palaces of the 1690s; and then FISCHER VON ERLACH and HILDEBRANDT. Little need be said about them here – of Fischer's brilliant centralizing church plans at Salzburg (Trinity, 1694–1702; Collegiate, 1694–1707), heralded by those by Caspar ZUCCALLI of 1685; of his Karlskirche in Vienna with its fantastic Trajan's Columns; of his restrained and courtly decoration; and of Hildebrandt's brilliant spatial interlocking and his fiery decoration (Upper Belvedere, Vienna, 1714–24). Meanwhile the great abbeys in the country were as busy rebuilding as the towns and the nobility: Melk (1702–14; by PRANDTAUER); St Florian (1686–1708; by CARLONE and then Prandtauer); Göttweig (1719 etc.; by Hildebrandt); Klosterneuburg (1730 etc.; by d'Allio). Particularly splendid are the libraries in the abbeys (Altenburg, 1740; Admont, c. 1745).

The Louis XVI or Robert ADAM style of the later C18 is represented in Vienna by the Academy of the Sciences (1753; by Jadot de Ville Issey) and the Josephinum (1783; by Canevale). The Gloriette, a large-scale eye-catcher in the park of Schönbrunn by Ferdinand von Hohenburg is, in spite of its early date (1775) in a neo-Cinquecento style. Neo-Grecian at its most severe are the Theseustempel (1819) and the Burgtor (1821), both by NOBILE (the latter originally designed by CAGNOLA).

C19 historicism is in full swing with the perfectly preserved Anif Castle near Salzburg (1838 etc), the church of Altlerchenfeld, Vienna (1848–61; by Eduard van der Nüll), in neo-Romanesque, and the Arsenal (1849–56; by Förster and others), also in a neo-Romanesque style. Shortly after, Vienna established herself as one of the centres of historicism on a grand scale with the abolition of the fortress walls of inner Vienna and the making of the Ringstrasse (begun 1859). Along this wide green belt a number of majestic public buildings were erected in various period styles: the Votivkirche (1856 etc.; by von Ferstel), in Gothic; the Opera (1861 etc.; by van der Nüll and Siccardsburg), in free Renaissance; the Town Hall (1872 etc.; by Ferdinand von Schmidt), in symmetrical Gothic; the Museums (1872 etc.; by SEMPER and Hasenauer), in Renaissance to Baroque; the Academy (1872 etc.; by Theophil von Hansen), in Renaissance; the Parliament (1873 etc.; also by von Hansen), in pure Grecian; the Burgtheater (1873 etc.; again by Semper and Hasenauer), in Renaissance; the University (by Ferstel), in a mixed Italian and French C16 style; and, finally, the Neue Hofburg (1881 etc.; by Semper and Hasenauer), again in Renaissance. There are also large blocks of flats as parts of the monumental, strung-out composition.

Vienna was one of the most important centres in the whole world when it came to abandoning historicism and creating a new idiom for the C20. The leaders were Otto WAGNER, whose Postal Savings Bank (1904) is remarkably fresh and enterprising, his pupil OLBRICH, whose Sezession (1898) blazed the trail – though more towards ART NOUVEAU than towards the C20 – and the two even younger men, HOFFMANN and LOOS. When the C20 style began to settle down and be accepted in the mid-twenties, a mild variety of it was applied to the many blocks of working-class flats, some of them vast, which the municipality of Vienna erected.

AXONOMETRIC PROJECTION. A geometrical drawing showing a building in three dimensions. The plan is set up truly to a convenient angle, and the verticals projected to scale, with the result that all dimensions on a horizontal plane and all verticals are to scale, but diagonals and curves on a vertical plane are distorted. *See figure 6*.

AZTEC ARCHITECTURE. The Aztec civilization which flourished in pre-Columbian Mexico (*c.* 1300–1520) has left remains of a notable religious architecture. Its most impressive monuments are the pyramids, built on an inhumanly vast scale, with flat tops to serve as ritual platforms approached by daunting ceremonial stairways and copiously decorated with monstrous, grimacing carved serpent heads. Good examples are at Teotihuacán and Tenayuca. The materials used were ADOBES faced with stone.

AZULEJOS. Glazed pottery tiles, usually painted in bright colours with floral and other patterns, much used on the outsides and insides of Spanish, Portuguese, and Central and South American buildings.

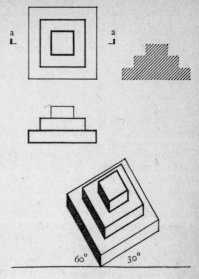

Fig. 6. Axonometric projection.
Plan; Section aa; Elevation

B

BAGUETTE (or BAGNETTE). A small moulding of semicircular section, like an ASTRAGAL; also a frame with a small BEAD MOULDING.

BAILEY. The courtyard of a castle; also called a *ward*.

BAKER, Sir Herbert (1862–1946), was born in Kent and remained an English countryman. Baker's most interesting work belongs to South Africa. He went out early, gained Cecil Rhodes's confidence, and built Groote Schuur for him in 1890 in the traditional Dutch Colonial idiom, and later private houses in Johannesburg, some very successful in an Arts and Crafts way (Stonehouse, 1902). His most prominent buildings were the Government House and Union Buildings in Pretoria (1905 onwards and 1910–13). Side by side with his friend LUTYENS he was called in at New Delhi, and was responsible there for the Secretariat Buildings and the Legislative Building (1912 etc.). His style is as imperially classical as Lutyens's, but much weaker, less original, and less disciplined. This is especially evident in his later London buildings (Bank of England, 1921; India House, 1925; South Africa House, 1930). He was more at ease where he could use a less elevated style and display a great variety of materials. This is why the War Memorial Cloister at Winchester College (1922–4) is one of his most successful buildings.

BALDACCHINO. A portable CANOPY, or a canopy on columns, usually over an altar (also CIBORIUM).

BALISTRARIA. In medieval military architecture, the cross-shaped opening in BATTLEMENTS and elsewhere for the use of the crossbow.

BALLFLOWER. A globular three-petalled flower enclosing a small ball; a decoration in use in the first quarter of the C14. *See figure 7.*

Fig. 7. Ballflower

BALLOON FRAMING. A method of timber-frame construction used in the U.S.A. and Scandinavia: the STUDS or uprights run from sill to eaves, and the horizontal members are nailed to them.

BALUSTER. A short post or pillar in a series supporting a rail or COPING and thus forming a *balustrade. See figure 79.*

BALUSTRADE, *see* BALUSTER.

BAPTISTERY. A building for baptismal rites containing the font; often separate from the church.

BAR TRACERY, *see* TRACERY.

BARBICAN. An outwork defending the entrance to a castle.

BARELLI, Agostino (1627–79). Born in Bologna, where he designed the Theatine church of S. Bartolomeo (1653), he later introduced the Italian Baroque style to Bavaria. He designed the Theatine church of St Cajetan, Munich (1653, completed by Enrico ZUCCALLI), on the model of S. Andrea della Valle, Rome. He also built the squarish central block of the electoral palace at Nymphenburg outside Munich (1663).

BARGEBOARDS. Projecting boards placed against the incline of the gable of a building and hiding the ends of the horizontal roof timbers; sometimes decorated. *See figure 8.*

BAROQUE ARCHITECTURE. The architecture of the C17 and part of the C18.

Fig. 8. Bargeboards

It is characterized by exuberant decoration, expansive, curvaceous forms, a sense of mass, a delight in large-scale and sweeping vistas, and a preference for spatially complex compositions. According to the number of these and kindred qualities present, a building or a national style of architecture may be called Baroque. The term applies fully to the C17 in Italy and to the C17 and part of the C18 in Spain, Germany, and Austria, but with limitations to the C17 in France (LE VAU, Versailles), the C18 in Italy (FONTANA, JUVARRA), and the late C17 and early C18 in England (WREN, HAWKSMOOR, VANBRUGH, ARCHER). For all these latter cases the term Baroque Classicism has been adopted to denote that they are instances of the Baroque tempered by classical elements. This is especially evident in England, where the swelling forms of Baroque plans and elevations were never favoured.

BARREL VAULT, *see* VAULT.

BARRY, Sir Charles (1795–1860). The most versatile of the leading Early Victorian architects, an excellent planner and an energetic, tough, and hard-working man. With some inherited money he travelled in 1817–20 through France, Italy, Greece, Turkey, Egypt, and Palestine, studying buildings and doing brilliant sketches. In 1823 he won the competition for St Peter's, Brighton, and then for some years did 'pre-archaeological' Gothic

churches, i.e., an inventive rather than a correct interpretation of the style. In 1824 he designed the Royal Institution of Fine Arts in Manchester – Grecian this time – and he followed this up with the Manchester Athenaeum (1836). But the Travellers' Club (1829–31) was a Quattrocento *palazzetto*, and this meant the beginning of the neo-Renaissance for England. With the Reform Club of 1837 his Renaissance turned Cinquecento, and with Bridgewater House (1847) a free, not to say debased, Cinquecento. This development from the reticent to the spectacular and from low to high relief permeates his work in general – see, now in the Northern Renaissance field, the development from Highclere (1837), itself far busier than his early work, to the Halifax Town Hall (1859–62), which is asymmetrical and a jumble of motifs. It was completed by Barry's son Edward M. Barry (1830–80), who built the Charing Cross and Cannon Street Hotels.

But Sir Charles's *magnum opus* is, of course, the Houses of Parliament, won in competition in 1835–6 and begun in 1839; it was formally opened in 1852. Its ground plan is functionally excellent, its façade to the Thames still symmetrical in the Georgian way, but its skyline completely asymmetrical and exceedingly well balanced, with its two contrasting towers and its flèche. Most of the close Perpendicular detail and nearly all the internal detail is by PUGIN, who was commissioned by Barry for the purpose.

BARTIZAN. A small turret projecting from the angle on the top of a tower or parapet. *See figure 9.*

BASEVI, George (1794–1845), was articled to SOANE. In 1816–19 he was in Italy and Greece. His first buildings are Grecian, but his best-known building, the Fitzwilliam Museum at Cambridge (begun 1836), already shows the trend towards classical harmony becoming, with clustered giant

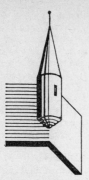

Fig. 9. Bartizan

columns and a heavy attic, more dramatic and indeed Baroque. It is the same trend which distinguishes the Beaux Arts style in France from the Empire style. Early in his career (*c.* 1825), Basevi also designed Belgrave Square (minus the corner mansions) and a number of country houses in various styles.

BASILICA. 1. In Roman architecture, an oblong building with double colonnades inside and a semicircular APSE at the end, used for public administration. Many basilicas were converted into Christian churches and thus the term came to be applied to churches, especially the seven Roman churches founded by Constantine. 2. In Early Christian and medieval architecture, an aisled church with a CLERESTORY and with or without a gallery. *See figure 10.*

BASKET ARCH, *see* ARCH.

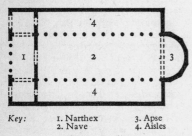

Key: 1. Narthex   3. Apse
            2. Nave   4. Aisles

Fig. 10. Basilica

BASTION. A projection at the angle of a fortification, from which the garrison can see and defend the ground before the ramparts.

BATTER. The inclined face of a wall.

BATTLEMENT. A PARAPET with alternating indentations or EMBRASURES and raised portions or *merlons*; also called *crenellation*. *See figure 18.*

BAUDOT, Anatole de (1834–1915). A pupil of LABROUSTE and VIOLLET-LE-DUC. His St Jean de Montmartre in Paris (1894–1902) is the first building where all the structural members, including the vaulting ribs, are of exposed reinforced concrete. Yet the character remains Gothic. It can be called the most successful demonstration of the union of old and new advocated by Viollet-le-Duc in his *Entretiens.*

BAUHAUS, *see* GROPIUS.

BAUTISTA, Francisco (1594–1679). A Spanish Jesuit priest who built churches for his order in Madrid and Toledo. That in Madrid, S. Isidro el Real (1629), is the most interesting, based on the plan of the Gesù in Rome, with a somewhat severe façade, the central element of which is repeated along the sides of the building. The church had considerable influence in Spain.

BAY LEAF GARLAND. Classical decorative motif used to enrich TORUS mouldings, etc. *See figure 11.*

Fig. 11. Bay Leaf garland

BAY WINDOW. An angular or curved projection of a house front filled by fenestration. If curved, also called a *bow window.* If on an upper floor only, called an *oriel* or *oriel window.*

BAYS. 1. Compartments of an interior, each separated from the other not by solid walls but by divisions marked in the side walls (columns or shafts) or in the ceiling (beams, transverse arches, etc.). 2. External divisions of a building marked by fenestration or buttresses.

BEAD MOULDING. A small cylindrical moulding enriched with ornament resembling a string of beads; used in the Romanesque period.

BEAKHEAD. A Norman decorative motif consisting of a row of bird, animal, or human heads biting a ROLL MOULDING. *See figure 12.*

Fig. 12. Beakhead moulding

BED MOULDING. A small moulding between the CORONA and the FRIEZE in any ENTABLATURE.

BEEHIVE HOUSE. A primitive structure, circular in plan and built of rough stones set in projecting courses to form a dome. Prehistoric examples, called *nuraghi*, have been found in Sardinia, and others of later date in Ireland and Scotland. They are still inhabited in South-east Italy (Apulia), where they are called *trulli*. The finest example of beehive construction is the tomb called the 'Treasury of Atreus' at Mycenae (C13 B.C.).

BEHRENS, Peter (1868–1940), started as a painter but after 1890 was attracted by design and the crafts, under the direct or indirect influence of the teachings of MORRIS. He designed typefaces, was one of the founders of the Vereinigte Werkstätten at Munich, and for them designed table glass among other things. In 1900 Ernst Ludwig, Grand Duke of Hesse, called him to Darmstadt (*see* OLBRICH). The house he designed for himself there in 1901 is original, vigorous, and

even ruthless. In 1907 he was appointed architect and consultant to the A.E.G. (General Electricity Company) in Berlin, and designed for them factories, shops, products, and even stationery. The factories are among the earliest anywhere to be taken seriously architecturally and designed without any recourse to period allusions. For more representational jobs he used a more representational style which has been called a 'scraped classicism' (offices in Düsseldorf for Mannesmann, 1911–12; German Embassy, St Petersburg, 1911–12). After the First World War his style paid tribute first to the then current Expressionism (offices for I. G. Farben, Höchst, 1920–4), then to the International Modern (Warehouse for the State Tobacco Administration, Linz, Austria, 1930).

BELANGER, François-Joseph (1744–1818). The most elegant Louis XVI architect and the leading French landscape gardener. Trained in Paris, he visited England in 1766. The following year he joined the Menus Plaisirs and in 1777 designed his masterpiece, the exquisite neo-classical Bagatelle in the Bois de Boulogne, Paris, which he built for the king's brother in sixty-four days to win a bet with Marie Antoinette. The garden, laid out between 1778 and 1780, was the most famous *jardin anglais* of the period. It was followed in 1784 by the *jardin anglo-chinois* at another of his pavilions, the Folie Saint James at Neuilly, and in 1786 by the last of his great landscape gardens, Méréville. In 1782 he designed a surprisingly advanced copper and iron dome for the Halle aux Blés, Paris, but it was not executed until 1808–13.

BELFAST ROOF, *see* ROOF.

BELFRY. Generally the upper room or storey in a tower in which bells are hung, and thus often the bell-tower itself, whether it is attached to or stands separate from the main building. Also the timber frame inside a church steeple to which bells are fastened. Derived from the old French *berfrei*

(= tower), the word has no connexion with 'bell'.

BELGIAN ARCHITECTURE. In the Middle Ages the Southern Netherlands belonged to the archdiocese of Cologne; hence Romanesque building drew its inspiration chiefly from Germany. The earliest building of major importance, St Gertrude at Nivelles (consecrated 1046) is, side by side with St Michael at Hildesheim, the best-preserved Ottonian church in the German orbit. The former St John at Liège was built to a central plan like Charlemagne's church at Aachen, the former Liège Cathedral had a west as well as an east chancel, St Bartholomew, also at Liège, has a typically German unrelieved façade block with recessed twin towers (cf. especially Maastricht), and the cathedral of Tournai has a trefoil east end (i.e., transepts with apsidal ends) on the pattern of St Mary in Capitol at Cologne; its group of five towers round the crossing may also be derived from Cologne.

Tournai had a great influence on the Early Gothic architecture of France (Noyon, Laon): the east end was rebuilt c. 1242, no longer on a German pattern but on that of such High Gothic cathedrals as Soissons and Amiens. The Gothic style in present-day Belgium was, in fact, imported from France; borrowings also occurred from Normandy and Burgundy, and as in other countries the Cistercians were among the pioneers. Orval of the late C12 is still Transitional, Villers (1210–72) is fully Gothic, as are the principal church of Brussels, Ste Gudule (begun before 1226, the façade C15), the beautiful chancel of St Martin at Ypres (1221 etc.), and Notre Dame at Tongres (1240 etc.). Later Gothic architecture in the Southern Netherlands first drew mainly on French inspiration, dominant at Hertogenbosch (c. 1280–1330) and in the chancel of Hal in the C14. But in the C15 Belgium, admittedly influenced by French Flamboyant as well as German 'Sondergotik', developed a splendid style of her own. The principal buildings are Notre Dame at Antwerp (completed 1518), St Rombaut at Malines, St Peter at Louvain (1425 etc.), and the Sablon Church at Brussels. Characteristic features are complicated lierne vaults of German derivation, proud towers – that of Antwerp 306 ft high, that of Malines about 320 ft and intended to be about 530 ft – and exceedingly elaborate Flamboyant fitments, such as rood screens.

The most spectacular castle is that of Ghent (inscribed 1180), with its oblong keep and its many towers along the curtain wall. But the sphere in which Belgium is in the forefront of European building is the town halls and guild halls of her prosperous towns. The Cloth Hall at Ypres (C13–C14), 440 ft long, is the grandest such building in all Europe, and there is the town hall of Bruges (tower c. 1280–1482, 350 ft high), then, ornately and lacily decorated, those of Brussels (1402 etc.), Louvain (1447 etc.), Ghent (1517), and Oudenarde (1527). Interiors were as rich as exteriors – see, for example, the magnificent chimneypiece in Courtrai Town Hall (1526). The names of the master masons are now mostly known: the family of the Keldermans is the most familiar. There are also plenty of medieval town houses preserved, Romanesque in stone (Tournai), Gothic most often in brick and frequently with crow-stepped gables (as early as the C13).

The Renaissance appeared in occasional motifs in paintings as early as 1500 and was more widely represented after 1510. The most important date for the promotion of the Renaissance spirit is 1517, when Raphael's cartoons for tapestries in the Sistine Chapel reached Brussels, where the tapestries were to be made. In the same year the Stadtholderess Margaret of Austria had additions built on to her palace at

Malines in the Renaissance style. Their relative purity is exceptional; the usual thing in the twenties and thirties is a happy-go-lucky mixing of Renaissance with traditional motifs, sometimes quite restrained (The Salmon, Malines, 1530–4), but mostly exuberant (The Greffe, Bruges, with its fabulous chimneypiece, 1535–7; the courtyard of the former Bishop's Palace, Liège, 1526). In churches the Renaissance was confined to details; the proportions and the vaults remained Gothic (St Jacques, Liège, 1513–38). A very influential element in architectural decoration was introduced in Antwerp in the forties and spread all over Northern Europe – the combination of STRAPWORK, inspired by Fontainebleau, and *grottesche*, inspired by ancient Roman excavations. Cornelis FLORIS and later Hans Vredeman de VRIES (d. after 1604) were its most eminent practitioners.

But Floris also designed the Antwerp Town Hall (1565 etc.), and this, though provided with a big, dominating gable in the northern style, is in its motifs entirely developed from BRAMANTE and SERLIO, i.e. the Italian (and French) Cinquecento. The former Granvelle Palace in Brussels (c. 1550) is also classical Cinquecento. However, the Jesuits, in their churches, clung to the Gothic well into the C17; an exception is St Charles Borromeo at Antwerp (1615–21), with a broad Mannerist façade and a tunnel-vaulted interior with arcades of columns in two tiers. True C17 architecture came in under the influence of Italy and France (domes such as Notre Dame de Montaigu, 1609 etc.; St Pierre, Ghent, 1629 etc.; Notre Dame de Hanswyck, Malines, 1663 etc.), and after c. 1650 developed into a characteristic Belgian Baroque, inspired largely by Rubens. Church façades are without towers and covered with sumptuous and somewhat undisciplined decoration (St Michael, Louvain, 1650–66; St John Baptist,

Brussels, 1657–77; St Peter, Malines, 1670–1709). Typical of the situation about 1700 are the houses round the Grand' Place in Brussels built after the bombardment of 1695 and with their gables basically still rooted in the Belgian past.

Of the C18 and early C19 little need be said; this period was dominated by French classicism (Royal Library, Brussels, c. 1750; Palais des Académies, Brussels, 1823–6). But in the later C19 Belgium found the way back to an exuberant Baroque. Poelaert's cyclopean Palais de Justice, Brussels (1866 etc.), is one of the most Baroque buildings of its time in Europe, though Poelaert could also work in a wild Gothic (Laeken Church, 1854 etc.). A generation later Belgium for the first time in her architectural history, and only for a few years, proved herself a pioneer; this was when attempts were being made to establish ART NOUVEAU as a viable architectural style. By far the most important architect in this movement was Victor HORTA of Brussels, and the key buildings are No. 6 rue Paul Émile Janson (designed 1892), the Hotel Solvey (1895 etc.), and the Maison du Peuple (1896 etc.), all of them with much of the undulating-line ornament of Art Nouveau, but also with a daring use of iron both externally and internally. Henri van de VELDE, though Belgian, belongs to international rather than Belgian Art Nouveau.

BELL GABLE, *see* BELLCOTE.

BELLCOTE. A framework on a roof to hang bells from; also called a *bell gable*.

BELVEDERE, *see* GAZEBO.

BEMA. The Greek word means a speaker's tribune or a platform. 1. Raised stage for the clergy in the apse of Early Christian churches. 2. In Eastern usage, a space raised above the nave level of a church, which is shut off by the ICONOSTASIS and contains the altar. 3. In synagogues, the elevated pulpit from which are read the

Pentateuch and Torah. Rabbinical authorities differ over its correct position: Maimonides (1204) maintains that the centre is correct, so does Moses Isserles of Cracow (c16), but Joseph Karo (1575) prescribed no fixed place. In modern times it has often been moved forward near the Ark for practical reasons. It is usually wooden and rectangular, and sometimes has a curved front and back, also open sides approached by steps.

BENCH-ENDS, see PEW.

BENEDETTO DA MAJANO (1442–97), was primarily a sculptor, but his Palazzo Strozzi, Florence (begun 1489), is a Renaissance masterpiece, a vast pile based on MICHELOZZO's Palazzo Medici-Riccardi, but with uniform RUSTICATION from the ground to the gargantuan projecting cornice. It was completed by Cronaca, otherwise Simone del Pollaiuolo, (1454–1508), who designed the noble arcaded CORTILE.

BENTLEY, John Francis (1839–1902). A pupil of Henry Clutton. Converted to Catholicism in 1861, he set up on his own in 1862. After a number of years spent mostly on designs for church furnishings and on additions and alterations, he built the Convent of the Sacred Heart at Hammersmith (1868 onwards) with a scrupulous simplicity and near-bareness; the serried chimneys are particularly impressive. Wider success came much later. Among the most memorable buildings are Holy Rood, Watford, a rich Gothic church, but also most intelligently thought out (1887 etc.), and St Francis at Bocking, Essex (1893). In 1894 he was commissioned to design Westminster Cathedral in London. The style here is Byzantine, the material brick with ample stone dressings and concrete for the domes. No iron is used: Bentley called it 'that curse of modern construction'. The campanile, asymmetrically placed, is the tallest church tower in London. The interior of the cathedral is superbly large in scale and ex-tremely sparing in architectural detail, though it was Bentley's intention to cover it with mosaics and slabs of variegated marbles. However, Philip WEBB admired it, bare as it was.

BERLAGE, Hendrikus Petrus (1856–1934), studied at the Zürich Polytechnic, then worked under CUYPERS. The building that made him famous, and is indeed a milestone in the development of Dutch architecture away from c19 historicism, is his Amsterdam Exchange (begun 1897). It does not mark a break with the past, but the treatment of period forms, derived from the Romanesque as well as the c16, is so free and the detail so original that it amounted to a profession of faith in an independent future. Specially characteristic are certain chunky, rather primeval details and others that are jagged and almost Expressionist. Berlage's style, indeed, prepared the way for the Expressionism of the so-called School of Amsterdam (see OUD). Berlage designed one building for England, the office building for Messrs Müller in Bury Street, London (1910–14). His last major work, the Municipal Museum in The Hague (1919–34), is less personal in style and rather reflects that of DUDOK.

BERNINI, Gianlorenzo (1598–1680). The dominating figure in Roman Baroque art. Primarily a sculptor, like MICHELANGELO, he was almost as universal a genius, being painter and poet as well as architect. He was born in Naples of a Neapolitan mother and Florentine father, Pietro Bernini, a late Mannerist sculptor of the second rank. The family settled in Rome c. 1605. Bernini spent the whole of his working life there, and no other city bears so strong an imprint of one man's vision and personality. His buildings and sculpture perfectly express the grandeur, flamboyance, and emotionalism of the Counter-Reformation. He was already famous as a sculptor by the age of twenty, but his long and uniformly successful career as an architect began with the election of Urban VIII (Barberini) in 1624. He was appointed architect to St Peter's five years later. But most of his important buildings belong to his middle age, mainly during the pontificate of Alexander VII (Chigi, 1655–67). By then his fame was so great that Louis XIV begged him to come to Paris to enlarge the Louvre. Unlike his neurotic contemporary and rival BORROMINI, he was well-balanced and extrovert in temperament, polished and self-assured in manner. Yet he was devout and deeply religious: an ardent follower of Jesuit teaching, he regularly practised the Spiritual Exercises of St Ignatius. He combined in an unusual if not unique degree a revolutionary artistic genius with the organizing ability of a man of affairs.

His first commissions (1624) were for the renovation of S. Bibiana and the baldacchino in St Peter's. Though interesting as an experiment, S. Bibiana suffers from a lack of assurance most uncharacteristic of its author and in striking contrast to the daringly original baldacchino (1624–33) he erected under Michelangelo's dome in the centre of St Peter's. With its gigantic bronze barley-sugar columns, buoyant scrolls, and dynamic sculpture, this showy masterpiece is the very symbol of the age – of its grandeur, luxury, and lack of restraint. And by its glorification of the twisted columns used in Constantine's basilica and traditionally connected with the Temple of Jerusalem it celebrates the continuity of the Church and its triumph over the Reformation.

Various other commissions followed: the façade and staircase of Palazzo Barberini, the remodelling of Porta del Popolo, the Cornaro Chapel in S. Maria della Vittoria. In the latter polychrome marbles, exaggerated perspective, and every trick of lighting and scenic illusion are exploited to heighten the dramatic effect of his marble group of the Ecstasy of St Teresa, placed as if behind a proscenium arch above the altar. But not until he was almost sixty did he get the chance to show his skill as a designer of churches, first at Castelgandolfo (1658–61), then at Ariccia (1662–4), and, finally and most brilliantly, at S. Andrea al Quirinale in Rome (1658–70), which perfectly realizes his conception of a church as a unified architectural setting for the religious mysteries illustrated by the sculptural decoration.

Of his two great secular buildings in Rome, Palazzo di Montecitorio (1650 onwards) and Palazzo Odescalchi (1664 onwards), the latter is by far the more important. It is composed of a richly articulated central part of seven bays with giant composite pilasters, between simple rusticated receding wings of three bays, and marks a decisive break with Roman tradition. It was very influential and became the model for aristocratic palaces all over Europe. Unfortunately, the composition was ruined by later alterations and enlargements. His gift for the monumental and colossal found supreme expression in the Piazza of St Peter's (1656 onwards). The conception is extremely simple and extremely original – an enormous oval surrounded by colonnades of free-standing columns with a straight entablature above. This not only helped to correct the faults of MADERNO's façade by giving it an impression of greater height but expressed with overwhelming authority and conviction the dignity, grandeur, and majestic repose of Mother Church. Bernini himself compared his colonnades to the motherly arms of the church 'which embrace Catholics to reinforce their belief'. The Piazza was to have been enclosed by a third arm, unfortunately never built, and the intended effect of surprise and elation on passing through the colonnades has now been idiotically destroyed by opening up the via della Conciliazione. The free-standing colonnades of the Piazza have been widely copied, from Greenwich to Leningrad. Bernini's last great work, the Scala Regia in the Vatican (1663–6), epitomizes his style – his sense of scale and movement, his ingenuity in turning an awkward site to advantage, his mastery of scenic effects (optical illusions, exaggerated perspectives, concealed lighting), and his brilliant use of sculpture to dramatize the climaxes of his composition. He here achieved the perfect Baroque synthesis of the arts.

BERTOTTI-SCAMOZZI, Ottavio (1719–90), the leading Palladian-Revival architect in Italy, built numerous houses in and around Vicenza, notably Palazzo Pagello-Beltrame (1780) and Palazzo Franceschini (1770, now the Questura), distinctly neo-classical versions of PALLADIO. He is more important as the editor of Palladio's work: *Le fabbriche e i disegni di Andrea Palladio raccolti e illustrati* (1776–83) and *Le terme dei Romani, disegnate da A. Palladio* (1797).

BÉTON BRUT. 'Concrete in the raw', that is, concrete left in its natural state when the FORMWORK has been removed. Sometimes special formwork is used to show clearly the timber graining on the concrete surface.

BIANCO, Bartolommeo (*c.* 1590–1657), a leading Baroque architect in Genoa, was born in Como, but was working in Genoa by 1619 when he began Palazzo Durazzo-Pallavicini. His best building is the University (1630–6), where he took full advantage of a steeply sloping site to produce a masterpiece of scenic planning with dramatic staircases and colonnaded courtyards on four levels.

BIBIENA, *see* GALLI DI BIBIENA.

BILLET. A Romanesque moulding consisting of several bands of raised short cylinders or square pieces placed at regular intervals. *See figure 13.*

BLIND (or BLANK) TRACERY. Tracery applied to the surface of walls, wood panels, etc., in Gothic buildings. *See also* ARCADE.

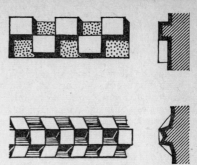

Fig. 13. Billet

BLOCKING COURSE. In classical architecture, the plain course of stone surmounting the CORNICE at the top of a building; also a projecting cornice of stone or brick at the base of a building.

BLONDEL, Jacques-François (1705–74). A minor architect but very influential as a writer and teacher. He ran his own school of architecture in Paris until he became Professor at the Académie royale de l'Architecture in 1756. Conservative in taste, he exalted the French tradition as exemplified by MANSART and PERRAULT and thus paved the way for neo-classicism. His publications include *L'Architecture française* (1752–6) and *Cours d'architecture* (1771–7).

BLONDEL, Nicolas François (1617–86), engineer and mathematician, was more interested in the theory than the practice of architecture. He expounded the rigidly classical and rationalist doctrines of the French Academy in his *Cours d'architecture* (1675, augmented ed. 1698). The Porte St Denis, Paris (1671), is his best surviving building.

BOASTED WORK. Stonework roughly blocked out preparatory to carving; also masonry finished with a boaster chisel.

BÖBLINGER. A family of South German masons of which the two most important members were Hans Senior and Matthäus. Hans (d. 1482) was a journeyman at Konstanz in 1435, then became foreman under Matthäus ENSINGER at St Mary, Esslingen, and in 1440 master mason of this church. Matthäus (d. 1505) was one of Hans's sons and was probably trained in Cologne. He was later at Esslingen with his father, and then at Ulm where, after three years, he became master mason of the Minster (1480). He was successor there to Ulrich and Matthäus Ensinger, and replaced Ulrich's design for the west tower with one of his own. His steeple was completed in 1881–90 and became the highest church tower in Europe (530 ft). However, Matthäus had to resign from the post and leave the town after cracks had appeared in the tower. He was called to a number of other places for consultation or to provide designs and supervise. Thieme-Becker's *Künstler-Lexikon* mentions eight more members of the family.

BODLEY, George Frederick (1827–1907), was of Scottish descent and George Gilbert SCOTT's first pupil (1845–c. 1850). Mostly but not exclusively a church architect, he always worked in the Gothic style; in his earlier works he was influenced by the French C13, later by English models. His style is as competent and knowledgeable as Scott's, but distinguished by a never-failing taste, by simplicity, and by great care for details, including the choice of those who were to do the furnishings and fitments. An early patron of MORRIS, he also started C. E. Kempe on his career. Among his earliest works are St Michael, Brighton (1859–61); St Martin, Scarborough (1861–2); All Saints, Cambridge (1863–4). In 1869 he went into partnership with Thomas Garner (1839–1906), another pupil of Scott's: the partnership lasted till 1898, though after 1884 the partners designed and supervised jobs individually. Among their most lavish works is Holy Angels, Hoar Cross, Staffordshire (1871–7). St Augustine, Pendlebury (1874), on the other hand, is one of the most monumental by virtue of its simplicity; instead of aisles, it has passages through internal buttresses, a motif derived from Albi and Spain and often repeated by the younger generation. Perhaps the noblest of all Bodley's churches is that of Clumber (1886–9), now standing forlorn in the grounds of the demolished mansion. Bodley also designed the chapel of Queens' College, Cambridge (1890–1), and buildings for King's College, Cambridge (1893). Among his pupils were C. R. Ashbee and Sir Ninian Comper.

BOFFRAND, Gabriel Germain (1667–1754), the greatest French Rococo architect, began as a sculptor, studying under Girardon in Paris (1681), but soon turned to architecture. He became the pupil and later the collaborator of J. H. MANSART. He was very prolific and made a large fortune, mainly by the speculative building of Parisian *hôtels* (e.g., Hôtels de Montmorency, 1712; de Seignelay, 1713; de Torcy, 1714), but he lost the bulk of it in the Mississippi Bubble of 1720. Like his contemporary de COTTE he had great influence outside France, especially in Germany (e.g., on the Residenz, Würzburg). His virtuosity is well seen in the Hôtel Amelot, Paris (1710), built round an oval court with rooms of various shapes and sizes, including a pentagon. The elevations, as always with Boffrand, are of the utmost simplicity and reticence, while the interior is of course very luxurious. His finest interior is probably that of the pavilion he added (c. 1737–40) to the Hôtel de Soubise (now the Archives Nationales), Paris. His Rococo ideal of elegant informality and sophisticated simplicity was realized in his Château de Saint Ouen, a brilliant and original conception consisting of a tiny Trianon-like pavilion of three rooms, set in a spacious courtyard formed by the guests' apartment, offices, stables, etc. He published *Livre d'architecture contenant les principes généraux de cet art* in 1745.

BOISERIE. French for wainscoting or panelling, but applied more strictly to C17 and C18 panelling elaborately decorated with shallow-relief carvings.

BOLECTION MOULDING. A moulding used to cover the joint between two members with different surface levels. It projects beyond both surfaces. *See figure 14.*

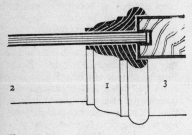

Key:
1. Bolection moulding
2. Panel
3. Frame

Fig. 14. Bolection moulding

BOND, *see* BRICKWORK.

BONNET TILE. A curved tile used for joining plain tiles along the HIPS of a roof.

BORROMINI, Francesco (1599–1667). The most original genius of Roman High Baroque architecture and the jealous rival of his almost exact contemporary BERNINI. A late starter, lonely, frustrated, and neurotic, he eventually committed suicide. Born at Bissone on Lake Lugano, the son of a mason, he began humbly as a stone-cutter, and went to Rome in his early twenties, and remained there for the rest of his life. Befriended by his distant relation MADERNO, he found employment as a stone-carver at St Peter's, mainly on decorative *putti*, festoons, etc. After Maderno's death (1629) he continued under Bernini, later becoming his chief assistant and occasionally contributing to the designs both at St Peter's and at Palazzo Barberini. But their relationship was uneasy. Himself a first-rate craftsman, Borromini despised Bernini's technical shortcomings; Bernini's success rankled. The two men parted for good in 1633 when Borromini's great opportunity came with the commission for S. Carlo alle Quattro Fontane. Despite its miniature size, S. Carlo (1638–46) is one of the most ingenious spatial compositions ever invented and displays Borromini's mastery of his art and revolutionary disregard for convention. The oval plan, emphasized by the honeycomb dome, is based on geometric units (equilateral triangles), but the swaying rhythm and sculptural effect of the undulating walls and restless, intertwined plastic elements produce an almost voluptuous effect. The concave–convex–concave façade was added in 1667. S. Carlo was quickly followed by S. Ivo della Sapienza (1642–60). Borromini's triangular planning system here produced a star-hexagon, which he worked out vertically with dynamic effect. The fantastic dome culminates in an extraordinary ZIGGURAT-like spiral feature.

His style reached its zenith at S. Ivo. Later buildings were either left unfinished or inhibited by complexities of site or by his having to take over plans by previous architects. Unfinished works include S. Maria dei Sette Dolori (*c.* 1655–66); the interior remodelling of S. Giovanni in Laterano (1646–9), which still lacks the intended nave vaulting; and S. Andrea delle Fratte (1653–65), where the dome is still without its lantern though the drum-like casing and three-storey tower outdo even S. Ivo in fantasy. At S. Agnese in Piazza Navona (1653–7) he took over from Carlo RAINALDI, changing the character of his interior designs by seemingly minor alterations and completely redesigning the façade on a concave plan. The dramatic grouping of high drum and dome framed by elegant towers is one of his best and most typical compositions, though he was dismissed as architect before its completion. An awkward site cramped his style at the Oratory of St Philip Neri (1637–50), remarkable mainly for its ingenious dual-purpose façade uniting chapel and monastic buildings. His domestic architecture is fragmentary but no less startling – *trompe l'œil* arcade at Palazzo Spada, river front and loggia at Palazzo Falconieri, grand *salone* at Palazzo Pamphili, and the library at the Sapienza. The latter was the prototype of many great c18 libraries.

He became increasingly unorthodox, and his last work, the Collegio di Propaganda Fide (*c.* 1660) shows a remarkable change of style towards monumentality and austerity, the capitals, for example, being reduced to a few parallel grooves. Its façade in via di Propaganda – heavy, oppressive, nightmarish – is unlike anything before or since. Reproached in his own day for having destroyed the conventions of good architecture, Borromini had little immediate influence in Italy except superficially in ornamentation. (His revolutionary spatial concepts were to bear abundant fruit later on in central Europe.) His style was too personal and eccentric, especially in its combination of Gothic and post-Renaissance elements. His Gothic affinities were noted by his contemporaries (e.g., Baldinucci), and indeed they went beyond a partiality for medieval features such as the SQUINCH, for his geometrical system of planning and emphasis on a dynamic skeleton brought him close to the structural principles of Gothic. Yet his blending of architecture and sculpture and his voluptuous moulding of space and mass tie him to the Italian anthropomorphic tradition.

BOSS. An ornamental knob or projection covering the intersection of ribs in a vault or ceiling; often carved with foliage. *See figures 15 and 85.*

BOULLÉE, Étienne-Louis (1728–99). A

Fig. 15. Boss

leading Romantic-Classical architect, he probably had more influence than LEDOUX, though he built little (the Hôtel Alexandre, Paris, 1766–8, is the most interesting survivor), and his treatise on architecture remained unpublished until as recently as 1953, for he had many and important pupils, such as J. N. L. Durand who wrote the most influential treatise of the Empire period. His best designs date from the 1780s and 1790s and are, if anything, even more megalomaniac than Ledoux's – e.g. a 500-ft-high spherical monument to Newton – and they are also, like Ledoux's, expressive or *parlantes* in intention despite their apparently abstract, geometrical simplicity. In his treatise he pleads for a felt, not a reasoned, architecture, and for character, grandeur, and magic.

BOW WINDOW, *see* BAY WINDOW.

BOWSTRING ROOF, *see* ROOF.

BOWTELL. A term in use by the c15 (e.g., William of Worcester's notes; mason's contracts) for a convex moulding. A form of ROLL MOULDING usually three-quarters of a circle in section; also called *edge roll*. *See figure 16.*

Fig. 16. Bowtell

BOX-FRAME. A box-like form of concrete construction, where the loads are taken on cross walls. This is suitable only for buildings consisting of repetitive small cells, such as flats or hostels. Sometimes called *cross-wall* construction. *See figure 17.*

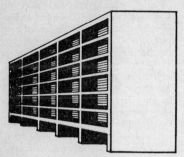

Fig. 17. Box-frame

BOX-PEW, *see* PEW.

BRACE, *see* ROOF.

BRACKET. A small supporting piece of stone, often formed of scrolls or VOLUTES, to carry a projecting weight. *See also* CORBEL.

BRAMANTE, Donato (Donato di Pascuccio d'Antonio, 1444–1514). The first of the great High Renaissance architects. He began under the shadow of ALBERTI and MICHELOZZO, and was profoundly influenced by LEONARDO DA VINCI, from whom he derived his interest in centrally-planned churches. In Rome he evolved a classic style of imposing monumentality which was to have a deep and lasting effect on the development of Italian architecture. PALLADIO declared that he 'was the first who brought good architecture to light'. He was born near Urbino, where he probably met the leading artists at the humanist court of Federigo da Montefeltro, Piero della Francesca, and FRANCESCO DI GIORGIO, to whom he presumably owed his interest in the problems of perspective. He is first recorded in 1477 painting perspective decorations on the façade of Palazzo del Podestà, Bergamo, and he later (1481) made a drawing which was engraved as a perspective model for painters. He entered the service of

Duke Ludovico Sforza *c.* 1479, for whom he worked at Vigevano as both decorative painter and architect. His first building of importance is S. Maria presso S. Satiro, Milan (begun 1482). Here he encased the tiny C9 Capella della Pietà in a drum decorated with niches flanked by slender pilasters, and crowned it with a rather chunky octagonal lantern. He entirely rebuilt the rest of the church on a Latin cross plan. Alberti's influence is apparent in the design for the façade (never completed), the use of shallow pilasters on the side wall and the barrel-vaulted nave. There was no room for a chancel so he feigned one in *trompe l'œil* painting and relief (still deceptive if seen from the right spot). Above the crossing he built a dome with coffered interior, the first since Roman times. He also built an octagonal sacristy, very richly decorated with carvings. In 1488 he was appointed consultant to Pavia Cathedral, but only the crypt was carried out according to his proposals. He designed a centrally planned east end for the Gothic church of S. Maria delle Grazie, Milan, spacious and airy internally, but with a lavish use of elegant but rather finicking carving on the exterior of the apses and the sixteen-sided drum which encases the dome (though much of this ornament may have been added without the warrant of his designs). For S. Ambrogio, Milan, he designed the Canons' Cloister (1492, only one wing built) and a further group of four cloisters (1497, two completed after 1576 to his plans). In the Canons' Cloister he used slender Corinthian columns with high friezes and boldly projecting impost blocks, and four columns in the form of tree trunks with the stumps of sawn-off branches protruding from the cylinders.

In 1499 the French invasion of Lombardy and the fall of the Sforzas forced him to flee to Rome, then the artistic centre of Italy. Apart from some frescoes, his first work in Rome was a cloister at S. Maria della Pace (1500), astonishingly different from anything he had previously designed. It has sturdy piers and attached Ionic columns derived from the Colosseum on the ground floor, and an open gallery on the first with alternate columns and piers supporting not arches but an architrave. The effect is wholly Roman in its quiet gravity. He became still graver and more Roman in his next building, the circular Tempietto of S. Pietro in Montorio, Rome (1502), the first great monument of the High Renaissance, which has a majestic solemnity belying its small size. Surrounded at the base by a Tuscan Doric colonnade with a correct classical entablature, it has no surface decorations apart from the metopes and the shells in the niches. It was intended to have been set in the centre of a circular peristyle which would have provided the perfect spatial foil to its solidity, for it is conceived in terms of volume rather than space, like a Greek temple. Here the Renaissance came closer to the spirit of antiquity than in any other building.

The election of Pope Julius II in 1503 provided Bramante with a new and wholly congenial patron who commissioned him to draw up a vast building plan for the Vatican and St Peter's. A range of buildings later incorporated in the Cortile di S. Damaso was promptly begun, with three tiers of superimposed arcades. Though massive, this was relatively modest in comparison with the scheme for the Cortile del Belvedere, a huge courtyard on three levels measuring about 950 ft by 225 ft, flanked by arcaded buildings, with a theatre at the lower end and a museum for classical antiquities with a central exedra closing the upper court. Work began at the museum end, but only the first storey was completed to his designs (much altered later). The only one of his works in the Vatican which survives intact is the handsome spiral ramp enclosed in a tower of the Belvedere (c. 1505). For St Peter's he proposed a church that would have been the *ne plus ultra* in centralized planning – a Greek cross with four smaller Greek crosses in the arms, roofed by a vast central dome as large as the Pantheon's with four smaller domes and four corner towers, all standing isolated in an immense *piazza*. The foundation stone was laid in 1506 and building was begun but little completed before the Pope's death in 1513 brought all work to a halt. The choir for S. Maria del Popolo, Rome (1505–9), is small in scale but grand in conception, with a massively coffered vault and shell-capped apse. He also designed and began Palazzo Caprini (1514, later altered out of recognition), with a heavily rusticated basement and five pedimented windows between coupled half-columns on the upper floor, a design which was to be widely imitated. The house was later acquired by RAPHAEL, who inherited his position as leading architect in Rome.

BRATTISHING. An ornamental cresting on the top of a screen or cornice.

Fig. 18. Battlements

BRAZILIAN ARCHITECTURE. Brazil was settled by the Portuguese early in the C16 and remained a Portuguese colony till 1807. The country became an independent empire in 1822, and a republic in 1889. Architecture during the colonial centuries remained dependent on Portugal; one of the earliest Baroque churches is S. Bento at Rio of 1652. The centres of the Baroque, however, are S. Salvador de Bahia and the towns of Minas Gerais, where gold was discovered in the late C17. At Bahia the Terceiros Church of 1703 is exuberantly CHURRIGUERESQUE; so is the decoration of the church of S. Francisco (1708 etc.). The architectural climax of Brazilian Baroque, however, is Ouro Preto near Belo Horizonte, with its many churches of the second half of the c18, mostly with two façade towers and elongated central plans. To the same group belongs the church of Bom Jesus at Congonhas do Campo (1777): sculpture here and in several of the Ouro Preto churches is by ALEIJADINHO.

A revulsion from the Baroque came only after 1815. French artists immigrated, including A. H. V. Grandjean de Montigny (1776–1850), who finished the Customs House at Rio in 1820. A little later, but still French Classical, is the theatre at Recife by Louis Vauthier (c. 1810–77), and the rather more American-Colonial-looking theatre at Belém do Pará (1868–78) with its attenuated giant portico. The neo-Baroque is best illustrated by the opera house at Manaus of 1890–6.

While all this had been first colonial and then peripheral, Brazil became one of the leading countries of the world in architecture after the Second World War. The Modern Movement had been introduced by the white cubic houses built from 1928 onwards by Gregori Warchavchik, who published his *Manifesto on Modern Architecture* in 1925. LE CORBUSIER visited Brazil briefly in 1929, and again in 1936, in connexion with the proposed new Ministry of Education at Rio. The building was begun to an amended plan by a group of young Brazilian architects in 1937. Among them were both Lucio COSTA and Oscar NIEMEYER, now the most famous Brazilian architects. Niemeyer is especially important for his early buildings at Pampulha, a club, a dance hall, and a casino of 1942, and a church of 1943. They are the earliest buildings in any country resolutely and adventurously to turn away from the international rationalism then just being accepted by progressive authorities and clients in

most countries. Instead, Niemeyer introduced parabolic curves in elevation, a tower with tapering sides, passages under canopies snaking their way from one building to another, a pair of monopitch roofs slanting downward to where they meet. Other architects whose names have become familiar are Marcelo and Milton Roberto, Affonso Reidy, and Rino Levi.

Lucio Costa's name became a household word overnight when in 1956 he won the competition for the plan of Brasilia, the new capital of Brazil (see COSTA). The principal buildings there are by Niemeyer: the hotel, the brilliant president's palace, the palaces of the three powers, and the ministry buildings. Niemeyer's centrally planned cathedral is not yet completed.

BREASTSUMMER, *see* BRESSUMER.

BRESSUMER. A massive horizontal beam, sometimes carved, spanning a wide opening such as a fireplace. Also the principal horizontal rail in a timber-framed house. *See figure 83.*

BRETTINGHAM, Matthew (1699–1769), was undistinguished, but had a large practice and built Holkham Hall to KENT's designs. He later claimed to have designed it himself. Few of his own works survive; Langley Park is probably the best. His son Matthew (1725–1803) was also an architect, equally successful and equally undistinguished.

BREUER, Marcel, was born at Pécs in Hungary, 1902. He studied at the Bauhaus (*see* GROPIUS) from 1920. In 1925 he was put in charge of the joinery and cabinet workshop, and in that year designed the first tubular steel chair. He went to London in 1935, to Harvard in 1937, and was in a partnership with Gropius 1937–40. His independent practice in America started effectively only after the Second World War. He was first commissioned to design private houses in New England. A sympathy with natural materials (rubble, timber), derived perhaps from his Bauhaus days, had already been apparent in some of his work in England. In the last ten years his practice has spread to other countries (Bijenkorf Store, Rotterdam, with Elzas, 1953; Unesco, Paris, with Zehrfuss and NERVI, 1953), and his style has followed the rather less rational and more arbitrary trend of architecture in general (Abbey of St John, Collegeville, Minnesota, 1953).

BRICKWORK. A *header* is a brick laid so that the end only appears on the face of the wall, while a *stretcher* is a brick laid so that the side only appears on the face of the wall.

English bond is a method of laying bricks so that alternate courses or layers on the face of the wall are composed of headers or stretchers only: *Flemish bond* is a method of laying bricks so that alternate headers and stretchers appear in each course on the face of the wall. *See figure 19.*

English bond

Header   Stretcher

Flemish bond

Fig. 19. Brickwork

BRISE-SOLEIL. A sun-break or check; now frequently an arrangement of horizontal or vertical fins, used in hot climates to shade the window openings.

BROACH SPIRE, *see* SPIRE.

BROACH-STOP, *see* STOP-CHAMFER.

BRODRICK, Cuthbert (1822–1905). A Yorkshire architect whose capital work is the Leeds Town Hall (1853–8), a grand edifice with a many-columned

dome, influenced by COCKERELL and of course WREN. More original is his Leeds Corn Exchange (1861–3), elliptical in plan, Italian Renaissance in style, and with little in the way of enrichment. He also did the wondrously big and heavy Grand Hotel at Scarborough in a style paying tribute to the then fashionable French Renaissance (1863–7), and the Town Hall of Hull (1862–6).

BRONGNIART, Alexandre-Théodore (1739–1813), a prominent neo-classical architect, was born in Paris and trained under J.-F. BLONDEL. In 1765 he began his very successful independent practice, designing the theatre at Caen (destroyed) and the Hotel de Montesson, Paris. For his private houses he adopted a graceful and unpedantic neo-classical style, the nearest equivalent in architecture to the sculpture of Clodion, who was several times employed to decorate them (e.g., Hôtel de Condé, Paris, 1781). But for the Capuchin convent in the Chaussée d'Antin, now Lycée Condorcet (1789, façade rebuilt 1864), he developed a much more severe manner, designing a colonnade of Paestum Doric columns for the cloister. His last important work was the Paris Bourse, an appropriately grandiose Corinthian building in the Imperial Roman style (begun 1807, altered and enlarged 1895).

BROOKS, James (1825–1901). A Gothic-Revival church architect whose directness of approach is comparable to BUTTERFIELD's; but where Butterfield is obstinate and perverse, Brooks excels by a simplicity which LETHABY called big-boned. His favourite material was stock brick, his favourite style that of the early C13 with lancet windows and apse. His principal churches are all in London: first a group in the poor north-eastern suburbs (St Michael, Shoreditch, 1863; Holy Saviour, Hoxton, 1864; St Chad, Haggerston, 1867; St Columba, Haggerston, 1867; and then, a little more refined, three individual masterpieces, among the best of their date in the country: the Ascension, Lavender Hill, 1874; the Transfiguration, Lewisham, 1880; and All Hallows, Gospel Oak, 1889. The latter was intended to be vaulted throughout.

BROSSE, Salomon de (1571–1626), was born at Verneuil where his maternal grandfather Jacques Androuet DU CERCEAU was building the *château*. His father was also an architect. He settled in Paris *c.* 1598. Unlike his relations in the Du Cerceau family and his predecessor BULLANT he conceived architecture in terms of mass and not merely of surface decoration. This plastic sense is evident in his three great *châteaux* of Coulommiers (1613), Luxembourg (1615, but enlarged and altered C19), and Blérancourt (1619). The latter is the finest, and was revolutionary in its day, being a free-standing symmetrical block designed to be seen from all sides. In 1618 he began the Palais du Parlement at Rennes, to which his feeling for sharply defined masses and delicacy of classical detail gives great distinction. His frenchified classicism is epitomized in the façade of St Gervais, Paris (1616), which combines Vignola's Gesù scheme with DELORME's frontispiece at Anet with three superimposed orders. He was the most notable precursor of François MANSART, whom he anticipated in some ways.

BROWN, Lancelot (nick-named Capability, 1716–83). The architect of several Palladian country houses, e.g., Croome Court (1751–2) and Claremont House (1770–2). But he is much more important as a landscape gardener. In 1740 he became gardener at Stowe where he worked on KENT's great layout, and in 1749 he became a consulting landscape gardener. Very soon he developed an artfully informal manner and devised numerous parks with wide expanses of lawn, clumps of trees, serpentine lakes, which provided a perfect setting for the neo-Palladian country seat. Nature was not fettered,

as in the formal schemes of LE NÔTRE, but tamed, and a thick planting of trees served both to conceal the bounds of the idyllic park and to protect it from the unimproved landscape beyond. His probably apocryphal remark on his lake at Blenheim, 'Thames, Thames you will never forgive me,' sums up his attitude. His parks were less an alternative to the formal garden than an alternative to nature which proved irresistibly appealing not only in England but also on the Continent. His best surviving parks are: Warwick Castle (*c.* 1750), Croome Court (1751), Bowood (1761), Blenheim (1765, much altered), Ashburnham (1767), Dodington Park (1764), and Nuneham Courtenay (1778).

BRUANT, Libéral (*c.* 1635–97), built the Hôtel des Invalides in Paris (1670–7), notable for the Roman gravity of its arcaded courts, and the highly original Salpêtrière Chapel in Paris (*c.* 1670). He was a greatly gifted architect who never achieved the success he merited.

BRUCE, Sir William (*d.* 1710), introduced the classical style into Scotland. He came into prominence after the Restoration, for which he had vigorously intrigued, and was rewarded with the lucrative Clerkship to the Bills (1660). He was created baronet 1668, and in 1671 appointed King's Surveyor and Master of Works in Scotland. His work at Holyroodhouse, Edinburgh (1671 onwards), is frenchified but still rather gauche. Kinross House (1685) and Hopetoun House (1698–1702) are more accomplished in the PRATT tradition.

BRUNEL, Isambard Kingdom (1806–59). The son of Sir Marc Isambard Brunel (1769–1849), who had been born in Normandy, had worked in the French Navy, then as city engineer in New York, and had settled in England in 1799; his most famous English work is the Thames Tunnel from Wapping to Rotherhithe (1824–43). The son was educated in Paris and trained in his father's office. In 1829 he designed the Clifton Bridge at Bristol, one of the noblest of English suspension bridges. He was also responsible for the Great Western line from London to Bristol, including the Box Tunnel. His best-known bridge is the Saltash Bridge, opened in 1859. He also built ships (the *Great Western*, which took only fifteen days to America, and the even larger *Great Eastern*) and, in addition, docks (Bristol, Monkwearmouth).

BRUNELLESCHI, Filippo (1377–1446), the first Renaissance architect and one of the greatest, as elegant and refined as Botticelli and as springlike. Far less dogmatic and antiquarian than his immediate successors, e.g., ALBERTI and MICHELOZZO, he was less concerned with the revival of antiquity than with practical problems of construction and the management of space. He, more than anyone else, was responsible for formulating the laws of linear perspective, and a preoccupation with the linear conquest of space characterizes his architecture. In his buildings the horizontals are marked by thin lines which seem to follow the guides of a perspective framework, while the verticals, columns, and fluted pilasters have a spidery, linear attenuation.

Born in Florence, he began as a goldsmith and sculptor, joining the Arte della Seta in 1398, then working for a goldsmith in Pistoia (silver altar, Pistoia Cathedral, *c.* 1399), and competing in 1401–2 for the second bronze door of the Florence Baptistery (he tied with Ghiberti but refused to collaborate with him). In 1404 he was admitted as a master to the Goldsmiths' Guild, and in the same year his advice was sought about a buttress for the cathedral in Florence. Sometime after 1402 he made his first visit to Rome, with Donatello, to study antique sculpture. He continued as a sculptor for a while, but gradually turned his attention exclusively to architec-

ture. In 1415 he repaired the Ponte a Mare at Pisa; in 1417 he advised on the projected dome of Florence Cathedral. His first major works, all in Florence, date from 1418 onwards – a domed chapel in S. Jacopo sopr'Arno (destroyed), the Barbadori Chapel in S. Felicità (partly destroyed), the Palazzo di Parte Guelfa (much altered, but the prototype Early Renaissance palace), and S. Lorenzo. While these were in progress he began, in 1420, to build his masterpiece, the dome of Florence Cathedral, and in 1421 the Ospedale degli Innocenti in Florence.

At S. Lorenzo he began with the sacristy (finished 1428), a cube roofed by a very elegant dome with narrow ribs radiating from the central lantern, a type of construction he called *a creste e vele* (with crests and sails), which neatly expresses its appearance of canvas stretched over the quadrant ribs. The whole interior is painted white, while taut bands of grey *pietra serena* outline the main architectural members; this is the first instance of this strikingly effective decorative scheme. The church itself he designed as a basilica, adding shallow transepts and also chapels attached to the side aisles. But he drew his inspiration not from Imperial Rome so much as the Tuscan Romanesque or proto-Renaissance of the C11–12.

He was commissioned to build the cathedral dome in partnership with Ghiberti who gradually slipped out of the picture. The dome is Gothic in outline with elegantly curved white ribs springing up to the centre, but it is essentially Renaissance in its engineering technique – herringbone brick-work in the Roman manner. The skeleton was completed in 1436, and a further competition held for the lantern – won this time by Brunelleschi alone. He designed the exquisite marble octagon which is perhaps the most successful part of the whole composition. In 1438 he designed the semicircular tribunes with shell-capped niches and coupled Corinthian columns which stand beneath the drum.

The Ospedale degli Innocenti, Florence (designed 1419, built 1421–44), is often claimed as the first Renaissance building. It consists of an arcade of slender, even spindly, Corinthian columns with blue-and-white glazed terracotta plaques between the arches, and a first floor with widely spaced pedimented windows above the centre of each arch. The wide spacing of the arches harks back to CII and CI2 Tuscan work, but the detail is distinctly Roman. The general effect would have been much more antique if, as he intended, similar structures had been erected on the other two sides of the *piazza* to make a forum in front of SS. Annunziata.

In 1429 he began the Pazzi Chapel in the cloister of S. Croce, Florence. The plan is more complex than that of the S. Lorenzo Sacristy: an atrium in the ratio of 1 : 3, the main building 2 : 3, and a square chancel. The interior decoration is more forceful than S. Lorenzo, with virile semicircular arcs of *pietra serena*, Corinthian pilasters, and, in the spandrels, glazed terracotta reliefs. The façade is odd, closer to the tribune of a basilica than a temple portico – slender Corinthian columns supporting a blank attic storey with shallow carved rectangular panels and coupled pilasters. It seems likely that this construction, which looks uncomfortably flimsy from the side, was intended to be continued round the whole cloister. In 1433 he went again to Rome for further study of antiquity, the immediate result of which was S. Maria degli Angeli, Florence, his most archaeological design, though unfortunately building stopped after three years and only the lower parts of the walls remain. It was the first centrally planned church of the Renaissance (an octagon with eight chapels surrounding the central space, sixteen-sided outside with flat walls and deep niches alternating). At S. Spirito, Florence (begun 1436), he reverted to the basilica Latin cross plan, but gave it an entirely new centralized emphasis by running an aisle round the whole church (the west section never built). Once again the proportions are straightforward – an arrangement of cubes, half cubes, and double cubes – creating that balance and feeling of tranquil repose which was among the chief aims of Renaissance architects. The classical ornamentation is correct and vigorous though sometimes employed in a slightly unorthodox fashion. Several other works have been attributed to him, notably the centre of Palazzo Pitti, Florence, which he may have designed shortly before his death. Though astylar it is clearly an Early Renaissance building, with its massive rusticated stonework inspired by Roman work and with proportions governed by a simple series of ratios.

Brunelleschi became the first Renaissance architect almost by accident. He seems to have been drawn towards ancient Rome less for aesthetic than for practical, engineering reasons. An eclectic empiricist, he hit by instinct on those ideas which were to be developed by his successors. Perhaps his greatest merit was to have preserved Early Renaissance architecture from the dry pedantry of archaeology and revivalism.

BRUTALISM. A term coined in England in 1954 to characterize the style of LE CORBUSIER at the moment of Marseille and Chandigarh, and the style of those inspired by such buildings: in England STIRLING & GOWAN; in Italy Vittoriano Viganò (Istituto Marchiondi, Milan, 1957); in America Paul RUDOLPH; in Japan Maekawa, TANGE, and many others. Brutalism nearly always uses concrete exposed at its roughest (BÉTON BRUT) and handled with overemphasis on big chunky members which collide ruthlessly.

BUCRANE (or BUCRANIUM). In classical architecture, a sculptured ox-skull, usually garlanded, often found in the METOPES of a Doric frieze. *See figure* 20.

Fig. 20. Bucranium

BULFINCH, Charles (1763–1844), came of a wealthy, cultivated Boston family. He graduated at Harvard and was, on his European journey in 1785–7, advised by JEFFERSON. His principal works are the Beacon Monument (1789) in Boston, a Doric column, 60 ft high; the State House at Hertford, Conn. (1792); the State House in Boston (1793–1800); and the Court House, also in Boston (1810). They are perhaps the most dignified American public buildings of their time. In Boston extensive street planning and the building of terraces of houses with unified façades was also done under Bulfinch's chairmanship. In his church plans (Holy Cross, 1805; New South Church, 1814) he was influenced by WREN, in his secular work by CHAMBERS and ADAM. From 1817 to 1830 Bulfinch was in charge of work on the Capitol in Washington.

BULLANT, Jean (c. 1520/25–78). His early, rather pedantic classical style is based on DELORME and the study of antiquity (he visited Rome c. 1540–5), but it rapidly acquired Mannerist complexities and, finally, in his late works for Catherine de' Medici, showed a fantasy similar to that of his rival DU CERCEAU. Much of his work has been destroyed. His additions to the Château of Écouen are early and illustrate his characteristically pedantic accuracy in classical details and no less characteristic misunderstanding of the spirit that stood behind them, as witness his most unclassical use of the colossal order. Mannerist features are striking in his bridge

and gallery at Fère-en-Tardenois (1552–62) and in the Petit Château at Chantilly (c. 1560). Of his work for Catherine de' Medici only his additions to Chenonceaux survive – the western arm of the forecourt and gallery over the bridge (c. 1576). He published *Reigle générale d'Architecture* (1563) and *Petit Traicté de Géométrie* (1564).

BULLET, Pierre (1639–1716), a pupil of F. BLONDEL, began in the classical academic tradition and did not display much originality until towards the end of his career at the Hôtels Crozat and d'Évreux in the Place Vendôme, Paris (1702–7). Built on irregular corner sites, they foreshadow the freedom and fantasy of Rococo architects in the shape and disposition of rooms.

BUNGALOW. A single-storey house. The term is a corruption of a Hindustani word, and was originally given to the light dwellings with verandas erected mainly for the British administrators. So many of these have been built in England by unqualified designers that certain areas have been opprobriously called 'bungaloid growths'.

BUNNING, James Bunstone, *see* LABROUSTE.

BUNSHAFT, Gordon, *see* SKIDMORE, OWINGS & MERRILL.

BUON or BON, Giovanni (c. 1355– c. 1443) and Bartolomeo (c. 1374– c. 1467), were father and son, and the leading sculptor-builders in early C15 Venice. They are known to have worked at S. Maria dell'Orto (1392), the Ca' d'Oro (1427–34), and the Porta della Carta of the Doge's Palace (1438–42). They were probably responsible for the design as well as the carved decorations.

BURGES, William (1827–81), trained in engineering, then in the offices of Blore and M. D. WYATT. He travelled in France, Germany, and Italy, and was always as interested in French as in English Gothic forms. In 1856, he won, with Henry Clutton (1819–93), the competition for Lille Cathedral, but in the event the building was not allotted to them. In 1859 he added the east end to Waltham Abbey, where for the first time the peculiar massiveness and heavy-handedness of his detail come out. He was a great believer in plenty of carved decoration, and specialized much less in ecclesiastical work than the other leading Gothic Revivalists. His principal works are Cork Cathedral (1862–76), still in a pure French High Gothic; the substantial addition to Cardiff Castle (1865); the remodelling of Castle Coch near Cardiff (c. 1875); the Harrow School Speech Room (1872); and his own house in Melbury Road, Kensington (1875–80). Hertford College, Connecticut, was also built to his designs (1873–80).

BURGHAUSEN, Hans von, see STETTHAIMER.

BURLINGTON, Richard Boyle, 3rd Earl of (1694–1753), was the patron and high priest of English PALLADIANISM and a gifted architect in his own right. He first visited Italy in 1714–15, but his conversion to Palladianism came after his return to London, which coincided with the publication of CAMPBELL's *Vitruvius Britannicus* and LEONI's edition of Palladio's *Four Books of Architecture*. He immediately replaced GIBBS with Campbell as architect of Burlington House and set out once more for Italy to study the master's buildings at first hand. He returned (1719) with his protégé William KENT, and for the next thirty years dominated the architectural scene in England. The widespread fashion for Palladio was largely due to his influence. He financed Kent's *Designs of Inigo Jones* (1727) and in 1730 published Palladio's drawings of Roman *thermae*. But there was a marked difference between his own and his followers' interpretation of the master. For him Palladianism meant a return to the architecture of antiquity as explained and illustrated by Palladio and he avoided, whereas his followers

blindly accepted, all the non-classical and Mannerist features in the master's style. Cold, intellectual, and aristocratic, he was described by Pope as a 'positive' man, and both the strength and weakness of Palladianism derive from his obsessive, puritanical urge to preach absolute classical standards – those just and noble rules which were in due course to 'Fill half the land with imitating fools' (Pope). His fastidious but dogmatic character is equally evident in his buildings, which became increasingly dry and pedantic. They have a staccato quality – an over-articulation or overemphasis of individual features – which suggests a formula-loving mind. His *œuvre* appears to have consisted in about a dozen buildings designed mostly for himself or friends, beginning in 1717 with a garden pavilion – the Bagno – at Chiswick, where he later built his best-known work, the ornamental villa based on Palladio's Rotonda (c. 1725). His only other important works to survive are the Dormitory, Westminster School, London (1722–30, rebuilt 1947) and the Assembly Rooms, York (1731–2, refronted 1828). This latter is an exact model of Palladio's Egyptian Hall, based on VITRUVIUS. In addition to his independent work, he may be credited as part author of several buildings by his protégé Kent, notably Holkham Hall.

BURN, William, see SHAW.

BURNHAM, David H. (1846–1912), came of an old Massachusetts family. His father moved to Chicago, and there, after several false starts, the son went into an architect's office, where he met J. W. ROOT. The two went into partnership, an ideal pair: Root was poetic and versatile, Burnham practical and a skilled administrator. Burnham and Root have an important share in the evolution of the so-called Chicago School. Their best-known buildings are the Monadnock Block (1889–91), still a load-bearing masonry structure, though severely direct and unornamented; the Masonic Temple (1891), with its twenty-two storeys the tallest building in the world at that time and with a complete steel skeleton (as introduced slightly before by HOLABIRD & ROCHE); and the Flatiron Building in New York (1902), the first New York skyscraper and again the tallest building at the time (290 ft). Burnham was made Chief of Construction for the World's Columbian Exposition in Chicago, which took place in 1893. Buildings were designed by HUNT, MCKIM, POST, SULLIVAN, and others. The most monumental of them were classical and columnar, and this demonstration of Beaux Arts ideals cut short the life of the Chicago School. Later Burnham concentrated more and more on planning: his plans for the District of Columbia (1901–2) are the start of comprehensive town planning in America. They were followed by the plan for Chicago (1906–9) and many others.

BURTON, Decimus (1800–81). The son of James Burton (1761–1837), a successful big London builder. As early as 1823 he designed the Colosseum in Regent's Park with a dome larger than that of St Paul's and a Greek Doric portico. It housed a panorama of London. In 1825 he began the Hyde Park Improvements which included the Hyde Park Corner Screen. He designed several housing estates (e.g., at Tunbridge Wells, 1828 etc.), the town of Fleetwood (1835 etc.), the great Palm Houses at Chatsworth (with PAXTON) and Kew (with R. Turner), many villas (including several in Regent's Park), the Athenaeum, London (1829–30), and a number of country houses.

BUSH-HAMMERING. A method of obtaining an even, rough texture on concrete after it has set, by using a bush-hammer with a specially grooved head which chips the surface.

BUTTERFIELD, William (1814–1900), a High-Church Gothic-Revivalist, was aloof in his life (a bachelor with a butler) and studious in his work. The peculiar aggressiveness of his forms – one jarring with the other – and of his colours – stone and multicoloured brick in stripes or geometrical patterns – was tolerated by the purists of the Cambridge Camden movement and their journal The Ecclesiologist, partly because he was their personal friend (he drew much for the Instrumenta Ecclesiastica of 1847), partly because he must have had a great power of conviction. His earliest church (and parsonage) of importance was Coalpit Heath (1844). This was followed by St Augustine's College, Canterbury, quieter than most of his work. The eruption of his fully developed personal style came with All Saints, Margaret Street, London (1849–59), a ruthless composition in red brick of church and accessory buildings on three sides of a small courtyard. The steeple is slender, noble, North German Gothic, and asymmetrically placed. St Matthias, Stoke Newington, London, followed in 1850–2 – yellow brick, with a nave crossed by two transverse arches; then St Alban's, Holborn, London, in 1863; Keble College, Oxford, in 1867–75; the Rugby School buildings in 1870–86; and many others. Nearly all his work, apart from that for colleges and schools, was ecclesiastical. An exception is the robustly utilitarian County Hospital at Winchester (1863). His early cottages (c. 1648–50) are also remarkably free from historicism. They are the pattern for WEBB's Red House.

BUTTRESS. A mass of masonry or brickwork projecting from or built against a wall to give additional strength.

Angle buttresses. Two meeting at an angle of 90° at the angle of a building.

Clasping buttress. One which encases the angle.

Diagonal buttress. One placed against the right angle formed by two walls, and more or less equiangular with both.

Flying buttress. An arch or half-arch transmitting the thrust of a vault or roof from the upper part of a wall to an outer support or buttress.

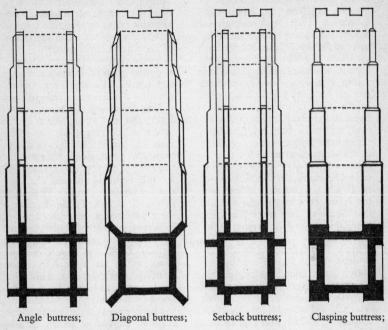

Angle buttress;   Diagonal buttress;   Setback buttress;   Clasping buttress;

Fig. 21. Buttress

Flying buttress

Setback buttress. A buttress set slightly back from the angle. *See figure 21.*

BYZANTINE ARCHITECTURE. The culmination of Early Christian architecture. This style developed after A.D. 330 when Constantine established the Imperial capital at Byzantium (renamed Constantinople) on the Bosphorus. The arts in Rome were then at a low ebb, but no efforts were spared to make the new capital as traditionally Roman as possible. Such a building as the aqueduct of Valens differs little from those built in the West during the previous 300 years. But gradually a new and original style emerged. Classical concepts, such as the ORDERS, were no longer observed; classical detail of

45

all kinds was coarsened and the lush relief decorations popular in Rome were abandoned in favour of flat, rather lacy ornaments. Early C5 churches in Cilicia (e.g., Kandirli and Cambazli), built in a mixture of Syrian and Roman styles, suggest that some of the new influences came from the East. The later C5 church of St John in Studion, Constantinople, also shows a tendency to depart from classical precepts. Yet classicism, or at least a desire to recapture the splendours of the classical past, was to remain a force of recurrent importance throughout Byzantine art, especially in the secular arts where the taint of paganism probably mattered less to early Christians. Very little is known of Byzantine domestic architecture, but recent excavations have revealed that the Imperial Palace in Constantinople was among the greatest buildings of its time.

In the C5 two forms of church were evolved: the BASILICA and the centrally planned church reserved for the shrines of martyrs. The latter, called *martyria*, were usually built on a Greek cross plan and were domed – the combination of a dome with a square base being a Byzantine introduction from the Near East. It was the achievement of C6 architects to combine these two forms of church and to create interiors in which a wholly unclassical play of void and solid, dark and light, produced an effect of mystery which is perhaps the most striking feature of the Byzantine church. The outstanding masterpiece of Byzantine church architecture, Haghia Sophia, Constantinople (built A.D. 532–7 by ANTHEMIUS OF TRALLES and ISIDORE OF MILETUS), shows this quality to perfection. But it was the mathematical and intellectual rather than the emotive qualities of Haghia Sophia that impressed contemporaries. 'Through the harmony of its measurements it is distinguished by indescribable beauty,' wrote Procopius. The same author commented that 'a spherical-shaped Tholos standing upon a circle makes it exceedingly beautiful'. At this time mathematics was considered the highest of the sciences, and Anthemius was a notable mathematician who believed that architecture was 'the application of geometry to solid matter'.

By the C9 symbolism began to play a greater part in Byzantine church architecture. The church was now regarded as a microcosm of all earth and sky, as the setting of Christ's life on earth, and at the same time as the image of the liturgical year. This complex triple symbolism was expressed in painted or mosaic decorations where the very colours used had an emblematic significance. The mystique of numbers also found reflection in church design. To the Byzantine these intellectual concepts were as important as the air of mystery created by screens and galleries dividing the well-lit central area from those surrounding it. The typical Byzantine church plan of a Greek cross inscribed in a square and capped by a central dome (evolved in C7) provided a perfect background for the display of this elaborate painted or mosaic decoration.

As early as the C5 the Byzantine style began to influence architecture in Italy, especially Ravenna (S. Giovanni Battista, S. Croce, and the so-called Mausoleum of Galla Placidia). The basilican S. Apollinare in Classe, Ravenna (c. 536–50), and the octagonal S. Vitale, Ravenna (c. 526–47), are among the greatest and least altered of all Byzantine buildings. Though erected by Byzantine architects, and probably by Byzantine masons as well, both reveal slight Western peculiarities, notably in the decoration of the exterior. Later, Western buildings began to show more radical departures from Byzantine precedents – e.g., S. Marco, Venice, with its very rich marble-clad exterior.

No new developments were made

after the C9. The types of plan evolved – notably the very popular Greek cross inscribed in a square – were repeated endlessly. After the C11 the beauty of their forms tended to be masked by an overabundance of painted decoration. But many fine churches were built, especially in Greece (Hosios Lukas in Phocis; Holy Apostles, Salonika; the Panagia in Athens) and as late as C13 and C14 in Serbia (Gracanica and Ljuboten).

C

CABLE MOULDING. A Romanesque moulding imitating a twisted cord. *See figure 22.*

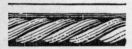

Fig. 22. Cable moulding

CABLED FLUTING, *see* FLUTING.

CAGNOLA, Marchese Luigi (1762–1833). A neo-classical architect who played a leading role in the Napoleonic transformation of Milan, designing the severe Ionic Porta Ticinese (1801–14) and the much richer Arco della Pace (1806–38). He also designed a Pantheon-like parish church at Ghisalba (*c.* 1830), a fantastic campanile crowned with CANEPHORAE supporting a dome at Urgnano (*c.* 1820), and his own many-columned Grecian villa Inverigo (begun 1813).

CAISSON. 1. A watertight chamber used in construction below water or in waterlogged ground. It can be a steel box which is floated into position and sunk, with a working space underneath kept dry by the use of compressed air, or a chamber without any bottom which carries on its top the beginning of a foundation to be sunk to the required depth. 2. A sunken panel in a flat or vaulted ceiling.

CALDARIUM. The hot-room in a Roman bath.

CALLICRATES was the leading architect in Periclean Athens, and with ICTINUS designed the Parthenon (447–442 B.C.). He probably designed and built the exquisite little Ionic temple of Athena Nike on the Acropolis, Athens (448–after 421 B.C.). He also built the south and central portion of the Long Walls from Athens to Piraeus, and perhaps restored part of the city walls.

CAMARÍN. A small chapel behind and above the high altar in Spanish churches. It is usually visible from the nave. The earliest example is in the church of the Desamparados in Valencia (1647–67).

CAMBER. To curve (a beam) either by sawing or by bending, so that the middle is higher than the ends. This is a good remedy for sagging tie-beams (*see* ROOF), as it gives them a slightly arched form.

CAMBODIAN ARCHITECTURE, *see* KHMER ARCHITECTURE.

CAME. A metal strip used for LEADED LIGHTS.

CAMERON, Charles (*c.* 1740–1812), was born in Scotland, visited Rome *c.* 1768, and published *The Baths of the Romans* in 1772. Nothing more is known of him until he was summoned to Russia in about 1774 by Catherine the Great, for whom he designed interiors at Tsarskoe Selo near Leningrad (1783–5) and other buildings, notably the Agate Pavilion. For the Grand Duke Paul he built the great palace at Pavlovsk (1781–96). In about 1787 he was superseded as architect-in-chief by his pupil Brenna, and when Catherine died in 1796 he was dismissed altogether from royal service. But he stayed on in Russia working for private patrons (e.g., Batourin Palace in Ukraine). He returned to favour after the death of Paul I, and in 1805 designed the naval hospital and barracks at Kronstadt. He was an admirer and close follower of Robert ADAM, especially in interior decoration, though lacking his finesse.

CAMPANILE. The Italian word for a bell-tower, usually separate from the main building.

CAMPBELL, Colen (d. 1729). Little is known about him until 1715 when he published the first volume of *Vitruvius Britannicus* and built Wanstead House (now demolished), which became the model for the English Palladian country house. He was probably responsible for Lord BURLINGTON's conversion to PALLADIANISM and was commissioned to remodel Burlington House, London (1718–19). Mereworth Castle (1722–5) is perhaps the best of the English versions of Palladio's Rotonda design. Houghton Hall (1721, executed with modifications by Ripley) is enormous and imposing, but Compton Place, Eastbourne (1726–7), is more elegant and refined.

CAMPEN, Jacob van (1595–1657). A leading exponent of Dutch PALLADIANISM, an unpretentious, placid, and economic form of classicism characterized by its use of brick mixed with stone and its straightforward, almost diagrammatic use of pilasters. The style is epitomized in his masterpiece the Mauritshuis, The Hague (1633–5), entirely Palladian in plan, with giant Ionic pilasters raised on a low ground floor and supporting a pediment, crowned with a typically Dutch hipped roof rising in a slightly concave line from the eaves. His great Town Hall in Amsterdam (now Royal Palace; 1648–55), built entirely of stone, is heavy and bourgeois. More original is the Nieuwe Kerk in Haarlem (1645) of the Greek-cross-in-square type. His domestic style had great influence, and was later introduced into England by Hugh MAY and others.

CANCELLI. In Early Christian architecture, a latticed screen or grille separating the choir from the main body of a church.

CANDELA, Felix (b. 1910), was born in Spain but lives in Mexico. He is one of the most resourceful concrete engineers of the age and is also important architecturally. Among his most significant works are the Church of Our Lady of Miracles (1953–5), an extreme example of mid-century Expressionism, and the Radiation Institute (1954), both at Mexico City.

CANEPHORA. A sculptured female figure carrying a basket on her head.

CANOPY. A projection or hood over a door, window, tomb, altar, pulpit, niche, etc.

CANTERBURY, *see* MICHAEL OF CANTERBURY.

CANTILEVER. A self-supporting projection without external bracing, e.g., a cantilever balcony, beam, or canopy. *See figure 23.*

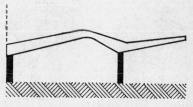

Fig. 23. Cantilever beam

CAP. The crowning feature of a windmill, usually a domical roof; also an abbreviation for CAPITAL.

CAPITAL. The head or crowning feature of a column.

Bell capital. A form of capital of which the chief characteristic is a reversed bell between the SHAFT or NECKING and the upper moulding. The bell is often enriched with carving.

Crocket capital. An Early Gothic form, consisting of stylized leaves with endings rolled over similar to small VOLUTES.

Cushion capital. A Romanesque capital cut from a cube, with its lower parts rounded off to adapt it to a circular shaft; the remaining flat face of each side is generally a LUNETTE. Also called a *block* capital.

Scalloped capital. A development of the block or cushion capital in which the single lunette on each face is elaborated into one or more truncated cones.

See also STIFF-LEAF; WATER-LEAF; *and, for capitals in classical architecture,* ORDER. *See figures 24 and 64.*

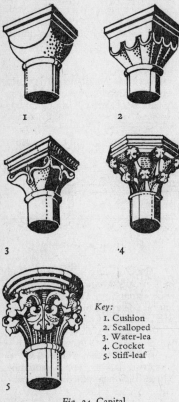

Key:
1. Cushion
2. Scalloped
3. Water-lea
4. Crocket
5. Stiff-leaf

Fig. 24. Capital

CARATTI, Francesco (d. 1679), was born at Bissone near Como, and went in 1652 to Prague, where he became the leading architect. His masterpiece is the Czernin Palace (1664 etc.), with a row of thirty giant attached Corinthian columns and a rusticated basement which breaks forward to provide bases for the columns and bulges out into a central porch. The strong chiaroscuro created by the projections makes this façade one of the most exciting of its time. He also built the Maria Magdalenenkirche, Prague (begun 1656).

CARLONE, Carlo Antonio (d. 1708), is the most important member of a large family of Italian artists working in Austria and South Germany. His masterpiece is the richly stuccoed interior of the Italianate Priory Church of St Florian (1686–1705). Other works include the Jesuitenkirche zu den Neun Chören der Engel, Vienna (1662), with a rather secular street façade, and the charming little pilgrimage church of Christkindl (1708–9), finished by PRANDTAUER, who was much indebted to Carlone.

CAROLINGIAN ARCHITECTURE takes its name from Charlemagne (King from 768, Emperor 800–14), and his descendants and the style extends in time from the late C8 into the C10, and in space through those countries which formed part of Charlemagne's Empire, especially France, Germany, and the Netherlands. Anglo-Saxon architecture in England and Asturian architecture in Spain stand outside this style, which is composite and the result of conflicting trends in these formative centuries of Western civilization. Charlemagne himself promoted a renaissance of Roman – i.e., Constantinian – Christianity. This is evident in poetry, in script, in illumination, and also in the plans and elevations of certain churches which follow Early Christian examples (St Denis, Fulda, etc.). But indigenous characteristics also make themselves felt and point forward to the ROMANESQUE: in this category are prominent towers, strongly stressed west ends and east ends (Centula, plan for St Gall), and also heavier, more massive members. The most spectacular building preserved from Charlemagne's time is the cathedral of Aachen.

CARR, John (1723–1807). A late and provincial exponent of PALLADIANISM, working mainly in Yorkshire.

He began life as a mason in his father's quarry near Wakefield, and in his twenties built Kirby Hall to the design of Lord BURLINGTON and Roger MORRIS. He was later associated with Robert ADAM in the building of Harewood House (begun 1759). From then onwards he designed and built many large country houses. He was unoriginal, but could be refined and dignified in a quiet way, e.g., Denton Park (c. 1778) and Farnley Hall (c. 1786). His largest and perhaps his best work is the Crescent at Buxton (1779–84), where he very successfully combined the younger WOOD's invention of the monumental residential crescent with the arcaded ground floor surmounted by giant pilaster order used by Inigo JONES at Covent Garden.

CARREL (or CAROL). A niche in a cloister where a monk might sit and work or read; sometimes applied to BAY WINDOWS.

CARTOUCHE. An ornamental panel in the form of a scroll or sheet of paper with curling edges, usually bearing an inscription and sometimes ornately framed.

CARYATID. A sculptured female figure used as a column, as on the Erechtheum. The term is also applied loosely to various other columns and pilasters carved wholly or partly in the form of human figures: ATLANTES (male caryatids), CANEPHORAE (females carrying baskets on their heads), HERMS (three-quarter-length figures on pedestals), Telamones (another name for Atlantes), and TERMS (tapering pedestals merging at the top into human, animal, or mythical figures). *See figure 25.*

CASEMATE. A vaulted room, with EMBRASURES, built in the thickness of the ramparts or other fortifications, and used as a barracks or battery, or both.

CASEMENT. I. The hinged part of a window, attached to the upright side of the window-frame. 2. The wide concave moulding in door and window JAMBS and between COM-

Fig. 25. Caryatid

POUND columns or piers, found in Late Gothic architecture. The term was in use by the middle of the C15 (William of Worcester's notes).

CASEMENT WINDOW. A metal or timber window with the sash hung vertically and opening outwards or inwards.

CASINO. 1. An ornamental pavilion or small house, usually in the grounds of a larger house. 2. In the C18 a dancing saloon, today a building for gambling.

CASSELS, Richard (c. 1690–1751). A German who settled in Ireland c. 1720 and became the leading architect of his day in Dublin. His surviving works conform to English PALLADIANISM, without any trace of his foreign origin: e.g., Tyrone House (1740–5) and Leinster House (1745) in Dublin, and his two great country houses, Carton (1739) and Russborough (1741).

CASTELLAMONTE, Carlo Conte di (1560–1641), was trained in Rome. He became architect to the Duke of Savoy in 1615 and played a large part in developing the city plan of Turin, where he designed Piazza S. Carlo (1637) and several churches. He began Castello di Valentino, Turin (1633), completed in the French style with a high hipped roof (1663) by his son Amadeo (1610–83), who succeeded him as court architect.

CASTELLATED. Decorated with BATTLEMENTS.

CASTLE. A fortified habitation. The planning and building of castles is primarily directed by the necessities of defence; it rarely extends as a whole into architecture proper, though certain features may. In the earlier Middle Ages the principal elements of castles were the donjon or KEEP and the hall in France and England, the Bergfrid and the Palas in Germany. The keep is a tower spacious enough to act as living quarters in time of war for the lord or governor and the garrison; the Bergfrid is a tower of normal proportions; the Palas is the hall-range. The earliest dated donjon is at Langeais (c. 990), the earliest surviving major hall at Goslar (mid C11). England built some hall-keeps, i.e., keeps wider than they are high (Tower of London). In France and Italy in the early C13 Roman precedent led to symmetrical compositions with angle towers and a gatehouse in the middle of one side. Some castles of Edward I in Britain took this over, and where in the late Middle Ages castles were still needed (south coast, Scottish border), they were often symmetrically composed. The rule in Britain at this time, however, was that castles could be replaced by unfortified manor houses. Towards the end of the Middle Ages the spread of firearms changed the castle into the fortress, with low BASTIONS for mounting cannon and no towers.

Fortress Elements

Casemate. Vaulted chamber in a bastion for men and guns.

Cavalier. Raised earth-platform of a fortress used for look-out purposes or gun placements.

Counterscarp. The face of the ditch of a fortress sloping towards the defender.

Demi-Lune, see Half-Moon.

Glacis. The ground sloping from the top of the rampart of a fortress to the level of the country around.

Half-Moon. Outwork of a fortress, crescent-shaped or forming an angle.

Hornwork. Outwork of a fortress with two demi-bastions.

Ravelin. Similar to a *Half-Moon.*

Redoubt. Small detached fortification.

Scarp. The side of the ditch of a fortress sloping towards the enemy.

Sconce. Detached fort with bastions.

CATHEDRA. The bishop's chair or throne in his cathedral church, originally placed behind the high altar in the centre of the curved wall of the APSE.

CATHEDRAL. Bishop's church, from CATHEDRA.

CAULCOLE. The stalk rising from the

leaves of a Corinthian capital and supporting one of the VOLUTES.

CAVALIER. In military architecture, a fort raised above the general lines of fortification to command the adjacent outworks.

CAVETTO MOULDING. A hollow moulding, about a quarter of a circle in section. *See figure 26.*

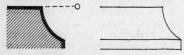

Fig. 26. Cavetto moulding

CELL. One of the compartments of a groin or rib VAULT, in the Romanesque period usually of plastered rubble, in the Gothic period of neatly coursed stones; the earliest known example is St Denis of 1140–4. Also called a *web*.

CELLA. The main body of a classical temple, excluding the portico.

CELURE. The panelled and adorned part of a wagon roof (*see* ROOF) above the ROOD or the altar.

CENOTAPH. A monument to a person or persons buried elsewhere.

CENTERING. Wooden framework used in arch and vault construction; it is removed (or 'struck') when the mortar has set.

CHAIR-RAIL (or DADO-RAIL). A moulding round a room to prevent chairs, when pushed back against the walls, from damaging their surface.

CHALET. A Swiss herdsman's hut or mountain cottage. The term is now loosely applied to any house built in the Swiss style.

CHALGRIN, Jean François Thérèse (1739–1811). A pupil of BOULLÉE and Rome scholar (1758–63). He began in the rather epicene neo-classical manner then current (e.g., in the work of SOUFFLOT), and reintroduced the basilican plan in his St Philippe-du-Roule, Paris (designed pre-1765, built 1772–84), which was very influential. But his masterpiece, the Arc de Triomphe, Paris (1806–35), is more Romantic-Classical in the style of Boullée, with its imperial symbolism and megalomaniac scale. He did not live to see it finished, and the sculptural decoration by Rude and others gives it a distinctly C19 appearance.

CHAMBERLIN, POWELL & BON. A London partnership, the members of which were born about 1920. The partners won the competition in 1952 for a City of London housing estate round Golden Lane, and this extensive scheme is not completed yet. They built an excellent warehouse at Witham in Essex (1953–5) and an excellent school (Bousfield School, London) in 1952–6. Their building for New Hall, Cambridge, is under construction (begun 1960), decidedly *outré* in its forms as the most recent work of the partnership tends to be. Their largest job in progress at present is for Leeds University.

CHAMBERS, Sir William (1723–96), the greatest official architect of his day in England, was born in Gothenburg, Sweden, the son of a Scottish merchant. At sixteen he joined the Swedish East India Company and for nine years made voyages to India and China. His architectural training began in 1749 in Paris under J.-F. BLONDEL, and was continued in Italy from 1750 until 1755, when he settled in London. He was an immediate success. His appointment (1756) as architectural tutor to the Prince of Wales established him in royal favour, and he became successively Architect to the King, jointly with Robert ADAM (1760), Comptroller (1769), and Surveyor General (1782). He was the first treasurer of the Royal Academy and took a leading part in its foundation. In 1770 the king allowed him to assume a knighthood on receiving the Order of the Polar Star from the King of Sweden.

His career was that of a supremely successful official and his buildings are extremely competent; fastidious in ornament, impeccable in the use of orders, but rather academic, despite his famous Pagoda in Kew Gardens, and much less spectacular than those of his rival Robert Adam. His style is scholarly but eclectic, based on English PALLADIANISM smoothed out and refined by the neo-classicism of SOUFFLOT and his contemporaries, whom he had known in Paris and with whom he afterwards kept in touch. Usually best on a small scale, his scholarly finesse is well illustrated by two of his earlier works, the Casino at Marino, Dublin (1757–69), an exemplary combination of strictly classical elements to fit a Greek cross plan, and the Pagoda at Kew (1757–62), in which he aspired to similar archaeological accuracy in another manner. His country houses are neo-Palladian in plan and composition – e.g., Lord Bessborough's villa, now a school, at Roehampton (*c.* 1760) and Duddingston House, Edinburgh (1762–4) – while the Strand façade of his largest and best-known work, Somerset House, London (1776–86), is a conscious imitation of a Palladian composition by Inigo JONES on the site. The courtyards and river façade display more vivacity and originality, and some of the interior decoration equals anything by Adam for elegant refinement. Though never as fashionable as Adam, he exerted great influence both as official head of his profession and through his numerous pupils. His *Treatise on Civil Architecture* (1759) became a standard work.

CHAMFER. The surface made when the sharp edge or ARRIS of a stone block or piece of wood, etc., is cut away, usually at an angle of 45° to the other two surfaces. It is called a *hollow chamfer* when the surface made is concave.

CHANCEL. That part of the east end of a church in which the main altar is placed; reserved for clergy and choir. From the Latin word *cancellus*, which strictly means the screen that often separated it from the body of the church. The term more usually describes the space enclosed and is applied to the whole continuation of the nave east of the CROSSING.

CHANCEL ARCH. The arch at the West end of a CHANCEL.

CHANTRY CHAPEL. A chapel attached to, or inside, a church, endowed for the celebration of Masses for the soul of the founder or souls of such others as he may order.

CHAPTERHOUSE. The place of assembly for abbot or prior and members of a monastery for the discussion of business. It is reached from the CLOISTERS, to whose eastern range it usually belongs, and in England is often polygonal in plan. *See figure 61.*

CHATRI. In Hindu architecture, an Umbrella-shaped dome. *See figure 27.*

Fig. 27. Chatri

CHEQUER-WORK. A method of decorating walls or pavements with alternating squares of contrasting materials (e.g., stone, brick, flint) to produce a chessboard effect.

CHEVET. The French term for the east end of a church, consisting of APSE and AMBULATORY with or without radiating chapels.

CHEVRON. A Romanesque moulding forming a zigzag; so called from the French word for a pair of rafters giving this form. *See figure 28.*

Fig. 28. Chevron

CHICAGO SCHOOL, *see* BURNHAM; HOLABIRD & ROCHE; JENNEY; ROOT; SULLIVAN; UNITED STATES ARCHITECTURE.

CHIMNEY BAR. The bar above the fireplace opening which carries the front of the CHIMNEY BREAST.

CHIMNEY BREAST. The stone or brick structure projecting into or out of a room and containing the flue.

CHIMNEY SHAFT. A high chimney with only one flue.

CHIMNEY STACK. Masonry or brickwork containing several flues, projecting above the roof and terminating in chimney-pots.

CHIMNEYPIECE, *see* MANTELPIECE.

CHINESE ARCHITECTURE. Except for pagodas, Chinese buildings have always been of wood, and thus very few examples of temples and none of private houses or palaces survive from before the Ming dynasty (1368–1644). Our knowledge of earlier buildings derives from paintings and low-reliefs. The loss is less grave than it would be in the West since Chinese traditionalism permitted little change in architectural principles or practice over the centuries. Excavations of neolithic sites reveal that from the beginning Chinese architecture was based on the column and that walls were used as protective screens rather than as structural members. Masonry vaults were used to roof tombs as early as the Han dynasty (206 B.C.–A.D. 220), but were not otherwise employed until the Yüan dynasty (1280–1368), when city gates were often vaulted. Temple roofs were invariably constructed of beams, whose length determined the width of the building.

Apart from some bridges (e.g., the Great Stone Bridge at Chao Hsien,

Hopei, of C6) and some Buddhist cave temples of the C5 and C6 – which can hardly be described as architecture, despite their decoratively carved doorways and interiors – the earliest buildings of importance to survive in China are the pagodas erected in the T'ang dynasty (618–906). The form was introduced with Buddhism from India but soon modified. They are usually on a square plan with successive storeys of diminishing width: decorations are derived from the structural elements of wooden architecture. The most notable surviving example is the Wild Goose Pagoda, Ch'ang-an, Shensi (701–5). Hexagonal or octagonal plans were preferred during the Sung period (960–1279), when the classic type was evolved – a tall tower of uniform width with roofs marking each storey. Stone and brick were the materials used, but decorations continued to be derived from wooden buildings, expecially the prominent and richly carved brackets. Many-storeyed pagodas of this type continued to be built until the C19, with few alterations save in the increasing elaborateness of the brightly coloured decorations. A fine example of the Sung dynasty is the South Pagoda at Fang-shan, Hopei (1117): a much prettified late example is the C18 Marble Pagoda in the Western Hills near Peking.

The earliest wooden building of importance to survive is the relatively small mid-C9 main hall of the temple Fo-kuang-ssu on Wu-t'ai-shan, which already foreshadows the essential elements of Chinese temple and palace architecture – columnar construction, with roofs of curving lines and wide eaves supported on intricately carved brackets. It is of one storey, as were all Chinese buildings except pagodas, though a purely decorative attic might occasionally be added to houses or palaces. The prototype of such buildings is already seen in the low-reliefs of the Han Dynasty. Present-day

Peking is a monument to the building mania and grandiose taste of the Ming. The Imperial City and the Forbidden City, with their rigidly symmetrical plans, gaily coloured palace pavilions and temples, though somewhat altered in later epochs, are a vast and imposing complex of courtyards, curving roofs, and white marble balustrading. The best preserved architectural group of the period is the Chih-hua-ssu temple, Peking, completed in 1444.

In the early C18 the Imperial Summer Palace, Yüan-ming-yüan (destroyed), was built under Jesuit influence in an imitation of Italian Baroque style. But this was a unique instance of Western influence; the traditional style persisted throughout the C19 and the drum-shaped Hall of Annual Prayers in the Temple of Heaven, Peking, one of the best-known Chinese buildings, was built as late as 1896. A change came after the Republican revolution of 1911, and European styles were adopted (e.g., the lecture hall of Nanking University in a pidgin-English neo-Georgian style). In the 1920s there was a so-called Chinese renaissance, when Chinese decorative features were applied to otherwise European-style buildings: the Municipal Government Building, Shanghai (1930), is among the worst examples, the Chung Sheng Hospital Shanghai, (1937), among the best. Since 1949 the INTERNATIONAL MODERN style has won increased support. The Chinese preference for single-storey buildings has been abandoned in favour of tall blocks, though these are limited to nine storeys in Peking for aesthetic reasons.

CHINOISERIE. European imitations or evocations of Chinese art which first appeared in the C17, became very popular in the C18 – especially in England, Germany, France, and Italy – and lingered on into the C19. Numerous PAGODAS were built in Europe. Of the larger buildings in the style the tea-house at Potsdam (1754–7); the

pavilion at Drottningholm, Sweden (1763–9); the Palazzina La Favorita, Palermo (1799); and the interior of the Royal Pavilion, Brighton (1802–21), are the most important.

CHOIR. The part of a church where divine service is sung.

CHURRIGUERA, José Benito de (1665–1725). The eldest of three architect brothers, the others being Joaquín (1674–1724) and Alberto (1676–1750). They came of a family of Barcelona sculptors specializing in elaborately carved retables and began in this way themselves; hence their peculiar architectural style with its lavish piling up of surface ornamentation, now known as the Churrigueresque style. Some of its more fantastic and barbaric features may have been inspired by native art in Central and South America. José Benito settled early in Madrid as a carver of retables (e.g., Sagrario in Segovia Cathedral) and did not turn architect until 1709, when he laid out the town of Nuevo Baztán, the most ambitious and original urban scheme of its period in Spain. His brother Joaquín's best works date from the next decade, e.g., Colegio de Anaya and Colegio de Calatrava at Salamanca. The youngest brother, Alberto, was the most talented, but did not emerge as an architect in his own right until after the death of his two elder brothers. The Plaza Mayor at Salamanca (begun 1729) is his first great work. San Sebastian, Salamanca, followed in 1731, but seven years later he left Salamanca and resigned as architect in charge. His last works are small but among his best: e.g., the parish church at Orgaz (1738) and the portal and façade of the church of the Assumption at Rueda (1738–47).

CIBORIUM, see BALDACCHINO.

CIMBORIO. The Spanish term for a LANTERN admitting light over a crossing tower (see CROSSING) or other raised structure above a roof.

CINCTURE. A small convex moulding round the SHAFT of a column.

CINQUEFOIL, *see* FOIL.

CIRCUS. 1. In Roman architecture a long oblong building with rounded ends and with tiered seating on both sides and at one end. 2. In the C18 a circular or nearly circular range of houses. 3. In modern town planning a circular road or street junction.

CLADDING. An external covering or skin applied to a structure for aesthetic or protective purposes. *See also* CURTAIN WALL.

CLAPBOARD. In the U.S.A. and Canada the term for WEATHERBOARD.

CLAPPER BRIDGE. A bridge made of large slabs of stone, some built up to make rough PIERS and other longer ones laid on top to make the roadway.

CLASSICISM. A style imitating, or inspired by, ancient Greece or Rome or by the classical trend in C16 Italy.

CLERESTORY (or CLEARSTORY). The upper stage of the main walls of a church, pierced by windows; the same term is applicable in domestic building. In Romanesque architecture it often has a narrow wall-passage on the inside.

CLÉRISSEAU, Charles-Louis (1721–1820). A French neo-classical draughtsman and architect who exerted a wide influence through his pupils and patrons, William CHAMBERS, Robert and James ADAM, and Thomas JEFFERSON. He also provided designs (not executed) for Catherine the Great. His own buildings are uninspired, e.g., the Palais de Justice, Metz (1778).

CLERK, Simon (d. *c.* 1489). Master mason of Bury St Edmunds Abbey from 1445 at the latest, and also of Eton College, *c.* 1455–60 (in succession to his brother John), and King's College Chapel from 1477 to 1485. Of his work at Bury nothing survives; at Eton and Cambridge he continued work, that is, he did not initiate, and so his style remains unknown to us. He is cited here as an example of the way distinguished masons were given responsibility in several places.

CLOCHER. The French term for a bell-tower.

CLOISTER VAULT. The American term for a domical VAULT.

CLOISTERS. A quadrangle surrounded by roofed or vaulted passages connecting the monastic church with the domestic parts of the MONASTERY; usually south of the NAVE and west of the TRANSEPT. *See figure 61.*

CLUSTERED PIER, *see* COMPOUND PIER.

COADE STONE. Artificial cast stone invented and successfully marketed in the 1770s by Mrs Eleanor Coade, and later by Coade & Sealy of London. It was widely used in the late C18 and early C19 for all types of ornamentation.

COATES, Wells (1895–1958). An English architect, memorable chiefly for his Lawn Road Flats in Hampstead, London (1933–4), one of the pioneer works in England in the massive concrete INTERNATIONAL MODERN style of the thirties.

COB. Walling material made of clay mixed with straw.

COCKERELL, Charles Robert (1788–1863), son of S. P. COCKERELL, studied under his father and assisted Sir Robert SMIRKE. From 1810 to 1817 he was abroad, first in Greece, Asia Minor, and Sicily, then in Italy. Keenly interested in archaeology, he was excellent at classical and modern languages; in Greece he worked on the discoveries of Aegina and Phigaleia. However, Cockerell combined his passion for Greek antiquities with a great admiration for WREN, and the result is a style which is the English parallel of the Paris Beaux Arts style of about 1840: grander than before, fond of giant orders and sudden solecisms, yet still firmly disciplined. Cockerell is an architects' architect, and PUGIN hated him passionately. Among his buildings the following only can be referred to: the Cambridge University (now Law) Library (1836–42) with its splendid coffered tunnel vault; the Taylorian (Ashmolean) Building in Oxford (1841–5); various branch buildings for the Bank of England, whose architect he became in 1833; and a number of insurance office buildings. He was Professor of Architecture at the Royal Academy, the recipient of the first Gold Medal of the Royal Institute of British Architects, and a member of the academies of Paris, Rome, Munich, Copenhagen, etc. He also wrote on the iconography of the west front of Wells Cathedral.

COCKERELL, Samuel Pepys (1754–1827), began in TAYLOR's office along with NASH. He acquired numerous surveyorships – Admiralty, East India Company, St Paul's, Foundling Hospital, etc. – but is remembered for his fantastic country house, Sezincote (1803), the first Indian-style building in England. Elsewhere he showed French influence of an advanced kind, e.g., west tower of St Anne's, Soho, London. In 1792 he restored Tickincote church in the Norman style, thus anticipating C19 restorations.

CODUCCI, Mauro (c. 1440–1504), a leading architect in late C15 Venice, was born at Lenna near Bergamo, and had settled in Venice by 1469. Like his rival LOMBARDO he achieved (though rather less successfully) a synthesis between the Renaissance and Veneto-Byzantine style with its rich surface decoration and mysterious spatial effects. His earliest known work is S. Michele in Isola (1469), the first Renaissance church in Venice, with a façade derived from ALBERTI's Tempio Malatestiano but capped by a semicircular pediment of Veneto-Byzantine inspiration. Between 1480 and 1500 he completed S. Zaccaria, with its very tall façade on which columns and niches are piled up on one another, and with classical ornament in most unclassical profusion. He was more restrained in S. Giovanni Crisostomo (1497–1504), the first centrally planned church in Venice

(cross-in-square). His main domestic building is Palazzo Vendramin-Calergi (c. 1500), with round-headed windows and rich marble cladding. He also designed the clock-tower and Procuratie Vecchie in Piazza S. Marco (1496–1500).

COFFERING. Decoration of a ceiling, a vault, or an arch SOFFIT, consisting of sunken square or polygonal ornamental panels. See also CAISSON.

COLLAR-BEAM, see ROOF.

COLONIA, Juan, Simón, Francisco, see SIMÓN DE COLONIA.

COLOSSAL ORDER. Any ORDER whose columns rise from the ground through several storeys.

COLUMN. An upright member, circular in plan and usually slightly tapering;

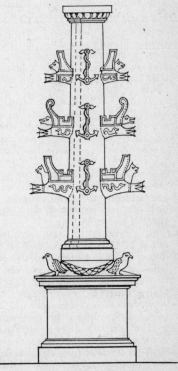

Fig. 29. Columna rostrata

in classical architecture it consists of base, SHAFT, and CAPITAL. It is designed to carry an ENTABLATURE or other load, but is also used ornamentally in isolation. *See figure 64.*

COLUMNA ROSTRATA. In Roman architecture, an ornamental column decorated with ships' prows to celebrate a naval victory. *See figure 29.*

COMMON RAFTER, *see* ROOF.

COMMUNION TABLE, *see* ALTAR.

COMPOSITE ORDER, *see* ORDER.

COMPOUND PIER. A pier with several SHAFTS, attached or detached, or demi-shafts against the faces of it; also called a *clustered* pier. *See figure 30.*

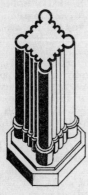

Fig. 30. Compound pier

CONCRETE. Cement mixed with coarse and fine aggregate (such as pebbles, crushed stone, brick), sand, and water in specific proportions. In some form it has been used for more than two thousand years, especially by the Romans. The discovery of Portland Cement in 1824 led to the great developments during the C19, and its use in structures of all kinds has largely revolutionized the shape of building today. *See also* PRECAST, PRESTRESSED, and REINFORCED CONCRETE.

CONFESSIO, *see* CRYPT.

CONSOLE. An ornamental bracket with a compound curved outline and usually of greater height than projection.

CONURBATION. A term used in town planning to denote a group of towns linked together geographically, and possibly by their function, e.g., the towns of the Black Country or the Potteries. The word was first used by Patrick GEDDES about 1910.

COPING. A capping or covering to a wall, either flat or sloping to throw off water.

CORBEL. A projecting block, usually of stone, supporting a beam or other horizontal member. *See figure 69.*

CORBEL TABLE. A range of CORBELS running just below the eaves; often found in Norman buildings.

CORBIE STEPS (or CROW STEPS). Steps on the COPING of a gable, used in Flanders, Holland, North Germany and East Anglia, and also in C16 and C17 Scotland.

CORDEMOY, J. L. de. An early Neoclassical theorist about whom very little is known except that he was a priest (prior of St Nicholas at La Ferté-sous-Jouars) and was not, as is sometimes said, identical with L. G. de Cordemoy (1651–1722). His *Nouveau traité de toute l'architecture* (1706) was the first to preach truth and simplicity in architecture and to insist that the purpose of a building should be expressed in its form. His ideas anticipated and probably influenced those of LAUGIER and LODOLI.

CORINTHIAN ORDER, *see* ORDER.

CORNICE. In classical architecture, the top, projecting section of an ENTABLATURE; also any projecting ornamental moulding along the top of a building, wall, arch, etc., finishing or crowning it. *See figures 42 and 64.*

CORONA. The vertical-faced projection in the upper part of a CORNICE, above the BED MOULDING and below the CYMATIUM, with its SOFFIT or under-surface recessed to form a drip.

CORPS DE LOGIS. The French term for the main building as distinct from the wings or pavilions.

CORTILE. The Italian term for a courtyard, usually internal and surrounded by ARCADES.

CORTONA, Pietro Berrettini da (1596–1669), painter and architect, second only to BERNINI in the history of Roman Baroque art, was born at Cortona, the son of a stone mason. Apprenticed to the undistinguished Florentine painter Commodi, he went with him to Rome c. 1612 and settled there. He can have received only superficial training in architecture, if any at all. First patronized by the Sacchetti family, for whom he designed the Villa del Pigneto (1626–36, now destroyed, but a landmark in villa design), he was soon taken up by Cardinal Francesco Barberini and his cultivated circle. Thereafter he had architectural and pictorial commissions in hand simultaneously. His first important building, SS. Martina e Luca, Rome (1635–50), is also the first great, highly personal, and entirely homogeneous Baroque church, conceived as a single plastic organism with a single dynamic theme applied throughout. It is notable especially for the pliable effect given to the massive walls by breaking them up with giant columns: these are not used to define bays or space, as they would have been by a Renaissance architect, but to stimulate the plastic sense. The decoration is extremely rich, even eccentric (e.g., the wildly undulating forms of the dome coffering), with here and there Florentine Mannerist traits. In contrast to Bernini he excluded figure sculpture entirely; he also excluded colour and had the interior painted white throughout.

His use of concave and convex forms in the façade of S. Maria della Pace, Rome (1656–7), is typically Baroque. More original is his application of theatre design to the *piazza*: he treated it as an auditorium, the side entrances being arranged as if they were stage doors and the flanking houses as if they were boxes. The gradual elimination of Mannerist ele-

ments from his style and his tendency towards Roman simplicity, gravity, and monumentality are apparent in the façade of S. Maria in Via Lata, Rome (1658–62). Comparison between his early and late works, notably the dome of S. Carlo al Corso, Rome (begun 1668), illustrates his remarkable progress from eccentricity and complexity, with effervescent decoration, to serene classical magnificence. Most of his grander and more ambitious schemes remained on paper (Chiesa Nuova di S. Filippo, Florence; Palazzo Chigi, Rome; Louvre, Paris). Though equally great as painter and architect he said that he regarded architecture only as a pastime.

COSMATI WORK. Decorative work in marble with inlays of coloured stones, mosaic, glass, gilding, etc., much employed in Italian Romanesque architecture, especially in and around Rome and Naples, C12–13. Roman marble workers of this period were known collectively as the Cosmati from the name Cosma, which recurs in several families of marble workers.

COSTA, Lucio, born 1902 at Toulon in France. Brazilian architect, planner, and architectural historian (in which capacity he works in the Commission for Ancient Monuments). An example of his excellent architectural work is the block of flats in the Eduardo Guinle Park at Rio (1948–54). As a planner he suddenly rose to fame by winning the competition for Brasilia, the new capital (Nova-Cap) of Brazil, in 1957. The plan is a formal one, yet not at all formal in the Beaux Arts sense. It has the shape of a bow and arrow or a bird, the head being the square with the two houses of parliament and the parliamentary offices, the tail being the railway station. Close to this are sites for light industry; nearer the head, but on the way along the straight monumental axis towards the station, follows the quarter of hotels, banks, theatres, etc., which lies at the junction of body and wings. The long curved wings (or the bow proper) are for housing; this area is divided into large square blocks, called *superquadre*, each with its freely arranged high slabs of flats, schools, church, etc.

COTTAGE ORNÉ. An artfully rustic building, usually of asymmetrical plan, often with a thatched roof, much use of fancy WEATHERBOARDING, and very rough-hewn wooden columns. It was a product of the picturesque cult of the late C18 and early C19 in England: an entire village of such cottages was built by NASH at Blaise Hamlet (1811). It might serve merely as an ornament to a park or as a lodge or farm labourer's house, but several, intended for the gentry, were built on a fairly large scale. Papworth's *Designs for Rural Residences* (1818) includes numerous designs.

COTTE, Robert de (1656–1735), an early Rococo architect, was instrumental in the diffusion abroad, especially in Germany, of French architectural and decorative fashions. He began under his brother-in-law J. H. MANSART, who established him professionally and whom he eventually succeeded as *premier architecte* (1709). His Parisian *hôtels* date from 1700 onwards, the most notable among those that survive being the Hôtel de Bouvallais (*c.* 1717) and the redecoration of François Mansart's Hôtel de la Vrillière, in which the gallery (*c.* 1719) is a Rococo masterpiece. He also worked extensively outside Paris (e.g., Palais Rohan, Strasbourg), and was frequently consulted by German patrons, for extensions to the *château* at Bonn and for Schloss Clemensruhe at Poppelsdorf, for example; but his designs or advice were not always accepted (e.g., at Schloss Brühl, Schloss Schleissheim, and the Residenz Würzburg).

COUPLED ROOF, *see* ROOF.

COVARRUBIAS, Alonso de (1488–1570), was a mason and decorative sculptor in a limpid, playful Early Renaissance style, though for structural members he still adhered to the Gothic tradition. He appears first as one of the nine consultants for Salamanca Cathedral in 1512, a sign of remarkably early recognition. From 1515 he did decorative work at Sigüenza. The church of the Piedad at Guadalajara (1526) is now in ruins, but the Chapel of the New Kings at Toledo Cathedral (1531–4) survives complete and is a delightful work. The fine staircase of the Archbishop's Palace at Alcalá is of *c.* 1530, the richly tunnel-vaulted Sacristy at Sigüenza of 1532–4. Covarrubias was master mason of Toledo Cathedral and architect to the royal castles (1537 etc.); see the courtyard of the Alcázar at Toledo.

COVER FILLET. A moulded strip used to cover a joint in panelling, etc.

COVING. 1. The large concave moulding produced by the sloped or arched junction of a wall and ceiling. 2. In the case of ROOD SCREENS the concave curve supporting the projecting ROOD LOFT.

COWL. A metal covering, like a monk's hood, fixed over a chimney or other vent, and revolving with the wind to improve ventilation.

CRADLE ROOF, *see* ROOF.

CREDENCE. A small table or shelf near the altar, on which the Sacraments are placed.

CRENELLATION, *see* BATTLEMENTS.

CREPIDOMA. The stepped base of a Greek temple.

CRESCENT. A concave row of houses.

CREST, CRESTING. An ornamental finish along the top of a screen, wall, or roof; usually decorated and sometimes perforated.

CRETAN AND MYCENAEAN ARCHITECTURE. Excavations have revealed the earliest examples of European architecture at Knossos and Phaestos in Crete. Although many of the discoveries are of controversial significance, and most of the proposed reconstructions are unconvincing, enough survives to reveal certain general characteristics. At both Knossos and Phaestos there were elaborate palaces, richly coloured and decorated with selinite revetments, destroyed in the (probably seismic) catastrophe of *c.* 1700 B.C. which marks the first break in Cretan history. The palaces built to replace them were more carefully integrated with the surrounding landscapes; they had hanging gardens, cool courtyards, and colonnaded walks. Planning seems to have been wilfully asymmetrical, and long corridors linked a bewildering series of tiny rooms with the grand MEGARA and pillared halls. Decorations proliferated, and both interiors and exteriors were boldly and brightly painted in a manner which must have been almost jazzy. Another dramatic destruction occurred *c.* 1400 B.C.; shortly afterwards Crete came under Mycenaean control.

The Mycenaeans of the Greek mainland developed their architecture under Cretan influence. They adopted the Cretan *megaron* and also the *tholos* or BEE-HIVE tomb, of which the best surviving example is the so-called 'Treasury of Atreus' at Mycenae (C15 B.C.). But between 1400 and 1200 B.C., when the Mycenaeans held the upper hand in the Greek world, they produced an architecture of greater monumentality and sophistication. The great cyclopean walls surviving at Mycenae and Tiryns reveal their engineering abilities. They developed the fortified acropolis as the civic and religious centre of the city. They began to use stone sculpture (e.g., the Lion Gate at Mycenae) as well as painting for decoration and, for especially fine rooms, incrustations of alabaster and lapis lazuli. But their most important achievement was in monumental planning. Abandoning the haphazard systems of the palaces at Knossos and Phaestos, they enhanced the majestic impact of the acropolis at Mycenae by arranging a succession of courtyards, staircases, and rooms on a single axis. The Mycenaeans were overthrown and their buildings destroyed by incursions from the north in the C12 B.C., but three Cretan–Mycenaean architectural elements – the *megaron*, the acropolis, and the axial plan – were destined to survive in GREEK ARCHITECTURE.

CROCKET. A decorative feature carved in various leaf shapes and projecting at regular intervals from the angles of spires, PINNACLES, canopies, gables, etc., in Gothic architecture. *See figure 31.*

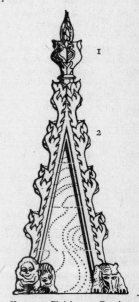

Key: 1. Finial 2. Crocket
Fig. 31. Crocket

CROCKET CAPITAL, *see* CAPITAL.

CROSS VAULT, *see* VAULT.

CROSS WINDOW. A window with one MULLION and one TRANSOM. *See figure 32.*

CROSSING. The space at the intersection of the nave, chancel, and transepts of a church; often surmounted by a crossing tower.

CROW STEPS, *see* CORBIE STEPS.

CRUCKS. Pairs of large curved timbers

Fig. 32. Cross window

used as the principal framing of a house. They take the place of both posts of the walls and rafters of the roof.

CRYPT. An underground chamber usually below the east end of a church; in early medieval times used for the burial of martyrs, saints, etc., and called a *confessio*.

CRYPTOPORTICUS. In Roman architecture, an enclosed gallery having walls with openings instead of columns; also a covered or subterranean passage.

CUPOLA. A DOME, especially a small dome on a circular or polygonal base crowning a roof or turret.

CURTAIL STEP. The lowest step in a flight, with a curved end.

CURTAIN WALL. 1. A non-load-bearing wall which can be applied in front of a framed structure to keep out the weather. There are now many types, manufactured from a variety of materials such as aluminium, steel, and glass; sections may include windows and the spaces between. *See figure 33.* 2. In medieval architecture the outer wall of a castle, surrounding it and usually punctuated by towers or BASTIONS.

CURVILINEAR TRACERY, *see* TRACERY.

CUSP. Projecting points formed at the meeting of the FOILS in Gothic TRACERY, etc. *See figure 46.*

CUTWATER. The wedge-shaped end of a pier of a bridge, so constructed to break the current of water.

CUVILLIÉS, François (1695–1768). One of the most accomplished Rococo

architects. Though he derived inspiration from the French Rococo, his decoration is much more exuberant than anything in France. His masterpiece, the Amalienburg in the park of Nymphenburg near Munich, has an easy elegance and gossamer delicacy which makes it the supreme secular monument of the Rococo. Born at Soigne-en-Hainaut, he entered the service of the exiled Elector Max Emanuel of Bavaria in 1708. As court dwarf, he travelled in the Elector's train through France, and in 1714 accompanied him on his return to Munich. Too small for the army, he began by working as a military architect and showed such promise that he was sent to Paris (1720–4) to study under J.-F. BLONDEL. In 1725 he was appointed Court Architect in Munich with EFFNER. He probably helped the Elector's brother in the decoration of Schloss Brühl near Cologne (1729) and designed the beautiful little house of Falkenlust in the park. His first work in Bavaria was the decoration of the Reiche Zimmer in the Residenz, Munich (1729–37, partly destroyed). In 1733 he provided designs for the abbey church of Schäftlarn and for Palais Königsfeld (now the Archbishop's Palace), Munich. His next work was the Amalienburg (1734–9).

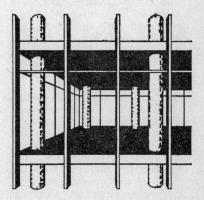

Fig. 33. Curtain wall

It is a single-storey building with a large circular room in the centre which makes the garden façade curve outwards gracefully. The carved wood and silvered decorations in the main rooms are of exquisite refinement and the colour schemes are remarkably subtle – a cool watery blue background in the centre, citron yellow in one of the side rooms, and straw yellow in the other. In 1747 he provided plans for Wilhelmstal, near Kassel (erected by C. L. du Ry). His last major work was the Residenztheatre, Munich (1751–3; partly destroyed 1944, restored 1958), one of the last insouciant extravaganzas of the Rococo, liberally decorated with exquisitely carved *putti*, caryatids, swags, trophies of musical instruments, and those frothy cartouches which characterize the style. In 1767 he completed the façade of the Theatine church of St Cajetan in Munich. He published a *Livre de cartouches* in 1738.

CUYPERS, Petrus Josephus Hubertus (1827–1921), the most important Dutch architect of the C19, studied at the Antwerp Academy and in 1850 became City Architect at Roermond. In 1852 he set up a workshop there for Christian art. In 1865 he went to Amsterdam, where he built his two most famous buildings, both in the Dutch brick Renaissance, and both restrained and without the exuberance of others working in the Northern Renaissance styles. The two buildings are the Rijksmuseum (1877–85) and the Central Station (1881–9). But the majority of Cuypers's works are neo-Gothic churches. It is hard to single out a few from the large total: they might be St Catharina, Eindhoven (1859); St Wilibrordus and Sacred Heart, both Amsterdam (1864–6 and 1873–80); St Bonifatius, Leeuwarden (1881); St Vitus, Hilversum (1890–2); and Steenbergen (1903). Cuypers also restored and enlarged the castle of Haarzuylen (1894–6).

CYCLOPEAN MASONRY. In pre-classical Greek architecture, masonry composed of very large irregular blocks of stone; also any polygonal masonry of a large size. *See figure 73.*

CYMA RECTA. A double-curved moulding, concave above and convex below, also called an *ogee moulding. See figures 34 and 42.*

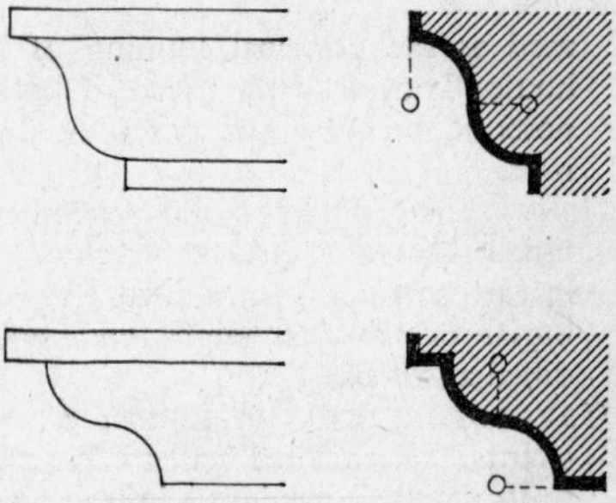

Fig. 34. Cyma recta; cyma reversa

CYMA REVERSA. A double-curved moulding, convex above and concave below; also called a *reverse ogee moulding. See figures 34 and 42.*

CYMATIUM. The top member of a CORNICE in a classical ENTABLATURE.

CZECHOSLOVAK ARCHITECTURE. In the Middle Ages art in Bohemia and Moravia formed part of German architecture. The country suddenly assumed international importance when Prague became the capital of Charles IV's empire. The new cathedral was begun by a French architect, Matthias of Arras, in 1341. His successor was the great Peter PARLER of Swabia, who started work in 1352. He is at his best in the porches and side chapels with their patterned rib-vaults including flying ribs. Links with the Decorated style in England seem probable but have never been proved. By Parler also is the church of Kutná Hora (Kuttenberg). The standard Gothic church of Czechoslovakia is the hall church of the German Late

Gothic type, examples of which are Brno (Brünn), Most (Brüx), and Louny (Laun). Two-naved churches were also built. The climax of medieval secular architecture is the Vladislav Hall in the Castle at Prague with its fantastic vault of intertwined curved ribs; this is by Benedict Rieth of Bavaria and was begun in 1487.

It is interesting that among the features of the Vladislav Hall there are also windows flanked by Renaissance pilasters. Bohemia took to the Renaissance as early as Hungary and Poland, and earlier than the more central countries such as France and Germany, neither of which possesses anything as purely and completely Italian and built as early as the Belvedere at Prague (1536). The oblong building, really a banqueting house, is the work of North Italian masons, and is surrounded by an arcade of slim columns. Arcaded courtyards became a hallmark of the later c16, as they did in Germany (Bučovice, 1566). Architects were nearly all Italians. In the c17 the Bohemian nobility built themselves palaces in Prague and in the country. The biggest are the Lobkowicz Palace at Roudnice (1652 etc.) and the Czernin Palace in Prague (1664 etc.), both by Francesco CARATTI. The Czernin Palace is twenty-nine

windows wide and four storeys high, with no pavilions or other projections, but with the heaviest diamond rustication on the ground floor and serried attached giant columns above. The change from this massed display to the splendidly curvaceous Bohemian c18 style was due to two members of the Bavarian DIENTZENHOFER family: Christian and Kilian Ignaz. Christian's principal works are the churches of St Niklas on the Kleinseite (Malá Strana) at Prague (1703 onwards) and Břevnow near Prague (1708 onwards). The source of the style is GUARINI, who designed a church near Prague, and there are also close relations to HILDEBRANDT's work. The most characteristic features are façades curving forward and backward, interlocked oval spaces inside, and skew- or three-dimensional arches.

Czechoslovakia once more came into the German orbit when she took up quite early the new style of the c20. The Ministry of Pensions by Havlíček & Honzík dates from 1928, and the building of Zlin for the Bata shoe factories and their housing from 1929 onwards resulted in a town nearly the size of the largest of the New Towns in England (60,000 inhabitants).

D

DADO. 1. In classical architecture, the portion of a PLINTH or PEDESTAL between the base and CORNICE; also called a *die*. *See figure 66.* 2. In modern architecture, the finishing of the lower part of an interior wall from floor to waist height.

DAGGER. A TRACERY motif of the Decorated style: a lancet shape, rounded or pointed at the head, pointed at the foot, and cusped inside. *See figure 35.*

Fig. 35. Dagger

DAIS. A raised platform at one end of a medieval hall, where the head of the house dined with his family circle.

DANCE, George (1741–1825), son of George Dance senior (d. 1768, architect of the Mansion House, London, 1739–52), went at seventeen to Italy for seven years with his brother Nathaniel, the painter, winning a gold medal at Parma in 1763 with some surprisingly advanced neo-classical designs. His early buildings are equally original and advanced, and might almost suggest an acquaintance with his more *avant-garde* French contemporaries, LEDOUX and BOULLÉE, because of his use of the elements of architecture as a means of expression rather than of abstract geometrical design. His first building after his return from Italy was the exquisitely pure and restrained All Hallows, London Wall (1765–7). This was followed by his daring and highly imaginative Newgate Prison, London (1769–78, demolished), the most original and dramatic building of its period in England. His ability appears to have

been quickly recognized, despite his unorthodoxy, for he was elected a founder member of the Royal Academy in 1768. His later buildings show no decline in originality or imagination: indeed, some of them anticipate SOANE – e.g., the Council Chamber of London Guildhall (1777, destroyed), in which the dome was treated like a parachute with fine lines radiating from the glazed opening in the centre, and the library of Lansdowne House, London (1792, completed by SMIRKE), which was lit by concealed windows in the semi-domed *exedrae* at either end of the long flat-vaulted room. After the turn of the century his style became increasingly austere and at Stratton Park (1803–4) and the College of Surgeons, London (1806–13), he foreshadowed the Greek Revival of SMIRKE and WILKINS. But his principal artistic legatee was his pupil Soane.

DANCING STEPS. Shaped steps on a turn, the tapered end being widened to give a better foothold; also called *Danced stairs* or *Balanced winders*.

DANISH ARCHITECTURE, *see* SCANDINAVIAN ARCHITECTURE.

DAVIS, Alexander Jackson (1803–92), who was born in New York, joined Ithiel Town (1784–1844) as a draughtsman and became a partner in 1829. Town had already designed the Connecticut State Capitol with a Greek Doric portico in 1827. The partners now designed more capitols of the same type, but with domes a little incongruously rising over the middle of the longitudinal blocks (Indiana, 1831; North Carolina, 1831; Illinois, 1837; Ohio, 1839). They are among the grandest of the Greek-Revival buildings in America. But Davis could also do collegiate Gothic (New York

University, Washington Square, 1832 etc.) and other versions of Gothic, and was versed in the cottage style too. At the same time he was interested in modern materials – he did an iron shop-front as early as 1835 – and was in fact an exceptionally versatile designer. He was one of the founders of the American Institute of Architects and of the villa estate of Llewellyn Park, New Jersey (1857).

DE SANCTIS, Francesco (1693–1740), designed the Spanish Steps in Rome (1723–5), the vast and fabulous external Baroque stairway of elegant, curvilinear design, mounting from Piazza di Spagna to S. Trinità dei Monti; a masterpiece of scenic town planning.

DECASTYLE. Of a PORTICO with ten fronted columns.

DECORATED STYLE. A phase of the Gothic style in England between the EARLY ENGLISH and the PERPENDICULAR. It begins in the 1290s and lasts into the second half of the C14, and is characterized first and foremost by the OGEE, a double or S-curve, which occurs chiefly in arches and in the TRACERY of windows. The other main characteristic is a maximum of decoration covering surfaces (e.g., in foliage DIAPERS) and encrusting arches, gables, etc.; the leaves are not naturalistic but stylized, with nobbly forms reminiscent of certain seaweeds. Spatially the Decorated style favours the unexpected vista, especially in diagonal directions. Principal works are the east parts of Bristol Cathedral and Wells Cathedral, the Lady Chapel at Ely, and screens (Lincoln), funerary monuments (Edward II, Gloucester; Percy Tomb, Beverley), stalls (Exeter), etc.

DEINOCRATES, a Hellenistic architect, contemporary with Alexander the Great, appears to have been the architect, with Paeonius, of the temple of Artemis at Ephesus (c. 356 B.C.). He is credited with the town plan of Alexandria and various other important undertakings, some of them rather

fanciful, e.g., the project to transform Mount Athos into a colossal statue of the king, holding in one hand a city and in the other a huge cup into which the mountain streams would be gathered and then cascade into the sea.

DELORME, Philibert (1500/15–1570), who was born in Lyon, the son of a master mason, went to Rome for three years, probably 1533–36, where he moved in high diplomatic-humanist circles but entirely misunderstood the point of Italian architecture. He was nothing if not original and as utterly French as his friend and admirer Rabelais. His buildings are notable for their ingenuity and sometimes outrageous experimentation. Almost everything he built has been destroyed, except for parts of Anet (Diane de Poitiers's house) and the tomb of Francis I in St Denis (begun 1547). The frontispiece of Anet (begun before 1550, now in the École des Beaux Arts, Paris) is a good example of his style, correct in detail and rather more monumental than that of his contemporary LESCOT. The chapel (1549–52) and entrance front (c. 1552) are still *in situ*. He had a great influence on the development of French architecture, partly through his books, *Nouvelles Inventions* (1561) and *Architecture* (1567). The decorative part of the screen in St Étienne-du-Mont, Paris, with its pierced balustrades and spiral staircase (c. 1545), is probably by Delorme.

DENTIL. A small square block used in series in Ionic, Corinthian, Composite, and more rarely Doric CORNICES. *See figures 42 and 64.*

DIAPER WORK. All-over surface decoration composed of a small repeated pattern such as lozenges or squares. *See figure 36.*

DIAPHRAGM ARCH. A transverse arch (*see* VAULT) across the nave of a church, carrying a masonry gable. Diaphragm arches divide wooden roofs into sections and were probably used to prevent fire spreading.

Fig. 36. Diaper work

DIASTYLE. With an arrangement of columns three diameters apart. *See also* ARAEOSTYLE; EUSTYLE; PYCNO-STYLE; SYSTYLE.

DIENTZENHOFER, Christian or Christoph, *see* DIENTZENHOFER, Kilian Ignaz.

DIENTZENHOFER, Georg (d. 1689). The eldest member of an important Bavarian family of Baroque architects. His main works are the Cistercian abbey church at Waldsassen (1685–1704, with A. Leuthner); the nearby pilgrimage church at Kappel (1685–9), built on an unusual trefoil plan with three minaret-like towers to symbolize the Trinity; and the church of St Martin, Bamberg (1686–93).

DIENTZENHOFER, Johann (*c.* 1665–1726), the son of Georg, studied in Rome until 1699, when he was called to build the Italianate cathedral at Fulda (1701–12). His most impressive church is the Benedictine abbey of Banz (1710–18), where his brother Leonhard (d. 1707) had built the conventual buildings; it has a complex ground plan based on a series of ovals and derived perhaps from GUARINI. His masterpiece is Schloss Weissenstein, Pommersfelden, one of the largest and finest of German Baroque palaces, built in the remarkably short period of seven years (1711–18), with vastly imposing *Treppenhaus* (for which the patron, Lothar Franz von Schönborn, sought the advice of HILDEBRANDT and also contributed ideas of his own), marble hall, gallery, hall of mirrors, and numerous richly stuccoed apartments.

DIENTZENHOFER, Kilian Ignaz (1689–1751), the most distinguished member of the Dientzenhofer family, was the son of Christian (1655–1722, a brother of Johann, who settled in Prague, where he built several churches, notably St Niklas on the Kleinseite, 1703–11, and St Margeretha, Břevnow, 1708–15). Trained first under his father, then under HILDEBRANDT, Kilian Ignaz soon became the leading Baroque architect in Prague. His style is sometimes a little theatrical, and he makes much play with contrasting concave and convex surfaces. His first independent building is the pretty little Villa Amerika, Prague (1720), with an almost Chinese roof in two tiers and very elaborate window surrounds. He also built the Palais Sylva-Tarouca, Prague (1749), on a much larger scale. His originality is best seen in his churches: the Thomaskirche, Prague (1723), with its intentionally jarring details; St Johann Nepomuk am Felsen, Prague (1730), with diagonally set towers on either side of the façade, a device he used again at St Florian, Kladno (*c.* 1750). He added a bold dome and towers to his father's St Niklas (1737–52). At the abbey church of Unter-Rotschow (1746–7) he showed for the first time a tendency towards classical restraint.

DIOCLETIAN WINDOW, *see* THERMAL WINDOW.

DIPTERAL. A term applied to a building with a double row of columns on each side.

DISCHARGING ARCH, *see* ARCH.

DISTYLE IN ANTIS. In classical architecture, a PORTICO with two columns between pilasters or ANTAE.

DODECASTYLE. Of a PORTICO with twelve frontal columns.

DOG-LEG STAIRCASE, *see* STAIR.

DOGTOOTH. Early English ornament consisting of a series of four-cornered stars placed diagonally and raised pyramidally. *See figure 37.*

DOME. A vault of even curvature erected on a circular base. The section can be

Fig. 37. Dogtooth

segmental, semicircular, pointed, or bulbous.

If a dome is to be erected on a square base, members must be interpolated at the corners to mediate between the square and the circle. They can be pendentives or squinches. A *pendentive* is a spherical triangle; its curvature is that of a dome whose diameter is the diagonal of the initial square. The triangle is carried to the height which allows the erection on its top horizontal of the dome proper. A *squinch* is either an arch or arches of increasing radius projecting one in front of the other, or horizontal arches projecting in the same manner. If squinches are placed in the corners of the square and enough arches are erected on them they will result in a suitable base-line for the dome. In all these cases the dome will have the diameter of the length of one side of the square. It can be placed direct on the circular base-line, when this is achieved, or a drum, usually with windows, can be interpolated. If the dome has no drum and is segmental, it is called a *saucer* dome.

Another method of developing a dome out of a square is to take the diagonal of the square as the diameter of the dome. In this case the dome starts as if by pendentives, but their curvature is then continued without any break. Such domes are called *sail vaults*, because they resemble a sail with the four corners fixed and the wind blowing into it.

A *domical vault* is not a dome proper. If on a square base, four webs (CELLS) rise to a point separated by GROINS (*see* VAULT). The same can be done on a polygonal base.

An *umbrella* or *parachute dome* is a dome on a circular base, but also divided into individual webs, each of which, however, has a base-line curved segmentally in plan and also curved in elevation. *See figure 38.*

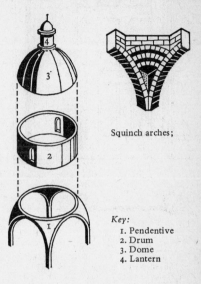

Squinch arches;

Key:
1. Pendentive
2. Drum
3. Dome
4. Lantern

Sail vault; Domical vault; Umbrella dome

Fig. 38. Dome

DOMICAL VAULT, *see* VAULT.

DONJON, *see* KEEP.

DOOR, *see figure 39.*

DORIC ORDER, *see* ORDER.

DORMER WINDOW. A window placed vertically in a sloping roof and with a roof of its own. The name derives from the fact that it usually serves sleeping quarters.

DORTER, *see* MONASTERY.

DOSSERET. The French term for an additional high block or slab set on top of an ABACUS and placed between it and the SPANDREL of the arch

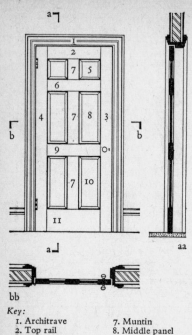

Key:
1. Architrave	7. Muntin
2. Top rail	8. Middle panel
3. Shutting stile	9. Lock rail
4. Hanging stile	10. Bottom panel
5. Top panel	11. Bottom rail
6. Frieze rail	

Fig. 39. Door

above; also called a *super-abacus*. Common in Byzantine work, and found in some Romanesque buildings. See IMPOST BLOCK, see also figure 40.

DOTTI, Carlo Francesco (*c.* 1670–1759). A leading Late Baroque architect in Bologna. His sanctuary of the Madonna di S. Luca, Bologna (1723–57), is a masterpiece of dramatic grouping, with a domed church built on an elliptical plan and a boldly undulating colonnade sweeping out from the main façade.

DOUBLE-FRAMED ROOF, *see* ROOF.

DOWNING, Andrew Jackson (1815–52), the son of a nurseryman and from the beginning an enthusiast for landscape and plants, became America's leading writer on landscape gardening, cot-

tages, and country houses, America's REPTON or LOUDON. His chief writings are *A Treatise on the Theory and Practice of Landscape Gardening*, 1841; *Cottage Residences*, 1842; *Notes about Buildings in the Country*, 1849; and *The Architecture of Country Houses*, 1850. For architectural commissions he was in partnership with Calvert Vaux (1824–95).

DRAGON BEAM, *see* OVERHANG.

DRAVIDIAN ARCHITECTURE, *see* INDIAN AND PAKISTANI ARCHITECTURE.

DRESSINGS. Stones worked to a finished face, whether smooth or moulded, and used around an angle, window, or any feature.

DRIPSTONE, *see* HOOD-MOULD.

DROP. The lower projecting end of a newel (*see* STAIR).

DROP ORNAMENT. A carved ornament in the form of a pendant.

DRUM. A vertical wall supporting a DOME or CUPOLA; it may be circular, square, or polygonal in plan.

DU CERCEAU. A family of French architects and decorators. Jacques Androuet the elder (*c.* 1520–*c.* 1584) was the founder of the dynasty; he is, and always was, more famous for his engravings than for his buildings, none of which survives. The châteaux Verneuil and Charleval were probably the best. But he was essentially an inventor of ornament, not an architect, and indulged in the most wanton and grotesque designs, generally in a Late Mannerist style. His first *Livre d'archi-*

Key: 1. Dosseret   2. Capital

Fig. 40. Dosseret

tecture (Paris, 1559) reveals his personal vein of fantasy and lack of refinement. It had considerable influence, and some of the more practical designs may even have been built. But he was best known for his *Les plus excellents bastiments de France* (1576–79). His son Baptiste (*c.* 1545–90) probably designed the Hôtel d'Angoulême, later de Lamoignon, Paris. His second son, Jacques Androuet the younger (*c.* 1550–1614), designed the Hôtel de Mayenne, Paris (*c.* 1605). Jean Du Cerceau (*c.* 1585–*c.* 1650), the son of Baptiste, designed two of the most typical Parisian houses of the reign of Louis XIII, the Hôtel de Sully and the Hôtel de Bretonville (destroyed); they are both remarkable for the richness of their elaborately carved decoration – sculptural friezes, pediments with scrolls and masks, and allegorical figures in niches.

DUDOK, William Marinus (b. 1884), was architect to the small town of Hilversum near Amsterdam from 1916. He designed many schools and other public buildings, and his style appears to be complete as early as 1921 (Dr Bavinck School, Public Baths): exposed brick; asymmetrical compositions of rectangular blocks, usually with a tower; long bands of low windows. The style reached its climax with the Hilversum Town Hall of 1928–30, internationally one of the most influential buildings of its date. Of Dudok's later buildings, the Utrecht Theatre (1938–41) and the Royal Dutch Steel Works at Velsen (Ijmuiden, 1948) are the most notable.

DUTCH ARCHITECTURE. Dutch Carolingian and Romanesque architecture looked to the Rhineland (Nijmegen, Maastricht, Roermond), Dutch Gothic architecture to France, especially Soissons and Brabant (cathedrals of Utrecht, 1254 etc. and Hertogenbosch, later C14 etc.). The national Gothic style of the late Middle Ages strangely heralds the Protestantism of the future, and not only in the whitewash

applied at that late date (The Hague Oude Kerk, Haarlem Oude Kerk, Dordrecht, Breda Grote Kerk, Zaltbommel). The most important secular monuments are the Binnenhof at The Hague (Great Hall, 1247) and, later, such town halls as that of Middleburg by Anthonis Keldermans from the Southern Netherlands.

Holland has some fine Early Renaissance monuments of the 1530s built by Italians, notably the tower of Ijsselstein Church and the courtyard of Breda Castle. Soon, however, this purity was replaced by a gay, boisterous national style with ornate gables and extensive play with brick and stone mixtures. It culminates in the work of Lieven de KEY at Haarlem and the churches by Hendrik de KEYSER in Amsterdam which are extremely interesting for their centralizing Protestant plans. At the same time as in England and France classical restraint replaced these 'Jacobean' displays. For this the earliest date is that of Jacob van CAMPEN's Coymans House at Amsterdam (1624), and in the thirties and forties there appeared plenty of outstanding classical buildings, especially van Campen's Mauritshuis at The Hague (1633), his magnificent Amsterdam Town Hall, now Royal Palace (1648 etc.), the Nieuwe Kerk at Haarlem (1645), and the Marekerk at Leiden (1639).

The architecture of the C18 and earlier C19 is of less international interest, but with BERLAGE and his Amsterdam Exchange (1897 etc.), in a style transitional between historicism and the C20, Holland reappeared in the forefront and has stayed there to the present day. Piet Kramer and de Klerk represent the Expressionism of the First World War, DUDOK and OUD the INTERNATIONAL MODERN style of the later twenties and thirties. Oud's work during and after the Second World War represents a turn away from rationalism, which took place in other countries as well, and the rebuilding of Rotterdam after the Second World War is one of the most striking examples of the recent concern with problems of the replanning of urban centres.

DWARF GALLERY. A wall-passage with small arcading on the outside of a building; usual in Romanesque architecture, especially in Italy and Germany.

E

EARLY ENGLISH. The first of the three phases into which the GOTHIC style in England is conventionally divided. It lasts from the adoption of the French Gothic to the end of the C13. Its principal characteristics, as against those of the contemporary French Gothic style, are: less emphasis on the vertical; the retention of much that had been English NORMAN usage (galleries instead of TRIFORIA); a preference for two sets of transepts, the main one and one farther east; LANCET WINDOWS, stiff-leaf CAPITALS, stiff-leaf vault BOSSES, and rib vaulting of more complex schemes than the French quadripartite one. Among the most important buildings are Wells, Lincoln, and Salisbury Cathedrals, Westminster Abbey, and the east transept of Durham Cathedral.

EASTER SEPULCHRE. A recess with TOMB-CHEST, usually in the north wall of a CHANCEL; the tomb-chest was designed to receive an effigy of Christ for Easter celebrations.

EAVES. The underpart of a sloping roof overhanging a wall.

ECHAL. In a synagogue, the fitting enclosing the Ark or cupboard in which are kept the rolls of the Law; often of wood. An ornate example of the C18 exists in London at Bevis Marks, in the form of a large tripartite REREDOS.

ECHINUS. An OVOLO MOULDING below the ABACUS of a Doric CAPITAL. See figure 64.

EFFNER, Joseph (1687–1745), born in Munich, was the son of the chief gardener to Max Emanuel, Elector of Bavaria, who sent him to be trained as an architect in Paris under BOFFRAND. In 1715 he was appointed Court Architect. He completed the Palace at Schleissheim (1715–27) and designed the magnificent *Treppenhaus*.

He also completed Schloss Nymphenburg outside Munich, converting the Italianate villa into a distinctly German Baroque palace (1716–28) and building several pavilions in the park; the Pagodenburg (1716, classical exterior with a Chinoiserie interior); the Roman Badenburg (1718); and the precocious picturesque Magdalenenklause (c. 1727).

EGAS, Enrique de (d. probably 1534), was the son either of Hanequin of Brussels, who built the upper parts of the towers of Toledo Cathedral and the Portal of the Lions (1452), or of Egas Cueman, Hanequin's brother, who was a sculptor and died in 1495. In 1497 Enrique became master mason of Plasencia Cathedral – where work, however, soon stopped and was later continued by JUAN DE ÁLAVA and FRANCISCO DE COLONIA – and in 1498 of Toledo Cathedral. Enrique's masterpieces are the hospitals of Santiago (1501–11), Toledo (1504–15), and Granada (begun 1504 and soon abandoned), where the North Italian Early Renaissance appears early and at its most delightful. He was consulted at the Seo of Zaragoza in 1500, and at Seville Cathedral in 1512, 1523, 1529, and 1534. He was also connected with the designs for the Royal Chapel at Granada (begun c. 1504), and was the designer of Granada Cathedral (begun 1523, but soon turned Renaissance from Enrique's Gothic by Diego de SILOE).

EGG AND DART (or EGG AND TONGUE). An OVOLO MOULDING decorated with a pattern based on alternate eggs and arrow-heads. See figure 41.

EGYPTIAN ARCHITECTURE. As Herodotus pointed out, the ancient Egyptians regarded the dwelling-house as a temporary lodging and the tomb as a

Fig. 41. Egg and dart

permanent abode. Houses were built of clay, sometimes but not always in the form of baked bricks; tombs and temples reproduced the elements of this domestic architecture on the grandest possible scale and in the most durable materials. Thus the bundles of papyrus stalks used as supports in mud huts were transformed into the majestic carved stone papyrus columns of the temples. No efforts were spared to secure the permanence of the tombs and their attendant temples by such devices as the use of the living rock and the steep BATTER of walls to resist earthquake shocks. The result is an architecture of inhuman, impersonal, and to this day daunting monumentality. Features peculiar to ancient Egyptian architecture include the PYRAMID, the OBELISK, the steeply battered PYLON, the symbolical lotus column, and incised relief decoration without any structural relevance.

The earliest large-scale work in stone is the funeral complex at Saqqara, built by the architect Imhotep for King Zoser, founder of the third dynasty (*c.* 2650–2600 B.C.) – a vast stepped pyramid almost 200 ft high, surrounded by a columned processional hall and other buildings to provide a habitation for the dead king and a realistic stage-setting for ritual, all enclosed by a niched limestone wall. The stepped pyramid was superseded by the regular pyramid, of which the most famous examples are at Giza, built for kings of the fourth dynasty (*c.* 2600–2480 B.C.). The collapse of the Old Kingdom (*c.* 2000 B.C.) created the first break in the history of ancient Egyptian architecture. There was a temporary revival in the period of the Middle Kingdom (1991–

1650 B.C.): earlier styles were slightly simplified and less durable materials were used (as in the pyramid of Sesostris I at Lisht). But not until the New Kingdom period (1570–1085 B.C.) were great buildings once again erected. The most notable monuments are the mortuary temple of Queen Hatshepsut at Deir el Bahari (*c.* 1480 B.C.), with its pillared halls, colonnades, and gigantic ramps connecting the different levels; the magnificent temple of Amon at Karnak (*c.* 1570–1085 B.C.); and the many-columned temple of Amon-Mut-Khons at Luxor (*c.* 1570–1200 B.C.), with its succession of rooms of diminishing size and increasing gloom. The final revival took place under the rule of the Ptolemies, whom Alexander the Great had established on the Egyptian throne. Numerous temples survive from this period (323–30 B.C.), still built in the traditional manner but slightly more elegant and less crushingly inhuman, e.g., the temple of Horus at Edfu and the temples on the island of Philae. For later architecture in Egypt *see* HELLENISTIC ARCHITECTURE and ISLAMIC ARCHITECTURE.

EIERMANN, Egon (b. 1909), was a pupil of POELZIG. By concentrating on industrial buildings, Eiermann managed to carry the INTERNATIONAL MODERN of the thirties through the Nazi years in Germany. Of his many post-war factories one of the finest is at Blumberg (1951). His international fame was established by the German Pavilion at the Brussels Exhibition of 1958, a perfect blend of crisp, clear, cubic, transparent blocks and their grouping in a landscape setting. The solution to the problem of grouping the new Kaiser-Wilhelm-Gedächtniskirche at Berlin (1959–62) with the dramatic neo-Romanesque ruin of the old is more questionable. Other recent buildings of special importance are the offices of the Essener Steinkohlen-Bergwerke, Essen (1958–60); the wholesale warehouses, etc., for Messrs Neckermann at Frankfurt (1958–61); and the German Embassy in Washington (1961–3).

EIFFEL, Gustave (1832–1923), the French engineer, is famous chiefly for the Eiffel Tower built for the Paris Exhibition of 1889. At 1010 ft, the Tower was the highest building in the world until the Chrysler and then the Empire State Buildings were erected in New York. The Eiffel Tower in its immensely prominent position in the centre of Paris marks the final acceptance of metal, in this case iron, as an architectural medium. Eiffel's iron bridges are technically and visually as important as the Eiffel Tower (Douro, 1876–7; Garabit Viaduct, 1880–4). He was also engineer to the Bon Marché store in Paris (1876), and to the Statue of Liberty in New York, both of which have remarkable iron interiors.

ELEVATION. The external faces of a building; also a drawing made in projection on a vertical plane to show any one face (or elevation) of a building. *See figure 6.*

ELIAS OF DEREHAM or DURHAM (d. 1245), was Canon of Salisbury and Wells and a confidant of Archbishops Hubert Walter and Stephen Langton, Bishop Jocelyn of Wells, Bishop Hugh of Lincoln, Bishop Poore of Salisbury, and Bishop des Roches of Winchester. He was present at the sealing of Magna Carta and at the translation of the relics of Thomas à Becket in 1220. He was, in addition, in charge of the King's Works at Winchester Castle and Clarendon Palace, and '*a prima fundatione rector*' of Salisbury Cathedral. *Rector* sounds like administrator rather than designer, but he was also paid for making a vessel for Salisbury Cathedral and is called *artifex* in connexion with the new shrine of Thomas à Becket; so he was certainly something of an artist, and it is likely that he was, like ALAN OF WALSINGHAM a hundred years later, a man capable also of designing buildings and of discus-

sing details constructively with the master masons.

ELIZABETHAN AND JACOBEAN ARCHITECTURE. The ascent to the throne of Elizabeth I (1558) is not really a break in the history of English architecture; the break took place during the years under Henry VIII when Italian Renaissance forms became the fashion. A less superficial understanding of what the Renaissance means began with the building of Old Somerset House in London about 1550. This, together with the survival of the Late Gothic belief in very large windows with MULLIONS and TRANSOMS and the adoption of the Netherlandish fashion of STRAPWORK ornament, produced the Elizabethan style. Longleat is the first complete example: others are Burghley House, Montacute, Wollaton, and Hardwick. The first fifteen years of the reign of James I brought no change. Among the principal buildings are Hatfield, Audley End, Bramshill. Plans of houses are often of E or H shape, if they do not have internal courtyards, as the largest have. Windows are usually very large and may dominate the walls. Gables, straight or curved in the manner of the Netherlands, are frequent. Wood and plaster decoration is rich and often over-extravagant. Ecclesiastical architecture was almost at a standstill, and even the ample Jacobean-looking church furnishings are usually Jacobean only in style but a little later in date.

ELL. In the U.S.A. a single-storey lean-to wing containing a kitchen. Ells were added in the C17 to WEATHERBOARDED, timber-framed buildings in New England.

ELMES, Harvey Lonsdale (1813–47). The son of James Elmes (1782–1862), architect and writer, a champion of the Elgin Marbles, of Keats, and of Wordsworth. James wrote on prison reform, and in 1823 edited the life and works of Wren. Harvey was a pupil of his father, and in 1836 won the competition for St George's Hall, Liverpool. Even though, in its grouping and its massing of columns, it is no longer of Grecian purity, the building is convincedly classical. It was completed brilliantly by C. R. COCKERELL after Elmes's death from consumption.

ELY, *see* REGINALD OF ELY.

EMBRASURE. A small opening in the wall or PARAPET of a fortified building, usually splayed on the inside.

ENCAUSTIC TILES. Earthenware tile glazed and decorated, much used in the Middle Ages and in Victorian churches for flooring.

ENCEINTE. In military architecture, the main enclosure of a fortress, surrounded by the wall or ditch.

ENGAGED COLUMN. A column attached to, or partly sunk into, a wall or PIER; also called an *applied column*.

ENGLISH ARCHITECTURE. *See* ANGLO-SAXON; DECORATED; EARLY ENGLISH; ELIZABETHAN AND JACOBEAN; GEORGIAN; GOTHIC REVIVAL; GREEK REVIVAL; NORMAN; PERPENDICULAR; QUEEN ANNE; STUART.

ENSINGER. A family of South German masons: the two most important members are Ulrich and Matthäus. Ulrich von Ensingen (d. 1419) was sufficiently distinguished by 1391 for the cathedral authorities at Milan to want to consult him; he refused the invitation. In 1392 he became master mason for Ulm Minster (begun 1377). He changed plan and elevation boldly and designed the west tower with its splendid porch. The upper parts of the tower were built to a changed design by Matthäus BÖBLINGER. In 1394 Ulrich went after all to Milan, but was not satisfied or able to convince the authorities, and so left in 1395. In 1399, in addition to his job at Ulm, he was put in charge of the continuation of the west tower at Strassburg. Here it was he who started the single tower instead of the two originally projected

and built the enchanting octagon stage. The spire, however, is by his successor Johann HÜLTZ. He also worked at Esslingen from *c.* 1400 onwards, and probably designed the west tower which was carried out (and probably altered) by Hans BÖBLINGER.

Ulrich had three sons who became masons. One of them is Matthäus (d. 1463), who first worked under his father at Strassburg, then became master mason at Berne, where he designed the new minster in 1420–1. From Berne he also undertook the job of master mason at Esslingen, but was replaced there in 1440 by Hans Böblinger. From 1446 he was master mason at Ulm. Of his sons three were masons.

ENTABLATURE. The upper part of an ORDER, consisting of ARCHITRAVE, FRIEZE, and CORNICE. *See figures 42 and 64.*

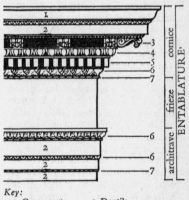

Key:
1. Cyma recta   5. Dentils
2. Fascia   6. Cyma reversa
3. Modillions   7. Astragal
4. Ovolo

Fig. 42. Entablature: Corinthian

ENTASIS. The very slight convex curve used on Greek and later columns to correct the optical illusion of concavity which would result if the sides were straight. Also used on spires and other structures for the same reason.

ENTRESOL, *see* MEZZANINE.

EQUILATERAL ARCH, *see* ARCH.

ERWIN VON STEINBACH (d. 1318), is one of the most famous medieval architects, because Goethe wrote his prose poem on Strassburg Cathedral, and especially its façade and steeple, round Erwin's name. According to an earlier inscription (which is not beyond suspicion), Erwin did indeed begin the façade in 1277. Documents refer to him under 1284 (?), 1293, and 1316. But during that time the steeple was not reached anyway, and even the lower part of the façade presupposes two changes of design. It is most likely that the happily preserved drawing for the façade known as B is Erwin's.

ESTÍPITE. A type of PILASTER tapering towards the base, extensively used in Spanish post-Renaissance architecture.

ETRUSCAN ARCHITECTURE. The main building materials were wood, rubble, clay (sometimes baked); stone was used only for the foundations of temples and secular buildings, for fortifications, and for tombs. As the Romans were anxious to erase all memory of the Etruscans very few of their buildings survive above ground level. Their most notable surviving constructions are city walls dating from C6 to C4 B.C. (Tarquinia, Chiusi, Cortona, etc.) – sometimes with handsome if rather heavy arched gateways – though most of these are later (e.g., Falerii Novi, *c.* 250 B.C.; Perugia, *c.* 100 B.C.). After C5 B.C. temples were built on a plan derived from Greece, but with rather widely spaced, stocky, wooden, unfluted columns, wooden beams, and richly modelled terracotta facings and ACROTERIA applied to them. Underground tombs were usually hewn out of the living rock; their interiors were very elaborately painted and occasionally decorated with stucco reliefs (e.g., Tomb of the Stucchi, Cerveteri, C3 B.C.).

EULALIUS designed the Church of the Holy Apostles, Constantinople (536–45, destroyed), the prototype Greek cross-plan church with five domes. It inspired S. Marco, Venice, and St Front, Périgueux.

EUSTYLE. With an arrangement of columns two and a quarter diameters apart. *See also* AEROSTYLE; DIASTYLE; PYCNOSTYLE; SYSTYLE.

EXEDRA. In classical architecture, a semicircular or rectangular recess with raised seats: also, more loosely, any APSE or niche or the apsidal end of a room.

EXTRADOS. The outer curve of an arch. *See figure 4.*

EYE-CATCHER. A decorative building, such as a sham ruin, usually built on an eminence in an English landscape park to terminate a view or otherwise punctuate the layout. *See also* FOLLY.

F

FACING. The finishing applied to the outer surface of a building.

FAN VAULT, *see* VAULT.

FANLIGHT. 1. A window, often semi-circular, over a door, in Georgian and Regency buildings, with radiating glazing bars suggesting a fan. 2. Also, less commonly, the upper part of a window hinged to open separately.

FANZAGO, Cosimo (1591–1678), was born at Clusone near Bergamo, but settled in Naples in 1608 where he became the leading Baroque architect. Trained as a sculptor, he also worked as a decorator and painter, and was interested less in planning than in decoration. His exuberant style is epitomized in the fantastic Guglia di S. Gennaro (1631–60), and in such effervescent façades as those of S. Maria della Sapienza (1638–41), S. Giuseppe degli Scalzi (*c.* 1660), and his vast unfinished Palazzo Donn'Anna (1642–4). His earlier buildings are more restrained and elegant, e.g., the arcades of the Certosa di S. Martino above Naples (1623–31).

FASCIA. A plain horizontal band, usually in an ARCHITRAVE, which may consist of two or three fasciae oversailing each other and sometimes separated by narrow mouldings. *See figures 42 and 64.*

FENESTRATION. The arrangement of windows in a building.

FERETORY. A shrine for relics designed to be carried in processions; kept behind the high altar.

FESTOON. A carved ornament in the form of a garland of fruit and flowers, tied with ribbons and suspended at both ends in a loop; commonly used on a FRIEZE or panel and also called a *swag. See figure 43.*

FIELDSTONE. The American word for rubble.

Fig. 43. Festoon

FIGUEROA, Leonardo de (*c.* 1650–1730), the creator of the Sevillian Baroque style, was the first to make use of the cut-brick construction in white or yellow walls surrounded with red trim so intimately associated with the city. His style is rich in an abundance of glazed tiles, patterned columns, SALOMÓNICAS, ESTÍPITES, tassels, foliated brackets, undulating cornices, statues of saints and caryatids and mermen. All his works are in Seville: e.g., Hospital de Venerables Sacerdotes (1687–97); Magdalena Church (1691–1709); Salvador Church (1696–1711); and the very ornate west entrance to S. Telmo (1724–34). S. Luis, the richest and finest Baroque church in Seville (1699–1731), is usually attributed to him. His son Ambrosio (1700–75) maintained his style in Seville (S. Catalina, 1732; chapel of the Cartuja, 1752–8; and Sacrament chapel in El Arahal, 1763–6), and the family tradition was carried on over the threshold of the neo-classical period by his grandson Antonio Matías (*c.*1734–96?), who built the elegant campanile at La Palma del Condado (1780).

FILARETE, Antonio Averlino (*c.* 1400–69), built little but played an important part in the diffusion of the Early Renaissance style. Born in Florence, he adopted the Greek name Filarete (lover of virtue) fairly late in life. He began as a sculptor and executed a bronze door for St Peter's (1443) in Rome. In 1451 he was commissioned by Francesco Sforza to build the Ospedale Maggiore in Milan, which he designed on a very elaborate symmetrical plan. He built only the first storey of the central block, a sturdy basement carrying an elegant Brunelleschian arcade. While in Milan he completed his *Trattato d'architettura*, which VASARI called the most ridiculous book ever produced; it circulated widely in manuscript but was not printed until the C19. Based partly on ALBERTI, it is important mainly for its designs of ideal and hopelessly impractical buildings and the elaborate plan for an ideal city, 'Sforzinda', which was to be blessed with every amenity, including a ten-storey tower of Vice and Virtue, with a brothel on the ground floor and an astronomical observatory on the top.

FILLET. A narrow, flat, raised band running down a shaft or along an arch or a ROLL MOULDING; also the uppermost member of a CORNICE, sometimes called a *listel*. *See figure 44*.

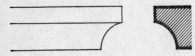

Fig. 44. Fillet

FINIAL. A formal ornament at the top of a canopy, gable, pinnacle, etc.; usually a detached foliated FLEUR-DE-LIS form. *See figure 31*.

FISCHER, Johann Michael (c. 1691–1766), the most prolific of South German Rococo architects, built no less than twenty-two abbeys and thirty-two churches. Though less gifted than his contemporaries NEUMANN and ZIMMERMANN, he had great sensitivity to spatial relationships and could obtain monumental effects. His masterpiece is the Benedictine abbey church at Ottobeuren (1744–67), with a fine soaring façade and magnificently rich interior frothing with effervescent decoration. The smaller church at Rott-am-Inn (1759–63) shows a tendency towards greater restraint and provides a perfect setting for the statues by Ignaz Günther. Other works include St Anne, Munich (1727–30), on an oval plan; the abbey church at Diessen (1732–9); the church at Berg-am-Laim (1738–51); the Benedictine abbey at Zwiefalten (1740–65), even larger than Ottobeuren and still richer inside; and finally, the Brigittine abbey church at Altomünster (1763–6).

FISCHER VON ERLACH, Johann Bernhard (1656–1723), a leading Baroque architect in Austria, was more restrained and intellectual than his rival HILDEBRANDT, but also more courtly and traditional. Born near Graz, he began as a sculptor and stucco worker, then went to Italy and trained as an architect under Carlo FONTANA in Rome from about 1682 to 1685, when he settled in Vienna; there he was eventually appointed Court Architect in 1704. His first building of note is Schloss Frain in Moravia (c. 1688–93), with an imposing oval hall. Italian influence, especially that of BORROMINI, is very evident in his three churches in Salzburg, the Dreifaltigkeitskirche (1694–1702), Kollegienkirche (1694–1707), and Ursulinenkirche (1699–1705). His masterpiece, the Karlskirche in Vienna (begun 1716), is a unique design with no antecedents and no successors, but his Roman memories are again quite explicit, notably in the opening theme of a Pantheon portico framed by a couple of Trajan's columns, expressive of his conscious striving after imperial grandeur. His secular buildings include the façade and *Treppenhaus*, with its monumental ATLANTES, of the Stadtpalais of Prinz Eugen, Vienna (1695–6); the Palais Batthyány-Schönborn, Vienna (1699–1706); the Palais Clam Gallas, Prague (1707–12); the Palais Trautson, Vienna (1710–16); and finally, the Hofbibliothek in the Hofburg, Vienna, which he began the year of his death (1723) and which was finished by his son Joseph Emanuel (1693–1742). This library is one of the most imposing interiors in Europe and illustrates his imperial manner at its grandiloquent best. He assumed the title 'von Erlach' on being knighted by the Emperor. His wide scholarship found expression in his *Entwurf einer historischen Architektur* (published Vienna 1721), which was the first architectural treatise to include and illustrate Egyptian and Chinese buildings, and which thus exerted a great influence on various later architectural exoticisms.

FLAMBOYANT. The late Gothic style in France. In Flamboyant TRACERY the bars of stonework form long wavy divisions.

FLÈCHE. A slender wooden spire rising from the RIDGE of a roof; also called a *spirelet*.

FLEUR-DE-LIS. French for lily-flower; originally the royal arms of France.

FLIGHT. A series of stairs unbroken by a landing.

FLITCROFT, Henry (1697–1769), was a protégé of Lord BURLINGTON, who procured him various posts in the Office of Works, where he eventually succeeded KENT as Master Mason and Deputy Surveyor. He was known as 'Burlington Harry'. Competent but uninspired, he was little superior to the 'imitating fools' who, according to Pope's prophecy, followed Lord Burlington's just and noble rules. His colossal west front at Wentworth Woodhouse (1735 etc.), the longest façade in England, illustrates the empty pomposity into which PALLADIANISM declined: Woburn Abbey is equally derivative (c. 1747). His town houses are more successful, notably 10 St James's Square, London (1734). St Giles-in-the-Fields, London (1731–3), is an unflattering imitation of St Martin-in-the-Fields.

FLORIS, Cornelis (1514/20–75). Primarily a sculptor but also the chief Renaissance architect in the southern Netherlands. The tall, grave, and classicizing Antwerp Town Hall (1561–5) is his masterpiece.

FLUSH BEAD MOULDING. An inset bead or convex moulding, its outer surface being flush with adjacent surfaces. *See figure 45.*

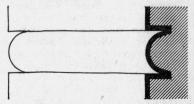

Fig. 45. Flush Bead moulding

FLUSHWORK. The decorative use of KNAPPED FLINT in conjunction with dressed stone to form patterns, such as TRACERY, initials, etc.

FLUTING. Shallow, concave grooves running vertically on the SHAFT of a column, PILASTER, or other surface. If the lower part is filled with a solid cylindrical piece it is called *cabled* fluting. *See figure 64.*

i: Detail of flowing tracery showing elaborate use of cusping

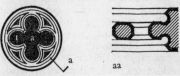

ii: Foil (aa: cusp in section)

Fig. 46

FLYING BUTTRESS, *see* BUTTRESS.

FOIL. A lobe or leaf-shaped curve formed by the CUSPING of a circle or an arch. The number of foils involved is indicated by a prefix, e.g., trefoil, multifoil. *See figure 46.*

FOLIATED. Carved with leaf ornament.

FOLLY. A costly but useless structure built to satisfy the whim of some eccentric and thought to show his folly; usually a tower or a sham Gothic or classical ruin in a landscape park intended to enhance the view or picturesque effect.

FONTAINE, Pierre François Léonard (1762–1853), the son and grandson of architects, became Napoleon's favourite architect and was largely responsible, with his partner PERCIER, for the creation of the Empire style. He studied in Paris under A. F. Peyre, then in Rome 1786–90. Percier joined him in Paris the following year, and they remained together until 1814. Their decorative style is well illustrated at Malmaison, where they worked for Napoleon from 1802 onwards, Joséphine's tented bedroom being completed in 1812. They extended the north wing of the Louvre to the Tuileries, and built the beautifully detailed Arc du Carrousel (1806–7) between the Tuileries and the Grande Galerie. Their joint works also include the rue de Rivoli, Paris (1801); the fountain in the Place Dauphine, Paris (1802); and much restoration and decoration at the royal *châteaux* (Fontainebleau, Saint-Cloud, Compiègne, Versailles) and at the Louvre, notably the Salle des Cariatides. Their influence spread rapidly throughout Europe mainly by means of their publications: *Palais, maisons, etc., à Rome* (1798) and especially their *Recueil de décorations intérieures* (1812). The most notable of Fontaine's independent works are the restoration of the Palais Royal, Paris (1814–31), including the Galerie d'Orléans) and the Hôtel-Dieu, Pontoise (1823–7).

FONTANA, Carlo (1634–1714), was born near Como but settled in Rome *c.* 1655. He began as assistant to CORTONA, RAINALDI, and BERNINI, working under the latter for ten years. His accomplished but derivative style is best seen in the façade of S. Marcello al Corso, Rome (1682–3), and in the many chapels he built in Roman churches: Cappella Cibo in S. Maria del Popolo (1683–7); baptismal chapel in St Peter's (1692–8). Less successful is the Jesuit church and college at Loyola in Spain. He restored and largely rebuilt SS. Apostoli, Rome (1702), and completed Bernini's Palazzo di Montecitorio, Rome, including the main entrance (1694–7). His secular buildings are undistinguished, e.g., Palazzo Spreti, Ravenna (1700), and Ospizio di S. Michele, Rome (1700–3). By industry and perseverance he became undisputed leader of his profession in Rome and was largely responsible for the classicizing, bookish academicism into which the Baroque style declined. He had an enormous influence all over Europe through his numerous pupils who included FISCHER VON ERLACH and HILDEBRANDT in Austria, GIBBS in England, and PÖPPELMANN in Germany.

FONTANA, Domenico (1543–1607), was born near Lugano, settled in Rome *c.* 1563, and became architect to Sixtus V (1585–90). His *magnum opus* is the Lateran Palace in Rome (1586), which displays his dry and monotonous style. He assisted Giacomo della PORTA in building the dome of St Peter's. In 1592 he settled in Naples, where he was appointed 'Royal Engineer' and obtained many large commissions including the Royal Palace (1600–2).

FORECHURCH, *see* ANTECHURCH.

FORMERET. In a medieval VAULT, the rib against the wall, known also as a *wall rib*.

FORMWORK. Commonly called *shuttering*, this is the temporary form that 'wet' concrete is poured into; it is constructed of braced timber or metal.

When the formwork is removed, the concrete is found to have the texture of the material imprinted upon its surface. The formwork may be re-used if the type of construction is suitable, as in walls or repeating floor BAYS.

FORTRESS, *see* CASTLE.

FORUM. In Roman architecture, a central open space usually surrounded by public buildings and colonnades: it corresponds to the Greek AGORA.

FOSSE. A ditch.

FOYER. The vestibule or entrance hall of a theatre.

FRAMED BUILDING. A structure whose weight is carried by the framework instead of by load-bearing walls. The term includes modern steel and reinforced concrete structures, as well as TIMBER-FRAMED (half-timbered) buildings. In the former the frame is usually encased within a FACING (or CLADDING) of light material; in the latter the infilling may be of WATTLE AND DAUB or of brick.

FRANCESCO DI GIORGIO MARTINI (1439–1501/2), a leading Early Renaissance theorist, wrote a treatise which, though not printed until the C19, exerted considerable influence, especially on LEONARDO DA VINCI, who owned a copy of it. He was born in Siena, the son of a poultry dealer, and trained as a sculptor and painter. Before 1477 he moved to Urbino and entered the service of Federigo da Montefeltro, who employed him as a medallist and military engineer. He wrote *c.* 1482 his *Trattato di architettura civile e militare*, based partly on VITRUVIUS (whom he translated or had translated) and ALBERTI, but showing a more practical attitude to the problems of architectural symbolism. Much of it is devoted to church planning: he produces a symbolic rationalization of the church with a long nave and centralized east end, and he also deals with the placing of the altar in a centralized church or tribune, stating the case for a central position to symbolize God's place in the universe, and for a peripheral position to symbolize his infinite distance from mankind.

His work as an architect is poorly documented. He probably contributed to the design of Palazzo Ducale, Urbino (perhaps the exquisitely beautiful loggia looking out over the surrounding hills). In 1485 he provided a model for the Latin cross church of S. Maria del Calcinaio, Cortona (completed 1516), a masterpiece of Early Renaissance clarity, harmony, and repose. He also provided a design for the austerely simple Palazzo del Comune, Jesi (1486; but much altered). Many other works have been attributed to him: S. Maria degli Angeli, Siena; S. Bernardino, Urbino; and Palazzo Ducale, Gubbio. He was also renowned as a designer of fortifications and war machinery.

FREESTONE. Any stone that cuts well in all directions, especially fine-grained limestone or sandstone.

FRENCH ARCHITECTURE. The earliest Christian buildings in France, such as the baptisteries of Fréjus, Mélas, Aix, and Marseille Cathedral, all dating from the C5, are of the same Early Christian type as baptisteries of that century in Italy and other Mediterranean countries. The origin of the plan types is Imperial Roman. Of the Merovingian and Carolingian periods little of importance is left, though French Carolingian buildings such as Centula (St Riquier) of 790–9 were at least as grand and important as their German counterparts.

The Romanesque style falls into regional groups cut across only by a type represented by some of the chief pilgrimage churches (St Martin, Tours, largely destroyed; St Sernin, Toulouse; Conques). These have transepts, usually with aisles, crossing towers, and ambulatories with radiating chapels. In elevation they have galleries, and they are all tunnel-vaulted, the tunnel vault being altogether the most usual system of vaulting in Romanesque France. It appears for the first time on a major scale at Tournus in Burgundy in the early CII. The plan of ambulatory with radiating chapels was also devised at that time or a little earlier, though it was based on Carolingian arrangements of a similar, if rudimentary nature. In its vaults Tournus is an exception: the grandest French churches of before and about the mid CII had as yet no confidence in major vaulting (St Remi, Reims, 1005–49; Jumièges in Normandy, c. 1040–67; St Étienne and Ste Trinité, Caen). This changed about 1060–70, and after that the French regional schools all have their particular vaulting arrangements. The schools are those of Burgundy, not unified in character (Cluny, Autun, and Vézelay, the latter groin-vaulted); of Auvergne, with a curious half-raised transept roof like a podium for the crossing tower, but otherwise very similar to the pilgrimage churches (Clermont-Ferrand, Issoire); of Poitou, with hall churches, i.e., churches with nave and aisles of the same height (Notre Dame la Grande, Poitiers; St Savin); of Provence, with high and narrow naves and aisles (Arles, St Paul-trois-Châteaux); and of the south-west, with domes over square bays (Cahors, Angoulême, Périgueux). In Burgundy and Provence detail is often inspired by ancient Rome. In the north of France double or single west towers are frequent, whereas façades in Poitou and farther south are towerless.

The Gothic style begins at St Denis and Sens about 1140. It is characterized by the pointed arch and the rib vault, neither, however, a Gothic invention. Pointed arches are frequent in Romanesque France, and rib vaulting seems to have originated at Durham just before 1100. Normandy took it over about 1110–20 (Caen), and from there the architect of St Denis must have derived the elegant vaults of his ambulatory: his two-tower façade also has Norman antecedents. The great Early Gothic cathedrals (Sens, c. 1140 etc.; Noyon, c. 1150 etc.; Laon, c. 1160 etc.; Paris, 1163 etc.) have sexpartite rib vaults, again, it seems, on a Norman pattern. They show a development to higher proportions, thinner members, larger openings, and less inert wall. Chartres, as rebuilt from 1194, turned Early Gothic into High Gothic. Its quadripartite rib vaults, tall arcades, tall clerestory windows, flying buttresses, and its replacement of the gallery by a low triforium band were taken over by Rheims, Amiens, and the later C13 cathedrals that were built as a sign of the spreading of royal France over the whole area of present-day France. This style remained the French standard for two centuries and more. Only in a few provinces did regional features manage to hold their own. Thus Poitou and also Anjou persisted with hall churches, even if their proportions and their spatial feeling changed in the Gothic direction. In the south a type established itself, probably on a Catalan pattern, with high proportions and inner chapels between buttresses instead of aisles (Albi, 1282 etc.). The Late Gothic style is called Flamboyant from the forms of the window tracery, similar to those of the English Decorated style. Flamboyant starts just before 1400 and is more a matter of decoration than of space.

Castle building is first characterized by the keep or donjon, turning very early from square or oblong to round or rounded. In consequence of the experience of eastern fortification during the Crusades the keep was given up about 1200 and systems were designed instead where defence is spread along the whole curtain wall, which is sometimes doubled and has many towers. Shortly after 1200 (Louvre, Dourdan) this new system was occasionally regularized and made into a symmetrical composition. In the course of the C15 the manor house or country house (Plessis-lès-Tours, 1463–72) began to replace the castle. The Flamboyant style created many splendid and ornate public and private buildings in the towns, such as the Law Courts of Rouen (1499–1509) and, the finest of all private houses, the House of Jacques Cœur at Bourges (1443 etc).

The Renaissance arrived early in France, but in a desultory way. Italians were working in Marseille in 1475–81. Odd Quattrocento details in painting occur even earlier. They also appear in architectural decoration, Easter Sepulchre (Solesmes, 1496). The earliest example of a systematic use of Quattrocento pilasters in several orders is Gaillon (1508). With François I full acceptance of such motifs as this is seen at Blois (1515 etc.) and in other *châteaux* along the Loire. The most monumental of them is Chambord (1519 etc.), a symmetrical composition with tunnel vaults inside, High Renaissance in derivation. The largest of the *châteaux* of François I is Fontainebleau (1528 etc.), and here, in the interior (François I Gallery, 1532 etc.), Mannerism in its most up-to-date Italian form entered France. By the middle of the C16 France had developed a Renaissance style of her own, with French characteristics and architects. The most important of them were LESCOT, who began the rebuilding of the Louvre in 1546, and DELORME. Delorme introduced the dome and proved himself an ingenious technician as well as a creator of grand compositions (Anet, *c.* 1547 etc.). BULLANT at Écouen (*c.* 1555 etc.) appears as Delorme's equal. His use of giant columns, internationally very early, had a great influence on France.

The wars of religion shook France so violently that little on a large scale could be built. The palace of Verneuil (begun *c.* 1565) was built slowly, while the palace of Charleval (begun 1573) was abandoned very soon. Both are by the elder DU CERCEAU, and both

show an overcrowding of the façades with restless and fantastical detail. The typically French pavilion roofs make their appearance here. Another example of the restlessness of these years is the town hall at Arras (1572).

With Henri IV things settled down. His principal contributions are *places* in Paris, i.e., town planning rather than palace architecture. The Place des Vosges (1605 etc.) survives entirely, the Place Dauphine fragmentarily, and the Place de France, the first with radiating streets (an idea conceived under Sixtus V in Rome) was never built. The elevations are of brick with busy stone DRESSINGS, a style which remained typical up to about 1630 (earliest part of Versailles, 1624). Henri IV's ideas on *places* as focal points of monumental town planning were taken up enthusiastically under Louis XIV and Louis XV, and reached their climax in the Paris of Napoleon III (Louis XIV: Place des Victoires, Place Vendôme, layout of Versailles).

The leading architects under Louis XIV were at the start François MANSART and LE VAU, then PERRAULT and Jules Hardouin MANSART. François Mansart (like Corneille in literature and Poussin in painting) guided France into that classical style to which she remained faithful till beyond 1800, though it looks as if Salomon de BROSSE, the leading architect under Louis XIII, had in his last work, the Law Courts at Rennes (begun 1618), preceded Mansart. Mansart is of the same fundamental importance in châteaux (Blois, 1635 etc.), town *hôtels* (Vrillière, 1635 etc.; Carnavalet, 1655), and churches. In church architecture de Brosse had started on tall façades crowded with Italian columns (St Gervais, 1616). Mansart toned them down to something closer to the Roman Gesù pattern, and he established the dome as a feature of ambitious Parisian churches (Visitation, 1632;

Minimes, 1636). His grandest church is the Val-de-Grâce begun in 1645 and continued by LEMERCIER. But Lemercier had preceded Mansart in the field of major domed churches: his Sorbonne church with its remarkably early grand portico of detached columns was begun in 1635. Le Vau was more Baroque a designer than Mansart, as is shown by his liking for curves, and particularly for ovals, externally and internally. His first Paris house is the Hôtel Lambert (*c.* 1640 etc.), his first country house Vaux-le-Vicomte (1657–61), with its domed oval centre saloon, where Louis XIV's team of Le Vau, Lebrun (the painter) and LE NÔTRE appeared together for the first time.

In 1665 Louis XIV called BERNINI to Paris to advise him on the completion of the Louvre. But Bernini's grand Baroque plans were discarded in favour of Perrault's elegant, eminently French façade with its pairs of slender columns and straight entablature in front of a long loggia (1667–70). J. H. Mansart was not an architect of the calibre of the others, but he was a brilliant organizer, and it fell to him vastly to enlarge and complete Versailles (1678 etc.). In Mansart's office the Rococo was created by younger designers (Pierre Lepautre) about 1710–15. It became essentially a style of interior decoration. Otherwise the difference between the C17 and C18 *hôtel* or country house is greater finesse and delicacy of detail, a more cunning planning of cabinets and major rooms, and a decrease in scale. The most impressive major work of the mid century is perhaps the planning and building of the new centre of Nancy by Héré (1753 etc.).

From the middle of the C18 onwards France turned to classicism, first in a moderate, still very elegant form in the works of A.-J. GABRIEL (Place de la Concorde, Petit Trianon), then from the 1770s onwards in a more radical way. The culmination is the designs of BOULLÉE and LEDOUX from the 1780s into the first years of the C19, with sturdy Tuscan or Greek Doric columns, large sheer surfaces of wall, tunnel vaults, and domes. The faith of this group of architects in elementary geometry has led to their rediscovery in the 1920s. With the Empire the ruthlessness of the style turned into grandeur, but France remained faithful to classicism in general, and the Gothic Revival never assumed the importance it possesses in England. On the other hand, France was early in the appreciation of iron and glass (LABROUSTE, VIOLLET-LE-DUC) and later of concrete (BAUDOT, PERRET).

The change from the classicism and, more generally, the historicism of the C19 to the new, entirely original style of the C20 was the work of a few creative architects in a number of countries. France was one of them, and the two architects who reached the new style before the First World War are GARNIER and PERRET. It is, however, characteristic of the strength of the French classical tradition that Perret in his later years turned to a basic classicism again.

FRENCH WINDOW. A long window reaching to floor level and opening in two leaves like a pair of doors.

FRET. A geometrical ornament of horizontal and vertical straight lines, repeated to form a band, e.g., a *key pattern*. See figure 47.

Fig. 47. Fret

FRIEZE. 1. The middle division of an ENTABLATURE, between the ARCHITRAVE and CORNICE; usually decorated but may be plain. *See figures 42 and 64*. 2. The decorated band along the upper part of an internal wall, immediately below the cornice.

FRONTISPIECE. The main façade of a building or its principal entrance BAY.

FRY, Maxwell (b. 1899). One of the pioneers in England of the INTERNATIONAL MODERN of the 1930s. His early buildings are private houses, dating from 1934 onwards. From 1934 to 1936 he was in partnership with GROPIUS. The most important outcome of this is the Impington Village College (1936). Of the major post-war work of the firm (now Fry, Drew & Partners), university and other buildings for Nigeria (Ibadan University College; Co-operate Bank, Ibadan, 1947–61), housing at Chandigarh (1951–4) and the new main offices for Pilkington's at St Helens (1961–4) should be mentioned.

FUGA, Ferdinando (1699–1782), was born in Florence and died in Naples. But his principal works are all in Rome, e.g., Palazzo della Consulta (1732–7), the façade of S. Maria Maggiore (1741–3), and Palazzo Corsini (1736 onwards), in which his sophisticated Late Baroque style is seen at its elegant best. In 1751 he settled in Naples, where he received several important commissions (Albergo de' Poveri, Chiesa dei Gerolamini), but his early virtuosity had by then faded into a tame classicism and his late works are notable mainly for their size.

FULLER, Richard Buckminster (b. 1895). After working in a variety of commercial jobs, he started work in 1922 on structural systems for cheap and effective shelter, light in weight as well as quick to erect and capable of covering large spans. The result was his *geodesic domes* developed after the Second World War. They have been made by him on the SPACE-FRAME principle in many different materials: timber, plywood, aluminium, paper board, PRESTRESSED CONCRETE, and even bamboo. The largest is at Baton Rouge, Louisiana: it has a diameter of 384 ft and was built in 1958.

FUNCTIONALISM. The creed of the architect or designer who holds that it is his primary duty to see that a building or an object designed by him functions well. Whatever he wishes to convey aesthetically and emotionally must not interfere with the fitness of the building or the object to fulfil its purpose.

G

GABLE. The triangular upper portion of a wall to carry a pitched roof; sometimes semi-circular or with curved sides. *See figure 48.*

Fig. 48. Gable. Dutch gable; Shaped gable

GABRIEL, Jacques-Ange (1698–1782). The greatest C18 architect in France and perhaps in Europe. His genius was conservative rather than revolutionary: he carried on and brought to its ultimate perfection the French classical tradition of François MANSART, bypassing, as it were, the Rococo. He resembled his great contemporary Chardin in his solid unostentatious good taste, which reached its highest pitch of refinement in small intimate buildings such as his Hermitage or Pavillon de Pompadour at Fontainebleau (begun 1748) and in his great masterpiece, the Petit Trianon in the park at Versailles (1763–9). The son of a successful architect, Jacques Gabriel (1667–1742) – who built several good Parisian *hôtels*, notably the Hôtel Peyrene de Moras (now the Musée Rodin), Paris, and who succeeded de COTTE as *Premier Architecte* and Director of the Academy – he was trained in Paris and never went to Italy. He worked under and with his father for the Crown, and in due course succeeded him as *Premier Architecte*. In this position he built exclusively for the king, Louis XV, and Mme de Pompadour. Additions and alterations to the various royal palaces – Fontainebleau, Compiègne,

Versailles – took up most of his time, but they lack inspiration, though the Opéra and his projected reconstruction of the Marble Court at Versailles are extremely elegant. His largest commissions outside Versailles were for the École Militaire, Paris (1751–8), and the layout of the Place de la Concorde, Paris (1755 etc.); while the two great palaces (Hôtel de Crillon and Ministère de la Marine, 1757–75) flanking his rue Royale – their façades with screens in the style of PERRAULT's great east front of the Louvre – are his most successful buildings on a monumental scale. The Pavillon Français, Versailles (1750), the small hunting-boxes or Pavillons de Butard (1750) and de la Muette (1753–4) and the Petit Château at Choisy (1754–6) foreshadow the civilized intimacy of his masterpiece. The Petit Trianon may owe something to the sober dignity of English PALLADIANISM, but the extreme elegance and refinement of this perfectly proportioned cubical composition is wholly French and achieves a serenity and distinction different in kind and quality from any other contemporary building.

GADROONED. Decorated with convex curves; the opposite of fluted (*see* FLUTING).

GALILEE. A vestibule or occasionally a chapel, originally for penitents and usually at the west end of a church. Sometimes called a NARTHEX or PARADISE.

GALILEI, Alessandro (1691–1737), born in Florence and trained there, went to England in 1714, but failed to attract any commissions. In 1731 he won the competition for the façade of S. Giovanni in Laterano, Rome, with a somewhat tight, severely classical design (executed 1733–6). He also designed the elegant Corsini Chapel in S. Giovanni in Laterano (1732–5) and the façade of S. Giovanni dei Fiorentini, Rome (1734).

GALLERY. In church architecture, an upper storey over an aisle, opening on to the nave. Also called a *tribune* and often, wrongly, a TRIFORIUM. Found as an exterior feature with continuous small open ARCADING in medieval Italian and German churches, and sometimes called a DWARF GALLERY.

GALLI DI BIBIENA. The leading family of QUADRATURA painters and theatrical designers in early C18 Italy. They came from Bibiena near Bologna. Several members of the family were spirited draughtsmen and accomplished painters of *trompe l'œil* architecture; a few were architects as well. Ferdinando (1657–1743) designed the church of S. Antonio Abbate, Parma (1712–16), with a very effective double dome. One of his sons, Giuseppe (1696–1757), worked as a theatrical designer in Vienna, and in 1748 designed the wonderfully rich interior of the theatre at Bayreuth; while another son, Antonio (1700–74), designed several theatres in Italy, of which only two survive: Teatro Communale, Bologna (1756–63), and Teatro Scientifico, Palazzo dell'Accademia Virgiliana, Mantua. A third son, Alessandro (1687–1769), became Architect-General to the Elector Palatine in Mannheim, where he built the opera house (destroyed) and began the fine Jesuit church (1733). The very elaborate stage designs by members of the family may have exerted some influence on JUVARRA and PIRANESI.

GAMBREL ROOF, *see* ROOF.

GARDEROBE. Wardrobe. Also the medieval name for a lavatory.

GARGOYLE. A water spout projecting from a roof, or the PARAPET of a wall or tower, and carved into a grotesque figure, human or animal.

GARNER, Thomas, *see* BODLEY.

GARNIER, Charles (1825–98), won the Grand Prix of the Academy in 1848, and went to Rome in the same year and to Athens in 1852. Back in Paris in 1854, he worked under Ballu. In 1861 he won the competition for the Opéra, and the building was completed in 1875. Prominently placed in one of HAUSSMANN's many grand *points de vue*, it is the most splendid incarnation of the Second Empire. The exterior, the ample staircase, the glittering foyer are frankly Baroque, and openly endeavour to beat the Baroque at its own game. At the same time Meyerbeer, Wagner, Verdi could not be heard in more sympathetic surroundings, since the building is most intelligently planned for its particular purpose of combining a setting for opera with a setting for social display. The same is true, in its own intentionally more meretricious way, of the Casino at Monte Carlo (1878), which, needless to say, had a universal influence in Romance countries on light-hearted resort architecture. Garnier's own villa at Bordighera (1872), with its asymmetrically placed tower, is Italianate and not Baroque.

GARNIER, Tony (1869–1948). When he gained the Prix de Rome in 1899 and duly went to Rome, he spent much of his time not measuring and studying ancient buildings, but working on the designs for a Cité Industrielle. These designs were submitted in 1904, exhibited and finally published in 1917. They represent a completely new approach to town planning, in radical opposition to the academic principles of town planning as taught by the École des Beaux Arts, principles of symmetry and imposed monumentality. Garnier instead gave himself a site that was imaginary and yet realistic, since it resembled the country near his native Lyon: he decided that his town should have 35,000 inhabitants, located industry, railway lines, station, town centre, and housing, and related them rationally to each other. Moreover, he proposed that all the building should be made essentially of concrete. He designed small houses of a quite novel cubic simplicity placed among trees, and some major buildings with the large CANTILEVERS which reinforced concrete had just begun to make possible, with glass and concrete roofs, etc. In 1905 Garnier was called by the newly elected mayor, Édouard Hérriot, to Lyon to be municipal architect. He built the slaughter-house in 1909–13, the stadium in 1913–16.

GÄRTNER, Friedrich von (1792–1847), the son of an architect, studied at the Munich Academy, then for a short time with WEINBRENNER, and after that in Paris with PERCIER and FONTAINE. In 1815–17 he was in Italy, and in 1819–20 in Holland and England. After that he held a chair at the Munich Academy. On a second journey to Italy in 1828 he was introduced to King Ludwig I of Bavaria, and from then was, side by side and in competition with KLENZE, the king's favourite architect. Gärtner's speciality was what the Germans call the *Rundbogenstil*, the style of round arches, be they Italian Romanesque or Italian Quattrocento: it is said that it was King Ludwig rather than Gärtner who favoured this post-classical style. In Munich Gärtner built the Ludwigskirche (1829–40), the State Library (1831–40), and the University (1835–40), all three in the Ludwigstrasse, and at its south end the Feldherrenhalle, a copy of the Loggia dei Lanzi in Florence (1840–4) and an essay in the Tuscan Gothic. In 1835–6 Gärtner was in Athens, where he designed the palace of the new king, a son of Ludwig.

GAU, Franz Christian (1790–1853), who was born in Cologne, went to Paris in 1810, and in 1815 with a Prussian grant to Rome, where he was a friend of the Nazarenes (Overbeck, Cornelius, etc.). In 1818–20 he was in Egypt and Palestine, but returned to Paris in 1821. Gau was more widely known during his lifetime as an Egyptian scholar than as an architect. Yet his Ste Clotilde (1846–57; completed by Ballu) is the one outstanding neo-Gothic church in Paris. The style is a rich High Gothic, the façade has two towers with spires like St Nicaise at Reims, and the roof construction is of iron.

GAUDÍ, Antoni (1852–1926), was born at Reus (Tarragona), where his father was a coppersmith and pot- and kettle-maker. So he grew up acquainted with metals, and it is not surprising that the savagery of his ornamental invention appeared first in metal railings and gates. Nor was the architecture of the building for which these were designed – the Casa Vicens at Barcelona – tame or imitative in the sense of C19 historicism. The house, built in 1878–80, is in fact a nightmarish farrago of Moorish and Gothic elements; indeed, Moorish and Gothic – and in addition, it seems, Moroccan – are the sources of Gaudí's style. The Casa Vicens was followed in 1883–5 by El Capricho, a house at Comillas in Northern Spain – equally crazy and less dependent on any past style.

In 1883 Gaudí was put in charge of the continuation of a large church in Barcelona, the Sagrada Familia, begun as a conventional neo-Gothic building. He did the crypt in 1884–91 and began the transept façade in 1891. By then he had been taken up by Count Güell, an industrialist who remained his faithful patron. His town house, the Palacio Güell, dates from 1885–9, and here there first appeared the parabolic arches and the wild roof excrescences which were to become part of Gaudí's repertoire. But far more fiercely extravagant than anything he or any architect had done before were the designs for the chapel of Sta Coloma de Cervelló which Gaudí began to build in 1898 for one of Count Güell's estates: it was never completed. It has a completely free, asymmetrical, jagged plan, with pillars set at a slant, warped vaults, an indescribable interplay of exterior and interior, and ostentatiously crude benches. For the Parque Güell, a park at Barcelona, begun in 1900, similar motifs were used, and in addition the snakily undulating back of a long seat running along the sides of a large open space was faced with bits of broken tile and crockery in arbitrary patterns as effective as any invented by Picasso (who lived at Barcelona during these very years, 1901–4).

In 1903 Gaudí began the upper part of the transepts of the Sagrada Familia. The lower part had gradually reached an ever freer interpretation of Gothic motifs, but the turrets at the top defeated comparison with anything architectural from the past or the present. Instead, comparisons with termite hills or with crustaceous creatures come naturally to mind. The ceramic facing is similar to that in the Parque Güell. Aesthetically as surprising and socially more so than any earlier building are Gaudí's two blocks of luxury flats, the Casa Battló and the Casa Milá (both begun 1905); for here was acceptance by wealthy Barcelonians of Gaudí's unprecedented architecture. The façades undulate, rise and fall, and are garnished with indescribable top excrescences and sharp, piercing, aggressive wrought-iron balconies. Moreover, the rooms have no straight walls, no right angles. The principles behind ART NOUVEAU (*see* HORTA, MACKINTOSH, Mackmurdo, van de VELDE), usually confined to decoration and mostly two-dimensional decoration, could not well be pushed to a further architectural extreme.

GAZEBO. A small look-out tower or summerhouse with a view, usually in a garden or park but sometimes on the roof of a house; in the latter case it is also called a *belvedere*.

GEDDES, Sir Patrick (1854–1932). If Raymond UNWIN was the greatest British town-planner of his day in practice, Geddes was the greatest in town-planning theory, a theory which he established in the present much-widened sense of the word, with emphasis laid on the necessity of preliminary surveys, on 'diagnosis before treatment', and on the dependence of acceptable town planning on sociological research bordering on biological work. Geddes was, in fact, a trained biologist and zoologist though he never took a degree. He was Professor of Botany at Dundee from 1889 to 1918, and of sociology at Bombay from 1920 to 1923. He was knighted shortly before his death. His principal work on town planning is *City Development* (1904).

GENELLI, Christian, *see* GILLY.

GEOFFREY DE NOIERS (active *c*. 1200), was called *constructor* of the choir of St Hugh at Lincoln Cathedral (begun 1192). The term may mean only supervisor, but more probably he is the designer of this epoch-making building. The design is, in spite of Geoffrey's name, entirely English not merely in its proportions and the curious layout of the east chapels, but especially in its vault, the earliest vault whose ribs make a decorative (and a very wilful) pattern rather than simply express their function.

GEORGIAN ARCHITECTURE starts with the rejection of the English Baroque of VANBRUGH and HAWKSMOOR, and with the revival of PALLADIANISM as it had first been introduced by Inigo JONES a hundred years before. The earliest architects are Colen CAMPBELL, Lord BURLINGTON, and KENT (the latter, however, much inspired by the Vanbrugh style as well). GIBBS continued rather in the WREN vein: he is chiefly remembered for his churches, which had much influence in America as well as in England. Palladianism ruled until modified by the more elegant and varied style of Robert ADAM, but essentially the Palladio tradition maintained its hold until the 1820s (NASH's Regent's Park terraces).

Georgian architecture is classical in its major exteriors; but on the smaller domestic scale it still has the sensible plainness of the QUEEN ANNE style. Interiors are more elaborate than exteriors; here also Palladianism was the rule at first, but it was handled with greater freedom and verve. A brief phase of ROCOCO followed about the middle of the century: then the enchantment of Robert Adam's delicate decoration captured nearly everybody. Grecian interiors were rare until about 1820, but Victorian licence and exuberance are already heralded in certain Regency interiors (Brighton Pavilion).

GERBIER, Sir Balthazar (1591?–1667), a Dutch-born Huguenot who settled in England in 1616, was courtier, diplomat, miniaturist, and pamphleteer as well as architect. He almost certainly designed the York Water Gate, Victoria Embankment Gardens, London (1626–7). Nothing else by him survives.

GERMAN ARCHITECTURE. After the Second World War many churches built between the C5 and the C9 were excavated. Most of them were on the simplest plans and on a small scale. Carolingian architecture is most magnificently represented by Aachen. Other surviving churches follow the simpler basilican type. However, from such evidence as the plan on vellum for new buildings at St Gall it can be assumed that much more complex types existed. In fact, excavations at Cologne have proved that a major building as complex as the plan for St Gall was in fact built. The plan of the abbey of Lorsch and the plan of Charlemagne's palace at Ingelheim, both known from excavations, are also very complex. The later C9 and the earlier C10 was a time of political crises and invasions, and little seems to have been built. This changed with the establishment of the Ottonian Empire in 962.

The first evidence of revival is the nunnery church of Gernrode (961 etc.) and the mighty WESTWORK of St Pantaleon at Cologne (964–80), and a first climax was reached with St Michael at Hildesheim (c. 1000–33). The designer of this church established the terms of reference of the German Romanesque style. He did so by looking back to Charlemagne's Centula in Picardy (790–9), whence came the doubling of the main external accent by a tower above the westwork (at Hildesheim a west choir), just like the crossing tower at the east end, and by double transepts as well. Moreover, the two towers were accompanied by thin stair turrets. From St Michael this design of groups much richer than those of France or England spread at once. In the mid C11 under the Salian emperors the Empire reached its climax, and German architecture for a short time was leading Europe. The foremost examples are Limburg-by-the-Hardt (1025–45), with one of the earliest proper two-tower façades; Speier Cathedral (c. 1030 etc.), with a system of mighty blank giant arches inside, derived from the exterior of the Imperial Roman Basilica at Trier; the Cathedral of Trier (c. 1030 etc.), an enlargement of another Imperial Roman building and one of the most original designs in all Romanesque architecture; and St Mary-in-Capitol at Cologne (consecrated 1065), with its monumental trefoil east end. The detail everywhere is extremely austere. These churches, emulated at the time only by Jumièges in Normandy, had much influence abroad: St Mary-in-Capitol on Tournai and ultimately Noyon, Trier on the motif of outer dwarf galleries as developed in Italy, and so on. None of them was originally vaulted, though, exceptionally, St Mary-in-Capitol may always have had tunnel vaults. Speier received its monumental groin vaults late in the C11. The remodelling of Speier at that time was immensely enriched by masons who are known to have come from Lombardy. In fact, the chief foreign influence in German C12 and early C13 architecture is North Italian. The most magnificent buildings of the High Romanesque are – apart from the *Pfalzen*, i.e., the palaces of the emperors with their great halls (first and foremost Goslar) – the abbey of Maria Laach (1093–1156), the parish churches of Cologne inspired by the trefoil plan of St Mary-in-Capitol, and the cathedrals of Mainz (*c* 1082 etc.) and Worms (*c.* 1160 etc.). At Worms the west end is an example of German Late Romanesque architecture at its most Baroque. The country did not take kindly to the French Gothic, and rather carried the Romanesque to its extreme: at Worms, for instance, a rose window of French Early Gothic derivation is used in a Romanesque context. When this part of Worms Cathedral was complete, the east parts of Reims and the west parts of Amiens Cathedrals already stood in all their High Gothic glory.

The Gothic style first appears in Germany in some Cistercian work of the early C13 (Ebrach, Walkenried, Maulbronn), in the east end of Magdeburg Cathedral (1209–31), and at Limburg-on-the-Lahn (*c.* 1215–40). The earliest rib vaults (Murbach, *c.* 1150) are Romanesque rather than Gothic and North Italian rather than French in type. Limburg is a most telling instance of Gothic forms (cf. Laon) being used to create a wholly Romanesque *ensemble*.

This situation changed only with St Elizabeth at Marburg (begun 1235) and the cathedral of Cologne (begun 1248). Cologne, largely built from the original plans in the C19, is a French building – with its total length of 450 ft and its inner height of 150 ft the boldest of all. The chancel was consecrated in 1322.

By then Germany had begun to develop a Gothic style of her own. It is already foreshadowed at Marburg,

where, about 1250, it was decided to build a hall church, i.e., with the aisles the same height as the nave. This, done in Romanesque contexts in Westphalia and Poitou, became the hallmark of the Gothic style in Germany. The Wiesenkirche at Soest is a specially noble and slender example of the first half of the C14 (1331 etc.) and the chancel of Schwäbisch Gmünd (1351 etc.) is the pattern for many outstanding South German buildings to come. The proportions of this type are high, the piers slim and often octagonal or round, and the eye can easily wander in all directions. The exteriors are plain and no more than envelopes for the interiors. Only the single tower creates a bold accent. Among these is the highest of all medieval towers, that of Ulm, not completed till the C19; 530 ft high, it leaves Salisbury's 404 ft far behind, and was only outdone by the New York skyscrapers etc. after 1900. Perhaps the most thrilling feature of the Late Gothic hall churches is their lierne vaults of net or star or even freer shapes, strangely similar to those of the early C14 in England. Superb examples are Nördlingen, Landshut, and Annaberg (as late as 1499 etc.)

By then Dürer had already been to Venice, and the first minor Renaissance details began to appear in his woodcuts. Altogether, just as in England, the Renaissance was taken over first as a style of decoration, though the first case of an attempted architectural *ensemble*, the Fugger Chapel at St Anna, Augsburg (1509–18), is very early. Another case of a complete *ensemble* is the palace at Landshut (1536 etc.), entirely dependent on Mantua and GIULIO ROMANO. Otherwise Renaissance forms were used primarily for such set-pieces as doorways. However, from about 1550 onwards, the Renaissance turned German. In the later C16 and the early C17 it was characterized by big gables, stubby columns, and much thick wood-carving inside. North Germany under Dutch influence was more elegant and perhaps less robust.

The German parallel to Inigo JONES is Elias HOLL, the architect of the Augsburg Town Hall (1615 etc.). Here for the first time, and paralleled in the Nuremberg Town Hall, the Renaissance was understood as a style, not just as an assembly of pretty motifs.

But the Thirty Years War interrupted the development, and at its end the Italian Baroque was adopted. This was soon naturalized and led to the German Baroque of *c.* 1700–60, which was responsible for many of the greatest achievements of the whole of C18 European architecture. The greatest names are SCHLÜTER in Berlin, influenced by BERNINI's palaces; the ASAM brothers in Bavaria, influenced by Bernini's ecclesiastical decoration; J. M. FISCHER and ZIMMERMANN, who built some of the grandest and most ingenious churches of Bavaria and Swabia; and NEUMANN, who developed under the influence of the Viennese HILDE-BRANDT, and whose work culminates in the churches of Vierzehnheiligen and Neresheim and the palaces of Würzburg and Bruchsal. The source of this German Baroque is predominantly the Italy of BORROMINI and GUARINI, and the combination of curved elements in the plans is inexhaustible. The decoration is unmistakably C18 and not C17, i.e., Rococo not Baroque: light colours, playful asymmetrical ornament, and eminently elegant sculpture.

The reaction against the artificiality and flippancy of this Rococo was bound up with a growing admiration for England. Such a building as the palace at Wörlitz in Anhalt of 1769–73 is strictly Georgian-Palladian. Landscape gardening appeared at the same time. Out of these two components, the classical and the romantic, the architecture of the late C18 and the early C19 was created, first by GILLY, who was inspired by the Paris of BOULLÉE and LEDOUX but at the same time possessed the greatest resources of originality, and then by SCHINKEL, KLENZE, and others. In Schinkel C19 historicism is already to the fore. Though he believed in the Grecian ideals, he built much in the Gothic style. In Klenze's work the Italian Quattrocento *palazzo* and the High Renaissance are added as sources, and after that the great fancy-dress ball of historicism was in full swing, with churches in the *Rundbogenstil*, that is to say an Early Christian to Italian Romanesque (Klenze, All Saints) and even Italian Quattrocento style and with the palace at Schwerin in French Renaissance (1844 etc.).

ART NOUVEAU, called in Germany *Jugendstil*, marked the break with historicism. It culminated about 1900 and was a few years later straightened out into the new wholly original style of the C20. The operative works are BEHRENS's from 1906 onwards (crematorium, Hagen; factories for the A.E.G., Berlin) and GROPIUS's Fagus Works (1910). In the second half of the twenties this style was more universally accepted in Germany than in most other countries.

GIBBERD, Frederick (b. 1908). One of the first in England to accept the INTERNATIONAL MODERN style of the 1930s (Pulman Court, Streatham, London, 1934–5). His best-known works after the Second World War are the plan and some of the chief buildings for the New Town of Harlow (1947 etc.); the Lansbury Market at Poplar, London (1950–1); and the buildings for London Airport (1950 etc.).

GIBBS, James (1682–1754). The most influential London church architect of the early C18. In contrast to his predominantly Whig and neo-Palladian contemporaries, he was a Scot, a Catholic, and a Tory with Jacobite sympathies, and had the unique advantage of training under a leading Italian architect, Carlo FONTANA. Born in Aberdeen he went to Rome *c.* 1703 to study for the priesthood, but left the Scots College after a year. He stayed on in Rome until 1709, and appears to have studied painting before turning to architecture. His first building, St Mary-le-Strand, London (1714–17), is a mixture of WREN and Italian Mannerist and Baroque elements. Rather surprisingly, he was then taken up by Lord BURLINGTON, though only to be dropped in favour of Colen CAMPBELL, who replaced him as architect of Burlington House. He had no further contact with the neo-Palladians and remained faithful to Wren and his Italian masters, although he absorbed into his eclectic style a few Palladian features. St Martin-in-the-Fields, London (1722–6), is his masterpiece, and was widely imitated, especially in its combination of temple-front portico and steeple rising from the ridge of the roof. The monumental side elevations of recessed giant columns and giant pilasters have windows with his characteristic GIBBS SURROUND.

His best surviving secular buildings are outside London: the Octagon, Twickenham (1720); Sudbroke Park, Petersham (*c.* 1720); Ditchley House (1720–5); and the Senate House (1722–30) and King's College Fellows' Building at Cambridge (1724–49). Several of these display his ebulliently Italian Baroque style of interior decoration at its sumptuous best. His last and most original building, the Radcliffe Library, Oxford (1737–49), is unique in England in showing the influence of Italian Mannerism. He exerted great influence both in Britain and in America through his *Book of Architecture* (1728), one of the plates from which probably inspired the White House in Washington.

GIBBS SURROUND. The surround of a doorway or window consisting of

alternating large and small blocks of stone, quoinwise, or of intermittent large blocks; sometimes with a narrow raised band connecting up the verticals and along the face of the arch. Named after the architect James GIBBS. *See figure 49.*

Fig. 49. Gibbs surround

GIL DE HONTAÑÓN, Juan (d. 1526), and Rodrigo (d. 1577), father and son. Juan is the designer of the last two Gothic cathedrals of Spain, Salamanca and Segovia: at Salamanca he was consulted in 1512 (with eight others) and made master mason; at Segovia he started the new building in 1525. An earlier work of his is the cloister of Palencia Cathedral (begun 1505). He was consulted in 1513 for Seville Cathedral and designed the new lantern, etc., also still Gothic (1517–19).

Rodrigo appears first in 1521 at Santiago, probably as an assistant of JUAN DE ÁLAVA; then, in 1526, as one of the five architects consulted on the projected vast collegiate church of Valladolid (the others are his father, his master, FRANCISCO DE COLONIA, and Riaño). He was master mason at Astorga Cathedral (1530 etc.), where he built the nave; at Salamanca Cathedral (1537 etc.), where the transepts must be his; at the cloister of Santiago (1538 etc.), where he followed Álava; at Plasencia Cathedral (1537 or 1544), where the contributions of various masons are obscure; and at Segovia Cathedral (1563 etc.), where the east end is his. His finest secular work is the PLATERESQUE façade of Alcalá University (1541–53). He also wrote a book on architecture which is known only at second-hand.

GILLY, Friedrich (1772–1800), came of a French Huguenot family which had moved to Berlin in 1689, and was the son of the architect David Gilly. In spite of his neo-classical convictions he started as a Gothic enthusiast, drawing the Marienburg in West Prussia (1794). The king bought one of the drawings and gave young Gilly a four-year travel grant which, because of the war, he could not take up. In 1796 the idea of a national monument for Frederick the Great was revived. The king had died in 1786, and in the following year the monument had first been suggested: Christian Genelli at once submitted a Greek Doric temple, a very early case of faith in Grecian ideals (*but see* LEDOUX and SOANE). Gilly now designed a great funerary precinct and in its centre, raised on a high platform, a much larger Greek Doric temple – a Parthenon for the Prussian king. The precinct is strikingly original and strikingly severe in its forms. It is true that Gilly leant on the most recent work of young Parisian architects and their model PIRANESI (e.g., in the tunnel-vaulted triumphal arch), but the absolutely unmoulded cubic shapes are all his.

The year after, he took up his grant, but went to France and England instead of Italy: what he drew in Paris shows the sympathies already indicated by the monument. On his return in 1798 Gilly was made Professor of Optics and Perspective at the newly founded Academy of Architecture. In the same year he did his design for a national theatre for Berlin; in spite of certain motifs derived from Paris it is perhaps the most unimitative design of the age. It seems easier to reach the

C20 from this unrelieved geometrical shape than from anything between Gilly and 1890. The functions of the various parts of the building are made perfectly clear, and the semicircular front in particular, taken from Legrand and Molinos's Théâtre Feydeau (which Gilly drew in Paris), was handed by him to Moller (Theatre, Mainz, 1829), and from there reached SEMPER.

GIOCONDO, Fra (*c.* 1433–1515). A Dominican friar, born in Verona. His main building is the Palazzo del Consiglio, Verona (1476–93), with its elegant Renaissance arcade and its two-light windows on the first floor placed in a Gothic manner above the columns. He was in Paris 1495–1505. In 1511 he published the first illustrated edition of VITRUVIUS. Appointed architect to St Peter's with RAPHAEL, he produced a very elaborate plan (unexecuted).

GIOTTO DI BONDONE (*c.* 1266–1337) was appointed master mason to the cathedral and city of Florence in 1334 on account of his fame as a painter. His architectural work was limited to the campanile of the cathedral, which he began in that year. The design was altered after his death.

GIULIO ROMANO (Giulio Pippi or Giulio Giannuzzi, 1492/9–1546), who was born in Rome, began as both painter and architect in the classical shadow of RAPHAEL, but soon developed a strongly personal and dramatically forceful Mannerist style. His first building, Palazzo Cicciaporci-Senni, Rome (1521–2), is in the tradition of BRAMANTE and Raphael but with significant variations, e.g., columns resting on a bold string course which appears to have swallowed up their bases, and tall oblong panels instead of pilasters, connected neither to an entablature nor to a base. In 1524 he went to work for Federigo Gonzaga at Mantua, where all his most notable buildings were constructed. Palazzo del Te (1526–31) was designed for Federigo's honeymoon and as a summer villa. One storey high, it is built around an enormous courtyard and looks on to a garden terminated by a semicircular pilastered colonnade. Much in the plan derives from ancient Rome by way of Raphael's Villa Madama, but the careful interrelation of house and garden is new. Still more revolutionary were the façades: one of them smooth, with the SERLIAN MOTIF repeated as a blind arcade towards the garden; the others excessively rough with irregular rustication, Tuscan columns, massive keystones and wilfully misused classical details (the centre triglyph of each intercolumniation looks as if it had slipped out of place). He decorated the interior with frescoes, mainly of an erotic nature. One room gives a key to his strange personality: it has only one door and no windows and the walls and ceiling are painted to represent the Fall of the Titans, so that the shape of the room is entirely effaced and the visitor finds himself engulfed in a cascade of boulders and gigantic nude figures some 14 ft high.

On the façade of his own house in Mantua (c. 1544) he again indulged in a truculently licentious misuse of classical detail, but this time with a different intention. It is elegantly aloof and sophisticated instead of oppressive and neurotic. For the Palazzo Ducale, Mantua, he designed the Cortile della Cavallerizza (c. 1544), with coupled twisted columns on the first floor and one wing pierced by arches and square windows to afford a view across a near-by lake. He also designed Mantua Cathedral (1545), with double aisles supported by sturdy Corinthian columns whose repeated drum-beat monotony draws the visitor towards the high altar – another instance of his preoccupation with the effect a building would make rather than with the perfection of its form. With him the history of Expressionism in architecture begins.

GOPURA. The elaborate high gateway to South Indian temples, characteristic of Hindu architecture. *See figure 50.*

Fig. 50. Gopura

GOTHIC ARCHITECTURE. The architecture of the pointed arch, the rib vault, the flying buttress, the walls reduced to a minimum by spacious arcades, by GALLERY or TRIFORIUM, and by spacious CLERESTORY windows. These are not isolated motifs; they act together and represent a system of skeletal structure with active, slender, resilient members and membrane-thin infilling or no infilling at all. The motifs are not in themselves Gothic inventions. Pointed arches had existed in ROMANESQUE Burgundy, southern France, and also Durham. Rib vaults had existed in Durham too; and the principle of flying buttresses as half-arches or half-tunnel-vaults under the roofs of aisles or galleries above aisles is also found in French and English Romanesque. Even the verticalism of Gothic churches is only rarely more pronounced than that of, say, St Sernin at Toulouse or Ely (both Romanesque churches). The earliest completely Gothic building is the lower part of the east end of St Denis Abbey, dating from 1140–4. For the development of the style in France and then in all other countries, *see* FRENCH; EARLY ENGLISH; GERMAN; SPANISH; etc.

GOTHIC REVIVAL. The movement to revive the Gothic style belongs chiefly to the late C18 and the C19. Before the late C18 it must be distinguished from the Gothic Survival, an unquestioning continuation of Gothic forms, which is of course largely a matter of out-of-the-way buildings. Of major buildings mostly churches are concerned, and St Eustache in Paris and the chapel of Lincoln's Inn in London were completed well within the C17. By then, however, the new attitude of Revival had also appeared – the conscious choice of the Gothic style in contrast to the accepted current style. The first cases are those of the finishing of Gothic buildings, cases of Gothic for the sake of conformity (flêche, Milan Cathedral; façade, S. Petronio, Bologna), but soon the choice was also made for new buildings, though rarely before *c.* 1720. Then cases multiply, at least in England (HAWKSMOOR), and with Horace Walpole's Strawberry Hill (*c.* 1750–70) the Gothic Revival became a fashion. It affected France and Germany in the later C18, and a little later also Italy, Russia, America, etc. With the growth of archaeological knowledge, the Gothic Revival became more competent but also more ponderous. For churches Gothic remained the accepted style well into the C20. Of public buildings, the epoch-making one was the Houses of Parliament in London (1834 etc.): other major examples are the Town Hall in Vienna, the Houses of Parliament at Budapest, the Law Courts in London, the University at Glasgow.

GRAND ORDER, *see* COLOSSAL ORDER.

GREEK ARCHITECTURE. Commenting on the buildings on the Acropolis at Athens, Plutarch remarked: 'They were created in a short time for all time. Each in its fineness was even then at once age-old; but in the freshness of its vigour it is, even to the present day, recent and newly wrought.' No better description of the aims and achievements of Greek architects has ever been written. Their ambition was to discover eternally valid rules of form and proportion; to erect buildings human in scale yet suited to the divinity of their gods; to create, in other words, a classically ideal architecture. Their success may be measured by the fact that their works have been copied on and off for some 2,500 years and have never been superseded. Though severely damaged, the Parthenon remains the most nearly perfect building ever erected. Its influence stretches from the immediate followers of its architects to LE CORBUSIER. Greek architecture was, however, predominantly religious and official. Whereas temples and public buildings were of the greatest magnificence, private houses seem to have been fairly simple single-storey affairs, built of cheap materials.

Although the technique of constructing arches was known to the Greeks and the materials used for building temples, after C6 B.C., were normally stone or marble, their architecture was TRABEATED and preserved many of the techniques of wooden construction. A deep respect for tradition led them to preserve as decorative elements in their stone buildings many of the constructional elements of wooden ones: TRIGLYPHS representing the end of cross beams, GUTTAE the pegs used for fastening them, and METOPES the space between them. They derived much from other Mediterranean civilizations – the plan of the temple from Crete by way of

Mycenae, the columnar form from Egypt, the capital from Assyria.

But the Doric temple form evolved in the late C7 B.C. was as original as it was typically Greek in its bold simplicity, unity of design, and use of decoration to emphasize (never to mask) structure. The earliest Doric temple to survive is that of Hera at Olympia (before 600 B.C.); it originally had wooden columns which were gradually replaced in stone. Fragments from the temple at Korkyra, Corfu (*c.* 600 B.C.), reveal that sculpture was already used for the pediments. Other notable early Doric temples include the Temple C at Selinunte in Sicily (mid C6 B.C.), the so-called Basilica at Paestum (*c.* 530 B.C.), and the temple of Zeus Olympios at Agrigentum in Sicily (*c.* 500–470 B.C.). In all these the columns are rather stocky and primitive-looking, partly because their smooth stucco coverings have flaked off. Much greater refinement marks the temple of Hephaistos, Athens (*c.* 449–444 B.C.). The summit was reached at the Parthenon (447–438 B.C.), with its perfect proportions and nicely balanced relation of sculpture to achitecture. Here, as in other Doric temples, great pains were taken to correct optical illusions by the subtle use of ENTASIS. The temple to Athena Nike (448–421 B.C.) and the Erechtheum (421–406 B.C.), also on the Acropolis, reveal a tendency towards the exquisite; and the latter, with its graceful Ionic capitals and wonderful CARYATIDS, also points towards a new appreciation of architectural movement.

A desire for richer ornamentation was manifested by the Mausoleum of Halicarnassus (355–330 B.C.), where the role of the sculptor was greater than that of the architect. The final stage of Greek architectural development may be illustrated by the Choragic Monument of Lysicrates, Athens (335–334 B.C.), of an almost over-bred elegance which seems to anticipate the C18, when, indeed, it became the most popular of all Greek monuments.

Although the main Greek achievement was in the evolution of the Doric temple, many other types of religious buildings were of great beauty. The grandest were the theatres, notably that of Dionysus under the Acropolis in Athens (C5 B.C., but much altered) and that at Epidaurus (*c.* 350 B.C.), which reveal as perfect a command of acoustics as of visual effects. Theatres of this type were much imitated, especially in Asia Minor, during the HELLENISTIC period. *See also* CRETAN AND MYCENAEAN ARCHITECTURE.

GREEK CROSS. A cross with four equal arms.

GREEK REVIVAL. Greek as against Roman architecture became known to the West only about 1750–60. It was at first regarded as primitive and imitated by only a few architects. The earliest example is a garden temple at Hagley by 'Athenian' STUART (1758). A Grecian fashion began only in the 1790s. Among the earliest believers in the positive value of the simplicity and gravity of the Greek C5 were LEDOUX and SOANE. The Greek Revival culminated in all countries in the 1820s and 1830s (SCHINKEL, SMIRKE, WILKINS, STRICKLAND, etc.).

GROIN. The sharp edge formed by the intersection of vaulting surfaces.

GROIN VAULT, *see* VAULT.

GROPIUS, Walter (b. 1883), studied at the Colleges of Technology of Berlin and Munich. He received his introduction to the C20 problems of architecture and the responsibilities of the architect in the office of Peter BEHRENS, who believed in the architect's duty to provide well-designed buildings for working in, and also well-designed everyday products. He spent the years 1907–10 with Behrens. The outcome of this was that Gropius, as soon as he had established a practice of his own (1910), submitted a memorandum to a powerful potential client on the mass-producing of housing and equipment. One year later he built, with Adolph Meyer (1881–1929), the Fagus factory at Alfeld, one of the earliest buildings in any country to be in full command of the elements of architecture which were to constitute the INTERNATIONAL MODERN style: glass curtain walling, unrelieved cubic blocks, corners left free of visible supports. For the Werkbund Exhibition at Cologne in 1914, Gropius produced, also with Adolph Meyer, a Model Factory and Office Building, equally radical in its statement of new principles. Apart from Behrens, Frank Lloyd WRIGHT was now a source of inspiration, for two publications about him had appeared in Berlin in 1910 and 1911. On the strength of the Werkbund Exhibition building, Henri van de VELDE, then head of the School of Arts and Crafts at Weimar, advised the Grand Duke to make Gropius his successor. Gropius accepted and, when the First World War was over, settled down at Weimar to convert the school into a completely new establishment, for which he coined the name Bauhaus (House of Building). This name alludes to Gropius's conviction that, as with the medieval cathedral, the building ought to be the meeting-place of all arts and crafts teaching; all should work towards this ultimate unity. He also believed that all artists should be familiar with crafts, and that the initial training of artists and craftsmen should be one and the same – an introduction to form, colour, and the nature of material. This part of the teaching programme, first worked out by Johannes Itten, was known as the Basic Course (*Vorkurs*).

Gropius, in the first years of the Bauhaus, was propelled by the ideas of William MORRIS on the one hand, by the enthusiasm of the Expressionists on the other. There are, indeed, a few works by him belonging to these first years which are entirely Expressionist in style, notably the jagged concrete monument to those killed in the March Rising (1921) and the large log-house for the timber manufacturer Adolf Sommerfeld (1921–2), the latter equipped by Bauhaus staff and students. But then in 1923, stimulated by contacts with the Dutch group of De Stijl (led by Theo van Doesburg), Gropius returned to the ideals of his early years. The Bauhaus turned from emphasis on craft to emphasis on industrial design, and Gropius's own style followed once again the line laid down by the Fagus factory. The principal monument of this change is the Bauhaus's own new premises at Dessau (1925–6), functionally planned and detailed. Other important designs of these flourishing years in Germany are those for a Total Theatre (1926) and the long slabs of 'rational' housing for Siemensstadt (1929).

The rising tide of National Socialism killed the Bauhaus, but Gropius had already left it in 1928. After Hitler assumed power, Gropius left Germany and, following a short spell of partnership with Maxwell FRY in London (1934–7) – the most influential outcome of which was the Impington Village College near Cambridge – he left for Harvard. The Impington College is the first of a type of informally grouped school buildings which after the Second World War has focused international attention on England. At Harvard Gropius's principal job was once again teaching. In accordance with his faith in cooperative work he started his own firm as the Architects' Collaborative – a group of younger men working with him in full freedom. Of the achievements of this cooperative the Harvard Graduate Centre (1949) and a block of flats for the Berlin Hansa Quarter (Interbau Exhibition, 1957) may be mentioned. Gropius's foremost recent work is the United States Embassy at Athens (1957–61).

GROTESQUE. Fanciful ornamental decoration in paint or stucco, resembling

ARABESQUE and used by the Romans on walls of buildings which, when discovered, were underground (i.e., in 'grottoes'), hence the name. It consists of medallions, sphinxes, foliage, etc., and was much used by painters and decorators from RAPHAEL onwards, especially during the C18.

GROTTO. An artificial cavern, usually with fountains and other water-works, and decorated with rock- and shell-work. It was especially popular in the C18.

GUARINI, Guarino (1624–83), was born in Modena and was a Theatine father, well known as a philosopher and mathematician, before he won fame as an architect. (He expanded Euclid and even foreshadowed Monge in his learned *Placita philosophica* of 1665.) Since he was first a mathematician and second an architect, his complex spatial compositions are sometimes difficult to understand by eye alone. But they are as exhilarating intellectually as artistically. All his important surviving buildings are in Turin, where he spent the last seventeen years of his life. His admiration of BORROMINI is very obvious in Collegio dei Nobili (1678) and Palazzo Carignano (1679), especially the latter with its oval saloon and undulating façade in the style of S. Carlo alle Quattro Fontane. To inflate Borromini's miniature church to palatial grandiloquence was daring enough, yet his originality had already carried him even farther in the Capella della SS. Sindone (1667–90) and in S. Lorenzo (1668–87). Both churches are crowned with fantastic and unprecedented cone-shaped domes. That of SS. Sindone is built of superimposed segmental arches that diminish in span as they ascend, the abstract geometric poetry of this free construction being emphasized by the diaphanous light which filters through the grids. The S. Lorenzo dome is equally unusual: it is composed of interlocking semicircular arches forming an octagon on a cir-

cular drum. The inspiration for this odd conception may have come from Hispano-Moresque architecture, perhaps from the similar dome in the mosque of al Hakim at Cordova (A.D. 965). Guarini's structural ingenuity was not confined to domes, and his other experiments, notably those with banded vaults and diagonal, forward-tilted, or three-dimensional arches, were to be very influential in Germany and Austria. None of his important buildings outside Turin has survived: e.g., SS. Annunziata and Theatine Palace in Messina (1660); Ste Anne-la-Royale, Paris (1662 onwards); St Mary of Altötting, Prague (1679); and S. Maria Divina Providencia, Lisbon. His influence was greatly increased by his *Architettura civile*, published posthumously in 1737: engravings from it were known from 1668 onwards.

GUAS, Juan (d. 1496). A Spanish mason of French descent, probably the designer of S. Juan de los Reyes at Toledo (1476 etc.). Towards the end of his life Guas was master mason of Segovia and Toledo Cathedrals. It is likely that the wildly Late Gothic façade of S. Gregorio at Valladolid is his (1487–96).

GUILLOCHE. A pattern of interlacing bands forming a plait and used as an enrichment on a moulding. *See figure 51.*

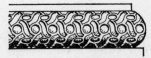

Fig. 51. Guilloche

GUIMARD, Hector (1867–1942), was professor at the École des Arts Décoratifs from 1894 to 1898. He is the best of the French ART NOUVEAU architects. At the beginning of his career (in 1893) he was influenced, it seems, by HORTA. His most remarkable building is the block of flats called

Castel Bérenger in Paris (1894–8). The use of metal, faïence, and glass-bricks is bold and inventive, though the exterior is of less interest. On the other hand his Métro stations (1899–1904) are nothing but exterior – open metal arches in extreme Art Nouveau shapes – a daring thing for an architect to design, and perhaps an even more daring thing for a client to accept.

GUTTAE. Small drop-like projections carved below the TENIA under each TRIGLYPH on a Doric ARCHITRAVE. *See figure 64.*

H

HADFIELD, George (c. 1764–1826), was born in Leghorn and trained at the Royal Academy Schools, London, winning the Gold Medal in 1784 and studying in Italy 1790–1. In about 1794 he went to America and was appointed in 1795 to supervise the construction of the new Capitol in Washington, replacing Stephen Hallet. He disapproved of the design (by Thornton) and Hallet's revisions, but the radical alterations he suggested, such as the introduction of a colossal order, were not approved and he was dismissed in 1798. He continued to practise in Washington and impressed his neo-classical taste on the new city, e.g., the City Hall, United States Bank, Fuller's Hotel, Gadsby's Hotel, Van Ness's mausoleum, and Arlington House whose imposing Paestum portico is one of the most splendid examples of the Greek Revival in America.

HAGIOSCOPE, *see* SQUINT.

HALFPENNY, William (Michael Hoare, d. 1755). His only surviving building of note is Holy Trinity, Leeds (1722–7), but he published some twenty architectural manuals for country gentlemen and builders which were enormously successful and influential. His designs are mostly Palladian but also include some rather ham-fisted attempts at Rococo sophistication, CHINOISERIE, GOTHIC REVIVAL, etc. *A New and Compleat System of Architecture* (1749) and *Rural Architecture in the Chinese Taste* (c. 1750) are among the best of his books.

HALF-TIMBERING, *see* FRAMED BUILDING *and* TIMBER-FRAMING.

HALL CHURCH. A church in which nave and aisles are of approximately equal height.

HAMMERBEAM, *see* ROOF.

HARDOUIN, *see* MANSART, Jules Hardouin.

HARDWICK, Philip (1792–1870), stopped practising in the course of the 1840s. His son and grandson were also architects. In 1815 he was in Paris, and he spent 1818–19 in Italy. His *œuvre* does not seem to have been large, but it is of high quality and varied interest. His most famous building today is Euston Station, with its majestic Greek Doric propylaea (1836–9) which became famous when it was infamously destroyed by the British Transport Commission. The station building was quite independent of the propylaea, whose spiritual function was that of a worthy introduction to that miracle of human ingenuity the London-to-Birmingham railway. The range of stylistic possibilities open to Hardwick was great, and he was remarkably good at all of them: a monumentally plain, strictly utilitarian classicism of brick and short Tuscan columns for the St Katherine's Dock warehouses (1827–8); an at the time most unusual restrained English Baroque for the Goldsmiths' Hall (1829–35); Jacobean for Babraham Hall, Cambridgeshire (1831); and a convincing and unaffected Tudor for Lincoln's Inn Hall and Library (1842–5). On the latter, PEARSON was assistant, and it is possible that the refined detailing is his; at all events, the building is effortlessly convincing and has no longer the character of romantic make-believe of early C19 Tudor imitations.

HARLING. The Scots term for ROUGH-CAST.

HARMONIC PROPORTIONS. A system of proportions relating architecture to music. The Ancients discovered that if two cords are twanged the difference in pitch will be one octave if the shorter is half the length of the longer, a fifth if one is two thirds of the other, and a fourth if the ratio is 3:4. It was therefore assumed that rooms or whole buildings whose measurements followed the ratios 1:2, 2:3, or 3:4 would be harmonious. Early Renaissance architects, notably ALBERTI, seized on this discovery as the key to the beauty of Roman architecture and also to the harmony of the universe. The idea was further developed by PALLADIO who, with the aid of Venetian musical theorists, evolved a far more complex scale of proportions based on the major and minor third – 5:6 and 4:5 – and so on.

HARRISON, Peter (1716–75). The only architect of distinction in pre-Revolutionary America. Born in England, he emigrated in 1740, and settled in Newport, Rhode Island, as a trader in wines, rum, molasses, and mahogany. He presumably taught himself architecture but quickly acquired competence in the Palladian style, as his first work shows – Redwood Library, Newport (1749–58), a timber building imitating rusticated stone. Other buildings show Gibbsian influence: King's Chapel, Boston (1749–58); Synagogue, Newport (1759–63). But he returned to Inigo JONES and the English Palladians for inspiration in his later works: Brick Market, Newport (1761–72), and Christ Church, Cambridge, Mass. (1760). He settled in New Haven, Mass., in 1761, and became Collector of Customs there in 1768, suffering some persecution in his later years as a loyalist and government official.

HASENAUER, Karl von, see SEMPER.

HAUSSMANN, Baron Georges-Eugène (1809–91). A Protestant from Alsace who became a lawyer and civil servant, he was ruthless, canny, and obstinate. Napoleon III made him Prefect of the Seine Department in 1853 and entrusted to him his sweeping plans for city improvement. Haussmann kept the post till 1870, and did as much as, or perhaps more than, the emperor expected. Haussmann's improvements follow the traditional principles of French town planning as established by Henri IV and developed by Louis XIV, and finally – Haussmann's direct model – by the so-called Artists' Plan of 1797: long straight boulevards meeting at *rond-points* are the principal motifs. It is often said that Haussmann made these boulevards to obtain good firing-lines in case of a revolution, but he was at least as much guided by traffic considerations (e.g., the connecting of railway stations) and was without doubt also passionately devoted to vistas towards monuments or monumental buildings such as the Arc de Triomphe or the Opéra.

HAWKSMOOR, Nicholas (1661–1736), the most original of English Baroque architects except VANBRUGH, came from a family of Nottinghamshire farmers. At eighteen he became WREN's amanuensis and was closely associated with him at Greenwich Hospital and other buildings until his death. Vanbrugh also found him an able assistant and employed him from 1690 onwards, notably at Castle Howard and Blenheim Palace. Indeed, he became more than just an assistant to both Wren and Vanbrugh, though it is impossible now to assess how much they owed to him. His independent works have great originality, and only his dour, capricious character and lack of push denied him greater opportunities and worldly success. Vigorous, odd, bookish, yet massively plastic in feeling, his style is a highly personal Baroque amalgam of Wren, classical Rome, and Gothic. Like Vanbrugh, but unlike Wren, his passion was for dramatic effects of mass, and he has been criticized for heaviness as a result. He began working on his own *c.* 1702 at Easton Neston, a compact rectangular building with a giant order all round; it combines Wren's grandeur and urbanity, and in some details foreshadows Vanbrugh. In 1711 he was appointed Surveyor under the Act for Building Fifty New Churches, and the six he designed himself form the bulk of his *œuvre*. All of them are minor masterpieces: St Anne's, Limehouse (1712–24), with its medieval steeple in classical dress; St Mary Woolnoth (1716–27), with its square within a square plan; St George's, Bloomsbury (1720–30), the most grandiose and least odd of all his buildings; and Christchurch, Spitalfields (1723–39), as perverse and megalomaniac as anything by Vanbrugh. His other buildings are only slightly less notable – the quadrangle and hall at All Souls', Oxford (1729), and the west towers of Westminster Abbey (1734), all in his neo-Gothic manner; and finally, the grim and austere circular Doric mausoleum at Castle Howard (1729), where he returned to Rome and BRAMANTE for inspiration.

HEADER, see BRICKWORK.

HEINZELMANN, Konrad (d. 1454), was at Ulm in the 1420s. He was called to Nördlingen in 1429 as master mason to design and build the church of St George, then to Rothenburg in 1428 to work on the church of St Jakob. In 1439 he went to Nuremberg, and there designed and began the beautiful chancel of St Lorenz.

HELLENISTIC ARCHITECTURE. The style developed in the Hellenistic kingdoms created out of the empire conquered by Alexander the Great (356–323 B.C.). The tendency towards greater elegance and elaboration in small buildings (e.g., Choragic Monument of Lysicrates, Athens) and a more richly sculptural and monumental style for large ones (e.g., Mausoleum of Halicarnassus and the Ionic temple of Artemis at Ephesus), already evident in early C4 GREEK ARCHITECTURE, was accelerated. The greatest Hellenistic city was Alexandria, laid out on a regular grid plan with numerous vast and very splendid buildings, none of which survives. The Ionic temple of Athena Polias, Priene (c. 335 B.C.), and of Artemis Leukophryene at Magnesia by Hermogenes (c. 130 B.C.) are representative of the style. Doric temples were still built, but the columns became much more slender and motifs from the Ionic order were introduced, as in the Temple of Hera Basileia at Pergamum (c. 150 B.C.). The richer Corinthian order was more to the taste of the new civilization: at Athens the great Olympeion (begun 174 B.C., though not completed until A.D. 131) is the first Corinthian building on the grand scale, and provides a piquant contrast to the sober solemnity of the Parthenon on the Acropolis above it.

Many of the finest Hellenistic buildings are civic rather than religious: the Bouleuterion at Miletus (174–65 B.C.) and various colonnaded walks like the recently restored Stoa in the Athenian AGORA (c. 150 B.C.). Military engineering was brought to a new height of efficiency and many forts and walls, with handsome crisply cut masonry and sometimes with arched gateways, survive both in Greece and in Asia Minor (e.g., Priene). Excavations have revealed that private houses were built on a much grander scale than before.

The Hellenistic style survived the conquest of Asia Minor by the Romans; indeed, Imperial Roman architecture may be regarded as its logical development. The main buildings of the two great Syrian sites, Baalbeck (the very rich Temple of Bacchus, courts, and portico, c. A.D. 120–200) and Palmyra (Temple of the Sun, c. A.D. 1; Temple of Baal, A.D. 131), are predominantly Hellenistic in feeling, though their vaults, arches, and domes are typically Roman.

HELM ROOF, see ROOF.

HENRY OF REYNS, Master of the King's Masons to Windsor Castle in 1243, and later to Westminster Abbey. He was dead, it seems, by 1253. This means he was King's Master Mason when Westminster Abbey was begun and so was probably its designer. Reyns sounds temptingly like Reims, and Reims Cathedral is, in fact, the stylistic source of much at Westminster (tracery, the wall-passages in the east chapels), together with work at Amiens and the Sainte Chapelle in Paris, only just completed when the abbey was begun. However, there are other features, such as the large gallery and the ridge-rib of the vault, which are entirely English and may make it more likely that Henry was an Englishman who had worked at Reims. Judging by style, Henry may also have designed the King's Chapel at Windsor Castle (built *c.* 1240).

HERLAND, Hugh (d. *c.* 1405). Carpenter in the king's service probably from *c.* 1350, and in charge of the king's works in carpentry from 1375, when William Herland, presumably his father, died. His *magnum opus* is the hammerbeam roof of Westminster Hall, done in the 1390s; it has a span of about 67 ft. He also worked for William of Wykeham (with WILLIAM OF WYNFORD) at New College, Oxford, and probably at Winchester College.

HERMS. Three-quarter-length figures on pedestals used decoratively in Renaissance and post-Renaissance architecture. *See also* TERM.

HERRERA, Juan de (*c.* 1530–97), travelled abroad, mainly in Italy, from 1547 to 1559. He was appointed to succeed Juan Bautista de TOLEDO at the Escorial in 1563, though he did not design any additions until after 1572: the infirmary and chapel (1574–82) were his main contributions. But his majestic if sometimes rather solemn and Italianate style is best seen at the Palace of Aranjuez (1569), at the Exchange at Seville (1582), and in his designs for Valladolid Cathedral (*c.* 1585), which were only partly exe-

cuted but had enormous influence, e.g., on Salamanca, Mexico, Puebla, and Lima Cathedrals.

HERRINGBONE WORK. Stone, brick, or tile work in which the component units are laid diagonally instead of horizontally. Alternate courses lie in opposite directions, forming a zigzag pattern along the wall-face.

HEWN STONE. The American term for ASHLAR.

HEXASTYLE. Of a portico with six frontal columns.

HILDEBRANDT, Johann Lukas von (1668–1745), a leading Baroque architect in Austria alongside FISCHER VON ERLACH, was born in Genoa, the son of a captain in the Genoese army and an Italian mother. Italian always remained his first language. He studied with Carlo FONTANA in Rome before settling in Vienna. He was appointed Imperial Court Engineer in 1701 and knighted by the emperor in 1720. His style is lighter than SCHLÜTER's and more Italianate than Fischer's, livelier too and homelier, with typically Viennese charm. He much admired GUARINI, as his early (1699) Dominican church at Gabel in North Bohemia shows. It has Guarini's characteristic three-dimensional arches and a complicated and imaginative Guarinesque plan (concave corners hidden by convex balconies, etc.). The influence of BORROMINI is evident in much of the carved decoration of his masterpiece, the Upper Belvedere in Vienna, built for Prince Eugen (1714–24). His secular buildings are notable for their oval and octagonal rooms (Schloss Racker, Hungary; Palais Starhemberg-Schönburg, Vienna) and for their ingeniously planned and spatially dramatic staircases (Palais Daun-Kinsky and the Belvedere, Vienna; Schloss Mirabell, Salzburg). He pointed the way forward to NEUMANN's masterpieces at Würzburg and Bruchsal. His best church is the Piaristenkirche, Vienna (1716, later modified by K. I. DIENTZENHOFER), octagonal in plan and bright, rhythmical, and Borrominesque inside.

HIP. The external angle formed by the meeting of two sloping roof surfaces. *See* ROOF *and figure 70*.

HIPPED ROOF, *see* ROOF.

HITTORF, Jakob Ignaz (1792–1867), was born at Cologne, went to Paris in 1810 with GAU and placed himself under PERCIER. He then worked under BELANGER just at the time when the latter was busy with the glass-and-iron dome of the Corn Market. In 1819–23 Hittorf travelled in Germany, England, and Italy. After that, till 1848, he was Royal Architect. His first major building, executed with his father-in-law Lepère, is St Vincent de Paul (begun 1824), still with an Ionic portico, but Early Christian rather than classical inside, with its two superimposed orders and its open roof. The exterior already shows the change from the pure classical to the new, grander, more rhetorical classical of the École des Beaux Arts as it culminated in Hittorf's Gare du Nord (1861–5). He also did extensive decorative work; laid out the Place de la Concorde in its present form (1838–40); built two Circuses (des Champs Élysées, 1839; Napoléon, 1851) with iron-and-glass domes; and, with Rohault de Fleury and Pellechet, designed the Grand Hôtel du Louvre – all of which proves his interest in new functions and new materials. Hittorf also made a name as an archaeologist, chiefly by his discovery of the polychromy of Greek architecture (1830), a 'Victorian' discovery shocking to the older generation of Grecian purists.

HOBAN, James (*c*. 1762–1831), was born in Ireland, emigrated to America after the Revolution, and was advertising in Philadelphia in 1785. But he settled in South Carolina until 1792, designing the State Capitol at Columbia (completed 1791, burnt down 1865), based on L'ENFANT's designs for the Federal Hall in New York. But he is remembered chiefly for the White House, Washington, which he designed in 1792, basing the front on a plate in GIBBS's *Book of Architecture*. He may also have had Leinster House, Dublin, in mind, though the White House is not, as has been suggested, a mere copy. It was built 1793–1801, and Hoban also supervised its rebuilding after 1814 (completed 1829). He also designed and built the Grand Hotel (1793–5) and the State and War Offices (begun in 1818), Washington. He ended his life as a solid and much respected councillor of that city.

HOFFMANN, Josef (1870–1956), was a pupil of Otto WAGNER in Vienna and one of the founders of the Wiener Werkstätten (1903), based on the William MORRIS conviction of the importance of a unity between architecture and the crafts. His style developed from ART NOUVEAU towards a new appreciation of unrelieved square or rectangular forms ('Quadratl-Hoffmann') – a change not uninfluenced by MACKINTOSH, whose furniture and other work had been exhibited by the Sezession (*see* OLBRICH) in 1900. The Convalescent Home at Purkersdorf outside Vienna (1903) is one of the most courageously squared buildings of its date anywhere in the world, and yet it possesses that elegance and refinement of detail which is the Viennese heritage. With his Palais Stoclet in Brussels (1905–11) Hoffmann proved that this new totally anti-period style of unrelieved shapes could be made to look monumental and lavish by means of the materials used – in this case white marble in bronze framing outside, mosaics by Gustav Klimt inside. Hoffmann later built many wealthy villas, some Austrian Pavilions for exhibitions, and also some blocks of flats, but his chief importance lies in his early works.

HOLABIRD & ROCHE. William Holabird (1854–1923) went to West Point in 1873–5 and to Chicago in 1875, where he took an engineering job in the office of W. Le B. JENNEY. In 1880 he formed a partnership with Martin Roche. Their Tacoma Building (1886–7), following Jenney's Home Insurance and going decisively beyond it, established steel-skeleton construction for skyscrapers (in this case of twelve storeys) and with it the Chicago School style. Their Marquette Building (1894) has the same importance stylistically as the Tacoma Building had structurally. Its horizontal windows and its crisp, unenriched mouldings pointed the way into the C20.

HOLFORD, Sir William, was born 1907 in South Africa. The leading town-planner in England, he is also widely recognized abroad, as witness his report on the development of Canberra (1957–8) and his presence on the jury for Brasilia (1957). In England his most brilliant design is that for the precinct of St Paul's Cathedral in London (1955–6), now in course of execution, with some unfortunate modifications. He was also reponsible for the post-war plan for the City of London (with Charles Holden, 1946–7).

HOLL, Elias (1573–1646). The leading Renaissance architect in Germany, where he holds a position parallel historically to that of his contemporaries Inigo JONES in England and de BROSSE in France. The son of an architect, he travelled in Italy, visiting Venice 1600–1, and presumably studied PALLADIO and other Italian Renaissance architects. He became city architect of Augsburg in 1602, and built his masterpiece, the Town Hall in Augsburg, between 1610 and 1620.

HOLLAND, Henry (1745–1806), began under his father, a Fulham builder, then became assistant to 'Capability' BROWN, whose daughter he married. His first independent work, Brooks's Club, London (1776–8), was quickly followed by his greatest, Carlton House, London, which he enlarged and altered for the Prince of Wales

(1783–5, demolished). Also for the Prince of Wales he built the Marine Pavilion at Brighton (1786–7), later transformed into the Royal Pavilion by NASH. His style owed something to both CHAMBERS and ADAM, with various Louis XVI elements added. Though lacking originality, the refined taste and 'august simplicity' of his interior decoration approached French neo-classicism in elegance. His best country houses are Southill (1795) and Berrington Hall (1778). He laid out and built Hans Town, Chelsea (1771 etc.), but this has been largely rebuilt.

HOOD-MOULD. A projecting moulding to throw off the rain, on the face of a wall above an arch, doorway, or window; can be called *dripstone* or *label*. *See also* LABEL-STOP *and figure 52.*

Fig. 52. Hood-mould

HORSESHOE ARCH, *see* ARCH.

HORTA, Baron Victor (1861–1947), a Belgian architect, studied in Paris in 1878–80, then at the Brussels Academy under Balat. He appeared in the forefront of European architecture with his Hôtel Tassel in the rue Paul-Émile Janson (designed 1892). This is the same year as that of van de VELDE's first exploration of ART NOUVEAU typography and design. The Hôtel Tassel is less startling externally, but its staircase with exposed iron supports, floral iron ornament, and much linear decoration on the wall is Art Nouveau architecture of the boldest. The Hôtel Tassel was followed by the particularly complete and lavish Hôtel

Solvay (1895–1900); the Maison du Peuple (1896–9), with a curved glass-and-iron façade and much structural and decorative iron inside the great hall; the store L'Innovation (1901); and several more private houses. Later Horta turned to a conventional classicism (Palais des Beaux Arts, Brussels, 1922–9).

HOWARD, Sir Ebenezer (1850–1928), started as a clerk in the City of London, rose to be a valued shorthand writer, and remained that nearly to the end. During a stay of five years in America (1872–7), he learned to know and admire Whitman and Emerson, and began to think of the better life and how it could be made to come true. In 1898 he read Edward Bellamy's utopian work *Looking Backward*, and this gave him the idea of his lifetime: that of the garden city which is an independent city and not a suburb – this is important – and is placed in the green countryside and provided with countrified housing as well as industry and all cultural amenities. His book *Tomorrow* came out in 1898, in 1899 the Garden City Association was founded, in 1902 the book was republished as *Garden Cities of Tomorrow*, and in 1903 Letchworth was started, to the design of Parker & UNWIN. This was the earliest of the garden cities and greatly influenced the post-war SATELLITE TOWNS of Britain. Howard was knighted in 1927.

HÜLTZ, Johann (d. 1449), was master mason of Strassburg Cathedral and as such designed the openwork spire with its fabulous spiral staircases. The work was completed in 1439. Hültz was the successor to Ulrich von ENSINGEN, who built the octagon (the stage below the spire).

HUNGARIAN ARCHITECTURE. Medieval architecture in Hungary reflects the events in various centres of the West. Sometimes inspiration came from one centre, sometimes from more than one. The sources for the Romanesque style are Lombardy (Pécs), Germany (Lébény, Jaák, Zsámbék), and France (Cistercians). National features can be traced, but are still minor. The same is true of the Gothic style, where the influence comes chiefly from Germany and Austria (City Parish Church, Budapest). The Renaissance arrived exceptionally early, thanks to King Matthias Corvinus (1458–90), and appears at Visegrád and Budapest before 1500. The C16 starts under the influence of the Turkish invasion, and in towns such as Budapest, Pécs, and Eger mosques, minarets, and baths can be seen. As a sign of the war against the Turks some fortresses were erected (Györ, etc.) by Italian engineers on the new Italian models. The Turkish occupation ended only in the late C17, and in the C18 Austrian and Bohemian Baroque held the stage. The best neo-classical architect of the first half of the C19 was Mihály POLLAK; the most conspicuous building of the later C19 the Gothic but symmetrical Parliament (1884 etc.) by Imre Steindl.

HUNT, Richard Morris (1827–95), came of a wealthy early Colonial family. They moved to Paris in 1843, and there Hunt joined LEFUEL's *atelier* and the École des Beaux Arts. He also worked on painting with Couture and on sculpture with Barye. He travelled widely before he was made an *inspecteur* under Lefuel on the Louvre in 1854. This first-hand knowledge of the French-Renaissance Revival he took back to America in 1855. He settled in New York and, side by side with his practice, ran an *atelier* on the Parisian pattern. But he returned to Europe again in the 1860s and only in 1868 finally came to rest. He designed the Tribune Building in New York (1873, one of the first with lifts), and then rich men's residences at Newport, in New York (W. K. Vanderbilt, 1878 onwards; J. J. Astor, 1893), and elsewhere (Biltmore, Ashville, N.C.,

1890). The French Renaissance remained his favourite style. Hunt was also the designer of the Administration Building at the Chicago Exposition of 1893 and the façade of the Metropolitan Museum, New York (built in 1900–2). He was one of the founders of the American Institute of Architects.

HURTADO, Francisco (1669–1725), one of the greatest Spanish Baroque architects, was quite the most exuberantly rich. His work is confined to interiors, which are of a fantasy unparalleled in Europe. Born and educated in Cordova, he became a captain in the army and possibly visited Sicily. He may have designed the Victoria *camarín* above the Mausoleum of the Counts of Buenavista, Málaga (1691–3). Most of his work is in Granada, where he designed the relatively simple *sagrario* or Sacrament Chapel for the Cathedral (1704–5). The Sacrament Chapel of the Cartuja (1702–20), walled with marble, jasper, and porphyry and containing a marble tabernacle supported by red and black salomónicas, is a masterpiece of polychromatic opulence. He called it 'a precious jewel', and claimed that there was nothing like it in all Europe. In 1718 he designed the very complex *camarín*, liberally decorated with grey-and-coral-coloured marble and lapis lazuli, for the Cartuja of El Paular, Segovia. He has also been credited with the design of the still more bizarrely rich sacristy of the Granada Cartuja (executed 1730–47 by Arévalo and Vázquez), where the tendency to muffle the structure in a riotous welter of ornament is taken to its final extreme.

HYPAETHRAL. Without a roof, open to the sky.

HYPERBOLIC PARABOLOID ROOF. A special form of double-curved shell, the geometry of which is generated by straight lines. This property makes it fairly easy to construct. The shape consists of a continuous plane developing from a parabolic arch in one direction to a similar inverted parabola in the other. *See figure 53.*

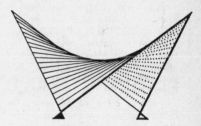

Fig. 53. Hyperbolic paraboloid

HYPOCAUST. The underground chamber or duct of the Roman system of central heating by means of air flues.

HYPOGEUM. An underground room or vault.

HYPOSTYLE. A hall or other large space over which the roof is supported by rows of columns giving a forest-like appearance.

HYPOTRACHELIUM. The groove round a Doric column between the SHAFT and the NECKING.

I

ICONOSTASIS. A screen in Byzantine churches separating the sanctuary from the nave and pierced by three doors; originally a lattice of columns joined by a decorated PARAPET and COPING. Since the C14–15 it has become a wooden or stone wall covered with icons, hence the name.

ICTINUS. The leading architect in Periclean Athens and one of the greatest of all time. With CALLICRATES he designed and built the Parthenon (447/6–438 B.C.), about which he later wrote a book, now lost, with Carpion. He was commissioned by Pericles to design the new Telesterion (Hall of Mysteries) at Eleusis, but his designs were altered by the three new architects who took over on the fall of Pericles. According to Pausanias he was also the architect of the Doric temple of Apollo Epicurius at Bassae, begun after the Great Plague of 430 B.C.

IMBREX. In Greek and Roman architecture, a convex tile to cover the join between two flat or concave roofing tiles.

IMPOST. A member in the wall, usually formed of a projecting bracket-like moulding, on which the end of an arch rests. *See figure 4.*

IMPOST BLOCK. A block with splayed sides placed between ABACUS and CAPITAL.

INDENT. A shape chiselled out in a stone slab to receive a brass effigy.

INDIAN AND PAKISTANI ARCHITECTURE. Nearly all buildings surviving from before the C16 Moghul conquest of the Indian sub-continent (modern India and Pakistan) are religious. The earliest buildings known are those associated with the rise of Buddhism – cave temples hollowed out of rocky mountainsides, with elaborate façades and halls lined with massive pillars, as at Karli (80 B.C.) and Ajanta (C4–5 A.D.). The Buddhists also built stupas, sacred mounds erected over relics and surrounded by walls with richly carved gateways, as at Sanchi where the finest of several stupas dates from CI A.D. In form the stupa symbolized the universe, with the hemispherical dome of the mound representing the sky.

Hindu temples survive in considerable numbers, distributed over the subcontinent. All reveal a love of very rich carved figurative decoration, usually of a sensuous and often of an overtly erotic character. Temple groups consist of a tall vimana or shrine, a columned hall and some minor buildings within a walled enclosure pierced by elaborate gates. Styles differ according to district rather than period, the three main styles being Northern, Chalukyan, and Dravidian. The principal northern Hindu temples include the group in Orissa (800–1200); the Great Temple, Bhubanesvar (C9, but with many later additions); and the group of thirty at Khajuraho. They are distinguished by the cactus-like curving roof-cones of the vimanas. The later Chalukyan temples have vimanas built on star-shaped (rather than square) plans, and the points of the star are surmounted by spires clustering round the roof cone and giving it a lively vertical emphasis – e.g., the group of temples at Belur (C12). Some Dravidian temples are cut out of the rock but, unlike earlier rock-cut or cave temples (e.g., Ajanta), in such a way that they are free-standing with all façades exposed – e.g., the Raths at Mamallapuram near Madras (C8). Other Dravidian temples, such as that at Tanjore (C10), rise like stepped pyramids above square bases.

The Jaina religion, an offshoot of Hinduism, produced numerous temples. One of the finest is the Temple of Vimala on Mount Abu (1032), with fantastically carved columns and beams inside. Of about the same date, the Great Sas Bahu temple appears like a mound of heavy decorative elements heaped on top of one another. Among later South Indian temples, that of Madura (C17) is perhaps the grandest.

Muslims from Afghanistan, who had made periodic incursions into India, established themselves in the north in the late C12 under the Ghorid dynasty, who created a capital at Delhi. They brought with them the ISLAMIC style. As in other lands subdued by Islam, temples were speedily converted into mosques, e.g., at Ajmer where a Jain college was masked by a façade decorated with geometrical carvings and Kufic script (1192). In Delhi itself a vast mosque, the Qutb-ul-Islam (1193), was built with a high minar which was to be much imitated in later Islamic architecture. Many other mosques were built under the Pathan dynasty – Jami Masjid, Jaunpur (1438–78), the Adinah Mosque, Gaur (1358–89), Jami Masjid, Ahmadabad (1424) – with Islamic decorations slightly modified by Hindu styles.

But it was not until after the establishment of the Moghul dynasty (1526) as the rulers of the greater part of India that the great Islamic monuments were erected. Indians were normally employed as architects and consequently the Islamic style of Persia and the Mediterranean countries was considerably modified. Better materials were used – finely jointed stonework, various coloured marbles, incrustations of semi-precious and sometimes precious stones – and an appearance of greater monumentality was obtained. At the same time the decorations were finished with jewel-like precision, even a coarse material like sandstone being carved with a delicacy usually reserved for ivory. Lace-like patterns were wrought out of marble panels for MUSHRABEYEH WORK (elaborate grilles). Thus Moghul architecture attained a unique combination of monumentality on a vast scale with miniaturist delicacy of detail. The two great Moghul patrons were Akbar (1556–1605) and his grandson Shah Jahan. Akbar built the remarkable new city of Fatehpur-Sikri (1568–75) and moved his capital there from nearby Agra. It incorporates the beautiful tomb of Sheik Salim Chisti, besides numerous pavilions. It was abandoned in 1585 and never reinhabited. Of Akbar's palace at Allahabad only the square audience hall with sixty-four columns has been preserved. Akbar's own tomb at Sikandara (1593–1613) is among the grandest in India – a massive red sandstone gateway inlaid with white marble opening into a garden which leads towards the tomb itself, a four-storey building encircled by an arcaded cloister and entered through a domed portal. Rich as they are, these monuments look almost severe in comparison with those built by Shah Jahan, most notably the Taj Mahal (1630–53) near Agra, the tomb of his favourite wife – grandiose in scale, exquisite in its opalescent colour, its refinement of carved and inlaid detail, perfectly balanced in its proportions and in the relationship of the mausoleum with its great bulbous dome to the four minars standing out from its corners, to the mosque and hall on either side, and to the great gateway which is separated from it by a garden crossed by ornamental canals. Other notable buildings of Shah Jahan's reign include the palace (1639–48) and the Jami Masjid (1644–58) in Delhi, the Pearl Mosque (1646–53) and the Royal Palace (1636) in Agra, and the two marble pavilions on an artificial lake at Ajmer. In mosques and monuments the bulbous dome first made its appearance and the elegant chatri received its classic form for the crowning of a minar. The palaces derive their beauty no less from their setting with gardens and water than from their architectural form and decoration. The works of the Moghul emperors were imitated by lesser potentates throughout India.

The British conquest of India introduced European styles, which were adopted for churches, administrative buildings, and town houses in the main centres. Neo-Palladian and GREEK REVIVAL styles were preferred until well into the C19 (Fort St George, Madras; Government House and Town Hall, Calcutta). But one of the most remarkable buildings is in the French C18 style, La Martinière, Lucknow (1795). In the Portuguese city of Goa, Iberian Baroque predominated. The last and largest notable monument of British rule was New Delhi, designed by Sir Edwin LUTYENS and Sir Herbert BAKER in an Imperial Roman style with occasional Moghul flourishes. The most noteworthy buildings erected since India and Pakistan achieved independence have been designed by LE CORBUSIER for Chandigarh.

INGLENOOK. A bench or seat built beside a fireplace, sometimes covered by the CHIMNEY BREAST.

INTARSIA. A form of mosaic made up of different coloured woods, popular in C15–16 Italy especially for the decoration of studies and small rooms in palaces and for the choirs of churches.

INTERCOLUMNIATION. The space between columns measured in diameters. Vitruvius established five main ratios, 1½D. Pycnostyle, 2D. Systyle, 2¼D. Eustyle, 3D. Diastyle, 4D. Araeostyle, of which Eustyle is the commonest.

INTERNATIONAL MODERN. A term coined in America to refer to the new architectural style of the C20, as created before the First World War by such architects as WRIGHT, GARNIER, LOOS, HOFFMANN, GROPIUS, and as accepted, at least in progressive circles, first in Central Europe in the course of the twenties and then in other countries of Europe and America from the late twenties onwards. The style is characterized by asymmetrical composition, unrelievedly cubic general shapes, an absence of mouldings, large windows often in horizontal bands, and a predilection for white rendering.

INTRADOS. The inner curve or underside of an arch; also called a *soffit*. See *figure 4*.

INWOOD, Henry William (1794–1843). The son of an architect (William Inwood, *c.* 1771–1843), with whom he designed his only building of note, St Pancras Church (1819–22), one of the great monuments of the Greek Revival in England. Every detail is faithfully copied from the Erechtheum, Tower of the Winds, Choragic Monument, and other famous Athenian buildings. Sometimes his archaeological material is rather recondite, but he always uses it with sensibility.

IONIC ORDER, *see* ORDER.

IRISH ARCHITECTURE. The most rewarding and original phase is that before the Normans, the phase of monastic communities where coenobites lived in round or square huts, stone-vaulted by pseudo-vaults of horizontally laid stones corbelled forward gradually. There were several oratories in such communities, tapering round towers and the glorious High Crosses. The most famous sites are Skellig Michael, Nendrum, Glendalough, Clonmacnois, and Monasterboyce. The buildings are mostly C10-11.

The Hiberno–Romanesque style has its most dramatic monument in Cormac's Chapel at Cashel (dated 1134); it has a tunnel-vaulted nave and a rib-vaulted chancel. There are plenty of monuments in the Norman style with only minor national characteristics. The Cistercians came in the 1140s, and the east end of Christ Church Cathedral, Dublin, shows their influence. The fully Gothic style in a wholly Early English version appears in the nave of Christ Church (connected with Wells and St David's) and the largely rebuilt St Patrick's Cathedral, also at Dublin. The most conspicuous Irish contribution to Gothic architecture is her friaries, mostly rurally sited; they have the tower between nave and chancel, which is also typical of English friaries.

Medieval architecture lasted into the C17. The English promoted such new towns as Londonderry, with its Gothic cathedral of 1628–33, and such houses as Carrick-on-Suir and Strafford's Jigginstown, both of the 1630s. Gothic gradually gave place to hipped roofs or parapets, and such buildings as Beaulieu and the Kilmainham Hospital of 1679 are entirely English in style. PALLADIANISM also bore an ample harvest in Ireland, the chief architects being Sir Edward Lovett Pearce, Richard Cassels, and Gandon. Examples are Castletown; Parliament House, Dublin, by Pearce; Powerscourt by Cassels; the Customs House and the Four Courts by Gandon; the house of the Provost of Trinity College, Caledon, by Nash; and many others. Ireland is indeed exceedingly rich in Georgian houses, though for lack of a function they are rapidly decreasing. In Dublin very much is still preserved, and the city may well claim to be the finest major Georgian city in the British Isles. If any Victorian buildings are to be singled out, they would again have to be essentially English ones: Cork Cathedral by Burges; Queen's University, Belfast, by Lanyon; and the Trinity College Museum by Deane & Woodward – all Gothic in style.

ISIDORE OF MILETUS assisted ANTHEMIUS OF TRALLES in the building of Haghia Sopia, Constantinople (A.D. 532–7), and was, like him, a geometrician who turned his attention to architecture. He is not to be confused with a younger Isidore, who heightened the dome of Haghia Sophia by 20 ft in 558.

ISLAMIC ARCHITECTURE. The origins are very obscure. The Bedouin Arabs, who were the original followers of Mohammed and responsible for the first Islamic conquests in Syria, Palestine, and Persia, were a nomadic people who lived in tents. In the cities they conquered they began by converting old buildings, and Christian churches became mosques; in Damascus a pagan temple transformed into a Christian church was incorporated in the Great Mosque (706–15). The earliest and one of the most beautiful of Islamic buildings is the Dome of the Rock, Jerusalem, built as a sanctuary (not as a mosque) on a circular plan (685–705, but much altered later, especially in 1561 when the exterior was cased in Persian tiles and the interior lined with marble). The first minarets were converted church towers in Syria, and that built at Kairouan, Tunisia (724–7), is modelled on such a tower. True to their nomadic origins the Umayyad rulers preferred desert residences to town palaces. Several survive as ruins – Qasr al-Hair (728–9); Mshatta near Amman, Jordania; and Qasr at-Tuba in the Wadi Ghadorf near Amman. In plan these groups of buildings were derived from Roman frontier stations. But both religious and secular buildings of the period incorporate elements which were to become distinguishing features of Islamic architecture: the horseshoe arch, tunnel vaults of stone and brick, rich surface decoration in carved stone, mosaic, and painting. During the Umayyad period the mosque took on its permanent architectural form, dictated by liturgical needs – minarets from which the faithful could be called to prayer; a wide courtyard with a central fountain for ablutions, with surrounding colonnades to give protection from the sun; a large praying chamber, marked externally by a dome (as a sign of importance) and internally by the mihrab or niche indicating the direction of Mecca, towards which the faithful must turn in prayer. The last survivor of the Umayyad dynasty became the founder of the Emirates at Cordova in Spain, where the early style of Islamic architecture was brought to perfection in the Great Mosque (786–990).

Under the Abbasids, who supplanted the Umayyads in 750, Persian influence began to dominate the Islamic world. The main achievements in architecture were the foundation of the new capital at Baghdad, built on a circular plan (762–7, now largely destroyed), and, slightly later, the smaller city of Raqqa, Syria, of which little survives except its richly decorated gateways. It was at this period that Islamic architecture began to depart radically from HELLENISTIC and BYZANTINE conventions. An elaborate court etiquette, derived from Persia and contrary to Bedouin ideas of informality, was introduced, and palaces were designed for the new caliphs on more formal and grandiose lines, e.g., the palaces at Ukhaidir and Samarra in Iraq. These large buildings were run up very quickly: stone was abandoned in favour of brick and there was much use of decorative stucco. The main c9 achievements were the Great Mosque of Kairouan, Tunisia (836); the mosque of Bu Fatata, Susa, Tunisia (850–1); the Great Mosque of Samarra, Iraq, with its strange ZIGGURAT-like minaret (c. 850); and the very well preserved mosque of Ibn Tulun, Cairo (876–7). Building materials were usually rough but dressed with intricate geometrical or floral surface decorations in painted stucco, mosaic, glazed tiles, or shallow relief carving. Local traditions influenced the decorative style in various regions (see INDIAN AND PAKISTANI; PERSIAN; TURKISH ARCHITECTURE).

In the original nucleus of the Islamic world the most notable later mosques are those at Tabriz, Persia (1204), Cairo (Mosque of Sultan Barquq, 1384), and Isfahan, Persia (1585). Most of the earlier religious buildings, including the Masjid-el-Aksa and the Dome of the Rock in Jerusalem, were also altered and more richly decorated in these centuries. In southern Spain a local style of great opulence was developed: its principal monuments are the Giralda tower, Seville (1159), and the Alhambra, Granada (1309–54).

ISOMETRIC PROJECTION. A geometrical drawing to show a building in three dimensions. The plan is set up with lines at an equal angle (usually 30°) to the horizontal, while verticals remain vertical and to scale. It gives a more realistic effect than an AXONOMETRIC PROJECTION, but diagonals and curves are distorted. See figure 54.

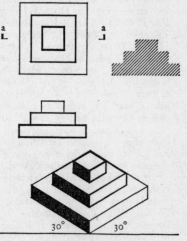

Fig. 54. Isometric projection
Plan; Section aa; Elevation

ITALIAN ARCHITECTURE. Early Christian churches in Italy are mostly of the basilican type: nave and aisles separated by columns carrying arches or straight entablatures, and an apse, sometimes flanked by two subsidiary chambers. Transepts are rare (St Peter's, S. Maria Maggiore, S. Paolo fuori le Mura), as are centrally planned buildings (S. Costanza, S. Stefano), which are usually found only as baptisteries (S. Giovanni in Laterano). The plans of these, with or without aisles, come straight from Imperial Roman architecture. On the other hand, major vaulting with tunnel or groin vaults, which the architects of Imperial Rome had handled with such supreme mastery, was given up entirely, probably for religious reasons of humility. Chancels preceding the apse are a Romanesque, not an Early Christian feature.

On the whole the Italian Romanesque is less enterprising than that of the north. Plans without transepts, i.e., with apses following nave and aisles immediately or with transepts not projecting externally, remain the rule. The architecture is divided into various regions. The most progressive are the north, close in architectural style to Germany, and in decoration and sculpture to Provence (Modena, begun 1099; S. Michele Pavia, Parma, after 1117; S. Ambrogio, Milan) and the south (S. Nicola, Bari, 1089 etc.; Trani, 1098 etc.). The north has heavy rib vaults which some scholars consider the earliest of the Middle Ages. In Sicily interesting mixtures with Norman and Saracen elements occur (Palermo, S. Giovanni degli Eremiti, Palace Chapel, Martorana, all of c. 1130–40; cathedrals of Cefalù, begun 1132, and Monreale, begun c. 1175). The French motif of the ambulatory with radiating chapels is rare (Aversa), but the south-west French and Early Byzantine motif of domed naves occurs (Molfetta, 1162 etc.). S. Marco in Venice begun 1063 stands outside the Italian regional traditions and belongs to Byzantine rather than Italian architecture. Tus-

cany developed a style already heralding the Quattrocento (S. Miniato, SS. Apostoli, Baptistery, all in Florence), though the largest Tuscan Romanesque church, Pisa Cathedral (1063 etc.) does not belong to this proto-Renaissance. However, the Leaning Tower with its tiers of outer arched galleries is Late Romanesque (1174 etc.), and so are such ornate façades as those of S. Michele and the cathedral of Lucca.

Italy took up the Gothic style slowly and with many reservations. The principal agents were the Cistercians (Fossanova, consecrated 1208; Casamari, consecrated 1217; S. Galgano, begun 1227), the court of the Emperor Frederick II, and the orders of friars. Frederick II's castles (Syracuse, Catania) of c. 1240 were square with round corner towers on Ancient Roman or perhaps current French suggestion (Dourdan). An exception is the most splendid of them, Castel del Monte, which is octagonal. Here, in the most unexpected way, Ancient Roman and current Burgundian-Gothic motifs meet. The most classical building of that moment in Italy was the Porta Capuana of about 1235. The earliest friars' church, St Francis at Assisi (begun 1228), is, oddly enough, patterned on the west French Early Gothic of Angers Cathedral: S. Francesco at Bologna (1236 etc.) followed, and this has an ambulatory. S. Andrea at Vercelli (1219 etc.), which is not a friars' church, reflects Laon Cathedral, but the spatial feeling is rather Romanesque than Gothic. The most interesting Italian church of the C13 is Siena Cathedral (c. 1230–60, radically altered 1369 etc.), with its hexagonal dome and its truly Italian Gothic façade by Giovanni PISANO (1284 etc.). The façade of Orvieto Cathedral follows that of Siena (c. 1310).

When the Gothic style had settled down in Italy, it soon transformed itself into something Italian – wider open, more static spaces, stress on horizontals, even round arches (S. Maria Novella, 1278 etc.; S. Croce, c. 1295 etc.; cathedral, 1296 etc.; Loggia dei Lanzi, 1376 – all in Florence). Only Milan in the north created in its cathedral an internal space and flamboyant external details of a kind not wholly alien to France or Germany (1386 etc.). S. Petronio at Bologna, emulating Milan in size, was started in 1390 to a plan and elevation mid-way between Milan and the Italian character. North Italy, and especially Venice, went on with flamboyant, purely Gothic detail, after Tuscany had embarked on the Renaissance (Porta della Carta, 1439 etc.; Ca' d'Oro, 1421 onwards, both in Venice). The climax of Venetian Gothic architecture is without question the Doge's Palace (1309 etc. and continued to the same design, 1423 etc.). Altogether secular buildings, and especially Town Halls, play an important part in Italian Gothic developments. The town-hall type with open ground floor and the main room above was international and common already in Romanesque times (Broletto, Como, 1216). The finest Gothic examples are Piacenza (1280 etc.) and Perugia (1283 etc.). More palace-like and with high slender towers are Siena (1288 etc.) and Florence (Palazzo Vecchio, 1298 etc.).

The Renaissance style was created by BRUNELLESCHI in Florence about 1420. Its earliest development is Tuscan, and it took a generation to establish it in Rome (Palazzo Venezia, c. 1470) and the north. ALBERTI, who was more in sympathy with ancient Roman architecture than most others, was instrumental in doing this. On the whole the Renaissance of the C15 (Quattrocento) prefers arcades of slender columns carrying arches, i.e., rather delicate members, and a graceful lively decoration. Examples of the former are Brunelleschi's earliest façade, that of the Foundling Hospital (1419 etc.) and such palace court-yards as that of MICHELOZZO's Palazzo Medici (1444 etc.) or the Ducal Palace at Urbino (1460s), which also has some of the most exquisite Quattrocento decoration. Palace façades, especially in Tuscany, are still forbidding, in direct continuation of the Trecento. Heavy rustication was favoured (Palazzo Medici, Palazzo Strozzi), though Alberti in his Palazzo Rucellai (1446 etc.) used a more elegant articulation by tiers of pilasters, and this was taken up by the Cancelleria in Rome (c. 1485 etc.). Church plans are usually longitudinal: Brunelleschi's with nave and aisles and slim arcades formed on Tuscan Romanesque patterns; Alberti's S. Andrea at Mantua aisleless, but with side-chapels, a system with a great future. But both Brunelleschi and Alberti and others as well (Giuliano da SANGALLO) favoured central plans and developed them in a variety of ways (Brunelleschi, S. Maria degli Angeli, 1434 etc.; Alberti, S. Sebastiano, Mantua, 1460 etc.; Sangallo, S. Maria delle Carceri, Prato, 1485 etc.).

Central Italians (MICHELOZZO, FILARETE) had introduced the Renaissance to Milan in the 1450s, and at the same time it appeared in Venice (Arsenal portal, 1457). In contrast to Central Italy, however, the north of Italy went in for extremely busy decoration of façades as well as interiors (Verona and Brescia Town Halls, Certosa of Pavia, Como Cathedral, 1470s to 1490s and after 1500). These façades had considerable influence on the Early Renaissance in transalpine countries. Even BRAMANTE, in his early years in Milan, used this rich and playful decoration, though at S. Maria presso S. Satiro it is rather Alberti (in Mantua) who inspired him. Bramante lived in Milan in the same years as LEONARDO DA VINCI, but it is impossible to say what their relationship was. Leonardo sketched architectural ideas, but did not build. Nearly all his church plans are of central types, and he reached unprecedented complexities. Bramante clearly was attracted by the same problem, even if none of the central churches of Lombardy can with certainty be ascribed to him (Lodi, Crema).

With Bramante's move from Milan to Rome in 1499 the High Renaissance was established, with more substantial and also more Roman forms and characters (St Peter's, Belvedere Court Vatican, Palazzo Caprini). RAPHAEL (Villa Madama), PERUZZI (Villa Farnesina), and GIULIO ROMANO were Bramante's successors, but the latter two soon turned away from his style to Mannerism. The solecisms of Giulio's Palazzo del Tè (1525 etc.) and his own house (1544), both at Mantua, are both eloquent and painful. At the same time MICHELANGELO designed in the Mannerist way (Medici Chapel and Laurentian Library, 1520s; exterior of St Peter's, 1546 etc.; and Porta Pia, 1561). Mannerism produced exquisite works (Farnese Palace, Caprarola, by VIGNOLA, 1547 etc.; Villa di Papa Giulio by Vignola, 1550 etc., Casino of Pius IV by LIGORIO, 1560, both Rome; Uffizi, Florence, by VASARI, 1550 etc.) as well as perverse ones (Casa Zuccari, Rome, 1590), but it never ruled unchallenged. In the north of Italy the Renaissance spirit was alive throughout the C16, as is demonstrated by buildings such as SANSOVINO's Library of S. Marco (1532 etc.) and Palazzo Corner (1532 etc.), SANMICHELE's palaces and city gates of Verona (1520s to 1550s), and PALLADIO's palaces inside and villas outside Vicenza. Though in the work of Palladio, especially his churches in Venice, Mannerist traits are easily discovered, most of his secular work must be classed as Renaissance. The problem of Vignola in Rome is similar, but whereas Palladio, where he is not Mannerist, belongs to the past, Vignola, where he is not Mannerist, points forward to the Baroque.

There can be no doubt that Vignola's Gesù (begun 1568) established a canon of church plan and elevation for the Baroque: chapels instead of aisles, transepts and a dome (S. Andrea della Valle, S. Carlo al Corso, etc.) The completion of St Peter's by MADERNA was also longitudinal. But the most interesting Baroque churches are those on central or elongated central plans. Vignola had used the oval as early as 1573, but it became a standard element only in the C17, varied inexhaustibly, especially by the greatest Roman Baroque architects BERNINI and BORROMINI. Bernini uses the oval longitudinally at S. Andrea al Quirinale, and RAINALDI uses a grouping of elements which gives the impression of a transverse oval at S. Agnese. The façade of this church, with its two towers and its concave centre, is by Borromini, whose façade of S. Carlino is even more complex in its use of concave and convex parts. There the interior carries the interaction of curves to the highest point it achieved in Rome, but the acme of spatial complications was reached by GUARINI at Turin. Bernini's work at St Peter's was concerned with decoration on the grandest scale (baldacchino, Cathedra Petri) and with the forecourt in front of Maderna's façade. The elliptical colonnades and their splaying-out connexion with the façade are both aesthetically and from the planning point of view equally satisfying.

In the field of major urban planning Rome had already taken the lead in the late C16, when the long streets radiating from the Piazza del Popolo had been laid out. In secular architecture Rome contributes less, though the open façade of the Palazzo Barberini and the giant pilasters of Bernini's Palazzo Odescalchi had much influence. For Baroque palaces

Genoa is the most interesting city.

As early as about 1700 Italy began to tone down the Baroque (FONTANA, then JUVARRA in Turin: Superga, 1717 etc.; Palazzo Madama, 1718 etc.) and in the Veneto a Palladian revival took place (Scalfarotti's S. Simeone, Venice, 1718 etc.; Preti's Villa Pisani, Strà, 1735 etc.).

The C19 has no really recognizable face in Italy. The C20 style started with SANT' ELIA's dreams of skyscrapers, but the new international style did not make itself felt until the early 1930s. Today Italian architecture is characterized by much talent but a lack of unified direction. The most important contribution is that of NERVI to the structural and aesthetic problems of wide spans.

IXNARD, Michel d' (1726–95), a French early neo-classical architect, worked mainly in the Rhineland. Born at Nîmes and trained in Paris, he became architect to the Elector of Trier. His main work is the very large, severe, and rather heavy abbey church of St Blasien in the Black Forest (1764–84), with a Doric exterior and solemn Corinthian rotunda.

J

JACOBSEN, Arne (b. 1902), whose style is the most refined and meticulous INTERNATIONAL MODERN, was initially influenced by ASPLUND's Stockholm Exhibition of 1930 and appeared as an International Modern architect with work of 1931, at a time when Copenhagen was reaching the climax of a classicism as refined and meticulous in its own way as Jacobsen's architecture was to be. He built chiefly private houses and housing until shortly before the Second World War, when he was also commissioned for work on a larger scale. The Town Hall of Aarhns (with Erik Møller, 1938–42) has a concrete skeleton tower. Søllerud, an outer suburb of Copenhagen, got a town hall by Jacobsen in 1939–42. The Munkegård School at Gentofte, another outer suburb of Copenhagen, is characterized by the many small play-yards between classrooms (1952–6). The Town Hall of Rødovre, yet another outer suburb of Copenhagen, is Jacobsen's most exquisite recent public building (1955–6), entirely unmannered, without any cliché or gimmick, nothing really but the formal apparatus of the International thirties, yet handled with an unparalleled precision and elegance. The same is true of his cylinder-boring factory at Aalborg (1957) and the S.A.S. Hotel at Copenhagen (1960; a tower block on a podium of the Lever House type, see SKIDMORE, OWINGS & MERRILL). Recently St Catherine's College at Oxford has been completed to Jacobsen's designs. During the fifties he also designed some fine and original furniture and cutlery.

JAMB. The straight side of an archway, doorway, or window; the part of the jamb which lies between the glass or door and the outer wall-surface is called a *reveal*.

JAMES, John (c. 1672–1746), built St George, Hanover Square, London (1712–25), with its hexastyle portico of free-standing giant columns and pediment. This idea was quickly taken up by HAWKSMOOR (St George, Bloomsbury) and GIBBS (St Martin-in-the-Fields). Wricklemarsh, Blackheath (1721), was his masterpiece, but it was demolished, like nearly all his work.

JAPANESE ARCHITECTURE. The earliest buildings are religious and date from after the introduction of Buddhism from China c. A.D. 550. As in China the usual building material was wood and the main structural element the column. The principle of the truss was never exploited, and thus the width of buildings was controlled by the lengths of timber available. Walls were merely protective screens, sometimes of material as flimsy as paper or cardboard. Although dependent on China for many seminal ideas, the Japanese produced a truly distinctive architectural style, more delicate in decoration if less monumental in scale. They also paid greater attention to the relation of buildings to landscape, not merely by designing exquisite artfully naturalistic gardens but also by taking advantage of sloping hillside sites for picturesque stairways linking one temple building to another (e.g., the Kurodanji Temple, Kyoto).

Among the earliest surviving buildings of importance are those of the Buddhist monastery, the Horyuji (C7, but much altered), comprising a Buddha hall and pagoda with cloister-like enclosure, library, and C10 lecture hall. The pillared hall is the prototype

Japanese temple. The pagoda is of five storeys, square in plan, with boldly projecting roofs above each floor, and crowned with a tall finial of metal rings and bells supported on a great central post about 100 ft high. Pagodas of this design remained popular throughout the centuries and a number of notable examples have survived. Temples maintained the general lines of the Horyuji, but with infinite variations in size and layout. Later periods showed a tendency to greater elaboration and sometimes to heaviness (e.g., Hokaiji Amidado, late C11). The Shinto shrines, some of which were rebuilt every few years, are much simpler than the Buddhist temples, and the oldest have thatched roofs of most elegant shape. Though they may be of little interest architecturally, their large and elaborately carved gateways are most impressive and some perpetuate the pre-Buddhist, indigenous Japanese style.

Houses are generally of simple design and of one storey. They are built on a rectangular plan rigidly controlled by a scale of proportion of which the basic unit is a mat measuring 6 ft × 3 ft. They are so designed that interior walls, usually of paper, may be moved to increase the size of rooms. Tea-houses, where the tea-drinking ceremony is performed, are like miniature private houses, set in beautifully planned gardens. Proportion, simplicity, and the eloquent use of natural materials are here all-important. The palace of the emperor at Kyoto consists of a group of pavilions distinguished from private houses only by larger and more elaborate roofs (like those of temples) and a different scale of proportions based on the imperial floor mat, which measured 7 ft × 3 ft 6 in.

One of the finest buildings is the C11 Byodo-in or 'Phoenix Hall' at Uji near Kyoto, originally erected as a villa beside a lotus lake but later transformed into a temple. This reflects influences from China of the Sung period, when elegance and grace were the artistic touchstone. As in all Japanese art, Chinese influences are often very strong, and Japan has preserved much of Chinese styles which have been destroyed on the mainland. Although most houses and temples are single-storey buildings, multi-storey houses are far less uncommon than in China: the soaring castle at Himeji (late C16) is of several storeys and possibly owes something to Western influence. Palaces and houses are generally distinguished less for their architecture than for their decorative fixtures – gilt metalwork applied to gable boards, brass caps affixed to the ends of projecting timbers, lacquer panels and wall paintings indoors – all wrought with exquisite artistry.

The westernization of Japan in the late C19 had a depressing influence on native architecture. But since the Second World War Japan has produced the most imaginative school of non-European architects, notably Junzo Sakakura, Kunio Maekawa, and Kenzo TANGE. They all go in for extremely massive concrete and bold heavily fanciful forms.

JAPELLI, Giuseppe (1783–1852), a leading Italian romantic architect and landscape gardener, was a true eclectic of a type rare in Italy, able to work happily in a wide range of styles. Beginning at the Café Pedrocchi, Padua (1816), in a very elegant version of neo-classicism, he then turned to a severe manner derived from the astylar backs of Palladian villas – e.g., Villa Vigodarzere, Saonara (1817) – then to a bold Grecian style for the Doric slaughterhouse in Padua (1821, now the Istituto d'Arte). After a visit to France and England he added a neo-Gothic wing to Café Pedrocchi (1837), and finally built the neo-Rococo Teatro Verdi, Padua (1847). His landscape parks are consistently in the English manner; most of them are in the Veneto (e.g., Saonara, Ca' Minotto, Rosà), but one of the finest was at Villa Torlonia, Rome (1840).

JEAN DE CHELLES. Architect of the south transept of Notre Dame in Paris (begun 1258). He died soon after. His successor and perhaps son, Pierre de Chelles, was still active in 1316, when he was called to Chartres Cathedral as a consultant.

JEAN D'ORBAIS. Probably the designer and first master mason of Reims Cathedral (begun c. 1211).

JEFFERSON, Thomas (1743–1826), legislator, economist, educationalist, and third President of the United States of America (1801–9), was also an able and immensely influential architect. The son of a surveyor, he inherited a considerable estate in Albermarle County, where in 1769 he chose a high romantic site for his own house, Monticello. He derived the plan from Robert Morris's *Select Architecture*, but modified it with reference to GIBBS and Leoni's edition of PALLADIO. It had porticos front and back and a great forecourt with octagon pavilions at the corners and square pavilions terminating the wings. It is very carefully thought out, both in its planning, on which he had strong personal views, and in its adaptation of Palladian elements. He was interested in Palladio mainly as the interpreter of Roman villa architecture, and looked back to Antiquity for the 'natural' principles of his architectural theory. In 1785, while he was in Europe, he was asked to design the Virginia State Capitol for Richmond. With the help of CLÉRISSEAU, he produced a temple design based on the Maison Carrée (16 B.C.) at Nîmes, but Ionic instead of Corinthian and with pilasters in place of half-columns on the flanks and rear. The Capitol (completed 1796) set a pattern for official architecture in the U.S.A. As Secretary of State to George Washington he played a leading part in planning the new federal capital in Washington from 1790 onwards. After he became President he entrusted LATROBE with the task of completing the new Capitol (1803, burnt 1814). Latrobe also assisted him with the University of Virginia, Charlottesville – a group of porticoed houses (each containing a professor's lodging and a classroom) linked by colonnades in a formal plan, with a great Pantheon at one end of the oblong composition (1817–26).

JENNEY, William Le Baron (1832–1907), was born in Massachusetts, studied at the École Centrale des Arts et Manufactures in Paris, was an engineer in the Civil War, and opened a practice in architecture and engineering in Chicago in 1868. In 1869 he published a book called *Principles and Practices of Architecture*. By far his most important building was the Home Insurance Building (1883–5), because its iron columns, iron lintels and girders, and indeed steel beams, prepared the way for the skeleton construction of the Chicago School (*see* HOLABIRD & ROCHE). Stylistically his work is of no value.

JIB DOOR. A concealed door flush with the wall-surface, painted or papered to correspond with the walls. The DADO and other mouldings are similarly carried across the door.

JOGGLE, JOGGLING. Masons' terms for a particular way of fitting stones together. *See figure 55.*

Fig. 55. Joggled joint

JOHNSON, Philip (b. 1906), lives in Connecticut. He became an architect only in middle age. His fame was first spread by the house he built for himself at New Canaan (1949) – very much in the style of MIES VAN DER ROHE – a cube with completely glazed walls all round. The siting is romantic, and perhaps in the years about 1950 one should already have been able to guess that Johnson would not remain faithful to Mies's principles. In the guest-house (1952) close to his own house vaults began to appear, inspired by SOANE, and the synagogue at Port Chester, New York (1956), made it clear that he would prefer variety, the unexpected effect, and elegance to the single-mindedness of Mies. Buildings of more recent years are the Museum at Fort Worth, Texas (1961), the Art Gallery for the University of Nebraska at Lincoln (1962), the New York State Theatre for the Lincoln Centre in New York (1962–4), and the indianizing shrine at New Harmony, Indiana (1960).

JOISTS. Horizontal timbers in a building, laid parallel to each other with their upper edges REBATED to receive the boards of a floor. The underside either forms the ceiling of the room below or has ceiling lathe nailed to it. In a large floor the main or *binding* joists are often crossed by smaller *bridging* joists which bear the floorboards. For a span exceeding about 15 ft, it was usual to insert one or more SLEEPERS to carry the joists, which would then run longitudinally.

JONES, Inigo (1573–1652), a genius far in advance of his time in England, imported the classical style from Italy to a still half-Gothic north and brought English Renaissance architecture to sudden maturity. He was the same age as Donne and Ben Jonson, and only nine years younger than Shakespeare. Born in London, the son of a Smithfield clothworker, he appears to have visited Italy before 1603, being then a 'picture-maker'. Not until 1608 is he heard of as an architect (design for the New Exchange in London), and his earliest known buildings date from later still. Meantime he had become a prominent figure at Court as a stage-designer for masques in the most lavish and up-to-date Italian manner. Many of his designs survive, of fantastic Baroque costumes and hardly less fantastic architectural sets, executed in a free, spontaneous style of draughtsmanship he had presumably picked up in Italy. In 1613 he went to Italy again, this time for a year and seven months, with the great collector Lord Arundel. He returned with an unbounded admiration for PALLADIO and a first-hand knowledge of Roman monuments unique in England at that date. (He met SCAMOZZI in Venice.)

From 1615, when he became Surveyor of the King's Works, until the Civil War in 1642 he was continuously employed at the various royal palaces. Immediately he built three startlingly novel buildings which broke uncompromisingly with the Jacobean past: the Queen's House, Greenwich (1616–18 and 1629–35); the Prince's Lodging, Newmarket (1619–22, now destroyed); and the Banqueting House, Whitehall, London (1619–22). The Queen's House is the first strictly classical building in England, though there was a long break in its construction (the foundations were laid in 1616, but the elevations and interior date from 1632–5). The Prince's Lodging, modest in size, set the pattern for the red-brick, stone-quoined, hipped-roof house with dormers, so popular later in the century. The Banqueting House is Jones's masterpiece; it perfectly expresses his conception of architecture – 'sollid, proporsionable according to the rulles, masculine and unaffected' – as well as his adoration of Palladio. But though every detail is Palladian it is not a mere imitation. Everything has been subtly transmuted and the result is unmistakably English: solid, sturdy, and rather phlegmatic. The Queen's Chapel, St James's Palace, London (1623–7), was also something new for England – a classical church, consisting of an aisleless parallelogram with a coffered segmental vault, a pedimented front, and a large Venetian window. Equally striking but more elaborate was the Bramantesque temple design he used for King James's hearse in 1625.

His principal buildings for Charles I have been destroyed, except for the Queen's House, Greenwich. This is an Italian villa sympathetically reinterpreted, whose chastity and bareness must have seemed daringly original. The upper-floor loggia is very Palladian, as is also the two-armed, curved open staircase to the terrace; but, as always with Jones, nothing is a direct copy. The proportions have been slightly altered and the general effect is long and low and very un-Italian. Inside, the hall is a perfect cube and symmetry prevails throughout. Also to the 1630s belong his great Corinthian portico at Old St Paul's, transforming the medieval cathedral into the most Roman structure in the country, and Covent Garden, the first London square, of which the church and a fragment of the square survive, the latter rebuilt. The square was conceived as one composition, the houses having uniform façades with arcaded ground floors and giant pilasters above (perhaps influenced by the Place des Vosges, Paris). In about 1638 he also produced elaborate designs for an enormous Royal Palace in Whitehall. These reveal his limitations and it is perhaps fortunate for his reputation that they were never executed.

1642 brought his brilliant career at Court to an end. He was with the king at Beverley, but nothing more is heard of him until 1645. Although his property was sequestrated he was pardoned in 1646 and his estate restored. From then onwards he seems to have swum quite happily with the political tide, working for the Parliamentarian Lord Pembroke. The great garden front at Wilton House was for long thought to have been built by him at about this date, but is now known to have been designed by his assistant Isaac de Caus (c. 1632). It was badly damaged by fire c. 1647 and the famous state rooms therefore date from about 1649, by which time Jones was too old to give much personal attention; he put it in the hands of his pupil and nephew by marriage, John WEBB. Nevertheless, the celebrated double-cube room, perhaps the most beautiful single room in England, epitomizes his style of interior decoration – gravity and repose combined with great opulence of heavy and rather French classical detail. Innumerable buildings have been attributed to Jones, of which a few may have had some connexion with him, notably the pavilions at Stoke Bruerne Park (1629–35). Though profound, his immediate influence was confined to Court circles. In the early C18 he largely inspired the Palladian revival of BURLINGTON and KENT.

JUAN DE ÁLAVA (d. 1537), a Spanish master mason on the verge of Late Gothic and Early Renaissance, appears first as consultant at Salamanca Cathedral in 1512 (with eight others) and Seville Cathedral in 1513 (with three others), in the latter year as master to the newly restarted work at Plasencia Cathedral (first with Francisco de Colonia, see SIMÓN DE COLONIA, who soon quarrelled with him). Then we come across him as the designer of the cloister of Santiago Cathedral (1521 onwards) and finally as master mason to Salamanca Cathedral after the death of Juan GIL DE HONTAÑÓN in 1526. S. Esteban at Salamanca (1524 onwards) is also by him; this and the work at Plasencia round the crossing are perhaps his finest.

JUBÉ. The French name for ROOD SCREEN.

JULIANUS ARGENTARIUS was probably the architect of S. Vitale, Ravenna (completed A.D. 547), built on a remarkably complex octagonal plan; as at Haghia Sophia in Constantinople, an effect of mystery is obtained by screening off aisles and galleries to produce a strong contrast in light and semi-darkness between the central area and the ambulatory. He may also have designed the similar church of SS. Sergius and Bacchus, Constantinople.

JUTTING, *see* OVERHANG.

JUVARRA, Filippo (1678–1736), born in Messina of a family of silversmiths, is the greatest Italian C18 architect and a brilliant draughtsman. His elegant and sophisticated Late Baroque buildings are as typical of their period as Tiepolo's paintings and equally accomplished; they have a Mozartian gaiety and fecundity of decorative invention. Trained in Rome under FONTANA (1703/4–14), he first won fame as a stage-designer, and this theatrical experience was to leave a mark on nearly all his subsequent work.

In 1714 he was invited to Turin by Victor Amadeus II of Savoy, who appointed him 'First Architect to the King'. Apart from a trip to Portugal, London, and Paris in 1719–20, he remained in Turin for the next twenty years. His output was enormous, ranging from churches, palaces, country villas, and hunting-lodges to the layout of entire new city quarters in Turin – not to mention work as an interior decorator and designer of furniture and the applied arts. Of his churches the Superga (1715–27) and the chapel of the Veneria Reale (1716–21), both near Turin, are spectacular,

the former being by far the grandest of all Italian Baroque sanctuaries, comparable with Melk in Austria and Einsiedeln in Switzerland. S. Filippo Neri (1715), S. Croce (1718 etc.), and the Carmine (1732–5, gutted during the war) in Turin are all very fine. His city palaces in Turin include Palazzo Birago della Valle (1716), Palazzo Richa di Covasolo (1730), and Palazzo d'Ormea (1730), while his work for the king is remarkable for the four great palaces and villas in or near Turin – Veneria Reale (1714–26), Palazzo Madama (1718–21), Castello di Rivoli (1718–21, but only partly executed), and his masterpiece Stupinigi (1719 etc.). In all these works he had the assistance of numerous highly skilled painters, sculptors, and craftsmen, who were summoned from all parts of Italy to execute his designs.

Though little development is discernible in his style, which is a brilliant epitome of current ideas rather than an original invention, it reached its fine flower in Stupinigi, especially in the great central hall whose scenic quality and skeletal structure suggest an influence from north of the Alps. In 1735 Juvarra was summoned to Spain by Philip V, for whom he designed the garden façade of S. Ildefonso near Segovia and the new Royal Palace in Madrid, executed with alterations after his death by G. B. SACCHETTI. He died suddenly in Madrid in January 1736.

K

KAHN, Louis, was born in 1901 on the Island of Ösel. He studied and lives at Philadelphia, and was internationally noticed only fairly recently, first with the Yale University Art Gallery (with D. Orr, 1951–3), then with the Richards Medical Research Building of the University of Pennsylvania (1957–60). The Art Gallery has for its main exhibition space a space-frame ceiling. The Medical Research Building has all ducts gathered in a number of sheer square towers projecting from and rising above the outer walls: the reason is said to be functional, but the effect is curiously dramatic and indeed aggressive – an original version of the so-called BRUTALISM which has come to the fore in the last ten years.

KAZAKOV, Matvey Feodorovich (1733–1812), the leading neo-classical architect in Moscow, began in the Baroque tradition but soon adopted an Imperial Roman style. He probably designed the rich Pashkov Palace, Moscow (1785–6). His main building is the Church of Ascension on the Razumovski estate (1790–3). He also built the Petrovski Palace near Moscow (1775–82), a curious Gothic or rather Russian medieval revival fantasy.

KEEL MOULDING. A moulding whose outline is like the keel of a ship – a pointed arch in section. *See figure 56.*

Fig. 56. Keel moulding

KEEP. The principal tower of a castle, containing sufficient accommodation to serve as the chief living-quarters permanently or in times of siege; also called a *donjon.*

KENT, William (1684–1748), painter, furniture designer, and landscape gardener as well as architect, was born in Bridlington of humble parents. He contrived to study painting in Rome for ten years and was brought back to London in 1719 by Lord BURLINGTON, whose friend and protégé he remained for the rest of his life. Whimsical, impulsive, unintellectual, in fact almost illiterate, he was the opposite of his patron – and as happy designing a Gothic as a classical building. Nevertheless, he allowed Burlington to guide his hand along the correct PALLADIAN lines in all his major commissions. His interior decoration is more personal, being, like his furniture, richly carved and gilt in a sumptuous manner deriving partly from Italian Baroque furniture and partly from Inigo JONES, whose Designs he edited and published in 1727.

He did not turn architect until after 1730, by which time he was well into his forties. His masterpiece Holkham Hall (1734 onwards, executed by BRETTINGHAM) was almost certainly designed largely by Burlington, whose hand is evident in the 'staccato' quality of the exterior and in the use of such typical and self-isolating features as the Venetian window within a relieving arch. The marble apsidal entrance hall, based on a combination of a Roman basilica and the Egyptian Hall of Vitruvius, with its columns, coffered ceiling, and imposing staircase leading up to the *piano nobile*, is one of the most impressive rooms in England. His lavishly gilt and damask-hung state apartments, elaborately carved and pedimented door-frames, heavy cornices and niches for antique marbles epitomize the English admiration for Roman magnificence. The Treasury (1734), 17 Arlington Street (1741), and 44 Berkeley Square (1742–4), all in London, are notable mainly for their interior decoration, especially the latter, which contains the most ingenious and spatially exciting staircase in London. His last building, the Horse Guards, London (1750–8) is a repetition of Holkham, with the unfortunate addition of a clock-tower over the centre: it was executed after his death by John VARDY. Through Burlington's influence Kent was appointed Master Carpenter to the Board of Works in 1726, and Master Mason and Deputy Surveyor in 1735. He is perhaps more important historically as a designer of gardens than as an architect. He created the English landscape garden, being the first to have 'leap'd the fence and seen that all nature is a garden'. This revolutionized the relation of house to landscape and led to less dramatic and forceful façades. From his time onwards the country house was designed to harmonize with the landscape, rather than to dominate and control it.

KENTISH RAG. Hard unstratified limestone found in Kent and much used as an external building stone on account of its weather-resisting properties.

KEY, Lieven de (c. 1560–1627), the first Dutch architect of note to work in the so-called 'Dutch Renaissance' style (similar to English Jacobean), was appointed city mason at Haarlem (1593), where he introduced the characteristic colourful use of brick with stone dressings (horizontal bands of stone, stone voussoirs set singly in brick above windows, etc.). His masterpieces are Leiden Town Hall (1595), the Weigh House, Haarlem (1597–8), and the Meat Market, Haarlem (1602–3).

KEY PATTERN, see FRET.

KEYSER, Hendrick de (1565–1621), the leading architect of his day in Amsterdam, where he was appointed city mason and sculptor in 1595, worked in a style somewhat similar to English Jacobean. His plain utilitarian churches had great influence on Protestant church design in the Netherlands and Germany, especially his last, the Noorderkerk in Amsterdam, built on a Greek cross plan (1620). His most important secular buildings are the Amsterdam Exchange (1608) and Delft Town Hall (1618). In domestic architecture he simplified and classicized the traditional tall, gable-fronted Amsterdam house, introducing the orders and reducing the number of steps in the gables.

KEYSTONE. The central stone of an arch or a rib vault; sometimes carved. See figure 4.

KHMER ARCHITECTURE. Under strong Indian influence an architectural style known as Khmer was developed in Cambodia between C7 and C13. The main site is Angkor, a vast deserted city from which all structures built in perishable materials have disappeared, leaving only a widely distributed complex of about 400 stone-built and brick-built temples, tombs, walls, bridges, and embankments among a series of artificial lakes. These buildings are almost oppressively rich in figurative sculpture, with long galleries containing well-preserved low reliefs. The most important, Angkor Wat (early C12), perhaps the largest temple in the world (208 ft high and covering 20,000 sq. ft), typifies the Khmer style: enclosed within a vast galleried wall on a square plan, with towers at the corners, it rises up like a fantastic mountain (a symbolic representation of Mount Meru upon which the world rests), with a group of five gigantic towers all of a bulging Hindu profile.

KING-POST, see ROOF.

KIOSK. A light open pavilion or summerhouse, usually supported by pillars and common in Turkey and Persia. European adaptations are used mainly in gardens, as band-stands, for example, or for small shops selling newspapers.

KLENZE, Leo von (1784–1864), a North German, was a pupil of GILLY in Berlin, and then of Durand and PERCIER and FONTAINE in Paris. He was architect to King Jérome at Cassel in 1808–13, and to King Ludwig I in Munich from 1816. Klenze was at heart a Grecian, but he was called upon to work in other styles as well, and did so resourcefully. His chief Grecian buildings are the Glyptothek, or Sculpture Gallery (1816–34) – the earliest of all special public museum buildings – and the Propylaea, both in Munich. The Propylaea was begun in 1846, a late date for so purely Grecian a design. Grecian also, strangely enough, is that commemorative temple of German worthies, the Walhalla near Regensburg (1830–42), which is in fact a Doric peripteral temple. But as early as 1816 (Palais Leuchtenberg) Klenze did a neo-Renaissance palace, the earliest in Germany, even if anticipated in France. This was followed by the Königsbau of the Royal Palace (1826) – which has affinities with Palazzo Pitti – and the freer, more dramatic Festsaalbau of the same palace (1833). In addition, Klenze's Allerheiligen Church, again belonging to the palace (1827), is – at the king's request – neo-Byzantine. *See also* GÄRTNER.

KLINT, P. V. Jensen (1853–1930), is famous chiefly for his Grundtvig Church at Copenhagen, won in competition in 1913 but, after further development of the design, begun only in 1921. With its steeply gabled brick façade, all of a stepped organpipe design, and with its interior, Gothic in feeling, it stands mid-way between the historicism of the C19 and the Expressionism of 1920, a parallel in certain ways to BERLAGE's earlier Exchange. The surrounding buildings, forming one composition with the church, are of 1924–6. Klint's son Kaare (b. 1888) is one of the most distinguished of the brilliant Danish furniture designers.

KNAPPED FLINT. Flints split in two and laid so that the smooth black surfaces of the split sides form the facing of a wall.

KNIGHT, Richard Payne (1750–1824), country gentleman and landscape-gardening theorist, began in 1774 to build Downton Castle for himself: rough, irregular (the plan is anti-symmetrical rather than asymmetrical), and boldly medieval outside, smooth, elegant, and distinctly neo-classical within, it is the prototype of the picturesque country house 'castle' which was to remain popular for half a century. In 1794 he published *The Landscape – a Didactic Poem* attacking 'Capability' BROWN's smooth and artificial style of landscape gardening. It was dedicated to Uvedale PRICE, who published a lengthy reply differing on points of detail. Knight's much longer *Analytical Enquiry into the Principles of Taste* (1805) examines the PICTURESQUE philosophically.

KNOBELSDORFF, Georg Wenceslaus von (1699–1753), was Court architect to Frederick the Great, whose eclectic tastes he faithfully mirrored. His public buildings were sternly Palladian, e.g., Opera House, Berlin (1741–3). At Schloss Sanssouci (1745–53) he adopted an elegant, predominantly French, Rococo manner; but here the guiding hand was that of Frederick himself, who should be regarded as its designer.

KREMLIN. A citadel or fortified enclosure within a Russian town, notably that in Moscow.

L

LA VALLÉE, Simon (d. 1642), son of an architect, settled in Sweden in 1637, becoming royal architect in 1639. He designed the Riddarhus in Stockholm (1641/2) derived from de BROSSE's Palais Luxembourg in Paris. He was succeeded as royal architect by his son Jean (1620–96), who travelled and studied in France, Italy, and Holland between 1646 and 1649. He completed his father's Riddarhus, built the Oxenstjerna Palace, Stockholm (1650), which introduced the Roman *palazzo* style, and designed the Katherinenkirka, Stockholm (1656), on a centralized plan probably derived from de KEYSER, as well as various palaces in Stockholm (e.g., for Field-Marshal Wrangel) and country houses (Castle Skokloster).

LABEL, *see* HOOD-MOULD.

LABEL-STOP. An ornamental or figural BOSS at the beginning and end of a HOOD-MOULD.

LABROUSTE, Henri (1801–75), a pupil of Vaudoyer and Le Bas, won the Grand Prix in 1824, and was in Rome 1824–30. After his return he opened a teaching *atelier* which became the centre of rationalist teaching in France. His rationalism appears at its most courageous in the interior of his only famous work, the Library of Ste Geneviève by the Panthéon in Paris (1843–50). Here iron is shown frankly in columns and vault, and endowed with all the slenderness of which, in contrast to stone, it is capable. Labrouste's is the first public, monumental building in which iron is thus accepted. The façade is in a nobly restrained Cinquecento style with large, even, round-arched windows, and there again, in comparison with the debased Italianate or the neo-Baroque of Beaux Arts type which just then was becoming current, Labrouste is on the side of reason. The London architect, J. B. Bunning (1802–63), in his Coal Exchange of 1846–9, recently criminally demolished, was as bold in his use of iron, but as an architect was undeniably lacking in the taste and discipline of Labrouste. In the 1860s Labrouste also built the reading-room and the stack-rooms of the Bibliothèque Nationale, again proudly displaying his iron structure.

LACUNAR. A panelled or coffered ceiling: also the sunken panels or COFFERING in such a ceiling.

LADY CHAPEL. A chapel dedicated to the Virgin, usually built east of the CHANCEL and forming a projection from the main building; in England it is normally rectangular in plan.

LANCET WINDOW. A slender pointed-arched window, much used in the early C13. *See figure 57.*

Fig. 57.
Lancet
window

LANGLEY, Batty (1696–1751), the son of a Twickenham gardener, published some twenty architectural books, mostly manuals for the use of country builders and artisans, e.g., *A Sure Guide to Builders* (1729); *The Builder's Compleat Assistant* (1738). But his fame rests on his *Gothic Architecture Restored and Improved* (1741) in which he formalized KENT's neo-Gothic into 'orders'. He built little, and none of his works survives.

LANTERN. A small circular or polygonal turret with windows all round, crowning a roof or dome. *See figure 38.*

LANTERN CROSS. A churchyard cross with lantern-shaped top; usually with sculptured representations on the sides of the top.

LASDUN, Denys (b. 1914), worked with Wells COATES 1935-7. From 1938 to 1948 he was a partner in Tecton. On the strength of his fertile imagination, his sincerity, and the force of his forms he has become one of the most impressive English architects of the post-war years. His principal buildings to date are flats at Bethnal Green, London (1956-9); luxury flats in St James's Place, London (1957-61); the Royal College of Physicians in Regent's Park, London (1960-4), Fitzwilliam House, Cambridge (1959 etc., not yet completed), and the buildings for the University of East Anglia at Norwich (1963 onwards).

LATIN CROSS. A cross with three short arms and a long arm.

LATROBE, Benjamin (1764-1820), the son of a Moravian minister in England, spent his boyhood and youth in England, in Germany, and again in England, where he worked under S. P. COCKERELL as an architect, and under Smeaton as an engineer. He must have been much impressed by SOANE's work. In 1793 he emigrated to America, where, after some years, he was taken up by JEFFERSON and did the exterior of the Capitol at Richmond, Va. In 1798 he moved to Philadelphia, and there built the Bank of Pennsylvania and in 1800 the Water Works (the latter largely an engineering job). The architecture of these two buildings was resolutely Grecian – the first examples of the Greek Revival in America – the former Greek Doric, and the latter Ionic. Of the same year 1799 is Sedgeley, the

earliest Gothic-Revival house in America. In 1803 Latrobe was called in at the Capitol in Washington, and there did some of his noblest interiors, with much vaulting in stone. The work dated from 1803-11, but the majority had to be redone after the fire of 1814, so what one now sees is mostly of Latrobe's maturity. But his most perfect work is probably Baltimore Cathedral (1804-18). Its interior in particular, on an elongated central plan, with the shallow central dome and the segmental tunnel vaults is as fine as that of any church in the neoclassical style anywhere. Latrobe had at the beginning submitted designs in Gothic as well as classical forms, the Gothic being the earliest Gothic church design in America. Latrobe was the first fully trained architect in the United States. Yet his engineering training made it possible for him, throughout his career, to work as well on river navigation, docks, etc. – a combination which was to become typical of American C19 architects.

LATTICE WINDOW. A window with diamond-shaped LEADED LIGHTS or with glazing bars arranged like an open work screen: also, loosely, any hinged window, as distinct from a SASH WINDOW.

LAUGIER, Marc-Antoine (1713-69), was a Jesuit priest and outstanding neo-classical theorist. His *Essai sur l'architecture* (1753) expounds a rationalist view of classical architecture as a truthful, economic expression of man's need for shelter, based on the hypothetical 'rustic cabin' of primitive man. His ideal building would have free-standing columns. He condemned pilasters and pedestals and all Renaissance and post-Renaissance elements. His book put neo-classicism in a nutshell and had great influence, e.g., on SOUFFLOT.

LAURANA, Luciano (*c.* 1420-79), was born in Dalmatia, and appeared in Urbino *c.* 1466 at the humanist court of Federigo da Montefeltro, which included Piero della Francesca and, later on, FRANCESCO DI GIORGIO. He was appointed architect of the Palazzo Ducale, Urbino (1468–72), for which he designed numerous chimney-pieces, doorcases, etc., of extreme refinement and elegance, anticipating and surpassing the C18 in delicacy. His masterpiece is the Florentine-style *cortile* in the Palazzo Ducale, with a light springy arcade of Corinthian columns echoed by shallow pilasters between the windows on the upper storey.

LE BLOND, Jean-Baptiste Alexandre (1679–1719), a minor Parisian architect, is of importance mainly because he introduced the French Rococo style into Russia. His masterpiece is the vast Peterhof Palace, St Petersburg (1716, later enlarged), decorated with typically French elegance and civilized reticence.

LE CORBUSIER (Charles-Édouard Jeanneret) was born 1887 at La Chaux-de-Fonds in French Switzerland. He worked in PERRET's office in Paris in 1908–9, then for a short time in that of BEHRENS in Berlin. The most influential and the most brilliant of C20 architects, of a fertility of formal invention to be compared only with Picasso's, he is restless and an embarrassingly superb salesman of his own ideas. It is no doubt relevant to an understanding of his mind and his work that he was and is an abstract or semi-abstract painter, comparable in some ways to Léger.

In Le Corbusier's early work three strains can be followed, continually interacting. One is the mass-production of housing (Dom-ino, 1914–15, Citrohan House, 1921; the abortive housing estate of Pessac, 1925). The second is town planning. Le Corbusier has published and publicized a number of total plans for cities with a centre of identical skyscrapers, symmetrically arranged in a park setting, with lower building and complex traffic routes between. They are less realistic than GARNIER's Cité Industrielle of 1901, but far more dazzling (Ville Contemporaine, 1922; Plan Voisin, 1925; Ville Radieuse, 1935; plan for Algiers, 1930). The third strain of Le Corbusier's early thought tends towards a new type of private house, white, cubist, wholly or partly on PILOTIS, with rooms flowing into each other. The earliest is the villa at Vaucresson (1922). Many followed, including the exhibition pavilion of the Esprit Nouveau at the Paris Exhibition of 1925, with a tree growing through the building. The most stimulating and influential villas were probably those at Garches (1927) and Poissy (1929–31). In the same years Le Corbusier did some designs for major buildings: for the League of Nations at Geneva (1927; not executed) and the Centrosojus in Moscow (1928). The designs had a great effect on progressive architects everywhere. Of major buildings actually erected two must be referred to: the Salvation Army Hostel in Paris (begun 1929) with its long curtain wall; and the Swiss House in the Paris Cité Universitaire (1930–2), introducing a random-rubble baffle wall to contrast with the usual white-rendered concrete. In 1936 Le Corbusier was called to Rio de Janeiro to advise on the new building of the Ministry of Education which was subsequently executed by COSTA, NIEMEYER, Reidy, and others. Their contribution has never been fully distinguished from his. In 1947 Le Corbusier was one of the group of architects to come to terms with the programme of the United Nations Headquarters in New York, and the Secretariat building, a sheer glass slab with solid, windowless end walls, is essentially his design.

At the same time, however, Le Corbusier began to abandon this rational smooth glass-and-metal style which until then he had been instrumental in propagating, and turned to a new anti-rational, violently sculptural, aggressive style which was soon to be just as influential. The first example is the Unité d'Habitation at Marseille (1947–52), with its heavy exposed concrete members and its fantastic roofscape. The proportions are worked out to a complicated system, called MODULOR, which Le Corbusier invented and pleads for. The Unité was followed by another at Nantes (1953–5) and a third at Berlin (for the Interbau-Exhibition, 1956–8). Le Corbusier's most revolutionary work in his anti-rational style is the pilgrimage chapel of Ronchamp not far from Belfort (1950–4), eminently expressive, with its silo-like white tower, its brown concrete roof like the top of a mushroom, and its wall pierced by small windows of arbitrary shapes in arbitrary positions. In his villas the new style is represented by the Jaoul Houses (1954–6), whose shallow concrete tunnel vaults soon became an international cliché. Of yet later buildings the Philips Pavilion at the Brussels Exhibition of 1958 had a HYPERBOLIC PARABOLOID ROOF, a form pioneered by M. Novitzki and the engineer Deitrich in the stadium at Raleigh, North Carolina (1950–3). At Chandigarh Le Corbusier laid out the town and built the extremely powerful Law Courts and Secretariat (1951–6), the influence of which proved to be strongest in Japan. At the same time he did some houses at Ahmedabad (1954–6) which, like the buildings of Chandigarh, are of extremely heavy, chunky concrete members. In 1957 Le Corbusier designed the Museum of Modern Art for Tokyo and the Dominican Friary of La Tourette (1957–60), a ruthlessly hard block of immense force. No one can say what his next buildings may look like.

LE MUET, Pierre (1591–1669), a *retardataire* Mannerist, published *Manière de bien bastir pour toutes sortes de personnes* (1623), an up-to-date version of DU CERCEAU's first book of architecture, containing designs suitable for different income groups but going farther down the social scale. His best surviving building is the Hôtel Duret de Chevrey, Paris (1635, now part of the Bibliothèque Nationale). His later buildings, e.g., Hôtel Tubeuf, Paris (1649), are more classical but never entirely free of Mannerist traits.

LE NÔTRE, André (1613–1700), the greatest designer of formal gardens and parks, was the son of a royal gardener. He studied painting and architecture as well as garden design, and was appointed Contrôleur Général des Bâtiments du Roi in 1657. The enormous park at Versailles (1662–90), with its vast *parterres*, fountains, sheets of water, and radiating avenues, is his masterpiece. It extends the symmetry of LE VAU's architecture to the surrounding landscape and provides a perfect setting for the building. He began at Vaux-le-Vicomte (1656–61) and later worked at St Cloud, Fontainebleau, Clagny, Marly, and elsewhere, mostly for Louis XIV.

LE PAUTRE, Antoine (1621–81), designed the Hôtel de Beauvais in Paris (1652–55), the most ingenious of all Parisian *hôtel* plans considering the awkward site. But he is best known for the engraved designs in his *Œuvres* (1652) of vast and fantastic town and country houses, which far exceed his contemporary LE VAU in Baroque extravagance. His influence is evident in the work of WREN and SCHLÜTER.

LE VAU, Louis (1612–70), the leading Baroque architect in France, was less intellectual and refined than his great contemporary MANSART. He was also less difficult in character and headed a brilliant team of painters, sculptors, decorators, gardeners, with whom he created the Louis XIV style at Versailles. He was a great *metteur-en-scène* and could produce striking general effects with a typically Baroque combination of all the arts. Born in Paris, the son of a master mason by whom he was trained, he first revealed his outstanding gifts in the

Hôtel Lambert, Paris (1639–44), where he made ingenious use of an awkward site and created the first of his highly coloured, grandiloquent interiors: the staircase and gallery are especially magnificent. In 1657 he was commissioned by Fouquet, the millionaire finance minister, to design his country house at Vaux-le-Vicomte. This is his masterpiece and by far the most splendid of all French *châteaux*. Here grandeur and elegance are combined in a manner peculiarly French, and no expense was spared. The *château* was built in about a year and the luxurious interior, decorated by Lebrun, Guérin, and others, and the gardens laid out by LE NÔTRE were finished by 1661. In the same year Fouquet was arrested for embezzlement, whereupon his rival Colbert took over his architect and artists to work for the king. Le Vau was commissioned to rebuild the Galerie d'Apollon in the Louvre (1661–2), decorated by Lebrun (1663). Work began on the remodelling of Versailles in 1669. Le Vau rose to the occasion, and his feeling for the grand scale found perfect expression in the new garden front. Unfortunately, this was ruined a few years later by Hardouin MANSART's alterations and extensions, and nothing survives at all of the interiors he executed with Lebrun; these included the most spectacular of all, the Escalier des Ambassadeurs. In the Collège des Quatres Nations, Paris (now the Institut de France, begun 1661), which was built at the expense of Cardinal Mazarin, he came closer than any other Frenchman to the warmth and geniality of the great Italian Baroque architects. The main front facing the Seine is concave, with two arms curving forward from the domed centrepiece to end in pavilions. The sense of splendour both in planning and decoration is no less typical than the occasional lack of sensitivity in the handling of detail.

LEADED LIGHTS. Rectangular or diamond-shaped panes of glass set in lead CAMES to form a window. In general use in domestic architecture until C18.

LEAN-TO ROOF, *see* ROOF.

LEDOUX, Claude-Nicolas (1736–1806), began as a fashionable Louis XVI architect, patronized by Mme du Barry, and developed into the most daring and extreme exponent of Romantic classicism in France. Only BOULLÉE among his contemporaries was his equal in imagination and originality, but most of Boullée's designs remained on paper. Neither was properly appreciated until recently. Despite its extreme geometrical simplicity their more advanced work is not abstract but expressive or *parlant*. Born at Dormans, Ledoux studied under J.-F. BLONDEL in Paris. He never went to Italy, though he was profoundly influenced by Italian architecture, especially by the cyclopean fantasies of PIRANESI. Though eccentric and quarrelsome, he was immediately and continuously successful and never lacked commissions. His first important buildings were the Hôtel d'Hallwyl, Paris (1766), the Château de Benouville (1770–77), and the Hôtel de Montmorency, Paris (1770–2), the last displaying his originality in planning on a diagonal axis, with circular and oval rooms.

In 1771 he began working for Mme du Barry and in the following year completed the Pavillon de Louveciennes, a landmark in the history of French taste. It was decorated and furnished throughout in the neoclassical style, the architectural treatment of the interior being confined to shallow pilasters, classical bas-reliefs, and delicate, honeycomb coffering. In 1776 he began the remarkable Hôtel Thélusson in Paris, approached through an enormous triumphal arch leading into a garden laid out in the English landscape manner. This typically Romantic-classical conception, in which the informality of the garden emphasized the stark simplicity and geometrical forms of the building, was repeated on a larger scale in the group of fifteen houses he built for the West Indian nabob Hosten in Paris (1792). They, too, were informally disposed in a landscape garden.

Success and official recognition appear to have stimulated rather than dulled his powers of invention, for his most advanced and original work dates from after he became an Academician and Architecte du Roi in 1773. His masterpieces are the massive and rigidly cubic theatre at Besançon (1775–84), with its unpedimented Ionic portico and, inside, a hemicycle with rising banks of seats surmounted by a Greek Doric colonnade. Odder still is his saltworks at Arc-et-Senans (1775–9), some of which still survives in a dilapidated condition. It is the supreme expression of his romantic feeling for the elemental and primeval. The glowering entrance portico is carved inside to emulate the natural rock out of which gushes water, presumably saline though also carved in stone. Even more extreme were the buildings he envisaged for his 'ideal city' of Chaux which were not, understandably, executed: one was to have been a free-standing sphere and another an enormous cylinder set horizontally.

His Paris toll-houses of 1785–9 are less extreme, but they illustrate the wide range of his stylistic repertoire. Of those that survive the most exciting is the Barrière de St Martin in Place de Stalingrad, a tall cylinder projecting out of a square block decorated with an inconsequential medley of motifs. His career came to an end with the Revolution (he was imprisoned during the 1790s) and he spent his last years preparing his designs for publication: *L'Architecture considérée sous le rapport de l'art, des mœurs et de la législation* (1804).

LEFUEL, Hector M. (1810–80), won the Grand Prix in 1839 and in the same year went to Rome. In 1854, at the death of Louis Visconti (1791–1853), he became chief architect to the Louvre, which Napoleon III had in 1851 decided to complete by large and elaborate links connecting it with the Tuileries. The neo-Renaissance fashion originated here and soon became international (cf. HUNT). Lefuel also designed the palace for the International Exhibition of 1855.

LEGRAND, J. B., *see* GILLY.

LEMERCIER, Jacques (*c.* 1580–1654), was the son of a master mason who worked at St Eustache, Paris. He studied in Rome *c.* 1607–14, bringing back to Paris the academic idiom of Giacomo della PORTA. Though he never quite succeeded in fusing this with his native French tradition, he ranks only just below MANSART and LE VAU in French classical architecture. If seldom inspired he was always more than competent. In 1624 he was commissioned by Louis XIII to plan extensions to the Louvre (the Pavillon de l'Horloge is the most notable of his additions), but his principal patron was Cardinal Richelieu, for whom he designed the Palais Cardinal (Palais Royal), Paris (begun 1633); the Sorbonne, Paris (begun 1626); the *château* and church of Rueil and the *château* and town of Richelieu (begun 1631). Only a small domed pavilion of the office block survives from the enormous Château Richelieu, but the town still exists as laid out by Lemercier in a regular grid with houses of uniform design built of brick with stone quoins. As a designer of *hôtels* he was remarkably ingenious, and his solution at the Hôtel de Liancourt, Paris (1623), became a prototype which was followed by nearly all his successors. His church of the Sorbonne (begun 1635) is perhaps his finest work and is one of the first purely classical churches in France. His dome at the Val-de-Grâce, Paris, where he took over from Mansart in 1646, is also most dramatic and effective.

L'ENFANT, Pierre Charles (d. 1825), a French architect and engineer who served as a volunteer major in the American army during the War of Independence, designed the old City Hall in New York and the Federal House in Philadelphia, but is remembered mainly for having surveyed the site and made the plan for the new federal capital in Washington, a grandiose conception based in some respects on Versailles. He would probably have been given the commission to design the Capitol and other buildings in Washington had he not become unmanageable. He was dismissed in 1792.

LEONARDO DA VINCI (1452–1519). The greatest artist and thinker of the Renaissance. His wide-ranging mind embraced architecture as well as many other fields of human activity. Although he built little or nothing, he provided a model for the dome of Milan Cathedral (1487, not executed), and during his last years in France produced a vast scheme for a new city and royal castle at Romorantin (not executed). But his influence was great, especially on BRAMANTE, who took over his interest in centralized churches. S. Maria della Consolazione at Todi (1508), begun by Cola da Caprarola, probably derived from one of his sketches by way of Bramante.

LEONI, Giacomo (c. 1686–1746), who was born in Venice, settled in England sometime before 1715, having previously been architect to the Elector Palatine. An apostle of PALLADIAN-ISM, he published the first English edition of Palladio's *Works* (1715) and at Queensberry House, London (1721, reconstructed 1792), provided the prototype English Palladian town house. His surviving buildings include Lyme Hall, Cheshire (1720–30); Argyll House, London (1723); and Clandon Park, Surrey (1731–5).

LESCOT, Pierre (1500/15–78). The son of a well-to-do lawyer, who gave him a good education. His only work to survive more or less intact is part of the square court of the Louvre (1546–51), which laid the foundations of French classicism. Essentially decorative, his style is very French and entirely lacks the monumentality of his Italian contemporaries. He had the great advantage of the sculptor Jean Goujon's collaboration, and his ornamental detail is therefore of the greatest refinement and delicacy. Though much altered, parts of his Hôtel Carnavalet, Paris (c. 1545–50), survive.

LESENE. A PILASTER without a base and capital often called a pilaster-strip and usually found on the exteriors of later Anglo-Saxon and early Romanesque churches. Although they were much used as decoration during the latter period, there is evidence in some Anglo-Saxon buildings to suggest that pilaster-strips as used by the Saxons were primarily functional. They served as bonding courses in thin rubble walls, and thus split up an unbroken expanse of wall, reducing cracking in the plaster and preventing longitudinal spread. The north nave wall at Breamore church shows long stones on end between flat stones, all clearly projecting some distance into the wall. This is a crude example of LONG AND SHORT WORK, but no claim can be made that the pilaster-strip and long and short work as used for QUOINS were evolved in any particular sequence. Other examples of the structural significance of the pilaster-strip are at Worth, where they are solid stone partitions, clearly of a piece with the long and short quoins, at Sompting and at Milborne.

LETHABY, William Richard (1857–1931), joined the office of Norman SHAW in 1877, became his trusted principal assistant, and set up on his own in 1889, helped on by Shaw. While he thus owed much to Shaw, as an artist and a thinker he owed more to MORRIS and Philip WEBB, on whom he wrote a book. He was as much an educator as a scholar and an architect, and indeed built very little.

Foremost among his buildings are Avon Tyrell in Hampshire (1891) and Melsetter on Orkney (1898), the church at Brockhampton in Herefordshire (1900–2) – probably the most original church of its date in the world – and the Eagle Insurance in Birmingham (1899), also of a startling originality, even if influenced by Webb. Lethaby was the chief promoter and the first principal of the London Central School of Arts and Crafts, which was established in 1894 on Morris's principles. It was the first school anywhere to include teaching workshops for crafts. Also in 1894, Lethaby (with Swainson) brought out a learned book on Haghia Sophia in Constantinople; in 1904 a general, very deeply felt book on medieval art; in 1906 and 1925 two learned volumes on Westminster Abbey; and in 1922 a collection of brilliant, convincedly forward-looking essays called *Form in Civilisation*.

LEVERTON, Thomas (1743–1824), the son of an Essex builder and not highly regarded in his own day, nevertheless designed some of the most elegant interiors in London, e.g., Nos. 1 and 13 Bedford Square (1780). His 'Etruscan' hall and other rooms at Woodhall Park (1778) are equally distinguished.

LIBERGIER, Hugues (d. 1263). A French master mason whose funerary slab is now in Reims Cathedral. He is called Maistre on it and is represented holding the model of the major parish church of Reims, St Nicaise, which he designed and began in 1231. He also has a staff, an L-square, and compasses.

LIERNE, *see* VAULT.

LIGHTS. Openings between the MULLIONS of a window.

LIGORIO, Pirro (*c.* 1500–83). Painter and archaeologist as well as architect. In 1550 he built the Villa d'Este, Tivoli, and laid out its wonderful formal gardens with elaborate fountains and water-works. His masterpiece is the exquisite little Casino di Pio IV (1558–62) in the Vatican gardens, Rome, one of the most elegant of Mannerist buildings. Also in the Vatican, he transformed the exedra in BRAMANTE's Cortile del Belvedere into a gargantuan niche.

LINENFOLD. Tudor panelling ornamented with a conventional representation of a piece of linen laid in vertical folds. One such piece fills one panel. *See figure 58.*

Fig. 58.
Linenfold

LINTEL. A horizontal beam or stone bridging an opening.

LISTEL, *see* FILLET.

LODGE. The medieval term for the masons' workshop and living-quarters, set up when a church, castle, or house was to be built. In the case of cathedrals and great abbeys it was often permanent, under a resident master mason, to maintain the fabric of the building.

LODOLI, Carlo (1690–1761). A Venetian priest and architectural theorist. His neo-classical and 'functional' ideas were published after his death by A. Memmo (*Elementi d'architettura lodoliana*, 1786), but they had been current for many years and were very influential, e.g., on Algarotti's *Saggio sopra l'architettura* (1753).

LOGGIA. A gallery open on one or more sides, sometimes pillared: it may also be a separate structure, usually in a garden.

LOMBARDO, Pietro (*c.* 1435–1515). A leading sculptor and architect in late C15 Venice. Though of exquisite sensitivity he stands outside the main development of Renaissance architecture. He was born at Carona in

Lombardy, hence his name. He appears to have visited Florence before 1464, when he is first recorded working in Padua as a sculptor. Soon after 1467 he settled in Venice. Between 1471 and 1485 he designed and carved decorations for the chancel of S. Giobbe, Venice, a work of strongly Florentine character. His next and most important work was S. Maria dei Miracoli (1481–9), in which he successfully blended the Veneto-Byzantine and Renaissance styles – marble panelling inside and out and a Byzantine dome, combined with crisply carved Renaissance ornament. To give an illusion of greater size he resorted to various *trompe l'œil* devices which he repeated on a larger scale, but with less success, on the façade of the Scuola di S. Marco (1488–90, upper storeys completed by CODUCCI). He also introduced into Venice the large architectural sepulchral monument with a classical framework and abundance of classically inspired sculpture. Here he was much assisted by his sons Antonio (*c.* 1485–1516) and Tullio (*c.* 1455–1532). Various Venetian palaces have been attributed to Lombardo, notably Palazzo Dario (*c.* 1487).

LONG AND SHORT WORK. Saxon QUOINS, consisting of long stones on end between flat ones, all bonded into the wall. The chancel arch JAMBS at Escomb (C7 or 8) may have a bearing on the origin of the technique; it may also have been evolved simultaneously and in association with pilaster-strip work (*see* LESENE). It is the insertion of the large flat stones which makes long and short work such a good bonding technique for corners, as in many cases they extend practically through the thickness of the walls; the upright blocks alone are subject to diagonal thrust.

Superficially long and short work is of two kinds:

a. the 'upright and flat' type, where the full size of the horizontal stone is visible on both flanks;

b. the long and short strip quoin, where the horizontal stones have been cut back, making them flush with the upright blocks.

This was a refinement in the process of finding a solid cornering for stone buildings, but is not necessarily an indication of a later date (e.g., Deerhurst of the early C10 has the 'upright and flat' type). The method of construction is the same for both kinds.

LONGHENA, Baldassare (1598–1682), the only great Venetian Baroque architect, was born in Venice of a family of stone carvers and was trained under SCAMOZZI. In 1630 he won a competition for the design of the *ex voto* church of S. Maria della Salute, with which he was to be occupied off and on for the rest of his long life (it was not finally consecrated until 1687). Standing on an imposing site at the entrance to the Grand Canal, this church is a masterpiece of scenographic design, with a vast buoyant dome anchored by huge Baroque scrolls to an octagonal base, and a very complex façade which directs the eye through the main door to the high altar. The interior is conceived as a series of dramatic vistas radiating from the centre of the octagonal nave. Longhena realized a similarly theatrical concept in the design of his imposing double staircase for the monastery of S. Giorgio Maggiore (1643–5), which had considerable influence on later architects. In the domestic field he was less adventurous: Palazzo Rezzonico (begun 1667) and Palazzo Pesaro (begun 1676) on the Grand Canal – both completed after his death – with heavily rusticated basements, abundance of carving, and deep recesses which dissolve the surface of the exterior in patterns of light and shade, are merely Baroque variations on SANSOVINO's Palazzo Corner. A tendency towards wilful exaggeration of sculptural detail in these works reaches its fantastic peak in the little church of the Ospedaletto

(1670–8), with a preposterously over-wrought façade bursting with *telamones*, giant heads, and lion masks. He has been credited with numerous villas on the mainland, but none is of much interest.

LONGHI, Martino the younger (1602–60), the most important member of a family of architects working mainly in Rome, was the son of Onorio Longhi (1569–1619) and the grandson of Martino Longhi the elder (d. 1591). He continued his father's work on S. Carlo al Corso, Rome, and began S. Antonio de'Portoghesi, Rome (1638). His major achievement is the façade of SS. Vincenzo ed Anastasio, Rome (1646–50), a powerfully dramatic, many-columned composition in which Mannerist devices are used to obtain an overwhelming high Baroque effect of grandeur and mass.

LOOS, Adolf (1870–1933), was born at Brno in Moravia, studied at Dresden, spent three crucial years in the United States (1893–6), and then worked in Vienna, strongly influenced by the doctrines just then expounded by Otto WAGNER. From the very first his designs (Goldmann shop interior, 1898) refused to allow any decorative features or any curves. His most important buildings are private houses of between 1904 (house, Lake Geneva) and 1910 (Steiner House, Vienna). They are characterized by unrelieved cubic shapes, a total absence of ornament, and a love of fine materials. In his theoretical writings, or rather his journalism, he was a rabid anti-ornamentalist, an enemy therefore of the Wiener Werkstätten and HOFFMANN, and a believer in the engineer and the plumber. His famous article called *Ornament and Crime* came out in 1908. As an architect, however, he wavered. His office building in the Michaelerplatz (1910) has Tuscan columns, his design for the Chicago Tribune competition of 1923 is a huge closely windowed Doric column; but smaller domestic jobs, such as the house for the Dadaist Tristan Tzara in Paris (1926), remained faithful to the spirit of 1904–10. Loos was not a successful architect, but he was influential among some of the *avant-garde* in Europe.

LOUDON, John Claudius (1783–1843), was apprenticed to a landscape gardener in Scotland, and educated himself the hard way. He settled in London in 1803, and at once began writing on gardening and agriculture. He also took up farming, made money and lost it, travelled on the Continent (1814 as far as Moscow, 1819–20 in France and Italy). His *Encyclopaedia of Gardening* came out in 1822, an *Encyclopaedia of Agriculture* in 1825, an *Encyclopaedia of Plants* in 1829, and the architecturally important *Encyclopaedia of Cottage, Farm and Villa Architecture* in 1833. This is the standard book if one wants to see what ideals and what styles of the past English country-houses followed, chiefly in the 1840s. Loudon also started and edited the *Gardener's Magazine* (1826 etc.) and the short-lived *Architectural Magazine* (1834). He was an exceedingly hard worker, labouring under great physical disabilities, and making and losing large sums of money.

LOUVRE. 1. An opening, often with a LANTERN over, in the roof of a hall to let the smoke from a central hearth escape; either open-sided, or closed by slanting boards to keep out the rain. 2. One of a series of overlapping boards or slips of glass to admit air and exclude rain. *See figure 59.*

LOW SIDE WINDOW. A window usually on the south side of the chancel, lower than the others, possibly intended for communication between persons outside the chancel and the priest within; perhaps also for the sanctus bell to be heard outside the church.

LOZENGE. A diamond shape.

LUCARNE. 1. A small opening in an attic or a spire. 2. A DORMER WINDOW.

LUDOVICE, João Frederico (Johann

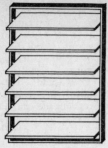

Fig. 59. Louvre

Friedrich Ludwig, 1670–1752), the leading Late Baroque architect in Portugal, was born at Hall in Swabia, the son of a goldsmith whose craft he practised first in Rome (1697–1701) then in Lisbon. In about 1711 the King of Portugal commissioned him to build a small convent at Mafra. Gradually the size of the project was enlarged, and the building finally became one of the largest in Europe (built 1717–70). It includes a royal palace, a vast church, and conventual buildings for 300 monks. Mafra derives mainly from High Baroque Rome with a few South German and Portuguese overtones: the church, liberally decorated with Italian statues, is especially impressive. His only other works of importance are the library of Coimbra University (1717–23) with a very rich *mouvementé* façade and the apse of Évora Cathedral (1716–46).

LUNETTE. A semicircular opening or TYMPANUM. The term can also be applied to any flat, semicircular surface.

LUTYENS, Sir Edwin (1869–1944), after a short time with George & Peto, was already in independent practice in 1889. In 1896 he designed Munstead Wood for Gertrude Jekyll, the gardener and garden designer who helped him in his career. A number of excellent country houses in the Arts and Crafts style followed (Deanery Garden, Sonning, 1899; Orchards, Godalming, 1899; Tigbourne Court, 1899; Folly Farm, Sulhampstead, 1905

and 1912), establishing Lutyens's originality and ability for coordinating forms. However, he was very early attracted by classicism, first of a William and Mary variety (Liberal Club, Farnham, 1894; Crooksbury, east front, 1899; Hestercombe Orangery, 1905), then of a grander neo-Georgian (Nashdom, Taplow, 1905) and a semi-Palladian, semi-English Baroque 'Wrenaissance' (Heathcote, Ilkley, 1906). Lutyens shared to the full the imperial *folie de grandeur* of the Edwardian years, and this made him the ideal architect for the last crop of really spectacular English country houses (Lindisfarne Castle, 1903; Castle Drogo, 1910–30), and of course for New Delhi. His Viceroy's House (1913 onwards) has a genuine monumentality and a sense of grandiose display which Baker in his buildings for Delhi never achieved.

However, classicism bogged Lutyens down in the end. In spite of extreme care for details of proportion and oddly impish details into which his former originality retreated, his later commercial buildings – Britannic House (1920 etc.) and the Midland Bank (1924 etc.) – stand outside the mainstream of European developments, whereas an earlier church by Lutyens such as St Jude's in the Hampstead Garden Suburb (1909–11) possessed a true originality and a sense of massing very rare in European ecclesiastical architecture of the time.

LYCH GATE. A covered wooden gateway with open sides at the entrance to a churchyard, providing a resting-place for a coffin (the word *lych* is Saxon for corpse). Part of the burial service is sometimes read there.

LYMING, Robert, carpenter, builder, and architect, designed the loggia and frontispiece of Hatfield House (1611). At Blickling Hall (*c.* 1625) he produced the last of the great Jacobean 'prodigy' houses in which Flemish ornamentalism and asymmetrical planning were completely anglicized.

M

MACHICOLATION. A gallery or PARA-PET projecting on brackets and built on the outside of castle towers and walls, with openings in the floor through which to drop molten lead, boiling oil, and missiles.

MACHUCA, Pedro (d. 1550), who began as a painter, worked in Italy and returned to Spain in 1520. His masterpiece, the Palace of Charles V in the Alhambra at Granada (1527–68), is very Italian in the RAPHAEL–GIULIO ROMANO style; indeed, it is larger and more complete than any Bramantesque palace in Italy. But various Spanish or PLATERESQUE features crept into his design, e.g., the garlanded window frames.

MACKINTOSH, Charles Rennie (1868–1928), studied at the Glasgow School of Art at the time when Glasgow painting had suddenly turned from a provincial past to new forms of considerable interest to people in England and even on the Continent. In 1893 and the following years he, his friend McNair, and the two Macdonald sisters, Margaret (later Mrs Mackintosh, 1865–1933) and Frances (later Mrs McNair), designed graphic work and repoussé metalwork in an ART NOUVEAU way, inspired by *The Studio* (which started in London in 1893) and especially by Jan Toorop, the Dutchman. In 1896 Mackintosh won the competition for the new building of the Glasgow School of Art and erected a building inferior to none of its date anywhere in Europe or America – on a clear rational plan, with the basic external forms equally clear and rational (e.g., the studio windows), but with a centre-piece of complete originality and high fancifulness, influenced by VOYSEY, by the Scottish castle and manor-house tradi-

tion, and even a little by the current English 'Wrenaissance'. The metalwork of the façade and much of the interior achieve a unification of the crisply rectangular with the long, delicate, languid curves of Art Nouveau. It is in this unique harmony that Mackintosh's greatness lies, and it explains the deep impression his furniture and furnishings made on Austrian architects when they became familiar with him, first through *The Studio* and then through an exhibition at the Sezession (*see* OLBRICH) in 1900. The Viennese were abandoning Art Nouveau excesses for a clearer, saner style, and Mackintosh both inspired and confirmed them.

Mackintosh had fully evolved his style in his interior work by 1899 – white lacquered chairs and cupboards, erect, elegant, clearly articulated, and with wistfully curved inlays in metal with pink, mauve, or mother-of-pearl enamel. There was no one else who could combine the rational and the expressive in so intriguing a way. His capital works at or near Glasgow are the tea-rooms for Mrs Cranston (Buchanan Street, 1897 etc.; Argyle Street, 1897 and 1905; Sauchiehall Street, 1904; Ingram Street, 1901, *c.* 1906, and *c.* 1911), now alas mostly destroyed or disused; two houses (Windyhill, Kilmacolm, 1899–1901, and Hill House, Helensburgh, 1902–3); a school (Scotland Street, 1906); and the library wing of the School of Art (1907–9) with its sheer, towering outer wall and its bewitchingly complex interior. In 1901 he had won second prize in a German publisher's competition for the house of an art-lover (Baillie Scott came first), and this consolidated his reputation abroad.

However, he was not an easy man,

and his erratic ways alienated clients. In 1913 he left the firm (Honeyman & Keppie) in which he had been a partner since 1904. He moved to Walberswick, then to London, then after the war to Port Vendres, and finally back to London, painting highly original, finely drawn landscapes and still-lifes, but never recovering an architectural practice.

MACKMURDO, Arthur H. (1851–1942), came from a wealthy family and had plenty of leisure to evolve a style of his own. In 1874 he travelled to Italy with RUSKIN. About 1880 he seems to have built his first houses. In 1882 he founded the Century Guild, a group of architects, artists, and designers inspired by Ruskin and MORRIS. The group began in 1884 to publish a magazine The Hobby Horse, which anticipated some of the features of book design recovered by Morris from the medieval past in his Kelmscott Press of 1890. As early as 1883, in the design for the cover of his book on Wren's City churches, Mackmurdo introduced those long flame-like or tendril-like curves which nearly ten years later were taken up, especially in Belgium, as a basis for ART NOUVEAU. But while in such two-dimensional designs, including a number for textiles (c. 1884), Mackmurdo is the lone pioneer of Art Nouveau, the furniture he designed from 1886 onwards and a stand for an exhibition at Liverpool, also of 1886, established him as the forerunner of VOYSEY in clarity of structure, elegance, and originality in the sense of independence of the past. Specially characteristic, on the exhibition stand, are the long, tapering posts with a far-projecting flat cornice. In 1904 Mackmurdo gave up architecture; later he concentrated on economic thought and writing, his ideas being similar to those of Social Credit.

MADERNO, Carlo (1556–1629), was born at Capolago on Lake Lugano, and had settled in Rome by 1588, beginning as assistant to his uncle Domenico FONTANA. He was appointed architect of St Peter's in 1603, when he also completed the façade of S. Susanna, Rome, a revolutionary design with which he broke away from the current rather facile and academic Mannerism and established his own lucid, forceful, and intensely dynamic style. S. Susanna and the majestic dome of S. Andrea della Valle, Rome, are his masterpieces, though he is best known for his work at St Peter's, where he had the unenviable job of altering MICHELANGELO's centralized plan by adding a nave and façade. Work began in 1607, and the façade was finished by 1612. Its excessive length is due to the later addition of towers, of which only the substructures were built and which now appear to form part of the façade. His Confessio before the high altar and his elegant fountain in the piazza are more successful. His secular buildings include Palazzo Mattei, Rome (1598–1618), and Palazzo Barberini, Rome (1626 onwards), though the latter was almost entirely executed after his death by BERNINI, who made various alterations, notably to the main façade.

MAEKAWA, Kunio, see TANGE.

MAILLART, Robert (1872–1940), a Swiss engineer, studied at the Zürich Polytechnic (1890–4), had jobs in various engineering firms, and then set up on his own (1902). He worked on the unexplored possibilities of reinforced concrete, and in the course of that work arrived at a new aesthetic for concrete, using it to span by curves, rather than merely as a new means of building post-and-lintel structures. His Tavenasa Bridge (1905) is the first in which arch and roadway are structurally one. He built many bridges afterwards, all of them of a thoroughbred elegance: the one across the Salzinatobel has a span of nearly 300 ft (1929–30). In 1908 he also began experimenting with concrete mushroom construction, at a time when this was being done independently in the United States; the technique involves a post and a mushroom top spreading from it that are one inseparable concrete unit. The first building of mushroom construction was a warehouse at Zürich (1910).

MANNERISM is in its primary meaning the acceptance of a manner rather than its meaning. Now Mannerism has also become a term to denote the style current in Italy from MICHELANGELO to the end of the C16. It is characterized by the use of motifs in deliberate opposition to their original significance or context, but it can also express itself in an equally deliberate cold and rigid classicism. The term applies to French and Spanish architecture of the C16 as well (DELORME; the Escorial), but how far it applies to the northern countries is controversial. Principal examples in Italy are MICHELANGELO's Medici Chapel and Laurentian Library, GIULIO ROMANO's works at Mantua, VASARI's Uffizi at Florence, and other works by these architects and LIGORIO, AMMANATI, Buontalenti, etc. PALLADIO belongs to Mannerism only in certain limited aspects of his work.

MANOR HOUSE. A house in the country or a village, the centre of a manor. Architecturally the term is used to denote the unfortified, medium-sized house of the later Middle Ages.

MANSARD ROOF, *see* ROOF.

MANSART, François (1598–1666), the first great protagonist of French classicism in architecture, holds a position parallel to Poussin in painting and Corneille in drama. He never went to Italy, and his style is extremely French in its elegance, clarity, and cool restraint. Though of scrupulous artistic conscience he was unfortunately both arrogant and slippery in his business relationships, and his inability to make and keep to a final plan not unnaturally enraged his clients. As a result, he lost many commissions. For the last ten years of his life he was virtually unemployed. He was seldom patronized by the Crown and never by the great nobility; his clients belonged mainly to the newly rich bourgeoisie, who had the intelligence to appreciate and the money to pay for his sophisticated and luxurious buildings.

Born in Paris, the son of a master carpenter, he probably began under de BROSSE at Coulommiers. By 1624 he had already established himself as a prominent architect in the capital. His early work derives from de Brosse, with Mannerist overtones in the style of DU CERCEAU, but his individual style began to emerge at the Château de Balleroy (1626), where the harmonious grouping of massive blocks achieves an effect of sober monumentality. His first masterpiece, the Orléans wing of the *château* at Blois (1635–8), would have been a grander and more monumental Palais Luxembourg had it ever been completed. Only the central block and colonnades were built. But these display to the full the ingenuity of planning, clarity of disposition, and purity and refinement of detail which distinguish his work. He also introduced here the continuous broken roof with a steep lower slope and flatter, shorter upper portion that is named after him. His style reached culmination at Maisons Lafitte (1642–6), the country house near Paris which he built for the immensely wealthy René de Longeuil, who apparently allowed him a completely free hand. (He pulled down part of it during construction in order to revise his designs!) It is his most complete work to survive and gives a better idea of his genius than any other. The oval rooms in the wings and the vestibule, executed entirely in stone without either gilding or colour, epitomize his suave severity and civilized reticence in decoration. His design for the Val-de-Grâce in Paris (*c.* 1645) is contemporary with Maisons Lafitte, but he was dismissed and replaced by LEMERCIER in 1646, when the building had reached the entablature of the nave and the lower storey of the façade. The conception appears to derive from PALLADIO's Redentore.

His other important buildings are Ste Marie de la Visitation, Paris (1632–4, now destroyed); the Hôtel de la Vrillière, Paris (1635–45), wholly symmetrical and the model for the classical type of Parisian *hôtel*; the Hôtel du Jars, Paris (begun 1648, now destroyed), in which he developed a freer, more plastic disposition of rooms which was to be very influential. His last surviving work is his remodelling of the Hôtel Carnavalet in Paris (1655). He was consulted by Colbert in the 1660s in connexion with the Louvre and a royal chapel at St Denis, but his designs were not executed.

MANSART, Jules Hardouin (1646–1708), the grand-nephew of François MANSART, by whom he may have been trained, owed more to LE VAU, whose grand manner he and Lebrun brought to perfection in the Galerie des Glaces at Versailles. He understood perfectly the artistic needs of Louis XIV's court and excelled as an official architect, being competent, quick, and adaptable. (He was appointed Royal Architect in 1675, *Premier Architecte* in 1685, and *Surintendant des Bâtiments* in 1699). His meteoric career aroused jealousy, and Saint-Simon accused him of keeping tame architects in a backroom to do all his work for him. He was certainly lucky in having such gifted assistants as Lassurance and Pierre Le Pautre, but he had real ability himself and a vivid sense of the splendour and visual drama required for a royal setting. From 1678 onwards he was in charge of the vast extensions to Versailles. These were disastrous externally, for he filled in the central terrace of Le Vau's garden façade and trebled its length. The stables, orangery, Trianon, and chapel are more successful. His Baroque tendencies

reached their height in the Invalides Chapel in Paris (1680–91), while the Place Vendôme (1698 etc.) illustrates his genius for the spectacular in town planning. Towards the end of his life, notably in a number of rooms at Versailles, Trianon, and Marly, which were redecorated under his direction in the 1690s, he veered away from Baroque splendours towards a lighter and more elegant style which marks the first step towards the Rococo.

MANTELPIECE. The wood, brick, stone, or marble frame surrounding a fireplace, frequently including an overmantel or mirror above; sometimes called *chimneypiece*.

MANUELINE STYLE. An architectural style peculiar to Portugal and named after King Manuel the Fortunate (1495–1521). *See* PORTUGUESE ARCHITECTURE.

MAQSURAH. A screen or grille of wood in a mosque to protect and separate the imam from the crowd.

MARKELIUS, Sven (b. 1889), is a Swedish architect and town-planner. City architect and planner to the city of Stockholm 1944–54, Markelius laid out the new suburb of Vällingby. Vällingby is not a SATELLITE TOWN, as it is not meant to have a completely independent existence, but is of an exemplary plan combining a truly urban-looking centre with peripheral housing of both high blocks of flats and small houses (1953–9).

MAROT, Daniel (*c.* 1660–1752), was the son of a minor French architect Jean Marot (*c.* 1619–79), who is chiefly remembered for his volumes of engravings *L'Architecture française* known as 'le grand Marot' and 'le petit Marot'. Born in Paris, Daniel emigrated to Holland after the Revocation of the Edict of Nantes (1685), becoming almost immediately architect to William of Orange. He developed an intricate style of ornamentation, similar to that of Jean Berain (see his *Nouvelles cheminées à panneaux de la manière de France*), and was involved among other things with the design of the palace at Zeist and the interior decoration and garden design at Het Loo. He followed William to England and designed the gardens and perhaps some of the furnishings and interior decoration at Hampton Court, but though he later described himself as 'Architect' to the King of England no buildings can be ascribed to him (Schomberg House, London, *c.* 1698, appears to have been strongly influenced by him). He died at the Hague, where he designed part of the Royal Library (1734–8) and Stadthuis (1733–9). He published his *Œuvres* in Amsterdam in 1712.

MARTIN, Sir Leslie (b. 1908), was Architect to the London County Council from 1953 to 1956, in succession to Sir Robert MATTHEW, and is now Professor of Architecture at Cambridge University. Under Martin the finest of all L.C.C. housing estates was built, that at Roehampton for a population of about 10,000. Some of the brightest young architects in England were at that time working in the L.C.C. office, and Martin gave them full scope. In the course of building the style of the scheme changed from one inspired by Sweden to that of LE CORBUSIER at Chandigarh, and Martin's own work in partnership with C. A. St J. Wilson has moved in the same direction – see, for example, the new building for Caius College, Cambridge (1960–2). Other recent work is College Hall, Leicester University (1958–61), and the new Oxford libraries (1961–4).

MARTINELLI, Domenico (1650–1718), quadratura painter and architect errant, who travelled widely and played an important part in the diffusion of the Italian Baroque style north of the Alps, was born in Lucca and ordained priest, but this did nothing to interfere with his wandering artistic career. His masterpiece is the Stadtpalais Liechtenstein in Vienna (1692–1705), which introduced the elaborate triumphal staircase which was to become an essential feature of Viennese palace architecture. He also designed the large but simpler Gartenpalais Liechtenstein, Vienna (1698–1711), and probably the Harrach Palais, Vienna (*c.* 1690), as well as the Invalidenhaus, Budapest (built 1721–37), and a house for Graf von Kaunitz, Austerlitz. It is said that he also worked in Warsaw, Prague, and Holland.

MATTHEW, Sir Robert (b. 1906), was Architect to the London County Council from 1946 to 1953, in the years in which the Council embarked on its exemplary housing and schools work. Matthew can be considered instrumental in establishing the progressive style of these buildings and the principles of variety in grouping, mixture of heights, and siting in landscape which have made the L.C.C. estates a pattern for the whole of Europe. Of recent buildings designed by the firm Robert Matthew, Johnson-Marshall & Partners the finest is New Zealand House, London (1958–63), while the most challenging is the Commonwealth Institute (1959–62), also in London, with its incorporation of the fashionable HYPERBOLIC PARABOLOID roof.

MAUSOLEUM. A magnificent and stately tomb. The term derives from the tomb of Mausolus at Halicarnassus.

MAY, Hugh (1622–84), the son of a Sussex gentleman and prominent among the virtuosi of the Restoration, imported the placid spirit of Dutch PALLADIANISM into England and helped, with PRATT, to establish the type of house later known, erroneously, as the 'Wren' type. Eltham Lodge, London (1663–4), is his only surviving work, a rectangular brick-built house with a central pediment and stone pilasters. He may also have designed Holme Lacy House, Hereford (begun 1673–4).

MAYAN ARCHITECTURE. The Maya

civilization of Central America (modern Yucatán and Guatemala), which flourished from about the C4 to C15 A.D., has left relics of an interesting architecture. Temples, public buildings, and private houses were disposed in spacious 'garden cities'. As in Peru, pyramids capped with temples were built – the largest is at Tikal, and there is a very fine example at Chichén Itzá. Carvings in wood and stone were abundant, as on the hieroglyphic staircase at Copán. The governor's palace at Uxmal, decorated with finely cut stone mosaics on the façades, has been called the most magnificent building erected in pre-Columbian America.

MCINTIRE, Samuel (1757–1811), was a self-trained architect of great ability and the outstanding example of the early American craftsman-builder tradition, though most of his work dates from after the end of the Revolutionary War in 1783. He was a wood-carver by trade and lived in Salem, Mass. With the help of Batty LANGLEY's books he taught himself the PALLADIAN style, which he adopted for his first houses, e.g., Pierce House (1779) and Derby House (1780 etc.) in Salem. His most ambitious effort was Salem Court House (1785, now demolished) with superimposed orders and a dome. In the 1790s he came under the influence of BULFINCH, from whom he picked up the ADAM style which he used in his later and finest houses (mostly destroyed, but there are rooms from them in the Boston and Philadelphia museums).

MCKIM, Charles Follen (1847–1909), studied first engineering at Harvard, then, in 1867–70, architecture in Paris at the École des Beaux Arts. On his return to the States he entered the office of H. H. RICHARDSON. When he set up his own practice, he went into partnership with W. R. Mead and a little later with Stanford WHITE. In 1878 they were all interested in Colonial architecture, a highly unusual thing at the time. To this was added almost at once a liking for the Italian Renaissance which was first introduced, it seems, by Joseph Merrill Wells, who entered the office in 1879 and died early, in 1890. The Italian Renaissance meant to them the High Renaissance, not the Baroque exuberance of classical motifs then current. A first proof of this new taste was the impressively restrained group of the Villard Houses in Madison Avenue (1882), the second the Boston Public Library (1887 etc.) with its façade by McKim, inspired by LABROUSTE's Ste Geneviève Library. McKim believed in interior enrichment on a grand scale, and for the library was able to call in Sargent and Puvis de Chavannes. For the Chicago exhibition of 1893, McKim did the Agriculture Building.

Later jobs include the Germantown Cricket Club (1891), decidedly American Colonial; the lavish Madison Gardens (1891), Spanish with a tall tower reminiscent of Seville; the Washington Triumphal Arch in New York in the style of the Étoile; Colombia University in New York with its library rotunda (1893) inspired by the Pantheon in Rome and JEFFERSON's Charlottesville (1817–26); the Morgan Library in New York (1903); and the Pennsylvania Railway Station also in New York (1904–10), a grandiose scheme echoing Imperial Roman *thermae*.

MEGARON. A large oblong hall, especially in Cretan and Mycenaean palaces; sometimes thought to be the ancestor of the Doric temple.

MENDELSOHN, Erich or Eric (1887–1953). The boldness of Mendelsohn's vision of a sculptural architecture emerged early in his many small sketches for buildings that are not functionally determined but are highly expressive with their streamlined curves. In the years of German Expressionism at and after the end of

the First World War, he was just once
enabled actually to build such a vision
(the Einstein Tower at Potsdam, 1919–
20); but vigorous curves carried round
corners also characterize his remodelling of the Mosse Building in Berlin
(1921), and appear much tempered by
the more rational spirit of the International Modern style of the later
twenties and the thirties in his excellent
Schocken stores for Stuttgart (1926)
and Chemnitz (1928). As expressive as
the Einstein Tower, but in terms of
multi-angular roof shapes instead of
curves, is another early work of Mendelsohn's, a factory at Luckenwalde
(1923). Mendelsohn visited the United
States in 1924 and was understandably
impressed by the expressive qualities
of the skyscrapers. Later Berlin buildings include the headquarters of the
Metal Workers' Union (1929) and
Columbushaus (1929–30). In 1933
Mendelsohn went to London and
joined Serge Chermayeff. A joint
work is the de la Warr Pavilion at
Bexhill (1935–6). But in 1934 he
moved on to Israel, and in 1941 finally
settled in the United States. In Israel he
built, among other things, the Hadassah University Medical Centre on
Mount Scopus, Jerusalem (1936–8), in
America the Maimonides Hospital at
San Francisco (1946–50).

MENGONI, Giuseppe (1829–77). Architect of the Galleria Vittorio Emanuele
in Milan, won in competition in 1861.
It was built in 1864–7, and is the
largest, highest, and most ambitious of
all shopping arcades. It is cruciform,
and the buildings through which it
runs take part in the free Renaissance
design of the *galleria*. Especially impressive is the façade towards the
Piazza del Duomo.

MERLON, *see* BATTLEMENT.

METOPE. The square space between two
TRIGLYPHS in the FRIEZE of a Doric
order; it may be carved or left plain.
See figure 64.

MEWS. A row of stables with living
accommodation above, built at the

back of a town house, especially in
London. They are now nearly all converted into houses or 'mews flats'.

MEXICAN ARCHITECTURE, *see* AZTEC
ARCHITECTURE, MAYAN ARCHI
TECTURE.

MEZZANINE. A low storey between
two higher ones; also called an
entresol.

MICHAEL OF CANTERBURY. A master
mason working *c.* 1300, first at
Canterbury for the cathedral, then in
London, where he was the first master
mason of St Stephen's Chapel (begun
1292) in the palace of Westminster
and probably its designer. A Walter
of Canterbury was in charge of work
at the palace in 1322. A Thomas of
Canterbury was working under him
in 1324 and, in 1331, probably after
his death, was put in charge of work
at St Stephen's Chapel. Thomas may
have died in 1336.

MICHELANGELO BUONAROTTI (1475–
1564). Sculptor, painter, poet, and one
of the greatest of all architects, he was
the archetype of the inspired 'genius' –
unsociable, distrustful, untidy, obsessed by his work, and almost pathologically proud – in fact, the antithesis
of the Early Renaissance ideal of the
complete man so nobly exemplified in
ALBERTI and LEONARDO. Deeply
and mystically religious, he was consumed by the conflicts and doubts of
the Counter-Reformation. As in his
life, so in his art, he rejected all the
assumptions of the Renaissance and
revolutionized everything he touched.
Nowhere was his influence so profound or so enduring as in architecture.
He invented a new vocabulary of ornament, new and dynamic principles
of composition, and an entirely new
attitude to space. His few dicta and his
drawings reveal that he conceived a
building as an organic growth and in
relation to the movement of the spectator. He made clay models rather
than perspective drawings, and appears to have eschewed the type of
highly finished design which could be

turned over to the builders ready for execution. He usually made considerable modifications as the building went up, and it is now impossible to tell exactly how his many incomplete works would have looked had he finished them or how he would have finally realized in stone those compositions which remained on paper – the façade of S. Lorenzo, Florence (1516), or the centrally planned S. Giovanni dei Fiorentini, Rome (1556–60).

His first work in architecture is the exterior of the chapel of Leo X in Castel Sant'Angelo, Rome (1514). In 1515 he received his first major commission, for the façade of BRUNELLESCHI's S. Lorenzo, Florence, which he conceived as an elaborate framework for more than life-size sculpture. In 1520, before his S. Lorenzo design was finally abandoned, he was commissioned to execute the Medici family mausoleum in the new sacristy of the same church, much of which was already built. He produced a revolutionary design in which, for the first time, the tyranny of the orders was completely rejected: windows taper sharply, capitals vanish from pilasters, tabernacles weigh down heavily on the voids of the doors beneath them. But the novelty of his design is less evident in this truculent misuse of the classical vocabulary than in the revolutionary conception of architecture which inspired it. He saw the wall not as an inert plane to be decorated with applied ornaments but as a vital, many-layered organism – hence the extraordinary form of the tabernacles with their strange elisions and recessions. The fact that he developed this new conception while the sacristy was in course of construction accounts for its many inconsistencies. The work was brought more or less to its present state by 1534 but never completed.

In 1524 he was commissioned to design a library for S. Lorenzo, Florence – the famous Biblioteca Laurenziana (reading-room designed 1525, vestibule 1526). The site determined its awkward shape and also limited the thickness of the walls. But he turned both these limitations to good effect, linking the structure to the decoration in a way never before achieved or imagined. Pilasters, which had hitherto been purely decorative elements applied to a structural wall, he used as the supports for the ceiling, while the cross-beams above the pilasters are echoed in mosaic on the floor so that the eye is drawn along the length of the room through a perspective of diminishing oblongs. He counteracted this longitudinal emphasis by stressing the verticality of the vestibule. Here the columns are set like statues in niches so that they appear to be merely decorative, though in fact they carry the roof. Other features are no less perverse – blind window-frames of aedicules with pilasters which taper towards the base, consoles which support nothing, and a staircase which pours forbiddingly down from the library on to the entrance level. There is no figure sculpture, but the whole interior is treated plastically as if it were sculpture.

In 1528–9 Michelangelo was employed on the fortifications of Florence, which he designed, with characteristic perversity, for offence rather than defence. In 1534 he left Florence for Rome, where he spent the rest of his life. His first Roman commission was for the reorganization of the Capitol, to provide a suitable setting for the ancient statue of Marcus Aurelius and an imposing place for outdoor ceremonies (begun 1539). He laid out the central space as an oval – the first use of this shape in the Renaissance – and designed new fronts for Palazzo dei Conservatori and Palazzo del Senatore (neither finished before his death). His designs were strikingly original, e.g., in their use of a giant order embracing two storeys, a device that was soon to become general. In 1546 he was commissioned to complete Antonio da SANGALLO's Palazzo Farnese. He converted the unfinished façade into one of the most imposing in Rome, redesigned the upper floors of the *cortile*, and planned a vast garden to link it with the Villa Farnesina on the far side of the Tiber (not executed). In the conception of this grandiose vista, as in his design for the Porta Pia (1561–5) at the end of a new street from the Quirinal, he anticipated the principles of Baroque town planning.

But his most important Roman commission was, of course, for the completion of St Peter's (1546–64). Here he was faced with the task of finishing a building begun by BRAMANTE and continued by Antonio da Sangallo. He reverted to the centralized plan of the former, but made it much bolder and stronger, and demolished part of the latter's additions. His work on the interior was entirely masked in the C17; on the exterior it is visible only on the north and south arms and the drum of the dome. (The dome itself is by della PORTA and differs substantially from MICHELANGELO's model.) But although his plans were much altered the church as it stands today owes more to him than to any other single architect. In his last years he designed the Capella Sforza, S. Maria Maggiore, Rome (c. 1560), on an ingenious plan rather coarsely executed after his death. He also provided plans for the conversion of the central hall of the Baths of Diocletian into S. Maria degli Angeli (1561), but here his work was completely overlaid in the C18.

The story of his architectural career is one of constant frustration. Not one of his major designs was complete at the time of his death. Yet his influence was none the less great. The Mannerists took from him decorative details which were gradually absorbed into the European grammar of ornament. But it was not until the C17 that architects were able to appreciate and began to emulate his dynamic control of mass and space. Significantly, his true heir was to be another sculptor architect, BERNINI.

MICHELOZZO DI BARTOLOMMEO (1396–1472), a sculptor and architect of extreme elegance and refinement, nevertheless lacked the genius of his great contemporaries Donatello and BRUNELLESCHI. Born in Florence, the son of Bartolommeo di Gherardo who hailed from Burgundy, he worked as assistant to Ghiberti (1417–24), then shared a studio with Donatello (1425–33). In the mid 1430s he began to turn his attention to architecture and succeeded Brunelleschi as Capomaestro at the cathedral in 1446. His first important works were for the Medici family. In about 1433 he added the graceful loggia wings to their castle-cum-villa at Careggi and eleven years later began the Palazzo Medici-Riccardi in Florence, the first Renaissance palace, with massive rusticated basement and slightly smoother rusticated upper floors capped by a prominent cornice. Behind this slightly forbidding fortress-like exterior there is an arcaded *cortile* derived from Brunelleschi's Ospedale degli Innocenti. His Villa Medici at Fiesole (1458–61) is lighter and more elegant in style.

Between 1444 and 1455 he designed the tribune, atrium, cloister, and sacristy of SS. Annunziata. The tribune (completed by ALBERTI) is centrally planned, inspired no doubt by Brunelleschi's S. Maria degli Angeli, but closer to an ancient Roman model, the temple of Minerva Medica. This was the first centralized building to be erected in the Renaissance, and it reflects both a desire to revive an antique form and a preoccupation with the circle as a symbol of the universe and eternity. At Pistoia he built the little church of S. Maria delle Grazie (1452), where he employed the Early Christian and Byzantine form of a square building with central dome and subsidiary domed chapels at the four

147

corners. In about 1462 he was in Milan, probably working on the Medici Bank. He also built the Portinari Chapel in S. Eustorgio, Milan (c. 1462), which owes much to Brunelleschi's S. Lorenzo sacristy. With this chapel he introduced the Renaissance style to Lombardy. From 1462 to 1463 he was in Dubrovnik, where he designed the Palazzo dei Rettori.

MIES VAN DER ROHE, Ludwig (b. 1886), worked under Bruno Paul, and then from 1908 to 1911 in Peter BEHRENS's office in Berlin. His earliest independent designs are inspired by SCHINKEL and the Berlin Schinkel Revival of the early C20 (Kröller House, 1912). At the end of the First World War he was, like GROPIUS, caught up in the frenzy and enthusiasm of Expressionism, and he designed then his revolutionary glass skyscrapers (1919–21). When Germany settled down to its rational responsible style of the later twenties and the early thirties, Mies van der Rohe excelled in this as well (housing, Berlin and Stuttgart, 1925–7). His true greatness as an architect was first revealed in the German Pavilion for the Barcelona Exhibition of 1929, with its open plan and masterly spatial composition, its precious materials – marble, travertine, onyx, polished steel, bottle-green glass – a sign of a striving after the highest quality and the most immaculate finishes. The planning principles of the Barcelona Pavilion were tested for domestic purposes in the Tugendhat House at Brno (1930), a private house.

From 1930 to 1933 Mies van der Rohe was director of the Bauhaus, first at Dessau and then when it moved to Berlin for its last harassed phase of existence. In 1938 he was made Professor of Architecture at the Armour Institute (now Illinois Institute) of Technology in Chicago. In 1939 he designed a complete new campus for the Institute, whose plan has since developed and whose buildings have grown. They are characterized by cubic simplicity – envelopes which easily adapt to the various requirements of the Institute – and a perfect precision of details, where every member makes its own unequivocal statement. These qualities pervade all Mies van der Rohe's work. 'I don't want to be interesting, I want to be good,' he said in an interview. The volume of his work, remarkably small until after the Second World War, has since grown considerably. Among private houses the Farnsworth House at Plano, Illinois (1950), must be mentioned; among blocks of flats the Promontory Apartments (1947) with a concrete frame, and Lake Shore Drive (1951) with a steel frame, both at Chicago; among office buildings, the Seagram Building in New York (1956–9), with a bronze and marble facing. They are all a final triumphant vindication of the style created in the early C20 and assimilated gradually in the thirties, and they do not participate in the neo-sculptural tendencies of the last ten or fifteen years.

MIHRAB. A prayer-niche facing Mecca in a mosque; first appears in the early C8.

MILLS, Robert (1781–1855), who was of Scottish descent, was discovered by JEFFERSON and articled to LATROBE, with whom he stayed from 1803 to 1808. His practice started in Philadelphia in 1808. He designed the former State House at Harrisburg in 1810 with a semicircular portico and a dome over the centre; a circular church at Charleston as early as 1804; an octagonal and a large circular one in Philadelphia in 1811–13 (the latter with 4,000 seats); and then the Washington Monument for Baltimore, an unfluted Doric column (1814–29). His principal later works are governmental buildings for Washington, all Grecian and competent (Treasury, 1836–9; Patent Office, 1836–40; Post Office, 1839 etc.), but his most famous work is the Washington Monument at Washington, won in competition in 1836 and completed only in 1884. It is an obelisk 555 ft high and was originally meant to have a Greek Doric rotunda at its foot. Mills also did engineering jobs and a number of hospitals. The Columbia Lunatic Asylum (1822) has none of the grimness of its predecessors. It is like a monumental hospital (Greek Doric portico), and has all wards to the south and a roof garden. It is of fireproof construction.

MINARET. A tall, usually slender tower or turret, connected with a MOSQUE. Minarets have one or more projecting balconies from which the muezzin calls the people to prayer. The first instance of a tower being utilized for this purpose was probably at Damascus in the early C8 (the Great Mosque). *See figure 60.*

Fig. 60. Minaret

MINBAR. The high pulpit in a MOSQUE.
MINOAN ARCHITECTURE, *see* CRETAN AND MYCENAEAN ARCHITECTURE.
MINSTER. Originally the name for any monastic establishment or its church, whether a monastery proper or a house of secular canons, it came to be applied to certain cathedral churches in England and abroad (e.g., York, Strassburg) and also other major churches (Ripon, Southwell, Ulm, Zürich).

MISERICORD (or MISERERE). A bracket on the underside of the seat of a hinged choir stall which, when turned up, served as a support for the occupant while standing during long services.

MNESICLES. A prominent architect in Periclean Athens. He designed the Propylaea, Athens (437–432 B.C., but never finished).

MODILLION. A small bracket or CONSOLE of which a series is frequently used to support the upper member of a Corinthian or Composite CORNICE, arranged in pairs with a square depression between each pair. *See figure 42.*

MODULE. 1. In classical architecture, half the diameter of a column at its base. 2. In modern architecture, any unit of measurement which facilitates prefabrication.

MODULOR. The system of proportion advanced by LE CORBUSIER in his *Le Modulor* (1951). It is based upon the human figure and is used to determine the proportions of building units.

MOGHUL ARCHITECTURE, *see* INDIAN AND PAKISTANI ARCHITECTURE.

MOLINOS, *see* GILLY.

MOLLER, Georg, *see* GILLY.

MONASTERY. Monasticism originated in Egypt, where the first men to choose a monastic life were hermits. A more organized monastic existence was conceived by St Pachomius (346): monks now still lived on their own like hermits, but so close together that they had a joint chapel and a joint refectory. Such monks are known as coenobites. This form of monasticism reached Europe by way of the South of France and from there entered Ireland (Skellig Michael). But the monastic architecture of medieval England and the Continent is that created in the C6 as the expression of the rule of the order established by St Benedict at Montecassino. Its first surviving complete expression is the plan of *c.* 820 made by a cleric of Cologne for St Gall in Switzerland; here we have the axial arrangement of ranges – the coenobites' layouts were haphazard – the cloister with its arcaded walks, the chapterhouse and dormitory in the east range, the refectory in the range opposite the church,

a Benedictine lay-brother who became the greatest Swiss Baroque architect. His masterpiece is the abbey church at Einsiedeln (begun 1719), a spatial composition of unusual complexity even for a Baroque architect. He also designed the parish church at Muri (1694–8), almost certainly the vast Benedictine abbey church at Weingarten (1714–24), with a façade much like Einsiedeln, and probably the church at Disentis (1696–1712).

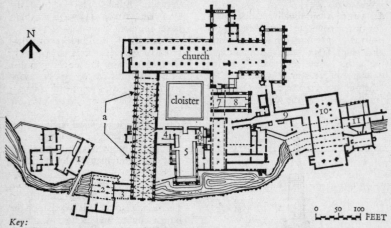

Key:
1. Guest houses
2. Lay brothers' infirmary
3. Reredorter
4. Kitchen
5. Monks' refectory
6. Warming house
7. Upstairs dormitory
   (shown by dotted lines)
8. Chapterhouse
9. Corridor
10. Infirmary hall
11. Infirmary chapel
a = storerooms

Fig. 61. Plan of Fountains Abbey

the stores in the west range. Abbots or priors usually lived near the west end as well, while the infirmary was beyond the claustral parts to the east. There were also a guest house, kitchens, brewhouse, bakehouse, smithy, corn-mills, stables, cowsheds, pigsties, etc., and workshops. In terms of architectural composition the monastery is infinitely superior to the medieval castle. *See figure 61.*

MONOLITH. A single stone, usually in the form of a monument or column.

MOOSBRUGGER, Caspar (1656–1725), born at Bregenz in the Voralberg, was

MORRIS, Robert (1701–54), a relation of Roger MORRIS, was a gifted writer on architectural theory. His books include *An Essay in Defence of Ancient Architecture* (1728), *Lectures on Architecture* (1734), and the posthumous *Select Architecture* (1755) which had a wide influence, e.g., on JEFFERSON's Monticello.

MORRIS, Roger (1695–1749). One of the most gifted and original exponents of PALLADIANISM, though of the CAMPBELL rather than the BURLINGTON school. Most of his work was done in association with the 9th Earl of Pembroke, an amateur architect whose share in his designs is difficult to assess; works include Marble Hill, Twickenham (1728), and the ornamental Palladian Bridge at Wilton (1736). Towards the end of his life he turned neo-Gothic at Inveraray Castle, Argyllshire (1746 etc.).

MORRIS, William (1834–96), was not an architect, but he holds an unchallengeable place in a Dictionary of Architecture because of his great influence on architects. This influence acted in three ways. Morris had begun by studying divinity, then for a short time turned to architecture and worked in the Oxford office of STREET, and subsequently in a desultory way learnt to paint under Rossetti. When he furnished his digs in London, and more so when, after his marriage, he wanted a house, he found that the architecture as well as the design of his day were not to his liking. So he got his friend Philip WEBB to design Red House for him, and this straightforward, red-brick, made-to-measure house had a great deal of influence. Secondly, as the result of the search for satisfactory furnishings, Morris and some friends created in 1861 the firm Morris, Marshall & Faulkner (later Morris & Co.), for which enterprise Morris himself designed wallpapers, the ornamental parts (and, rarely, the figure work) of stained glass, chintzes (i.e., printed textiles), and later also carpets, tapestries and woven furnishing materials, and in the end (1890–6) even books and their type and decoration (Kelmscott Press).

All his designs shared a stylized two-dimensional quality which contrasted with the then prevailing naturalism and its unbridled use of depth; but they also possessed a deep feeling for nature which itself contrasted with the ornamental work of a few slightly older English reformers (PUGIN; Owen Jones). These qualities impressed themselves deeply on younger architects of Norman SHAW's office and school, so much so that some of them took to design themselves. However, they might not have gone so far, if it had not been for Morris's third way of influencing architects, his lectures, which he began in 1877 and continued till his death. They were impassioned pleas not only for better, more considered design, but for abolishing the ugliness of towns and buildings and of the things made to fill buildings, and for reforming the society responsible for towns, buildings, and products. Morris was a socialist, one of the founders of organized socialism in England. That he was also a poet would not be of relevance here if it were not for the fact that his poetry and his prose romances developed from an avowed medievalism to a strongly implied social responsibility for the present. At the same time the medievalism, displayed, for example, by the self-conscious use of obsolete language, is a reminder of the medievalism – admittedly more adapted and even transmuted – of his designs. There is, indeed, a medievalism even in Morris's theory, for his socialism is one of labour becoming once more enjoyable handicraft. And although Morris fervently believed, harking back again to the Middle Ages, that all art ought to be 'by the people for the people', he could never resolve the dilemma that production by hand costs more than by machine, and that the products of his own firm therefore (and for other reasons) were bound to be costly and not 'for the people'. It needed a further reform and a revision of this one essential tenet of Morris's to arrive at the C20 situation where architects and artists design for industrial production and thereby serve the common man and not only the connoisseur. But Morris started the movement, and it was due to him that artists such as van de VELDE or BEHRENS turned designers, and that architects like VOYSEY did likewise. It was also due to him that the criteria of two-dimensional design rose from C19 to C20 standards. Webb's work for Morris had the same effect on furniture design.

MOSAIC. Surface decoration for walls or floors formed of small pieces or *tesserae* of glass, stone, or marble set in a mastic. The design may be either geometrical or representational. Mosaic reached its highest pitch of accomplishment in Roman and Byzantine buildings.

MOSLEM ARCHITECTURE, *see* ISLAMIC ARCHITECTURE.

MOSQUE. A Moslem temple or place of worship. The primitive mosque at Madinah, built by Mohammed in 622, was the prototype: a square enclosure, surrounded by walls of brick and stone, partly roofed. By the end of the C7 all the chief ritual requirements of a congregational mosque had been evolved.

MOTTE. A steep mound, the main feature of many C11 and C12 castles *See* MOTTE-AND-BAILEY.

MOTTE-AND-BAILEY. A post-Roman and Norman defence system consisting of an earthen mound (the *motte*) topped with a wooden tower, placed within a BAILEY with enclosure ditch, palisade, and the rare addition of an internal bank.

MOUCHETTE. A curved DAGGER tracery motif in curvilinear TRACERY, especially popular in the early C14. *See figure 62.*

Fig. 62. Mouchette

MOULDINGS. The contours given to projecting members. *See* Bead, Cable, Keel, Ogee, Roll, Wave moulding; Beakhead; Billet; Bowtell; Chevron; Dogtooth; Hood-mould; Nailhead.

MOZARABIC. The adjective applied to North Spanish architecture built by Christian craftsmen under Moorish influence and having many Islamic features such as the horseshoe ARCH.

MUDÉJAR. The adjective applied to Spanish architecture produced by Christian or Moorish craftsmen under Moorish influence and retaining a distinctly Islamic style with such features as the horseshoe ARCH. Mudéjar motifs persisted in Spanish Gothic architecture and are also to be found in the PLATERESQUE buildings of the C16.

MULLION. A vertical post or other upright dividing a window or other opening into two or more LIGHTS.

MUNTIN. The vertical part in the framing of a door, screen, panelling, etc., butting into, or stopped by, the horizontal rails. *See figure 39.*

MUSHRABEYEH WORK. Elaborate wooden lattices used to enclose the upper windows in Islamic domestic architecture.

MUTULE. The projecting square block above the TRIGLYPH and on the SOFFIT of a Doric CORNICE.

MYCENAEAN ARCHITECTURE, *see* CRETAN AND MYCENAEAN ARCHITECTURE.

MYLNE, Robert (1734–1811), a contemporary and rival of Robert ADAM, descended from a long line of Scottish master masons. He was trained by his father in Edinburgh, then went to Paris (1754) and Rome (1755–8), where he had amazing success by winning First Prize at the Accademia di S. Luca in 1758. But he did not fulfil this early promise. His first work after settling in London (1759) was to be his most famous, Blackfriars' Bridge (1760–9, demolished), in which he introduced elliptical arches. Thereafter he worked extensively both as architect and engineer. His largest country house Tusmore (1766–9, altered by W. Burn 1858), was neo-Palladian. More elegant and original is The Wick, Richmond (1775), a small suburban 'box', while his façade of the Stationers' Hall, London (1800), shows him at his most neo-classical.

N

NAILHEAD. An Early English architectural enrichment consisting of small pyramids repeated as a band. *See figure 63.*

Fig. 63. Nailhead

NAOS. The sanctuary or principal chamber of a Greek temple, containing the statue of the god.

NARTHEX. In a Byzantine church, the antechamber to the NAVE, from which it is separated by columns, rails, or a wall; used by penitents, candidates for baptism, and catechumens, and not to be confused with the porch, which opens on to the street. In a general medieval sense, an enclosed covered ANTECHURCH at the main entrance, especially if the direction is transverse and not east–west and several bays deep; sometimes called a GALILEE. *See figure 10.*

NASH, John (1752–1835), London's only inspired town-planner and the greatest architect of the PICTURESQUE movement. He was the exact opposite of his contemporary SOANE, being self-confident and adaptable, socially successful and artistically conservative, light-handed and slipshod in detail, but with an easy mastery of general effects on a large scale. Again, unlike Soane, he was an architect of exteriors rather than interiors. The son of a Lambeth millwright, he was trained under TAYLOR, but quickly struck out on his own and by 1780 was building stucco-fronted houses, then a novelty in London. In 1783 he went bankrupt, retired to Wales and recovered, then joined the landscape gardener REPTON, with whom he developed a fashionable country-house practice. His output was enormous and in every conceivable style – classical (Rockingham, 1810), Italian farmhouse (Cronkhill, *c.* 1802), castellated Gothic (Ravensworth Castle 1808; Caerhays Castle, 1808), even Indian and Chinoiserie (Brighton Pavilion, 1815). He also built thatched cottages (Blaise Hamlet, 1811). With their fancy-dress parade of styles and irregular planning and silhouettes, these buildings epitomize the Picturesque in architecture. The same picturesque combination of freedom and formality marks his greatest work, the layout of Regent's Park and Regent Street in London (1811 onwards), a brilliantly imaginative conception foreshadowing the garden city of the future. He was already sixty, but still had the enthusiasm and organizing ability to carry the whole scheme through, and he lived to see it finished. The park is sprinkled with villas and surrounded by vast terraces and crescents of private houses built palatially with grandiose stucco façades. There are also cottage terraces and make-believe villages of barge-boarded and Italianate villas. Of his Regent Street frontages nothing now remains except the eye-catcher, All Souls, Langham Place (1822–5). During the 1820s he also planned Trafalgar Square, Suffolk Street, and Suffolk Place, built Clarence House, and Carlton House Terrace, and began Buckingham Palace, all in London. But he shared in his royal patron's fall from public favour, was suspected of profiteering and sharp practice, and his career came to an abrupt end when George IV died in 1830. He was dismissed from Buckingham Palace (completed by Edward Blore) and from the Board of Works of which he had been one of the Surveyors General since 1813. His reputation remained under a cloud for the next fifty years or more.

NAVE. The western limb of a church, that is, the part west of the CROSSING; more usually the middle vessel of the western limb, flanked by AISLES.

NAZZONI or NASONI, Niccolo (d. 1773), who was born near Florence, settled in Portugal (1731), where he became one of the leading Baroque architects. His main work is São Pedro dos Clérigos, Oporto (1732–50), a large and impressive church on an oval plan with a very richly decorated façade, embraced by a bold pattern of ascending staircases.

NECKING. A narrow MOULDING round the bottom of a CAPITAL between it and the shaft of the column.

NEEDLE SPIRE, see SPIRE.

NEO-CLASSICISM. A style which emerged in the C18 in reaction to the excesses of Late BAROQUE and ROCOCO. It aimed at recapturing the sober magnificence of the antique world and producing an architecture embodying the 'noble simplicity and tranquil greatness' which Winckelmann regarded as the outstanding qualities of antique art. Neo-classical buildings are solid, linear, and generally rather severe. They tend towards archaeological precision in the use of the ORDERS, though in some instances classical revivalism became a means towards greater simplicity and rigidity, rather than an end in itself. Several of the theorists of the movement (LAUGIER, LODOLI, LEDOUX) wished to abandon all decoration, even classical decoration.

English PALLADIANISM of the early C18 may be regarded as the first phase of the movement; but by the mid C18 Palladio's interpretation of classical precedents was abandoned, and architects went direct to ancient buildings for inspiration. Such architects as SOUFFLOT, ADAM, and

CHAMBERS studied Imperial Roman architecture at first hand. The measured drawings of Greek Doric buildings which began to be published after the mid-century (e.g., Stuart and Revett's *Antiquities of Athens*, 1762) exerted little immediate influence, but they later contributed to the GREEK REVIVAL, which constituted the final phase of the neo-classical movement.

NERVI, Pier Luigi (b. 1891), took his degree in civil engineering in 1912, but he had a long wait before he was allowed to establish himself as what he undoubtedly is, the most brilliant concrete designer of the age. Nervi is as inventive and resourceful a technician as he is aesthetically sensitive an architect. He is, moreover, an entrepreneur and a university professor, a combination which would be impossible, because it is not permitted, in Britain.

The stadium in Florence was built in 1930–2; it seats 35,000, has a cantilever roof about 70 ft deep and an ingenious flying spiral staircase sweeping far out. In 1935, for a competition for airship hangars, he produced his idea of a vault of diagonally intersecting concrete beams with very massive flying-buttress-like angle supports. Such hangars were built at Orbetello from 1936 onwards. A second type with trusses of precast concrete elements was carried out at Orbetello in 1940. 1948 is the date of Nervi's first great exhibition hall for Turin. The concrete elements this time are corrugated, an idea which went back to experiments of 1943–4. The second hall followed in 1950, again with a diagonal grid. The building of 1952 for the Italian spa of Chianciano is circular, and has a grid vault. By this time Nervi's fame was so firmly established that he was called in for the structure of the Unesco Building in Paris (1953–6). His also is the splendid structure of the Pirelli skyscraper in Milan (1955–8; *see also* PONTI) – two strongly tapering concrete pillars from which the floors are cantilevered. With Jean Prouvé as the other consultant engineer, Nervi was responsible for the enormous new exhibition hall on the Rond-point de la Défense in Paris (1958): a triangle, each side 710 ft long, with three triangular sections of warped concrete roof, rising to a height of 150 ft.

Nervi's most recent buildings are the Palazzetto dello Sport in Rome (1959), circular with V-shaped supports for the dome all round; the Palazzo dello Sport, also in Rome (1960), with a 330-ft span and seating 16,000; and yet another exhibition hall for Turin (1961), a square with sides 520 ft in length, supported on sixteen enormous cross-shaped piers.

NESFIELD, Eden, see SHAW.

NEUMANN, Johann Balthasar (1687–1753), the greatest German Rococo architect, was a master of elegant and ingenious spatial composition. He could be both wantonly sensuous and intellectually complex, frivolous and devout, ceremonious and playful. His churches and palaces epitomize the mid-c18 attitude to life and religion. But despite their air of spontaneity, few works of architecture have been more carefully thought out. His designs are as complex as the fugues of Bach; and for this reason he has been called an architect's architect.

The son of a merchant, he was born in Bohemia but worked mainly in Franconia, where he began in a cannon foundry and graduated to architecture by way of the Prince Bishop's artillery. He visited Vienna and Milan (1717–18), and soon after his return began the Bishop's new Residenz in Würzburg, consulting HILDEBRANDT in Vienna and de COTTE and BOFFRAND in Paris about his designs. The influence of Hildebrandt is very evident in the finished palace, which was executed under a succession of five bishops over some sixty years, though it was structurally complete by about 1744. His main achievements here are

the Hofkirche or Bishop's Chapel (1732–41) and the magnificent ceremonial staircase leading up to the Kaisersaal (designed 1735). This staircase is one of his most original and ingenious conceptions, second only to his superb staircase at Bruchsal (1731, destroyed in the Second World War). He later designed the imposing staircase at Schloss Brühl near Cologne (1744–8). These ceremonial staircases formed the most important single element in each palace and are at the same time masterpieces of engineering ingenuity and exhilarating spatial play.

He was also much employed as a church architect, designing the parish church at Wiesentheid (1727), the St Paulinkirche, Trier (1732–57), and the Kreuzkapelle at Etwashausen (1741). In 1743 he began his great masterpiece, the pilgrimage church of Vierzehnheiligen, where the foundations had already been built by a previous architect. His first task was to accommodate his own ideas to a somewhat inconvenient plan and this provided a spur to his genius. He worked out a remarkably complicated scheme based on the grouping of ovals, both in the vaulting and in the ground plan, which provides a breathtakingly exciting spatial effect, enhanced by the foaming and eddying Rococo decoration. Nowhere did the *mouvementé* quality of Rococo architecture find better expression: not only the statues but even the columns seem to be executing an elegant minuet.

In the larger abbey church at Neresheim (begun 1745) he had a much freer hand and his plan is much simpler, though also based on ovals. By the use of very slender columns to support the large central dome he achieved an almost Gothic airiness. His last work of importance, the Marienkirche at Limbach (1747–52), is on a much smaller scale, but is unusual for him in being no less elaborately decorated on the exterior than inside.

NEUTRA, Richard (b. 1892), is Austrian

by birth and studied in Vienna. In 1912–14 he worked under LOOS, and in 1921–3 he was with MENDELSOHN in Berlin. In 1923 he emigrated to Chicago, but finally settled down at Los Angeles in 1925. He became one of the chief propagators of the new European style in America. His work is predominantly domestic, and mostly of a wealthy and lavish kind. His forte is a brilliant sense for siting houses in landscape and linking building and nature; many of his houses are indeed on a scale rarely matched in Europe (house in the desert, Colorado, 1946). Neutra has also designed some excellent schools and, recently, some religious and commercial buildings. His style is essentially that of his youth; it is unchanged in its direction by the anti-rational tendencies of the last ten or fifteen years.

NEW TOWNS. Those towns designed in the British Isles under the Act of 1946 – eight in the London region (Harlow, Crawley, Stevenage, etc.) and six in other parts of England, Scotland, and Wales. More are now being added. Although most of them have an existing town or village as a nucleus, they are entirely independent units, with populations of about 60,000 to 80,000. The development of these planned towns over the years has been of very great interest from sociological, architectural, and planning points of view.

NEWEL, see STAIR.

NIEMEYER, Oscar (b. 1907), studied in his home town Rio de Janeiro, then worked in the office of Lucio COSTA and received his diploma in 1934. In 1936 he belonged to the team of Brazilian architects working with LE CORBUSIER on the new building for the Ministry of Education at Rio. He built the Brazilian Pavilion for the New York World Fair of 1939 with Costa, but only came fully into his own with the casino, club, and church of St Francis at Pampulha outside Belo Horizonte (1942–3). Here was a completely new approach to architecture, admittedly for non-utilitarian purposes: parabolic vaults, slanting walls, a porch canopy of a completely free double-curving form – a sculptural, frankly anti-rational, highly expressive style. The style suited Brazil with its past of the extremest Baroque; it also became one of the elements in that general turn away from rationalism which is principally familar in Le Corbusier's buildings after the Second World War.

Niemeyer was made architectural adviser to Nova Cap, the organization instituted to create Brasilia, the new capital, and in 1957 became its chief architect. He designed the hotel in 1958 and the exquisite president's palace in the same year. The palace has a screen of freely and extremely originally shaped supports in front of its glass façade, and Niemeyer has varied this theme in other buildings at Brasilia as well (Law Courts). The climax of the architectural composition of the capital is the Square of the Three Powers, with the Houses of Parliament – one with a dome, the other with a saucer-shaped roof – and the sheer, quite unfanciful skyscraper of the offices between. The slab blocks of the various ministries are also deliberately unfanciful. Niemeyer certainly varies his approach according to the spiritual function of buildings. Thus the cathedral of Brasilia, circular, with the excelsior of a bundle of curved concrete ribs rising to the centre, is highly expressive; the block of flats for the Interbau Exhibition in Berlin (Hansa Quarter, 1957) is rational, without, however, lacking in resourcefulness; and Niemeyer's own house outside Rio (1953) is a ravishing interplay of nature and architecture.

NOBILE, Pietro (1773–1854), a neo-classicist of a rather archaeologizing tendency, worked in Vienna (Theseustempel, a miniature of the Haiphesteion, Athens, built to house a statue by Canova, 1820–3; the Burgtor,

1824) and in Trieste (S. Antonio, 1826–49).

NOOK-SHAFT. A shaft set in the angle of a PIER, a RESPOND, a wall, or the JAMB of a window or doorway.

NORMAN ARCHITECTURE is not the architecture of Normandy, but the architecture of Britain from the Norman conquest or just before to the advent of the GOTHIC style, i.e., ROMANESQUE architecture in Britain. The style, from its first appearance at Westminster Abbey as rebuilt by Edward the Confessor (*c.* 1045 etc.), is the direct continuation of that of Jumièges, Mont St Michel, and the churches of Caen: internally with arcade, gallery (ample or small, with large or subdivided openings towards the nave), CLERESTORY, and open timber roof; externally with two façade towers and a square crossing tower (Canterbury, Southwell). The volume of building was enormous. Nearly every cathedral and abbey church was rebuilt, and most of the bishops and abbots came from Normandy. But apart from the system of Normandy, there are also interesting variations of divers origin: the mighty single west tower of Ely on the pattern of Germany; the giant niches of the façades of Tewkesbury and Lincoln, also on German patterns; the gallery tucked in below the arch of the arcade (Jedburgh); and the giant round piers of Tewkesbury and Gloucester, per-haps on a Burgundian pattern (as at Tournus). Ornament is prevalently geometrical (zigzag, CRENELLATION, chain, reel, and similar motifs). Figure sculpture is rarely concentrated on the portals as in the French royal domain (York, Chapterhouse of St Mary); its connexions are rather with the west of France and with Lombardy.

In only one respect does England appear to lead in the European Romanesque style: in the vaulting of Durham Cathedral. For while England has no parallel to the mighty tunnel vaults of so many French naves and the groin vaults of so many German naves, Durham was rib-vaulted from the beginning (1093), and hers seem to be the earliest rib vaults not only of northern Europe but possibly of Europe altogether. While it may be that some of the elementary rib vaults of Lombardy are in fact of earlier date, those of Durham are without question infinitely more accomplished, and they and their descendants in France (Caen, St Étienne; Beauvais) led to the triumphant adoption of rib vaulting at St Denis and in the whole Gothic style, first in France and then everywhere.

NORWEGIAN ARCHITECTURE, *see* SCANDINAVIAN ARCHITECTURE.

NYMPHAEUM. Literally a 'temple of the nymphs' but generally a Roman pleasure-house, especially one containing fountains and statues.

O

OBELISK. A tall tapering shaft of stone, usually granite, monolithic, of square or rectangular section, and ending pyramidally; much used in ancient Egypt.

OCTASTYLE. Of a portico with eight frontal columns.

OCULUS. A round window.

ŒIL-DE-BŒUF WINDOW. A small circular window, similar to that which lights the small octagonal vestibule at Versailles known as the Œil-de-bœuf.

ŒILLET. In medieval architecture, a small opening in fortifications through which missiles could be discharged.

OFF-SET. The part of a wall exposed horizontally when the portion above it is reduced in thickness; often sloping, with a projecting drip mould on the lower edge to stop water running down the walls, e.g., in Gothic buttresses. Also called the water-table. See WEATHERING.

OGEE. A double-curved line made up of a convex and a concave part (s or inverted s).

OGEE ARCH, see ARCH.

OGEE MOULDING, see CYMA RECTA and CYMA REVERSA.

OGIVE. The French name for a pointed arch; hence ogival, a term applied to French Gothic architecture, but no longer used.

OLBRICH, Joseph Maria (1867–1908), studied at the Vienna Academy, gained the Rome prize in 1893, returned to work under Otto WAGNER, and in 1897–8 built the Sezession in Vienna, the premises of a newly founded society of the young progressive artists of Austria and the work which immediately established Olbrich's reputation. The little building, with its strongly cubic walls and its delightful hemispherical openwork metal dome, is both firm in its basic shapes and

fanciful in its details. It is this unusual combination of qualities which attracted Ernst Ludwig Grand Duke of Hessen to Olbrich. So in 1899 Olbrich was called to Darmstadt and there, on the Mathildenhöhe, built the studio house (Ernst Ludwig Haus) and some private houses, including one for himself. The group of houses, some of them by other members of the group of artists assembled at Darmstadt (e.g., BEHRENS), was first built and furnished and then, in 1901, presented as an exhibition, the first of the kind ever held. Later Olbrich added another exhibition building and a tower, the Hochzeitsturm (1907). His last major building was the Tietz department store at Düsseldorf, the closely set uprights of whose façade, deriving from Messel's Wertheim store in Berlin, were very influential.

Olbrich's historical role is among those who succeeded in overcoming the vegetable weakness of ART NOUVEAU by providing it with a firmer system of rectangular co-ordinates. The other leading architects working in this direction were HOFFMANN and MACKINTOSH. Both Mackintosh and Olbrich succeeded in preserving the fancifulness of Art Nouveau sinuosity within this new, more exacting framework, whereas Hoffmann, and of course Behrens to a still greater extent, moved right away from Art Nouveau.

OLMSTEAD, Frederick Law (1822–1903), the principal landscape architect of America after DOWNING's death and America's leading park designer, studied engineering and travelled widely in America, Europe, and even China, before being made superintendent for the Central Park to be formed in New York (1837). He visited European parks in 1859, then for a while supervised a mining estate in California (1863–5) and at that time suggested making the Yosemite area a reserve, and finally returned to the Central Park job in 1865. Olmstead also planned the parks system of Boston, the Niagara reserve, millionaires' estates, and the campus of the newly founded Leland Stanford University at Palo Alto. Among his pupils the most important was his nephew John Charles Olmstead (1852–1920).

OPISTHODOMOS. The enclosed section at the rear of a Greek temple, sometimes used as a treasury.

OPTICAL REFINEMENTS. Subtle modifications to profiles or surfaces to correct the illusion of sagging or disproportion in a building. See ENTASIS.

OPUS ALEXANDRINUM. Ornamental paving of coloured marbles arranged in geometrical patterns.

OPUS INCERTUM. Roman walling of concrete faced with irregularly shaped stones.

OPUS QUADRATUM. Roman walling of squared stones.

OPUS RETICULATUM. Roman walling of concrete faced with squared stones arranged diagonally like the meshes of a net.

ORANGERY. A garden building for growing oranges, with large windows on the south side, like a glazed LOGGIA.

ORATORY. A small private chapel, usually in a house.

ORCHARD, William (d. 1504), master mason, was probably designer of Bishop Waynflete's Magdalen College at Oxford (1468 etc.). The initials W.O. in the ingenious vault of the Divinity School, completed in the 1480s, allow this to be attributed to him, and if so, the similarity in design of the vaults of the Divinity School and the chancel of Oxford Cathedral make him a likely candidate for this even more ingenious vault. Both are characterized by the pendants which look like springers built on non-existing piers between a nave and aisles. It is a technically daring, highly original, and visually most puzzling solution.

ORDER. 1. In classical architecture, a column with base (usually), shaft, capital, and entablature, decorated and proportioned according to one of the accepted modes – Doric, Tuscan, Ionic, Corinthian, or Composite. The simplest is the Tuscan, supposedly derived from the Etruscan-type temple, but the Doric is probably earlier in origin and is subdivided into Greek Doric and Roman Doric, the former having no base, as on the Parthenon and the temples at Paestum. The Ionic order originated in Asia Minor in the mid c6 B.C. The Corinthian order was an Athenian invention of c5 B.C., but was later developed by the Romans, who provided the prototype for the Renaissance form. The Composite order is a late Roman combination of elements from the Ionic and Corinthian orders. The Doric, Tuscan, Ionic, and Corinthian orders were described by VITRUVIUS, and in 1540 SERLIO published a book on the orders which established the minutiae of the proportions and decorations for Renaissance and later architects. See figure 64.

2. Of a doorway or window, a series of concentric steps receding towards the opening.

ORIEL, see BAY WINDOW.

ORIENTATION. The planning of a building in relation to the rising sun, especially of West European churches which are usually orientated east–west with the altar at the east end. But there are many exceptions, e.g., St Peter's, Rome, which is orientated west–east.

ØSTBERG, Ragnar (1866–1945). His international fame derives entirely from his Stockholm City Hall (begun 1909, completed 1923), a building transitional – like BERLAGE's and KLINT's work – between c19 historicism and the c20. The City Hall makes

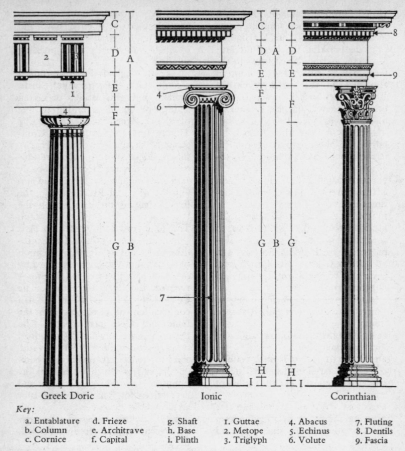

Greek Doric   Ionic   Corinthian

Key:

a. Entablature	d. Frieze	g. Shaft	1. Guttae	4. Abacus	7. Fluting
b. Column	e. Architrave	h. Base	2. Metope	5. Echinus	8. Dentils
c. Cornice	f. Capital	i. Plinth	3. Triglyph	6. Volute	9. Fascia

Fig. 64. Order

extremely skilful use of elements of the Swedish past, Romanesque as well as Renaissance. Its exquisite position by the water suggested to Østberg certain borrowings from the Doge's Palace as well. But these motifs are converted and combined in a highly original way, and the decorative details, rather mannered and attenuated, are typical of the Arts and Crafts of Germany, Austria, and Central Europe in general about 1920. The City Hall was very influential in England in the twenties.

Østberg had studied in Stockholm (1884–91) and travelled all over Europe as well as in America (1893–9). He was professor at the Stockholm Konsthögskola in 1922–32.

OUBLIETTE. In medieval architecture, a secret dungeon reached only through a trapdoor above, and into which a prisoner could be dropped and, presumably, forgotten.

OUD, J. J. P. (b. 1890), worked for a short time under Theodor Fischer in Germany in 1911. In 1915 he met

Tuscan   Roman Doric   Composite

Theo van Doesberg and with him and RIETVELD became one of the pillars of the group De Stijl. Architecturally this group stood for an abstract cubism in opposition to the fanciful School of Amsterdam with its Expressionist compositions (de Klerk, Piet Kramer). There exist designs by Oud in a severely cubic manner which date from as early as 1917 and 1919. In 1918 he was made Housing Architect to the City of Rotterdam, a position he retained until 1927. His most important estates are one at Hoek van Holland (1924–7) and the Kiefhoek Estate (1925–30). Later Oud mellowed, abandoned the severity of his designing, and helped to create that curiously decorative, somewhat playful Dutch style which was nicknamed locally Beton-Rococo. The paramount example is the Shell Building at The Hague (1938–42).

OVERDOOR, *see* SOPRAPORTA.

OVERHANG. A system of timber construction, dating from the C15, in which the upper storey is thrust out over the lower by weighting the overhang of the JOISTS with the upper wall and thereby strengthening them. Overhanging is also known as *oversailing* or *jutting*. An overhang on all four sides of a building needs strong cornerposts. Upon each is projected the *dragon beam* from the centre of the house, which in turn receives the shortened rafters on both sides. All the rafters are mortised into the main beams. On their outer projecting ends is placed the cill of the walling for the next storey. Sometimes curved braces are slotted into the lower framing to strengthen the rafters. *See also* ROOF.

OVERSAILING, *see* OVERHANG.

OVERSAILING COURSES. A series of stone or brick courses, each one projecting beyond the one below it.

OVOLO MOULDING. A wide convex moulding, sometimes called a quarter-round.

P

PADSTONE, *see* TEMPLATE.

PAGODA. A Buddhist temple in the form of a tower, usually polygonal, with elaborately ornamented roofs projecting from each of its many storeys; common in India and China and, as CHINOISERIE, in Europe.

PAINE, James (*c.* 1716–89), was born and lived in London, but worked mainly as a country-house architect in the Midlands and North. Solid and conservative, he carried on the neo-Palladian tradition of BURLINGTON and KENT: he and Sir Robert TAYLOR were said to have 'nearly divided the practice of the profession between them' during the mid-century. His houses are practically planned and very well built, with dignified conventional exteriors and excellent Rococo plasterwork inside, e.g., Nostell Priory (begun *c.* 1733) and the Mansion House, Doncaster (1745–8). Later on he showed more originality. At Kedleston (begun 1761, but soon taken over by ADAM) he had the brilliant idea of placing in sequence the antique basilica hall and a Pantheon-like circular saloon. At Worksop Manor (begun 1763, but only a third built) he envisaged a gigantic Egyptian Hall, and at Wardour Castle (1770–6) he designed a magnificent circular staircase rising towards a Pantheon-like vault. But by this date he had been superseded in the public eye by Robert Adam, and his reputation and practice declined rapidly. As a result of some domestic trouble during his last years he retired to France, where he died. Most of his work is illustrated in his two volumes of *Plans, Elevations and Sections of Noblemen's and Gentlemen's Houses* (1767 and 1783).

PALLADIAN WINDOW, *see* SERLIANA.

PALLADIANISM. A style derived from the buildings and publications of PALLADIO. Its first exponent was Inigo JONES, who studied Roman ruins with Palladio's *Le antichità di Roma* and his buildings in and around Vicenza (1613–14), and introduced the style into England. Elsewhere in northern Europe, especially Holland (van CAMPEN) and Germany (HOLL), Palladian elements appear in buildings – temple fronts, the SERLIANA window, etc. – but here the leading influence was SCAMOZZI rather than Palladio. The great Palladian revival began in Italy and England in the early C18: in Italy it was confined to Venetia, but affected churches as well as secular buildings; in England it was purely domestic. The English revival, led by CAMPBELL and Lord BURLINGTON, was at the same time an Inigo Jones revival. Numerous books were published under Burlington's aegis and these provided a set of rules and exemplars which remained a dominant force in English architecture until late in the C18. From England and Venetia, Palladianism spread to Germany (KNOBELSDORFF) and Russia (CAMERON and QUARENGHI). At Potsdam accurate copies of Palladio's Palazzo Valmarana and Palazzo Thiene were built in the 1750s under the influence of Frederick the Great and his courtier, the Paduan Count Algarotti. From England the style also spread to the U.S.A. in the 1760s (JEFFERSON). Outside Italy the Palladian revival was concerned mainly with the use of decorative elements. Little attention was paid to Palladio's laws of HARMONIC PROPORTIONS except in Italy, where his ideas on this subject were examined by BERTOTTI-SCAMOZZI and elaborated by a minor architect, Francesco Maria Preti (1701–84).

PALLADIO, Andrea (1508–80). The most influential and one of the greatest Italian architects (see PALLADIANISM). Smooth, elegant, and intellectual, he crystallized various Renaissance ideas, notably the revival of Roman symmetrical planning and HARMONIC PROPORTIONS. An erudite student of ancient Roman architecture, he aimed to recapture the splendour of antiquity. But he was also influenced by his immediate predecessors, especially BRAMANTE, MICHELANGELO, RAPHAEL, GIULIO ROMANO, SANMICHELI, and SANSOVINO, and to some extent by the Byzantine architecture of Venice. His style is tinged with MANNERISM, and it was understandably thought to be 'impure' by later neo-classical architects and theorists.

The son of Piero dalla Gondola he was born in Padua and began humbly as a stone mason, enrolled in the Vicenza guild of bricklayers and stone masons in 1524. Then, in about 1536, he was taken up by Giangiorgio Trissino, the poet, philosopher, mathematician, and amateur architect, who encouraged him to study mathematics, music, and Latin literature, especially VITRUVIUS, and nicknamed him Palladio (an allusion to the goddess of wisdom and to a character in a long epic poem he was then writing). In 1545 Trissino took him to Rome, where he studied the remains of ancient architecture for two years. On returning to Vicenza he won a competition for the remodelling of the Early Renaissance Palazzo della Ragione or Basilica and work began in 1549. He surrounded it with a two-storey screen of arches employing a motive derived from SERLIO but henceforth called Palladian. This columned screen gives to the heavy mass of the old building a grandeur wholly Roman and an airy elegance

no less distinctively Palladian. It established his reputation, and from 1550 onwards he was engaged in an ever-increasing series of overlapping commissions for palaces, villas, and churches.

The first of his palaces in Vicenza was probably Palazzo Porto (begun *c.* 1550), on a symmetrical plan derived from ancient Rome, with a façade inspired by Raphael and Bramante but much enriched with sculptured ornament. Soon afterwards he began the more original Palazzo Chiericati (completed in the late C17). This was built not in a narrow street but looking on to a large square; so he visualized it as one side of a Roman forum and designed the façade as a two-storey colonnade of a light airiness unprecedented in C16 architecture. In Palazzo Thiene (begun *c.* 1550, but never completed) he used a dynamic combination of rectangular rooms with a long apsidal-ended hall and small octagons similar to those of the Roman *thermae*. For the convent of the Carità in Venice (planned 1561, but only partly executed) he produced what he and his contemporaries supposed to be a perfect reconstruction of an ancient Roman house; it also contains a flying spiral staircase, the first of its kind. But while his plans became ever more archaeological, his façades broke farther away from classical tradition towards Mannerism, probably the result of a visit to Rome in 1554. Thus the façade of Palazzo Thiene gives an impression of massive power, emphasized by the rustication of the whole wall surface. It has rusticated Ionic columns on either side of the windows – barely emerging from chunky bosses – heavy quoins and *voussoirs* which contrast with smooth Corinthian pilasters. Palazzo Valmarana (begun 1566) is a still more obviously Mannerist composition with a mass of overlapping pilasters and other elements which almost completely obscure the wall surface. The end bays are disquietingly weak, no doubt intentionally. But only in the Loggia del Capitano (1571) did he wilfully misuse elements from the orders. The Loggia is by far his richest building, with a mass of *horror vacui* relief decoration. His last building in Vicenza was the Teatro Olimpico (begun 1580 and finished by SCA-MOZZI) – an elaborate reconstruction of a Roman theatre.

His villas show no similar process of development. In the 1550s he evolved a formula for the ideal villa – a central block of ruthlessly symmetrical plan, decorated externally with a portico and continued by long wings of farm buildings, either extended horizontally or curved forwards in quadrants, as at La Badoera (*c.* 1550–60), and linking the villa with the surrounding landscape. On this theme he composed numerous variations – from the elaboration of La Rotonda (begun *c.* 1550), with its hexastyle porticos on each of its four sides, to the simplicity of La Malcontenta (1560) and Fanzolo (*c.* 1560–5), where the windows are unmarked by surrounds and the decoration is limited to a portico on the main façade, to the stark severity of Poiana, where columns are replaced by undecorated shafts. The use of temple-front porticos for houses was a novelty (Palladio incorrectly supposed that they were used on Roman houses). Sometimes they are free-standing but usually they are attached; and at Quinto (*c.* 1550) and Maser (1560s) he treated the whole central block as a temple front. The relation of the portico to the rest of the building and the sizes of the rooms inside were determined by harmonic proportions.

Temple fronts and harmonic proportions also play an important part in his churches, all of which are in Venice: the façade of S. Francesco della Vigna (1562), and the churches of S. Giorgio Maggiore (begun 1566) and Il Redentore (begun 1576). The latter two appear inside to be simple basilicas, but as one approaches the high altar the curves of the transepts opening out on either hand and the circle of the dome overhead produce a unique effect of expansion and elation. Both churches terminate in arcades screening off the choirs and adding a touch of almost Byzantine mystery to the cool classical logic of the plan.

In 1554 Palladio published *Le antichità di Roma* and *Descrizione delle chiese ... di Roma*, of which the former remained the standard guide-book for 200 years. He illustrated Barbaro's *Vitruvius* (1556) and in 1570 published his *Quattro libri dell'architettura*, at once a statement of his theory, a glorification of his achievements, and an advertisement for his practice. (His drawings of the Roman *thermae* were not published until 1730, by Lord BURLINGTON.)

He was the first great professional architect. Unlike his most notable contemporaries, Michelangelo and Giulio Romano, he was trained to build and practised no other art. Though he was erudite in archaeology and fascinated by complex theories of proportions, his works are surprisingly unpompous and unpedantic. But the rules which he derived from a study of the ancients, and which he frequently broke in his own work, came to be accepted almost blindly as the classical canon, at any rate for domestic architecture.

PALMETTE. A fan-shaped ornament composed of narrow divisions like a palm leaf. *See figure 3.*

PANTHEON DOME. A shallow dome similar to that of the Pantheon in Rome, though not necessarily open in the centre.

PANTILE. A roofing tile of curved S-shaped section.

PARADISE. 1. An open court or ATRIUM surrounded by porticos in front of a church (some medieval writers gave this name to the atrium of Old St Peter's). 2. The garden or cemetery of a monastery, in particular the main cloister cemetery (e.g., Chichester Cathedral, where the cloister-garth on the south side is called the 'paradise'). PARVIS seems to be a corruption of *paradisus*.

PARAPET. A low wall, sometimes battlemented, placed to protect any spot where there is a sudden drop, for example, at the edge of a bridge, quay, or house-top.

PARCLOSE. A screen enclosing a chapel or shrine and separating it from the main body of the church so as to exclude non-worshippers.

PARGETTING. Exterior plastering of a TIMBER-FRAMED building, usually modelled in designs, e.g., vine pattern, foliage, figures; also, in modern architecture, the mortar lining of a chimney flue.

PARKER, Barry, *see* UNWIN.

PARLER. The most famous family of German masons in the C14 and early C15. The name is confusing, as *Parlier* is German for the foreman, the second-in-command, in a masons' lodge and can thus occur in reference to masons not members of the family. The family worked in South Germany, chiefly Swabia, and in Bohemia, chiefly Prague. More than a dozen members are recorded. The most important ones are Heinrich I and his son Peter. Heinrich I was probably *Parlier* at Cologne, and then became master mason at Schwäbisch-Gmünd, one of the most important churches in Germany for the creation of the specifically German Late Gothic style (*Sondergotik*). It is likely that he designed the operative part, the chancel, a design on the hall church principle which had great influence. A Heinrich of the same family, quite possibly he, also designed the chancel at Ulm (begun 1377).

Peter (d. 1399) was called to Prague in 1353, aged only twenty-three, to continue the cathedral begun by Matthias of Arras (*c.* 1340). He com-pleted the chancel and went on to the west, working first on a synthesis of the French cathedral plan with the hall principle of Gmünd and its consequences. In the chapels farther west he developed interesting and fanciful lierne vaults, curiously similar to English ones built a generation and more earlier. He probably designed and worked also at Kuttenberg and Kolin.

The Parlers, and especially Peter, also exercised great influence through the sculptural work of their lodges. Another member of the family, Johann, was master mason of the town of Freiburg from 1359 and perhaps designed the chancel of the minster there (1354–63). Yet another, again called Heinrich of Gmünd, was at Milan Cathedral in 1391–2 ('Enrico da Gamondia'), but left under a cloud, having been unable to win the authorities over to his ideas. The Hans of Freiburg ('Annes de Firimburg') who, also in vain, made a report to the Milan authorities earlier in 1391 may be yet another Parler.

PARQUET. Flooring of thin hardwood (about $\frac{1}{4}$ in. thick) laid in patterns on a wood subfloor and highly polished. Inlaid or plated parquet consists of a veneer of decorative hardwood glued in patterns to squares of softwood backing and then laid on a wood sub-floor.

PARVIS(E). 1. In France the term for the open space in front of and around cathedrals and churches; probably a corruption of *paradisus*, *see* PARADISE. 2. In England a term wrongly applied to a room over a church porch.

PATERA. A small, flat, circular or oval ornament in classical architecture, often decorated with ACANTHUS leaves or rose petals. *See figure 65.*

PATIO. In Spanish or Spanish American architecture, an inner courtyard open to the sky.

PAVILION. An ornamental building, lightly constructed, often used as a pleasurehouse or summerhouse in a

Fig. 65. Patera and rosette

garden, or attached to a cricket or other sports ground; also a projecting subdivision of some larger building, usually square and often domed, forming an angle feature on the main façade or terminating the wings.

PAXTON, Sir Joseph (1801–65), the son of a small farmer, became a gardener and in 1823 worked at Chiswick in the gardens of the Duke of Devonshire. The Duke discovered his exceptional ability and in 1826 made him superintendent of the gardens at Chatsworth. He became a friend of the Duke, with him visited Switzerland, Italy, Greece, Asia Minor, Spain, etc., and in 1854 became Liberal M.P. for Coventry. He designed greenhouses for Chatsworth, the largest being 300 ft long (1836–40), tried out a new system of glass and metal roof construction in them, laid out the estate village of Edensor (1839–41), and so, in 1850–1, moved into architecture proper by submitting, uninvited, his design for a glass-and-iron palace for the first international exhibition ever held. The Crystal Palace was truly epoch-making, not only because this was the most direct and rational solution to a particular problem but also because the detailing of this 1,800-ft-long building was designed in such a way that all its parts could be factory-made and assembled on the site – the first ever example of PRE-FABRICATION. Paxton was also nominally responsible for a few large country houses (Mentmore, Ferrières, for members of the Rothschild dy-

nasty), but they were partly or largely designed by his son-in-law. He was, further, one of the founders of the *Gardener's Chronicle*, and was interested in public parks as well as private grounds (Birkenhead, 1843–7).

PEARSON, John Loughborough (1817–97), was a pupil of Ignatius Bonomi, SALVIN, and HARDWICK. Under Hardwick he worked on the Hall of Lincoln's Inn, where one may well discover his hand in the niceness of the detailing. In 1843 he set up practice, and almost at once was commissioned to design small churches. His first important church is St Peter, Kennington Lane, Lambeth, London (1863–5), French Gothic and vaulted throughout, the ribs of stone, the webs of brick. This building displays his faith in truth in building and in a nobility owed to the religious purpose. Pearson also designed country houses – e.g., Quar Wood, Gloucestershire (1857), which is Gothic, and Westwood, Sydenham, London (1881), which is French Renaissance – but essentially he is a church architect and a Gothicist. His best churches of the 1870s and 1880s are among the finest of their day not only in England but in Europe. Their style is C13 Franco-English, their decorative detail extremely sparing, and their spatial composition quite free and unimitative. Examples are St Augustine, Kilburn Park, London (1870–80); St John, Red Lion Square, London (1874, demolished); Truro Cathedral (1879–1910); St Michael, Croydon (1871); St John, Upper Norwood, Surrey (1880–1); Cullercoats, Northumberland (1884). He was also surveyor to Westminster Abbey.

PEBBLEDASH, *see* ROUGHCAST.

PEDESTAL. In classical architecture, the base supporting a column or colonnade; also, more loosely, the base for a statue or any superstructure. *See figure 66.*

PEDIMENT. In classical architecture, a low-pitched GABLE above a PORTICO,

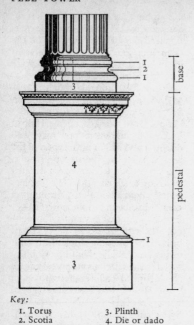

Key:
1. Torus
2. Scotia
3. Plinth
4. Die or dado

Fig. 66. Pedestal: Corinthian

formed by running the top member of the ENTABLATURE along the sides of the gable; also a similar feature above doors, windows, etc. It may be straight-sided or curved segmentally. An *open pediment* is one where the sloping sides are returned before reaching the apex. A *broken pediment* has a gap in the base-moulding. *See figure 2.*

PELE-TOWER. A term peculiar to northern England and Scotland, signifying a small tower or house suitable for sudden defence.

PENDANT. A BOSS elongated so that it hangs down; found in Late Gothic vaulting and, decoratively, in French and English C16 and early C17 vaulting and also stucco ceilings. *See figure 67.*

PENDENTIVE. A concave SPANDREL leading from the angle of two walls to the base of a circular DOME. It is one of the means by which a circular

dome is supported over a square or polygonal compartment (*see also* SQUINCH), and is used in Byzantine (Haghia Sophia, Istanbul) and occasionally Romanesque architecture (Périgueux), and often in Renaissance, Baroque, and later architecture. *See figure 38.*

PENTHOUSE. A subsidiary structure with a lean-to-roof (*see* ROOF); also a separately roofed structure on the roof of a high apartment block.

PERCIER, Charles (1764–1838), studied in Paris under A. F. Peyre and in Rome (1786–92) with his future partner P. F. L. FONTAINE. They worked together from 1794 until 1814, becoming the leading architects in Paris under Napoleon and creating the Empire style in decoration. For their joint works and publications, *see* FONTAINE.

PERGOLA. A covered walk in a garden usually formed by a double row of posts or pillars with JOISTS above and covered with climbing plants.

PERIPTERAL. Of a building, surrounded by a single row of columns.

PERISTYLE. A range of columns surrounding a building or open court.

PERPENDICULAR STYLE, the last phase of the GOTHIC style in England, starts in a few places about 1330 and becomes accepted from about 1360 onwards. Whereas the EARLY ENGLISH ruled for about a century and the DECORATED for not much more than half, the Perpendicular remained current, without essential modifications, to the Reformation, i.e., for nearly two

Fig. 67. Pendant

hundred years. The style is characterized by the stress on straight verticals and horizontals, by slender, vertically subdivided supports and large windows, by window tracery with little fantasy and inventiveness. The signature tune is the panel motif, which is simply an arched panel with the arch cusped. This occurs in rows and tiers everywhere in the tracery, and almost as frequently in blank-wall decoration. Whether the style was created in St Stephen's Chapel in Westminster Palace, the chapterhouse of St Paul's Cathedral, or the south transept of Gloucester Cathedral is controversial. In vaulting the Perpendicular first favours lierne vaults, therein following the inventions of the Decorated, and later fan vaults, introduced about 1350–60 either in the cloisters at Gloucester or in the chapterhouse at Hereford. For the Early Perpendicular the chancel of Gloucester Cathedral is the most important work; for the time about 1400 the nave of Canterbury and the nave of Winchester; for the Late Perpendicular St George's Chapel at Windsor, King's College Chapel at Cambridge, and the chapel of Henry VII at Westminster Abbey (and its predecessor, the chancel vault of Oxford Cathedral). But for the Perpendicular style parish churches are as significant as the major buildings so far noted. The grandest of these are in Suffolk and Norfolk, in Somerset (especially towers), and in the Cotswolds, demonstrating the riches which the wool and cloth trade made for the middle class.

PERRAULT, Claude (1613–88), a doctor by profession and amateur architect, was partly if not mainly responsible for the great east front of the Louvre in Paris (begun 1667), one of the supreme masterpieces of the Louis XIV style. LE VAU and the painter Lebrun were also members of the committee appointed to design this façade. It owes something to BERNINI's rejected pro-

ject for the Louvre, and is notable for its great colonnade or screen of paired columns. He also designed the Observatoire, Paris (1667), and brought out an edition of VITRUVIUS (1673). His brother Charles (1626–1703) was a theorist and Colbert's chief assistant in the Surintendance des Bâtiments.

PERRET, Auguste (1874–1954). The son of the owner of a building and contracting firm. After studies under Guadet he and two brothers joined the firm which was known from 1905 as Perret Frères. His first outstanding job was the house No. 25b rue Franklin near the Trocadéro in Paris, a block of flats on an interesting plan; it has a concrete structure with the concrete members displayed and ART NOUVEAU faience infillings. Next came a garage in the rue Ponthieu (1905), even more demonstratively expressing its concrete frame. The Théâtre des Champs Élysées (1911–14) was originally designed by van de VELDE, but in its final form it is essentially Perret's, and its distinguishing feature is again the proud display of its concrete skeleton. Details, however, are decidedly classical, even if with a minimum of traditional motifs, and Perret was subsequently to develop in that direction. Nevertheless, until the mid-twenties bold concrete experiments still prevailed: the 65-ft arches across the vast workroom of the Esders tailoring establishment (1919), and the decorative concrete grilles of the windows and the concrete excelsior of the steeple of the churches of Notre Dame du Raincy (1922–3) and of Montmagny (1926). Examples of Perret at his most classical – basically the successor to the most restrained French C18 style – are the Museum of Public Works (1937, though with a brilliant curved flying concrete staircase inside) and the post-war work for Amiens (skyscraper 1947) and Le Havre (1945 etc.). The latter includes Perret's last work, the strange centrally planned church of St Joseph.

PERRON. An exterior staircase or flight of steps usually leading to a main, first-floor entrance to a house.

PERSIAN ARCHITECTURE. The nomadic peoples of Persia produced no architecture until after their conquest of Babylon in 539 B.C. The only notable example of the succeeding period is the palace group at Persepolis (518–c. 460 B.C.), which reveals Assyrian influence in the extensive use of animal sculpture for the capitals of columns and in the use of large-scale relief decorations. Relief decorations in brightly coloured glazed brickwork (now in the Louvre, Paris) were also employed at Susa. The Hall of a Hundred Columns at Persepolis, so far as it can be reconstructed, shows that other elements were derived from Egypt though treated with greater lightness and elegance. Buildings erected under the Sassanian dynasty (226 B.C.–A.D. 642) were constructed of bricks and decorated with carved stucco; vaults and domes were much employed, as in the palace at Ctesiphon (A.D. 550). Other partially surviving Sassanian buildings of note are the palaces at Sarvistan (A.D. 350) and at Feruz-Abad (A.D. 223–41).

Persia made an important contribution to the development of ISLAMIC architecture, notably in the design of the cruciform mosque (in which an often very high vaulted niche is placed in each of the four walls of the court), e.g., the Friday Mosque in Isfahan (C12) and Majid-i Shah, Isfahan (1616). The Persians made great use of internal and external revetments of glazed tiles of great beauty. Also they developed the domed tomb-chamber, the most notable being the mausoleum of Uljaitu, Sultaniyeh (c. 1309–13).

PERUVIAN ARCHITECTURE. Vast and impressive remains of stone-built civil, religious, funerary, and military buildings survive in the Andes mountains. It is impossible to estimate their age with any precision; they have been dated variously between c. 13,000 B.C. and c. 3000 B.C., but are now thought to be much later, probably from towards the beginning of the Christian era. Walls were built of huge blocks of finely cut masonry fitted together without cement; doors and windows usually taper towards the top. Small and usually circular sepulchral buildings (kullpis and chullpas) were roofed with slabs of stone. The most important of the early sites is Machu Picchu. Buildings at Chanchan incorporate much carved stone and stucco relief decoration. Numerous large terraced monuments (stepped pyramids with flat tops), built of ADOBES and containing labyrinths of passages and cells, have survived – e.g., Huaca Juliana, Huaca Trujillo, and the Aramburu group, near Lima. The Inca Empire, which succeeded the more primitive cultures (1438–1532), introduced a greater air of sophistication, evident in the buildings of its capital, Cuzco.

PERUZZI, Baldassare (1481–1536). One of the best High Renaissance architects in Rome. His works are much indebted to BRAMANTE and RAPHAEL, but have an almost feminine delicacy which contrasts with the monumentality of the former and the gravity of the latter. Born in Siena, he began as a painter under Pinturicchio. In 1503 he went to Rome, where he was employed by Bramante and assisted him with his designs for St Peter's. He probably built S. Sebastiano in Valle Piatta, Siena (c. 1507), a centralized Greek cross church derived from Bramante. His first important work was the Villa Farnesina, Rome (1508–11), one of the most exquisite of all Italian houses both for its architecture and for its interior decoration (frescoes by Peruzzi himself, Raphael, GIULIO ROMANO, Sodoma, and Ugo da Carpi), which combine to make it the outstanding secular monument of the High Renaissance. The plan is unusual: a square block with an open loggia in the centre of the garden front and projecting wings. The main rooms are on ground level. The façade decoration is rich with two superimposed orders of pilasters crowned with a boldly carved frieze of *putti* and swags in which the attic windows are set.

On Raphael's death (1520) Peruzzi completed his S. Eligio degli Orefici, Rome, and succeeded him as architect of St Peter's. In 1527 he fled from the Sack of Rome to Siena, where he was appointed city architect, but returned soon afterwards. With Antonio da SANGALLO the younger he began the Villa Farnese, Caprarola, on an unusual pentagonal plan (*c.* 1530, completed by VIGNOLA). His last work, Palazzo Massimo alle Colonne, Rome (1532–6), is perhaps his most interesting, for its unorthodox design seems to echo the uneasy atmosphere of Rome in the years after the Sack. The façade is curved; there is a disturbing contrast between the ground floor with its deeply recessed loggia and the papery-thin upper part, with shallow window surrounds on the first floor and curious flat leathery frames round those on the floors above. In the *cortile* the sacrosanct orders are wilfully misused. The self-confidence of the High Renaissance has here given way to the sophisticated elegance and spiritual disquiet of Mannerism.

PEW. A fixed wooden seat in a church, in use at least by the C14. In medieval times pews were partially enclosed at the ends next to the aisles with *bench-ends*, which sometimes rise above the WAINSCOT and terminate in carved FINIALS (*see* POPPYHEAD). A *box-pew* is one with a high wooden enclosure all round and a small door; it is essentially a Georgian type.

PHAROS. A Roman lighthouse.

PIANO NOBILE. The main floor of a house, containing the reception rooms. It is usually higher than the other floors, with a basement or ground floor below and one or more shallower storeys above.

PIAZZA. 1. An open space, usually oblong, surrounded by buildings. 2. In C17 and C18 England, a long covered walk or LOGGIA with a roof supported by columns.

PICTURESQUE. Originally a landscape or building which looked as if it had come out of a picture in the style of Claude or Gaspar Poussin. In the late C18 it was defined in a long controversy between Payne KNIGHT and Uvedale PRICE as an aesthetic quality between the sublime and the beautiful, characterized in the landscape garden by wild ruggedness (chasms, dark impenetrable woods, rushing streams, etc.), and in architecture by interesting asymmetrical dispositions of forms and variety of texture – as in the COTTAGE ORNÉ and Italianate or castellated Gothic country houses of John NASH.

PIER. 1. A solid masonry support, as distinct from a COLUMN. 2. The solid mass between doors, windows, and other openings in buildings. 3. A name often given to Romanesque and Gothic pillars varying from a square to a composite section (*see* COMPOUND PIER).

PIERMARINI, Giuseppe (1734–1808), the leading neo-classical architect in Milan, trained in Rome under VANVITELLI and settled in Milan in 1769. His most famous work is the façade of Teatro della Scala, Milan (1776–8). He also built several vast palaces, all rather severe with long façades on which ornament is reduced to a bare minimum, e.g., Palazzo Reale, Milan (1773), Palazzo Belgioioso, Milan (1779), and Villa Reale, Monza (1780).

PIERRE DE MONTEREAU (or MONTREUIL) (d. 1267), was master mason of Notre Dame, Paris, in 1265. The High Gothic work at St Denis Abbey, begun in 1231, is ascribed to him. On his tombstone he is called *doctor lathomorum*.

PIGAGE, Nicolas de (1720–96), was born at Lunéville and trained in Paris, visited France and Italy, and in 1749 became architect to the Elector Palatine Carl Theodor, for whom all his best work was executed. His masterpiece is Schloss Benrath near Düsseldorf, a large pavilion, apparently of one storey (but in fact of three), somewhat similar to Sanssouci at Potsdam, and decorated internally in the most exquisitely refined and restrained Rococo manner that hovers on the verge of Louis XVI classicism. At Schwetzingen he laid out the Elector's garden (1766), and built a miniature theatre and various follies, including a mosque, a romantic water castle, and a bath-house with a mirror ceiling.

PILASTER. A shallow PIER or rectangular column projecting only slightly from a wall and, in classical architecture, conforming with one of the ORDERS.

PILASTER-STRIP, see LESENE.

PILGRAM, Anton (d. *c.* 1515), was mason and sculptor first at Brno and Heilbronn (at Heilbronn he did the high-spired tabernacle for the Holy Sacrament), and later at St Stefan in Vienna, where the Organ Foot (1513) and the pulpit (1514–15) are his, both very intricate in their architectural forms and both including a self-portrait of the master.

PILLAR. A free-standing upright member which, unlike a COLUMN, need not be cylindrical or conform with any of the orders.

PILLAR PISCINA, see PISCINA.

PILOTIS. A French term for pillars or stilts that carry a building, thereby raising it to first-floor level and leaving the ground floor open.

PINNACLE. A small turret-like termination crowning spires, buttresses, the angles of parapets, etc.; usually of steep pyramidal or conical shape and ornamented, e.g., with CROCKETS. *See figure 78.*

PIRANESI, Giovanni Battista (1720–78), who was mainly an engraver of views of Roman antiquities and an architectural theorist, exerted a profound influence on the development of the neo-classical and Romantic movements. Born in Venice, he was trained as an engineer and architect, and settled in Rome *c.* 1745. His highly dramatic views of Roman ruins and imaginative reconstructions of ancient Rome helped to inspire a new attitude to antiquity. In *Della magnificenza ed architettura de' Romani* (1761) he championed the supremacy of Roman over Greek architecture and in *Parere sull' architettura* (1765) advocated a free and imaginative use of Roman models for the creation of a new architectural style. He put his theories into practice only once, not very successfully, at S. Maria del Priorato, Rome (1764–6), which combines an antique flavour with allusions to the Knights of Malta, who owned the church; but it lacks the power and imagination of his engravings.

PISANO, Nicola (d. *c.* 1280), and his son Giovanni (d. shortly after 1314), the greatest Italian sculptors of their generation, are also recorded as architects. In the case of Nicola we have no documents, but tradition (VASARI) and some stylistic arguments; in the case of Giovanni we are on firmer ground. He appears as master mason of Siena Cathedral in 1290 and at Siena some years earlier, during the time when the cathedral received its Gothic façade. About 1296 he moved to Pisa and was there probably also master mason. Andrea Pisano (d. 1348–9) is not a relation of Giovanni. He is the finest Italian sculptor of the generation following Giovanni's and was also an architect. As such he is traceable in records of Florence Cathedral as master mason probably after Giotto's death in 1337, and at Orvieto Cathedral also as master mason from 1347. However, at Orvieto by that time the most important sculptural and architectural work on the façade was over, and at Florence also nothing architectural can be attributed to him with certainty.

PISCINA. A stone basin in a niche near the altar for washing the Communion or Mass vessels; provided with a drain and usually set in or against the wall south of the altar. A free-standing piscina on a pillar can be called a *pillar piscina*.

PLATERESQUE. Literally 'silversmith-like', the name is given to an ornate architectural style popular in Spain during the C16. It is characterized by a lavish use of ornamental motifs – Gothic, Renaissance, and even Moorish – unrelated to the structure of the building to which it is applied. The main practitioners, many of whom were sculptors as well as architects, included Diego de SILOE, Alonso de COVARRUBIAS, Rodrigo GIL DE HONTAÑÓN.

PLINTH. The projecting base of a wall or column pedestal, generally CHAMFERED or moulded at the top. *See figures 64 and 66.*

PODIUM. 1. A continuous base or plinth supporting columns. 2. The platform enclosing the arena in an ancient amphitheatre.

POELZIG, Hans (1869–1936), studied at the College of Technology in Berlin, and in 1899 was appointed to a job in the Prussian Ministry of Works. In the next year, however, he became Professor of Architecture in the School of Arts and Crafts at Breslau, and in 1903 its director. He stayed till 1916, then became City Architect of Dresden (till 1920), and after that Professor of Architecture in the College of Technology and the Academy of Arts in Berlin. In 1936 he accepted a chair at Ankara, but died before emigrating.

His first building of note was the water tower at Posen (Poznan), built in 1910 as an exhibition pavilion for the mining industry. It is of iron framing with brick infilling and details of exposed iron inside. Of 1911–12 are an office building at Breslau, with the motif of bands of horizontal windows curving round the corner – a motif much favoured in the 1920s and 1930s – and a factory at Luban, equally advanced in its architectural seriousness and its grouping of cubic elements. During and immediately after the First World War Poelzig was one of the most fertile inventors of Expressionist forms, chiefly of a stalagmite or organ-pipe kind. These fantastic forms characterize his House of Friendship (1916), designed for Istanbul, his designs for a town hall for Dresden (1917), and those for a Festival Theatre for Salzburg (1919–20), none of which was executed. However, he did carry out the conversion of the Grosses Schauspielhaus for Berlin (1918–19), with its stalactitic vault and its highly Expressionist corridors and foyer. Later buildings were more conventionally modern (the enormous office building of 1928 for the Dye Trust, I.G. Farben, at Frankfurt and the equally enormous building (1929) for the German Broadcasting Company in Berlin).

POINTED ARCH, *see* ARCH.

POINTING. In brickwork, the strong mortar finishing given to the exterior of the joints.

POLISH ARCHITECTURE of the Middle Ages is at first colonial architecture following German patterns and in the C15 becomes an integral part of German Late Gothic architecture. Wroclaw (Breslau) and Gdansk (Danzig) were German cities, and the churches of Cracow also can be understood only in conjunction with southern Germany and Bohemia. The Gothic town hall of Torun (Thorn) is one of the grandest of the Middle Ages anywhere, and the University of Cracow one of the most interesting of medieval university buildings.

As was the case in Bohemia and Hungary, the Renaissance reached Poland early and was welcomed. The Early Renaissance parts of the Wawel (castle) of Cracow were begun as early as 1502 and the domed chapel of King Sigismond attached to Cracow

Cathedral in 1517; the architects in both cases were Italians. Specially characteristic of the indigenous later C16 and early C17 style are lively top crestings instead of battlements. Many of the architects were still Italian and later again German. Poland has proportionately more Italian, i.e., Renaissance, churches in the C16 and early C17 than Germany.

The Italian church type of the Gesù in Rome was taken over before 1600, and Poland contributed much to the Italianate Baroque of the later C17. The plans of the C18, with their predilection for elongated central themes, show affinities with Bohemia and once more South Germany. Baroque palaces start with Wilanow and the Krasinski Palace at Warsaw in the last quarter of the C17 and culminate in the plans of PÖPPELMANN and other architects of the Electors of Saxony, Kings of Poland. Neo-classicism has left several exceptionally fine buildings in Poland: Ujazdow near Warsaw, including the Lazienki Palace with its excellent interiors; the remodelled interiors of the palace of Warsaw; the grand Wilno Cathedral; Wilno Town Hall; and a number of town and country houses. English influence appeared in picturesque gardens and their furnishings from the 1770s onwards (Arkadia, Nieborow).

POLLAK, Leopoldo (1751–1806), who was born and trained in Vienna, settled in Milan in 1775 and became an assistant to PIERMARINI. His masterpiece is the Villa Belgioioso Reale (1793), a very large and very grand but strangely Frenchified version of PALLADIO, with a rusticated basement, giant Ionic order, and lavish use of sculpture. He also built several villas near Milan and laid out their gardens in the English style, e.g., Villa Pesenti Agliardi, Sombreno (c. 1800).

POLLAK, Mihály (1773–1855), the leading Hungarian classicist, was born in Vienna. His father was an architect, and his step-brother was Leopoldo POLLAK. He studied under his brother in Milan and settled down in Budapest in 1798. His style is moderate, never *outré*, and not very personal. Occasionally he also used Gothic features (Pecs, Cathedral, or Fünfkirchen, 1805 etc.). He built large private houses and country houses, but his *chefs-d'œuvre* are public buildings, notably the Theatre and Assembly Room (completed 1832), the Military Academy (Ludoviceum, 1829–36), and the National Museum with its Corinthian portico and its splendid staircase (1836–45).

PONTI, Gio (b. 1891), designer and architect, was also a painter and draughtsman in the twenties. His drawing reflects the style of the Vienna Sezession (*see* OLBRICH), and his designs for porcelain of around 1925 may also be inspired by the Wiener Werkstätten. Ponti is a universal designer: his *œuvre* includes ships' interiors, theatrical work, light fittings, furniture, and products of light industry. Most of his best work in these fields dates from after the war, e.g., the famous very delicately detailed rush-seated chair (1951). His fame as an architect rested for a long time on three buildings: the Faculty of Mathematics in the Rome University City, dated 1934 and one of the *incunabula* of International Modern architecture in Italy (though preceded by Terragni's few buildings); and then the two twin office buildings (1936 and 1951) designed for the Montecatini Company, both in Milan. The first, with its subdued modernity and its elegant detail, was a pioneer work and at the same time very personal, the second is more conventional. Ponti's finest building is the Pirelli skyscraper in Milan (1955–8), built round a hidden structural concrete core by NERVI; the building is 415 ft high, a slender slab of curtain walling with the long sides tapering to windowless ends.

PONZIO, Flaminio (1560–1613), official

architect to Pope Paul V (Borghese), was able but rather unadventurous; he never developed far beyond the Late Mannerist style in which he was trained. His most notable work is the Cappella Paolina in S. Maria Maggiore, Rome (1605–11), very richly decorated with sculpture and panels of coloured marbles and semi-precious stones. He also built the very long façade of Palazzo Borghese, Rome (1605–13), and the handsome Acqua Paola fountain on the Janiculum (1612).

PÖPPELMANN, Mathaeus Daniel (1662–1736), the architect of the Zwinger at Dresden, a Baroque masterpiece, was born at Herford in Westphalia and began at the court of the Elector of Saxony in Dresden, being appointed Court Architect in 1705. For a state visit in 1709 he built a temporary wooden amphitheatre which the Elector, Augustus the Strong, then decided to replace with a stone construction, the Zwinger. Pöppelmann was sent off to gather ideas in Vienna and Italy, and the building thus owes something both to the Viennese Baroque of HILDE-BRANDT and to Rome and Pozzo's *Prattica della perspettiva*. But it could hardly be more original in general conception – a vast space surrounded by a single-storey gallery linking two-storey pavilions and entered through exuberant frothy gateways – the whole composition resembling a giant's Meissen table-centre. Only a section was carried out (1711–22, damaged 1944 but now rebuilt). His other buildings are far less exciting: Japanisches Palais, Dresden (begun 1715, finished by other architects, and destroyed in the Second World War); the 'Indian' Schloss, Pillnitz (1720–32, with Z. Longuelune), with Chinoiserie roofs and painted figures of Chinamen under the eaves.

POPPYHEAD. An ornamental termination to the top of a bench or stall-end, usually carved with foliage and fleur-de-lis-type flowers, animals, or figures. A poppyhead is in fact a FINIAL.

PORCH. The covered entrance to a building; called a PORTICO if columned and pedimented like a temple front.

PORTA, Giacomo della (*c.* 1537–1602), a Mannerist architect of Lombard origin working in Rome, is notable mainly as a follower of MICHELANGELO, whom he succeeded as architect of the Capitol. Here he finished the Palazzo dei Conservatori to Michelangelo's design with slight alterations (1578) and also built the Palazzo del Senatore (1573–98) with rather more alterations. He followed VIGNOLA as architect of the Gesù, Rome, designing the façade (1573–84), which was destined to be copied for Jesuit churches throughout Europe. In 1573–4 he became chief architect at St Peter's, where he completed Michelangelo's exterior on the garden side and built the minor domes (1578 and 1585) and the major dome (1588–90) to his own design. The large dome is his masterpiece, though it is rather more ornate and much nearer in outline to the dome of Florence Cathedral than Michelangelo's would have been. He also built the Palazzo della Sapienza (begun *c.* 1575); the nave of S. Giovanni dei Fiorentini (1582–92); S. Andrea della Valle (1591, completed by MADERNO 1608–23); Palazzo Marescotti (*c.* 1590), and the very splendid Villa Aldobrandini, Frascati (1598–1603).

PORTCULLIS. A gate of iron or iron-inforced wooden bars made to slide up and down in vertical grooves in the JAMBS of a doorway; used for defence in castle gateways.

PORTE-COCHÈRE. A porch large enough for wheeled vehicles to pass through.

PORTICO. A roofed space, open or partly enclosed, forming the entrance and centrepiece of the façade of a temple, house, or church, often with detached or attached columns and a PEDIMENT. It is called *prostyle* or *in antis* according to whether it projects from or recedes into a building; in the latter case the columns range with the front wall. According to the number of fronted columns it is called *tetrastyle* (4), *hexastyle* (6), *octastyle* (8), *decastyle* (10), or *dodecastyle* (12). If there are only two columns between pilasters or antae it is called *distyle in antis*.

PORTUGUESE ARCHITECTURE. Until about 1500 Portugal participates in the development of Spanish architecture: there are Roman remains (temple at Évora); S. Frutuoso de Montélios is a C7 church on a Greek cross plan with horseshoe apses and domes, clearly inspired by Byzantium; Lourosa is MOZARABIC of 920; and the principal monuments of the Romanesque style also have their closest parallels in Spain. They are the cathedrals of Braga (begun *c.* 1100) and Coimbra (begun after 1150), inspired by Santiago de Compostela, in the style of the so-called pilgrimage churches of France: high tunnel-vaulted naves, arcades and galleries, and no clerestory lighting. On the other hand, they have no ambulatories. Individual buildings of special interest are the Templars' church of Tomar of the late C12, with a domed octagonal centre and a lower sixteen-sided ambulatory, and the Domus Municipalis of Braganza, a low irregular oblong with rows of short arched windows high up.

The Romanesque style died hard; the cathedral of Évora (begun 1186) is still pre-Gothic. The Gothic style was introduced by the Cistercians, and the outstanding Early Gothic building is Alcobaça (begun 1178) on the pattern of Clairvaux and Pontigny, i.e., with ambulatory and radiating chapels forming an unbroken semicircle. Its tall rib-vaulted interior is one of the noblest of the order in all Europe. The monastic quarters are well preserved and very beautiful too. But Alcobaça is an exception, for, generally speaking, the Gothic style does not begin in Portugal until the mid C13. Among the most important buildings are a number of friars' churches (S. Clara, Santarém) and a number of cathedral cloisters (Coimbra, Évora, Lisbon – all early C14).

But Portuguese architecture comes properly into its own only with the great enterprise of Batalha, a house of Blackfriars commemorating the battle of Aljubarrota. It was begun in 1388 with a vaulted nave of steep Spanish proportions and an east end of the type peculiar to the Italian friars. But in 1402 a new architect appeared, called Huguet or Ouguete, and he introduced a full-blown Flamboyant, i.e., a Late Gothic style, mixed with many reminiscences of the English PERPENDICULAR. The façade, the vaults of cloister and chapterhouse, and the chapel of João I are his work. He also began a large octagon with seven radiating chapels east of the old east end, but this was never completed. Here, as in the link with the old east end, the vaults are of complex English types. The climax of the Late Gothic in Portugal is the MANUELINE STYLE, named after King Manuel I (1495–1521). It is the parallel to the Spanish style of the Reyes Católicos and, like it, springs from the sudden riches pouring in from overseas. But whereas the Spanish style is essentially one of lavish surface decoration, the most significant works of the Manueline style show a transformation of structural members as well, especially a passion for twisted piers. These appear at Belem, a house of the order of the Jerónimos (1502 etc.) – together with richly figured vaults and ample surface incrustation – and also at Setúbal (1492 etc.). In addition there are the wildly overdecorated doorways and windows of Golegã and Tomar (1510 etc.). The portal to the unfinished east chapels of Batalha suggests East Indian inspiration. The leading masters were one Boytac, a Frenchman, at Setúbal and Belem, Mateus Fernandes in the portal of Batalha, and Diogo de ARRUDA in the nave and the windows of Tomar.

But Tomar also contains the most important examples in Portugal of the Italian Renaissance in its Roman Cinquecento forms. The buildings in question are the cloister and the church of the Conception (both *c.* 1550). But, as in Spain, the Renaissance had arrived earlier and in playful Quattrocento forms. Among cathedrals the Cinquecento style is represented by Leiria (1551 etc.), the work of Afonso Álvares. His nephew Baltasar designed the Jesuit church of Oporto (*c.* 1590–1610) with its typically Mannerist, high and restless twin-tower façade. Also as in Spain, the Baroque was long in coming, but when it came it was less wild than in the neighbouring country; it influenced Brazil considerably (e.g., the Seminary at Santarém, 1676). The leading Baroque architects are João Turriano (1610–79) and João Antunes (1683–1734), and the most completely Baroque town is Aveiro. Octagonal and round plans are typical of Portuguese Baroque churches. The climax of the Baroque is well within the C18. It appears in the buildings of Niccolò Nasoni (d. 1773), a native of Italy – such as the palace of Freixo and several churches at Oporto – and the buildings of J. F. LUDOVICE (*c.* 1670–1752), a native of Germany – such as the grand abbey of Mafra (1717–70) and the chancel of Évora Cathedral (1716–46).

Opposition to the Baroque set in about the middle of the C18. There were two centres: Oporto, where the large hospital is by John CARR of York (design 1769) and the Terceiros Church has decoration inspired by Robert ADAM; and Lisbon, where rebuilding (to a plan) after the disastrous earthquake of 1755 was done on French principles. The most spectacular piece of the rebuilding is the Terreiro do Paço, the large square facing the Tejo.

POST, George Browne (1837–1913), graduated in civil engineering and then worked in HUNT's office. He conducted his own practice from 1860 and started again after the war in 1868. Post was an eclectic, without commitment to any one style in particular. He was interested in structure and planning, and late in life was partly responsible for evolving the standard American hotel plan with a bath to every room, a system which is complete in the Statler Hotel at Cleveland (1911–12). He did a number of millionaires' residences (Cornelius Vanderbilt, 1889 and 1895) and several prominent office buildings in New York, e.g., the Equitable Building of 1869 (the first with lifts), the New York Times and Pulitzer Buildings (both 1889), and the St Paul Building (1897–9) which, with its twenty-two storeys, was the tallest in New York at that time.

POST, Pieter (1608–69), was a leading exponent of Dutch PALLADIANISM, an unpretentious, placid, and economic form of classicism, characterized by its use of brick with stone dressings and straightforward, almost diagrammatic use of pilasters. His masterpiece is the Huis-ten-Bosch near The Hague (1645–7), but the small Weigh-house at Leiden (1657), with its Tuscan pilasters on a rusticated base and supporting a simple pediment, is more typical. His style, like that of his contemporary van CAMPEN, had great influence, and was later imported into England by Hugh MAY and others.

POSTERN. A small gateway, sometimes concealed, at the back of a castle, town, or monastery.

POWELL & MOYA (A. J. Philip Powell and John Hidalgo Moya, b. 1921 and 1920) established themselves by winning the City of Westminster competition for the large housing estate in Pimlico, later named Churchill Gardens (1946). The clarity, precision, and directness of their style has been maintained in all their later work, such as the Mayfield School in Putney, London (1956), the Princess Margaret Hospital at Swindon (1957 etc.), the ingenious sets for Brasenose College, Oxford (1956 etc.), and the Festival Theatre at Chichester (1962).

PRANDTAUER, Jakob (1660–1726), was the architect of Melk (1702–14), perhaps the most impressive of all Baroque abbeys. The church, with its undulating façade, many-pinnacled towers, and bold dome, is clasped between two long ranges of monastic buildings which stretch forward to form a courtyard. Prandtauer took every advantage of the unusually dramatic site above the Danube to create a picturesque group of buildings which seems to rise out of the rock. The interior of the church (completed by other architects) is rich and *mouvementé*, with an almost Gothic sense of height. Prandtauer's other works are less exciting: the church at Sonntagberg (1706–17), a smaller version of Melk; the handsome open stairway and Marmorsaal at St Florian (1708); alterations to the Gothic cathedral at St Pölten (1722); and town houses in St Pölten.

PRATT, Sir Roger (1620–84), a gentleman amateur, learned and widely travelled, was the most gifted of JONES's followers. His few buildings were very influential, but have all been destroyed or altered. At Coleshill (1650, now destroyed), Kingston Lacy (1663–5, altered by BARRY), and Horseheath (1663–5, destroyed) he invented the type of house later erroneously called the 'Wren' type. Clarendon House, London (1664–7, destroyed), was the first great classical house in London and was widely imitated and copied, e.g., at Belton House, Lincolnshire, by Stanton (1684–6).

PRECAST CONCRETE. Concrete components cast in a factory or on the site before being placed in position.

PREFABRICATION. The manufacture of whole buildings or components in a factory or casting yard for transportation to the site.

PRESBYTERY. The part of the church which lies east of the choir and where the high altar is placed.

PRESTRESSED CONCRETE. A development of ordinary REINFORCED CONCRETE. The reinforcing steel is replaced by wire cables in ducts, so positioned that compression can be induced in the tension area of the concrete before it is loaded. This is done by stretching or tensioning the cables before or after casting the concrete. It results in more efficient use of materials and greater economy.

PRICE, Sir Uvedale (1747–1829), landscape gardening theorist, was a friend of REPTON and R. P. KNIGHT, whom he joined in a revolt against the 'Capability' BROWN style. In reply to Knight's poem *The Landscape* he published a three-volume *Essay on the Picturesque* (1794), which defined the PICTURESQUE as an aesthetic category distinct from the Sublime and the Beautiful as defined by Burke. His approach was more practical than Knight's and laid great stress on the need for landscape gardeners to study the works of the great landscape painters.

PRIMATICCIO, Francesco (1504/5–70), was primarily a decorative painter and sculptor and, as such, head of the First School of Fontainebleau. His few buildings date from towards the end of his career, notably the Aile de la Belle Cheminée at Fontainebleau (1568) and the Chapelle des Valois at St Denis, largely built after his death and now destroyed.

PRINCIPAL, *see* ROOF.

PROFILE. The section of a MOULDING or, more generally, the contour or outline of a building or any part of it.

PRONAOS. The vestibule of a Greek or Roman temple, enclosed by side walls and a range of columns in front.

PROPYLAEUM. The entrance gateway

to an enclosure (usually temple precincts), as on the Acropolis at Athens.

PROSCENIUM. 1. In a Greek or Roman theatre, the stage on which the action took place. 2. In a modern theatre, the space between the curtain and orchestra, sometimes including the arch and frontispiece facing the auditorium.

PROSTYLE. Having free-standing columns in a row, as often in a PORTICO.

PSEUDO-DIPTERAL. In classical architecture, a temple planned to be DIPTERAL but lacking the inner range of columns.

PSEUDO-PERIPTERAL. In classical architecture, a temple with porticos consisting of only pilasters or columns in relief.

PTEROMA. In a Greek temple, the space between the walls and colonnades.

PUGIN, Augustus Welby Northmore (1812–52). His father, Augustus Charles (1762–1832), came from France to London in 1798, became a draughtsman in the office of NASH and later a draughtsman and editor of books on Gothic architecture (*Specimens*, 1821 onwards; *Gothic Ornaments*, 1831). The son helped on these, but soon received decorative and then architectural commissions. He designed furniture for Windsor Castle and stage sets for the theatre (*Kenilworth*, 1831) before he was twenty. He found himself shipwrecked off the Firth of Forth in 1830, got married in 1831, lost his wife one year later, got married again in 1833, lost his second wife in 1844, got married once more in 1849, and lost his mind in 1851.

He had a passion for the sea, and, after his conversion to Catholicism in 1834, a greater, more fervent passion for a Catholic architecture, which had to be Gothic of the richest 'Second Pointed', i.e., late C13 to early C14 in style. He leaped to fame and notoriety with his book *Contrasts* (1836), a plea for Catholicism illustrated by brilliant comparisons between the meanness, cruelty, and vulgarity of buildings of

his own day - classicist or minimum Gothic – and the glories of the Catholic past. Later he wrote more detailed and more closely considered books (*The True Principles of Pointed or Christian Architecture*, 1841, etc.), and in them showed a deeper understanding than anyone before of the connexions between Gothic style and structure and of the function of each member. From these books he even appears a founder father of FUNCTIONALISM, though this is true only with qualifications.

His buildings mostly suffer from lack of means. He was rarely allowed to show in stone and wood the sparkling lavishness he could achieve on paper. He was as interested in furnishings, altars, screens, stained glass, metalwork, as in the building itself. This is how BARRY got him to work for the Houses of Parliament, where not only the Gothic details of the façades but even such fitments as inkstands and hatstands were designed by Pugin. He was a fast and ardent draughtsman. Perhaps his best churches are Cheadle in Staffordshire (1841–6), the cathedral of Nottingham (1842–4), and St Augustine, Ramsgate (1846–51), which he paid for himself and which stands next to his own house. As against earlier neo-Gothic churches, Pugin's are usually archaeologically correct, but often have their tower asymmetrically placed, and this started the calculated asymmetry of most of the best English C19 church design.

PULPIT. An elevated stand of stone or wood for a preacher or reader, which first became general in the later Middle Ages (the AMBO was used in the early Middle Ages). Often elaborately carved, and sometimes with an acoustic canopy above the preacher called a *sounding board* or *tester*. Occasionally found against the outside wall of a church.

PULPITUM. A stone screen in a major church erected to shut off the choir from the nave. It could also be used as a backing for the return choir stalls.

PULVIN. In Byzantine architecture, a DOSSERET above the capital supporting the arch above.

PULVINATED. Convex in profile; a term usually applied to a FRIEZE.

PURBECK MARBLE. A dark conglomerate from the Isle of Purbeck capable of receiving a high polish. In fashion in England from the later C12 onwards and favoured particularly in the C13. Used for COMPOUND PIERS in churches. Purbeck shafts in conjunction with shafts of normal limestone give a striking effect of light and dark. Also used for effigies all over England.

PURLIN, see ROOF.

PYCNOSTYLE. With an arrangement of columns set $1\frac{1}{2}$ times their diameter apart. See ARAEOSTYLE; DIASTYLE; EUSTYLE; SYSTYLE.

PYLON. In ancient Egyptian architecture, the rectangular, truncated, pyramidal towers flanking the gateway of a temple; also, more loosely, any high isolated structure used decoratively or to mark a boundary.

PYRAMID. In ancient Egyptian architecture, a sepulchral monument in the form of a huge stone structure with a square base and sloping sides meeting at an apex: also, more loosely, any structure of this form.

Q

QUADRANGLE. A rectangular court-yard enclosed by buildings on all sides and sometimes within a large building complex. The arrangement is often found in colleges and schools.

QUADRATURA. *Trompe l'œil* architectural painting of walls and ceilings. In the C17 and C18 it was frequently executed by travelling painters who specialized in it and were known as *quadraturisti*.

QUADRIGA. A sculptured group of a chariot drawn by four horses, often used to crown a monument or façade.

QUARENGHI, Giacomo (1744–1817), a very prolific architect, was much admired and patronized by Catherine II of Russia. Born near Bergamo, he went to Rome in 1763 to study painting, but soon turned to architecture. He designed the interior of S. Scolastica, Subiaco (1770–7), in a light, elegant vein of neo-classicism. In 1776 he accepted an invitation to St Petersburg where he spent the rest of his life. His most important building is the English Palace, Peterhof (1781–9), a sternly aloof Palladian house with no decorations apart from a vast projecting portico on one side and a recessed loggia on the other. He employed a similar formula for the State Bank (1783–8, altered) and the Academy of Sciences (1783–7), both in Leningrad. The Hermitage Theatre, Leningrad (1782–5), is smaller and richer.

QUARRY (or QUARREL). A small, usually diamond-shaped pane, or a square one placed diagonally, with which medieval-leaded windows were glazed. The term can also apply to any small quadrangular opening in the TRACERY of a window. The word probably derives from the French *carré*. Various devices and patterns were painted on quarries, particularly during the Perpendicular period.

QUATREFOIL, *see* FOIL.

QUEEN ANNE ARCHITECTURE normally covers the age of William and Mary as well. In building on the grand scale these are the decades of the English Baroque, the decades of Greenwich and Chatsworth, of VAN-BRUGH (Castle Howard, Blenheim) and HAWKSMOOR (Easton Neston), with displays of giant columns and often highly original, self-willed details. On the smaller domestic scale the so-called Wren type of house persisted (*see* STUART ARCHITECTURE). The most important churches are Hawksmoor's. They are of the early Georgian years, but in style belong to the pre-Georgian phase, and are as interesting for their details as for the variety of their spatial solutions. 'Queen Anne' is also the name for the style of about 1870 propagated chiefly by Norman SHAW. It is, in fact, a mixture of the semi-Dutch style of *c*. 1630–60, William and Mary, and Queen Anne.

QUEEN-POST, *see* ROOF.

QUIBIA. The direction in which every Moslem turns when he prays: originally towards Jerusalem, but changed by Mohammed in 624 to Mecca.

QUIRK. A sharp v-shaped incision in a moulding and between mouldings.

QUOINS. The dressed stones at the corners of buildings, usually laid so that their faces are alternately large and small. From the French *coin* (corner). *See figure 68.*

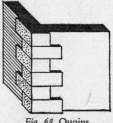

Fig. 68. Quoins

R

RADBURN PLANNING. A planning idea originated in the United States after the First World War by a group including Lewis Mumford, Clarence Stein, Henry Wright, and others. It was first tried out at Radburn, New Jersey. The main object of the plan is the complete segregation of traffic and pedestrians. Areas known as superblocks are ringed by roads from which cul-de-sac service roads lead to the interior. All paths and walks linking the blocks with each other and the town centre pass over or under the roads. Examples of towns planned under some such system are Vällingby, near Stockholm, and Cumbernauld, one of the New Towns in Scotland.

RAGUZZINI, Filippo (d. 1771). The most original and spirited Rococo architect in Rome, where he built the hospital and church of S. Gallicano (1725–6) and Piazza di S. Ignazio (1727–8). The latter is a masterpiece of scenic town planning.

RAINALDI, Carlo (1611–91), was born and lived in Rome. Son of a minor architect, Girolamo Rainaldi (1570–1655), he came into his own only after his father's death. He evolved a typically Roman grand manner notable for its lively scenic qualities and for its very personal mixture of Mannerist and North Italian features with the High Baroque style of his great contemporaries, especially BERNINI. With his father he began S. Agnese in Piazza Navona, Rome, on a conservative Greek cross plan in 1652, but was dismissed in the following year when BORROMINI took over the work. His principal buildings are all in Rome – S. Maria in Campitelli (1663–7); the façade of S. Andrea della Valle (1661–5); the exterior apse of S. Maria

Maggiore (1673); and the artfully symmetrical pair of churches in Piazza del Popolo, S. Maria in Monte Santo and S. Maria de' Miracoli (1662 etc.), which punctuate the beginning of the three main streets radiating into the centre of the city (Bernini replaced him as architect of the former in 1673).

RAINWATER HEAD. A box-shaped structure of metal, usually cast iron or lead, and sometimes elaborately decorated, in which water from a gutter or parapet is collected and discharged into a down-pipe.

RAMP. 1. A slope joining two different levels. 2. Part of a staircase handrail which rises at a steeper angle than normal, usually where winders (*see* STAIR) are used.

RAMPART. A stone or earth wall surrounding a castle, fortress, or fortified city for defence purposes.

RAMSEY, *see* WILLIAM OF RAMSEY.

RAPHAEL (Raffaello Sanzio, 1483–1520). The greatest exponent of High Renaissance classicism in architecture as well as in painting. His buildings are few, but they quickly took their place beside ancient Roman buildings and the late works of BRAMANTE as architectural models. Though he owed much to Bramante, his style is sweeter, softer, and simpler. Born in Urbino, he was trained as a painter under Pietro Perugino at Perugia. An early painting of *The Betrothal of the Virgin* (1504, Brera Gallery, Milan) is dominated by a domed building, which reveals an exquisite sensitivity to architecture and a particular interest in centrally planned structures. In 1508 he settled in Rome, where he was almost immediately employed by Pope Julius II to paint the Stanza della Segnatura in the Vatican, including

The School of Athens with its wonderful architectural perspective of coffered vaults. His first building is S. Eligio degli Orefici, Rome (1509, completed by PERUZZI 1526), a small, centrally planned Greek cross church with a dome of crystalline perfection. The interior, painted pure white, with only the barest minimum of architectural decoration in grey, has an austerity and clarity of form which epitomizes the religious feeling of the Renaissance. He designed Palazzo Vidoni-Caffarelli, Rome (c. 1515, later enlarged in height and length), and probably Palazzo Costa, Rome (demolished), and Palazzo Pandolfini, Florence (c. 1520). These derive from Bramante's Palazzo Caprini with notable variations, e.g., unbroken horizontal lines of rustication on the basement and at Palazzo Costa alternate triangular and segmental pediments above the windows on the first floor, between clusters of three pilasters.

In 1515 he was appointed Superintendent of Roman Antiquities and probably proposed a scheme (also attributed to Bramante) for measuring and drawing all the Roman remains and restoring a large number of them. The most notable result of his archaeological interests was the design for Villa Madama, Rome (begun c. 1516, but never completed), with a circular courtyard and numerous apsed and niched rooms inspired by the Roman *thermae*. The only part completed was decorated with exquisitely subtle stucco reliefs and GROTESQUE paintings by Giovanni da Udine and GIULIO ROMANO, derived from such Imperial Roman buildings as Nero's Golden House. Here Raphael re-created the elegance of Roman interior decoration as effectively as Bramante had reproduced the solemnity and monumental grandeur of Roman architecture. He was appointed architect of St Peter's (1515) with Fra GIOCONDO and A. da SANGALLO, and drew up a basilican

variant to Bramante's plan. His last work was the centrally planned Chigi Chapel in S. Maria del Popolo, Rome (1519), which was completed by the sculptor-architect Lorenzo Lotti (1490–1541).

RASTRELLI, Bartolommeo Francesco (1700–71), the leading Rococo architect in Russia, was the son of an Italian sculptor who went to St Petersburg with LE BLOND in 1716. He studied in Paris under de COTTE and his style is, with occasional Russian overtones, purely French. In 1741 he was appointed official architect to the Tsarina Elizabeth Petrovna, for whom all his main buildings were designed: Summer Palace, St Petersburg (1741–4, destroyed); Anichkov Palace on the Nevski Prospekt, St Petersburg (1744); Peterhof (1747–52), a colossal enlargement of Le Blond's building with lavish if slightly over-ripe Rococo decoration inside; the Cathedral of St Andrew, Kiev (1747–67); and the curious Russo-Rococo Smolny Convent, St Petersburg (1748–55). His masterpieces are the Great Palace, Tsarskoe Selo, now called Pushkino (1749–56), and the Winter Palace, St Petersburg (1754–62), both with immensely long façades, and both painted turquoise-blue with white trim. But he is seen at his best in the delicate little pavilions he designed for Tsarskoe Selo. He was an exquisite miniaturist, usually forced to work on a heroic scale.

RAVELIN. In military architecture, an outwork formed of two faces of a salient angle and constructed beyond the main ditch and in front of the CURTAIN WALL.

RAYMOND, Antonin, *see* TANGE.

RAYMOND DU TEMPLE (active c. 1360–1405). Master of the King's Works in Masonry, and also master mason of Notre Dame in Paris. The king was godfather to his son.

REAR ARCH. The arch on the inside of a wall spanning a doorway or window opening.

REAR VAULT. The small vaulted space between the glass of a window and the inner face of the wall, when the wall is thick and there is a deep SPLAY.

REBATE. A continuous rectangular notch or groove cut on an edge, so that a plank, door, etc. may be fitted into it.

REDAN. A small RAVELIN.

REDMAN, Henry (d. 1528), was the son of the master mason of Westminster Abbey, and is first found working there in 1495. He succeeded his father at the Abbey in 1516 and also worked for the king, holding the post of King's Master Mason from 1519, jointly with William VERTUE, and in the end alone. He was called in with Vertue for an opinion at King's College Chapel, Cambridge, in 1509, and again appears with him at Eton for the design of Lupton's Tower in 1516. He was also Cardinal Wolsey's architect, and may have designed Hampton Court. At Christ Church, Oxford (Cardinal College), he was, jointly with John Lebons or Lovyns, in charge from the beginning (1525).

REEDING. Decoration consisting of parallel convex mouldings touching one another.

REGINALD OF ELY (d. 1471). First master mason, and so probably the designer, of King's College Chapel, Cambridge (begun 1446). However, his design did not include the present fan vaulting; it seems that he intended a lierne vault (*see* VAULT) instead. Reginald in all probability designed Queens' College too (1446 etc.), and perhaps the archway of the Old Schools (begun 1470), now at Madingley Hall.

REGULUS. The short band between the TENIA and GUTTAE on a Doric ENTABLATURE.

REINFORCED CONCRETE. Since concrete is strong in compression and weak in tension, steel rods are inserted to take the tensile stresses which, in a simple beam, occur in the lower part; the concrete is thus reinforced.

RENAISSANCE. The Italian word *rinascimento* (rebirth) was already used by Renaissance writers themselves to indicate the restoration of ancient Roman standards and motifs. Today the term means Italian art and architecture from *c.* 1420 (BRUNELLESCHI) to the mid C16. It was replaced by MANNERISM and BAROQUE, though the old mistaken custom is still occasionally found of extending Renaissance to include the Baroque. In countries other than Italy the Renaissance started with the adoption of Italian Renaissance motifs, but the resulting styles – French Renaissance, German Renaissance, etc.– have little in common with the qualities of the Italian Renaissance, which are details of ancient Roman derivation and a sense of stability and poise. *See also* BELGIAN; CZECHOSLOVAK; DUTCH; FRENCH; GERMAN; HUNGARIAN; ITALIAN; POLISH; RUSSIAN; SPANISH; SWISS architecture.

RENNIE, John (1761–1821), son of a farmer, was trained by an inventive millwright and then at Edinburgh University. In 1784 he was put in charge of installing the new Boulton & Watt steam engine at the Albion Works in London. In 1791 he set up in business on his own. He was first interested in canals (Kennet and Avon), later also in fen drainage, harbours and docks, lighthouses, and also bridges. He designed the Plymouth Breakwater (begun 1806) and Waterloo Bridge (1810), as well as other London bridges. His sons George (1791–1866) and Sir John (1794–1874) were both famous engineers too.

RENWICK, James (1818–95), the son of an English engineer who emigrated to America and became the most prominent man in his field in the United States, graduated at Columbia College, New York, and became famous as an architect of churches (Grace Church, Broadway, 1843 etc. St Patrick's Cathedral, 1853–87). His other best-known buildings are the sweetly picturesque neo-Norman

Smithsonian Institution in Washington (1846), and Vassar College, an essay in a free Renaissance mixture (1865).

REPTON, Humphry (1752–1818), the leading English landscape gardener of the generation after BROWN, was a contemporary of PRICE and KNIGHT, with whose defence of wildness and ruggedness, however, he did not agree. The innovation of his layouts, an innovation which pointed forward into the C19, is the treatment of the garden close to the house not naturally and picturesquely, but formally with parterres and terraces, to which in his late work he added such 'Victorian' motifs as rose-arbours, aviaries, etc. He also was responsible for a certain amount of architectural work though this was mostly left to his sons John Adey (1775–1860) and George (1786–1858). Repton had lived as a country gentleman until a financial setback forced him to make a living out of his passion for gardening. He was at once successful, and the total of parks and gardens treated by him is in the neighbourhood of two hundred. He wrote *Sketches and Hints on Landscape Gardening* in 1795, *Observations on the Theory and Practice of Landscape Gardening* in 1803, *An Inquiry into the Changes of Taste in Landscape Gardening* in 1806, and *Fragments on the Theory and Practice of Landscape Gardening* in 1816. The term 'landscape gardening' is his.

REREDOS. A wall or screen, usually of wood or stone, rising behind an altar, and as a rule decorated.

RESPOND. A half-PIER bonded into a wall and carrying one end of an arch; often at the end of an ARCADE.

RETABLE. An altar-piece, either painted or carved, standing at the back of an altar.

RETAINING WALL. A wall, usually battered, which supports or retains a weight of earth or water; also called a *revetment*.

RETICULATED, *see* TRACERY.

RETRO-CHOIR. The space behind the high altar in a major church.

RETURN. The side or part which falls away, usually at right angles, from the front or direct line of a structure. Two particular uses of the term are: *a.* that part of a dripstone or HOOD-MOULD which, after running downwards, turns off horizontally; *b.* the western row of choir stalls which runs north–south, set against the screen at the west end of the choir.

REVEAL. That part of a JAMB which lies between the glass or door and the outer wall surface. If cut diagonally, it is called a SPLAY.

REVETMENT, *see* RETAINING WALL.

REYNS, *see* HENRY OF REYNS.

RIB. A projecting band on a ceiling or vault, usually structural but sometimes purely decorative, separating the CELLS of a groined VAULT.

RIBBON DEVELOPMENT. The construction of continuous strings of houses along main roads. This was responsible for much spoliation of the English countryside during the first quarter of this century, but was largely halted by the passing of the Ribbon Development Act of 1935.

RIBERA, Pedro de (*c.* 1683–1742), the leading Late Baroque architect in Madrid, carried the CHURRIGUERESQUE style to its ultimate point of elaboration. In the neo-classical period he was held up for derision by one authority, who published a complete list of his buildings as an object lesson to students, with the result that his *œuvre* is unusually well documented. Of Castilian origin, he began working for the city council of Madrid in 1719, and became its official architect in 1726. With the exception of the tower of Salamanca Cathedral (*c.* 1738) and a chapel attached to S. Antonio, Ávila (1731), all his buildings are in Madrid. His most celebrated work is the doorway to the Hospicio S. Fernando (*c.* 1722), an overpowering extravaganza of boldly and somewhat coarsely carved draperies, festoons, top-heavy *estípites*, urns, and flames rising in staccato leaps above the roof-line. In 1718 he built the little church of the Virgen del Puerto, which has an exterior like a garden pavilion, with a picturesque bell-shaped spire, and an octagonal interior with a *camarín* behind the altar. Other works include the Toledo Bridge (1723–4), with elaborately carved tabernacles perched above the arches; the Montserrat Church (1720, incomplete); and S. Cayetano (1722–32, incomplete).

RICCHINO, Francesco Maria (1583–1658). The most important Lombard architect of the early Baroque. His S. Giuseppe in Milan (1607–30) broke away from the prevailing academic Mannerism as decisively as did MADERNO's S. Susanna in Rome (1603). Both in its plan (a fusion of two centralized units) and in its aedicule façade S. Giuseppe is entirely forward-looking. Nearly all his later churches have been destroyed. Of his surviving works the best are the concave façades of the Collegio Elvetico, Milan (1627), and the Palazzo di Brera, Milan (1651–86), with its noble courtyard.

RICHARDSON, Henry Hobson (1838–86), studied at Harvard, and then studied architecture at the École des Beaux Arts in Paris (1859–62), where, after the Civil War, he returned to work under LABROUSTE and then HITTORF. Back at Boston he started a practice, and in 1870 won the competition for the Brattle Square Church, in 1872 that for Trinity Church. These established him as an original, and at the same time a learned architect. His favourite style was a very massive, masculine Romanesque, inspired by architects such as VAUDREMER. But the tower of the Brattle Square Church, with its frieze of figures right below the machicolated top, is Romanesque only in so far as it is round-arched. In 1882 he travelled in Europe, and only then saw French and North-Spanish Romanesque buildings at first hand. The Romanesque suited him as a style: it was direct and powerful, and thus capable of fulfilling American requirements. Rockfaced rustication was also a favourite with him. In fact, he was always attracted by utilitarian jobs. The most monumental of these is the Marshall Field Wholesale Building in Chicago (1885). He also designed small railway stations in the eighties. Before then he had done some small libraries (North Easton, 1877; Quincy, 1880), two buildings for Harvard (Sever Hall, 1878, which is remarkably independent of any stylistic imitation; Austin Hall, 1881, which is Romanesque), and also some private houses (the shingle-faced, very original and forward-pointing Stoughton House at Cambridge, 1882–3; the Glessner House at Chicago, 1885). Richardson was a *bon vivant*, a designer of zest and conviction. His Romanesque was soon widely imitated – to its detriment – but helped greatly in liberating America from the indiscriminate imitation of European revivals. Among his pupils were MCKIM and WHITE, and he also influenced ROOT and SULLIVAN decisively.

RICKMAN, Thomas (1776–1841), moved late from medicine and business into architecture. From sketching and writing about old churches he went on to open a practice as an architect. This was in 1817, the year in which he also published some lectures under the title *An attempt to discriminate the Styles of Architecture in England*. This little book established our terms Early English, Decorated, and Perpendicular. As an architect Rickman is less interesting. His most familiar building (with Henry Hutchinson, a former pupil, as his partner) is New Court, St John's College, Cambridge (1826–31), with the attached so-called Bridge of Sighs. Rickman was a Quaker, but late in life turned Irvingite.

RIDGE. The horizontal line formed by

the junction of two sloping surfaces of a roof. *See figure 69.*

RIDGE-RIB, *see* VAULT.

RIETH, Benedikt (d. 1534). German mason working as Master of the King's Works in Bohemia. His *chef-d'œuvre* at Prague is the Wladislav Hall in the castle with its intricate lierne vault, including curved ribs, and and its curious italizing details of windows and doorways, Quattrocento in style, but including strange Gothic twists. This work must belong to the years 1485–1502. By Rieth also is the Royal Oratory in Prague cathedral, fancifully Late Gothic (*c.* 1490–3). It has ribs in the form of naturalistically imitated branches. At St Barbara Kuttenberg Rieth altered the existing plans for the nave and aisles, and designed the net vault, a vault whose ribs form a net of lozenges (1512 etc.).

RIETVELD, Gerrit Thomas (1888–1964), was the son of a joiner to whom he was apprenticed. He was later in the cabinet-making business. He came into contact with De Stijl in 1919. His most famous design for a building is the Schroeder House, at Utrecht (1924). With the growth of rationalism in architecture he was eclipsed, but once more received work when, in the Fifties, the style of the Twenties began to be revived.

RINALDI, Antonio (*c.* 1709–90). One of the leading Late Rococo architects in Russia. His main works are the Chinese Palace, Oranienbaum (1762–8), with a pretty Chinoiserie interior, and the Marble Palace, Leningrad (1768–72), derived from JUVARRA's Palazzo d'Ormea, but rather more austere and classical, faced with red granite and grey Siberian marble.

RISER, *see* STAIR.

ROBERT DE LUZARCHES. The master mason who began Amiens Cathedral in 1220.

ROCOCO ARCHITECTURE. The Rococo is not a style in its own right, like the BAROQUE, but the last phase of the Baroque. The great breaks in European art and thought take place at the beginning of the Baroque and again at the beginning of Neo-classicism. The Rococo is chiefly represented by a type of decoration initiated in France, by lightness in colour and weight where the Baroque had been dark and ponderous, and, in South Germany and Austria, by a great spatial complexity, which, however, is the direct continuation of the Baroque complexity of BORROMINI and GUARINI. The new decoration is often asymmetrical and abstract – the term for this is *rocaille* – with shell-like, coral-like forms and many c- and s-curves. Naturalistic flowers, branches, trees, whole rustic scenes, and also Chinese motifs are sometimes playfully introduced into *rocaille*. In French external architecture the Rococo is only noticeable by a greater elegance and delicacy. England has no Rococo, apart from occasional interiors. But the playful use of Chinese, Indian, and also Gothic forms in garden furnishings can well be ascribed to Rococo influence.

RODRÍGUEZ, Ventura (1717–85), the leading Spanish Late Baroque architect, began under SACCHETTI at the Royal Palace, Madrid, and was employed by the Crown until 1759. His first important work was the Church of S. Marcos, Madrid (1749–53), built on an oval plan derived from BERNINI's S. Andrea al Quirinale, Rome. In 1753 he built the Transparente in Cuenca Cathedral. In 1760 he became professor at the Madrid academy and his work began to assume a more dogmatic appearance. The Royal College of Surgery, Barcelona (1761), is almost gaunt in its severe renunciation of ornament. His noblest work is the façade of Pamplona Cathedral (1783), with a great Corinthian portico flanked by square towers, archaeologically correct in detail yet still reminiscent of early C18 Rome.

ROLL MOULDING. Moulding of semi-circular or more than semicircular section.

ROMAN ARCHITECTURE. Whereas GREEK ARCHITECTURE is tectonic, built up from a logical series of horizontals and verticals (the Doric temple has been called 'sublimated carpentry'), Roman architecture is plastic with much use of rounded forms (arch, vault, and dome), so that buildings tend to look as if they had been made of concrete poured into a mould. In Greek and Hellenistic architecture the column was the most important member; in Rome the column was frequently degraded to merely decorative uses, while the wall became the essential element. Hence the Roman predilection for the PSEUDO-PERIPTERAL temple (Temple of Male Fortune, Rome, mid CI B.C.; Maison Carrée, Nîmes, 16 B.C.), for the Corinthian order, and for elaborately carved ENTABLATURES and other ornamentation. It was the development of concrete used in conjunction with brick that made possible the construction of the great Roman domes and vaults. Concrete proved as economical of material as of labour, since the masons' rubble could be used for filling. Surfaces were either stuccoed or clad in marble. The earliest concrete dome is C2 B.C. (Stabian Baths, Pompeii), while the earliest large-scale concrete vault is that of the Tabularium in Rome of 78 B.C., where the half-columns are used ornamentally – the first instance of the divorce of decoration and function. The concrete barrel vault on a colossal scale appears in Domitian's Palace, Rome (late CI A.D.). Later vaulted buildings of importance include the Baths of Caracalla (c. A.D. 215), Baths of Diocletian (A.D. 306), and the Basilica Nova of Maxentius (A.D. 310-13), all in Rome.

Roman architecture reached its apogee in the Pantheon, Rome (c. A.D. 100-25, with a dome 141 ft in diameter), which is both a feat of engineering and a masterpiece of simple yet highly satisfying proportions – it is based on a sphere, the height of the walls being equal to the radius of the dome. Comparison of the Pantheon with the Parthenon reveals the contrast between the tectonic and extrovert nature of Greek and the plastic, introvert nature of Roman architecture. This is equally evident in the most typically Roman of all buildings, the BASILICA, which, with its interior colonnades, is like a Greek temple turned outside in. Other typically Roman buildings are: THERMAE, with their rich decoration and complicated spatial play; AMPHITHEATRES, of which the Colosseum, Rome (A.D. 69-79) is the largest; triumphal arches, a purely decorative type of building of which the earliest recorded examples were temporary structures of the C2 B.C. Always of the Corinthian or Composite ORDER, these arches vary from the relative severity of that at Susa near Turin to the elaboration of that at Orange in the south of France (c. 30 B.C.). City gateways were hardly less profusely decorated, e.g., Porta Nigra at Trier (late C3 or early C4 A.D.).

Hadrian's fantastic sprawling villa at Tivoli (c. A.D. 123) illustrates almost the whole range of Imperial Roman architecture at its sophisticated best. Indeed it is perhaps over-sophisticated already. The last great architectural monument of the Roman Empire is Diocletian's Palace at Split in Yugoslavia (c. A.D. 300), built after the Pax Romana had begun to disintegrate. Yet even here the Roman genius for experimentation was still at work. Certain decorative elements, e.g., engaged columns standing on isolated corbels, anticipate the language of BYZANTINE ARCHITECTURE.

ROMANESQUE ARCHITECTURE. The style current until the advent of GOTHIC. Some experts place its origins in the C7, others in the C10:

the former view includes CAROLIN-GIAN in Romanesque architecture, the latter places the beginning of Roman-esque at the time of the rising of the Cluniac order in France and the Ottonian Empire in Germany. The first view also includes ANGLO-SAXON ARCHITECTURE, the second identifies the Romanesque in Britain with the NORMAN.

The Romanesque in the northern countries is the style of the round arch. It is also characterized by clear, easily comprehended schemes of plan-ning and elevation, the plan with staggered apses (*en échelon*) at the east end of churches, the plan with an ambulatory and radiating chapels, plans (mainly in Germany) with square bays in nave, transepts, and chancel, and square bays in the aisles one quarter the area. The composi-tions of the walls also stress clearly marked compartments, e.g., in the shafts which in Norman churches run from the ground right up to the ceil-ing beams.

The Early Romanesque had not yet the skill to vault major spans. Experi-ments began about 1000, but remained rare till after 1050. Then various sys-tems were developed which differen-tiate regional groups: tunnel vaults in France, often pointed (Burgundy, Provence), and also in Spain; groin vaults in Germany; domes in the south-west of France; rib vaults at Durham and in Italy. The spread of the rib vault and the pointed vault, however, is usually a sign of the ap-proaching Gothic style. In the ex-teriors the two-tower façade plus a tower over the crossing is most typical of England and Normandy, whereas screen façades with no towers are characteristic of the south of France, and a multitude of towers over the west as well as the east parts is typical of Germany.

ROMANO, *see* GIULIO ROMANO.

ROOD. Originally the Saxon word for a cross or crucifix. In churches this was set up at the east end of the nave, flanked by figures of the Virgin and St John. It was usually wooden, and fixed to a special beam stretching from RESPOND to respond of the chancel arch, above the ROOD LOFT. Some-times the rood is painted on the wall above the chancel arch.

ROOD LOFT. A gallery built above the ROOD SCREEN, often to carry the ROOD or other images and candles; approached by stairs either of wood or built in the wall. Rood lofts were introduced in the C15, and many were destroyed in the Reformation.

ROOD SCREEN. A screen below the ROOD, set across the east end of the nave and shutting off the chancel.

ROOF

Elements

Braces. Diagonal subsidiary timbers inserted to strengthen the framing of a roof. They can be straight or arched (the arched brace is a refined version of the CRUCK), and connect either a tie-beam with the wall below, or a collar-beam with the rafters below.

Collar-beam. A tie-beam applied higher up the slope of the roof.

Hammerbeam. A horizontal bracket roof, usually projecting at the wall plate level, to carry arched braces and struts, and supported by braces. Ham-merbeams lessen the span and thus allow shorter timbers. They also help to reduce lateral pressure.

King-post. The middle upright post in a roof TRUSS connecting the tie-beam or collar-beam with the RIDGE.

Principals. The main rafters of a roof, usually corresponding to the main bay divisions of the space below.

Purlin. A horizontal timber laid parallel with the wall plate and the ridge beam some way up the slope of the roof, resting on the principal rafters and forming an intermediate support for the common rafters.

Queen-posts. A pair of upright posts placed symmetrically on a tie-beam (or collar-beam), connecting it with the rafters above.

Rafter or *common rafter*. A roof timber sloping up from the wall plate to the RIDGE.

Strut. A timber, either upright, connecting the tie-beam with the rafter above it, or sloping, connecting a King- or Queen-post to the rafter.

Tie-beam. The horizontal transverse beam in a roof, connecting the feet of the rafters, usually at the height of the wall plate, to counteract the thrust.

Wall plate. A timber laid longitudinally on the top of a wall to receive the ends of the rafters.

Wind-braces. Short, usually arched, braces connecting the purlins with the principal rafter and the wall plate, and fixed flat against the rafters. Wind-braces strengthen the roof area by increasing resistance to wind pressure. They are often made to look decorative by foiling and cusping.

See figure 69.

Types

A *Belfast* or *bowstring roof* is constructed with curved timber trusses and horizontal tie-beams, connected by light diagonal lattices of wood.

A *coupled* roof is constructed without ties or collars, the rafters being fixed to the wall plates and ridge pieces.

A roof is *double-framed* if longitudinal members (such as a ridge beam and purlins) are used. Generally the rafters are divided into stronger ones called principals and weaker subsidiary rafters.

A *gambrel roof* terminates in a small gable at the ridge; in America the name is given to a roof with a double pitch like a *mansard* roof.

A *helm roof* has four inclined faces joined at the top, with a gable at the foot of each.

A *hipped roof* has sloped instead of vertical ends.

A *lean-to roof* has one slope only and is built against a higher wall.

A *mansard roof* has a double slope, the lower being longer and steeper than the upper; named after François MANSART.

A *saddleback roof* is a normal pitched roof. The term is most usual for roofs of towers.

In a *wagon roof*, by closely set

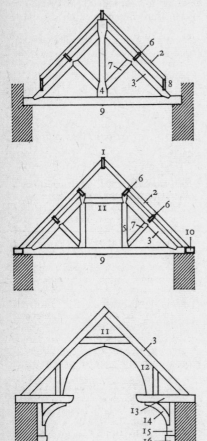

Key:
1. Ridge
2. Common rafter
3. Principal rafter
4. King-post
5. Queen-post
6. Purlin
7. Strut
8. Sole plate
9. Tie-beam
10. Wall plate
11. Collar-beam
12. Arched brace
13. Hammerbeam
14. Brace
15. Wall post
16. Corbel

Fig. 69. Roof: Elements

rafters with arched braces, the appearance of the inside of a canvas over a wagon is achieved. Wagon roofs can be panelled or plastered (ceiled), or left uncovered. Also called a *cradle roof*.

See HYPERBOLIC PARABOLOID ROOF *and figure 70*.

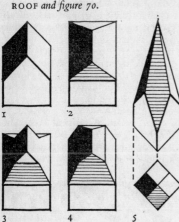

Key:
1. Saddleback   4. Mansard
2. Hipped   5. Helm
3. Gambrel

Fig. 70. Roof: types

ROOT, John Wellborn (1850–91), was born in Georgia, went to school near Liverpool and studied at Oxford. He then took an engineering degree at the University of New York. In 1871 he went to live at Chicago. There he met BURNHAM and went into partnership with him, a suitable partnership to which Burnham contributed his organizational acumen and interest in planning, Root his resourcefulness and his aesthetic accomplishments, which included not only drawing but also music. On the work of the partnership *see* BURNHAM.

RORICZER. A family of C15 German masons, master masons of Regensburg Cathedral for three generations. Wenzel died in 1419. His style was so clearly influenced by Prag and the PARLER that he must have been trained in their lodge. The surviving drawing of the west front of the cathedral may be his. Konrad, his son, is mentioned as master mason to the cathedral in 1456 and 1474. Concurrently, he had the same job at St Lorenz in Nuremberg (*see* HEINZELMANN) from *c.* 1455 onwards. At Regensburg he probably designed the triangular porch. He was consulted for St Stefan in Vienna in 1462, and for the Frauenkirche in Munich in 1475. He must have died *c.* 1475. His son Matthäus was Konrad's second-in-command at Nuremberg from 1462 to 1466. He wrote an important small book on how to set out Gothic finials (published 1486), was also master mason of Regensberg Cathedral, and died shortly before 1495, whereupon his brother Wolfgang was appointed his successor. Wolfgang was executed for political reasons in 1514.

ROSE WINDOW (or WHEEL WINDOW). A circular window with FOILS or patterned TRACERY arranged like the spokes of a wheel.

ROSETTE. A rose-shaped PATERA. *See figure 65*.

ROSSELLINO, Bernardo (1409–64), was primarily a sculptor. As an architect he began under ALBERTI, carrying out his designs for Palazzo Rucellai, Florence (1446–51), and his restoration and alterations to S. Stefano Rotondo, Rome. He designed the *cortile* of Palazzo Rucellai, and in 1451 was appointed architect to Pope Nicholas V, for whom he designed the east end of a completely new St Peter's (never completed). His chief works are the palace and cathedral at Pienza (1460–3), commissioned by Pope Pius II (Piccolomini). The former is a heavier and much less subtle version of Palazzo Rucellai, the latter a not unattractive cross between Alberti's Tempio Malatestiano, Rimini, and S. Maria Novella, Florence. Palazzo Venezia, Rome (1455), has sometimes been attributed to him.

ROSSI, Giovanni Antonio de' (1616–95).

A prolific Roman High Baroque architect. His most important work is in the domestic field, e.g., the grandiose Palazzo Altieri, Rome (1650–4 and 1670–6), and the smaller, more elegant Palazzo Asti-Bonaparte, Rome (c. 1665), which set a pattern for C18 architects in Rome. In his ecclesiastical work he showed a preference for oval plans and lavish sculptural decoration. His Cappella Lancellotti in S. Giovanni in Laterano, Rome (c. 1680), and S. Maria in Campo Marzo, Rome (1676–86), are minor masterpieces of Roman High Baroque.

ROSSI, Karl Ivanovich (1775–1849). The leading architect in post-1815 St Petersburg where he was responsible for replacing the Greek revival style of VORONIKHIN and ZAKHAROV with a much juicier Rome-inspired brand of classicism. The son of an Italian ballerina, he was trained in Russia and visited Italy only in 1802. Until 1816 he worked mainly in Moscow, but his principal buildings are in Leningrad: the huge and richly Roman General Staff Arch, built on a parabolic plan in Palace Square (1819–29); the Alexander Theatre (1827–32); and the Senate and Synod (1829–34). But he is perhaps less important for these buildings than for the town planning around them.

ROTUNDA. A building (often surrounded by a colonnade) or room circular in plan and usually domed, e.g., the Pantheon.

ROUGHCAST. An external rendering of rough material, usually applied in two coats of cement and sand on to which gravel, crushed stone, or pebbles are thrown before the second coat is dry; also called *pebbledash*.

RUBBLE MASONRY. Rough unhewn building stones or flints, generally not laid in regular courses. *Coursed rubble* is walling with the stones or flints roughly dressed and laid in deep courses.

RUDOLPH, Paul (b. 1918), was a pupil of GROPIUS at Harvard. Since 1958 he has been head of the school of architecture at Yale University, New Haven, for which he designed the new building (1961–3). This unmistakably belongs to the trend often termed BRUTALISM, but Rudolph – like SAARINEN and Philip JOHNSON – is one of those who do not feel compelled to adhere to one style in all their designs, even those of the same years, though this in no way impairs his sincerity. Rudolph's other principal buildings are the Sarasota High School (1958–9), Cocoon House, Siesta Key, Florida (1960–1), and the fortress-like Endo Laboratories at Garden City, New York (1961–4).

RUNNING DOG. A classical ornament often used in a frieze, similar to the wave ornament. It is sometimes called a *Vitruvian scroll. See figure 71.*

Fig. 71. Running dog

RUSKIN, John (1819–1900), was not an architect, but the source of an influence as strong on architecture as it was on the appreciation of art. This influence made itself felt in two ways: by the principles which Ruskin tried to establish, and by the styles whose adoption he pleaded for.

As for the former, they are chiefly the principles of the *Seven Lamps of Architecture*, which came out in 1849: Sacrifice (architecture, as against mere building, takes into account the venerable and beautiful, however 'unnecessary'); Truth (no disguised supports, no sham materials, no machine work for handwork); Power (simple grand massing); Beauty (only possible by imitation of, or inspiration from, nature); Life (architecture must express a fullness of life, embrace boldness and irregularity, scorn refinement, and also be the work of men as men, i.e., handwork); Memory (the greatest glory of a building is its age, and we must therefore build for perpetuity); Obedience (a style must be universally accepted: 'We want no new style', 'the forms of architecture already known are good enough for us'). From this last point, Ruskin proceeded to list the styles of the past which are perfect enough to be chosen for universal obedience. They are the Pisan Romanesque, the Early Gothic of West Italy, the Venetian Gothic, and the earliest English Decorated. This last, the style of the late C13 to early C14, had in fact been the choice of PUGIN, of the Cambridge Camden Movement (see BUTTERFIELD), and of SCOTT. But Ruskin's next book on architecture was *The Stones of Venice* (1851–3), which, being in praise of the Venetian Gothic, led admirers of Ruskin to imitate that style – J. P. Seddon, J. Prichard, early STREET, early E. Godwin. But *The Stones of Venice* also contains the celebrated chapter *On the Nature of Gothic*, which for the first time equated the beauties of medieval architecture and decoration with the pleasure taken by the workman in producing them. This was the mainspring that released the work of MORRIS as creator of workshops and as social reformer.

RUSSIAN ARCHITECTURE sets out as a branch of BYZANTINE ARCHITECTURE: stone churches from the C11 to the C16 have the characteristic motifs of the inscribed cross and the five domes. The principal apse is flanked by subsidiary apses, and occasionally there are also subsidiary outer aisles. There must also have been many log-built churches, but none is preserved earlier than the C17.

The Renaissance came to Russia remarkably early. Ivan the Great (1462–1505) was married to a Byzantine princess educated in Rome. A North Italian architect, Aristotile Fioravanti, was brought to Moscow, and another Italian, Alevisio Novi,

arrived shortly before the death of Ivan. He built the Cathedral of St Michael in the Kremlin with Renaissance detail such as the Venetian semicircular shell-gables. But in plan and elevation – inscribed cross and five domes – the Russian tradition was retained by both men, and by others building in the C16. However, a new indigenous type, derived probably from early wooden churches, appeared at Kolomenskoe in 1532, a type with a much simpler central plan and a tall, octagonal, central tower with spire. This type was made more and more decorative in the course of the C16, and invaded the Kremlin in the shape of the fabulous Cathedral of St Basil (1555–60), which is overcrowded with motifs, just as contemporary buildings of the Renaissance–Mannerism of Germany and England can be. The plan, with eight instead of four domed subsidiary spaces round the central tower, is novel too.

Mannerism like this continued throughout most of the C17, until the next foreign assault, that of the Baroque, brought final westernization. The architects were Italian or German (SCHLÜTER, SCHÄDEL, TRESSINI). This Russian Baroque culminated in the work of RASTRELLI at Peterhof, Tsarskoe Selo, and the Winter Palace at St Petersburg in the mid C18. Altogether, it was the palace now that dominated instead of the church. In the churches Baroque forms were applied to versions of traditional Russian concepts. The palaces were appointed inside with a great luxury of precious materials. The turn to the neo-classical style came no later than in most other countries, with the Academy and the Marble Palace at Leningrad by the Frenchman Vallin de la Mothe and the Italian RINALDI. Only a little later Russian architects began to replace foreigners, and STAROV's round tower at Nikolskoe (1774–6) is as severely neo-classical in the new Parisian sense as anything of the same date in the west. Starov had, in fact, studied in Paris and Italy.

Concurrently CAMERON brought the style of Robert ADAM. Grecian in design, again influenced by France, are Thomas de Thomon's Exchange (1804), ZACHAROV's Admiralty (1806), and VORONIKHIN's Mining Academy (1811). Altogether, Leningrad can be considered of all towns the one with the most consistent and the most sweeping classicist character. Meanwhile, churches remained less exactly classical, and the Cathedrals of the Virgin of Kazan and of St Isaac, both at Leningrad, carry their domes as a token both of classicism and of the Russian tradition. The Picturesque in garden furnishings (ruins, etc.) hit Russia in the late C18, and produced the historicism of the C19, as in other countries. What is peculiar to Russia is an Ancient Russian Revival starting, it seems, in the 1830s.

Events of the C20 are the short-lived adherence of Russia to the most advanced architectural concepts of the early 1920s (Lissitzky, Wesnin, Ladovski), and then the enforced return to a grandiloquent classicism (Red Army Theatre, Moscow University, Moscow Underground). Recently this classicism has been disavowed, and large-scale housing programmes with prefabricated elements show Russia at one with Western interests and viewpoints.

RUSTICATED COLUMN. A column whose SHAFT is interrupted by plain or rusticated square blocks. *See figure 72.*

RUSTICATION. Masonry cut in massive blocks separated from each other by deep joints, employed to give a rich and bold texture to an exterior wall and normally reserved for the lower part of it. Various types have been used: *cyclopean* (or *rock-faced*), with very large rough-hewn blocks straight

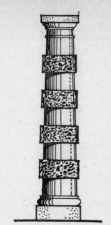

Fig. 72. Rusticated column

from the quarry (or artfully carved to look as if they were); *diamond-pointed*, with each stone cut in the form of a low pyramid; *smooth*, with blocks, neatly finished to present a flat face, and chamfered edges to emphasize the joints; *vermiculated*, with the blocks carved with shallow curly channels like worm tracks. Sometimes it is simulated in stucco or other compositions, e.g., by PALLADIO. *See figure 73.*

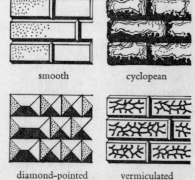

smooth   cyclopean

diamond-pointed   vermiculated

Fig. 73. Rustication

S

SAARINEN, Eero (1910–60), the son of Eliel SAARINEN, went with his father to the United States, but spent part of his study years in Paris (1929–30). In 1931–4 he was at Yale, in 1935–6 back in Finland. His important works are all of the post-war years, and taken together they are admirable for their variety and their sense of visual and structural experiment. The General Motors' Technical Centre at Warren, Michigan (1948–56), has severely rectangular buildings in the style of MIES VAN DER ROHE, plus a circular auditorium with a shallow aluminium-roofed dome, and a highly original water tower 132 ft high as a vertical accent. The Kresge Auditorium of the Massachusetts Institute of Technology at Cambridge (1953–5) has a warped roof on three supports, and the chapel there has undulating inner brick walls and a central opening in a dome whose top is of an abstract-sculptural form. The chapel of Concordia Senior College (1953–8) has a steeply pointed, decidedly Expressionist roof, while the Yale University Hockey Rink (1953–9) has a central arch of double curve spanning the length, not the width of the building. The Trans-World Airline's Kennedy Terminal (1956–62), with its two dramatically outward-swinging arches, is consciously symbolic of flight and has elements inside of almost GAUDÍ-like heavy curving. After that the T. J. Watson Research Centre at Yorktown, New York (1957–61), is, with its 1000-ft curved shape, perfectly crisp and unemotional; but the Ezra Stiles and Morse Colleges at Yale (1958–62), a unified composition, have the stepping-for-ward–backward-and-upward movement so characteristic of Louis KAHN's Medical Research Building in Phila-delphia, begun one year earlier. Saarinen's last fling was the Dulles Airport for Washington (1958–63), with a long down-curving roof ridge on lines of closely set, heavy and out-ward-leaning concrete supports. Saari-nen also designed the United States Embassies in London (1955–61) and Oslo (1959 etc.).

SAARINEN, Eliel (1873–1950). His most famous building is the railway station at Helsinki, which was built in 1905–14 after a competition he won in 1904. The style is inspired by the Vienna Sezes-sion (see OLBRICH), but in a highly original version, and the building takes its place in the series of outstand-ing Central European railway stations characteristic of the years from the end of the C19 to the First World War (Hamburg begun 1903; Leipzig, 1905; Karlsruhe, 1908; Stuttgart, 1911). Saarinen took part in the Chicago Tribune competition of 1922, and his design, though unsuccessful, was much admired. As a result he left Finland and emigrated to the United States, where his best-known buildings are Cran-brook School (1925 etc., 1929 etc.) and Christ Church, Minneapolis (1949).

SACCHETTI, Giovanni Battista (1700–64). A pupil of JUVARRA, whom he followed to Spain and whose designs he executed for the garden façade of the palace La Granja at S. Ildefonso (1736–42). His main work is the Royal Palace, Madrid (begun 1738), where he greatly enlarged Juvarra's scheme by reference to BERNINI's Louvre project: the result is imposing, almost overpowering and rather top-heavy. He also laid out the area of the city surrounding the palace.

SACCONI, Count Giuseppe (1853–1905). His *magnum opus* is the National

Monument to Victor Emmanuel II in the centre of Rome, won in competition in 1884. Among other works the Assicurazioni Generali in Piazza Venezia, Rome (1902–7) might be mentioned.

SADDLE BARS. In CASEMENT glazing, the small iron bars to which the lead panels are tied.

SADDLE STONE, see APEX STONE.

SADDLEBACK ROOF, see ROOF.

SAKAKURA, Junzo, see TANGE.

SALLY-PORT. A POSTERN gate or passage underground from the inner to the outer works of a fortification.

SALOMÓNICA. The Spanish word for barley-sugar column, a feature much used in Spanish Baroque architecture.

SALVI, Nicola (1697–1751), designed the Trevi Fountain in Rome (1732–62), a Late Baroque masterpiece. It consists of a classical palace-façade, based on a Roman triumphal arch; this is set on an enormous artificial outcrop of rock out of which fountains gush into a lake-size basin at the bottom. Marble tritons and Neptune in a shell preside over the whole fantastic composition.

SALVIN, Anthony (1799–1881), who came of an old North Country family, was the son of a general. A pupil of NASH, he was a recognized authority on the restoration and improvement of castles, and his work in that field includes the Tower of London, Windsor, Caernarvon, Durham, Warwick, Alnwick, and Rockingham. But he by no means devoted himself exclusively to castles, though he was emphatically a domestic rather than an ecclesiastical architect. The range of styles used by him includes the sober Tudor of Mamhead in Devon (1828, a remarkably early use of the Tudor style), the lush Italian Renaissance interiors of Alnwick (1854 etc., not designed but approved by him), and the elaborate Jacobean of Thoresby, Nottinghamshire (1864–75). But his most stunning building is quite an early one: Harlax-ton in Lincolnshire (1834 etc.), which is in an elaborate, indeed grossly exuberant, Elizabethan. The building was carried on by W. Burn.

SANCTUARY. Area around the main altar of a church (see PRESBYTERY).

SANFELICE, Ferdinando (1675–1750), a leading Neapolitan architect of his day, was spirited, light-hearted, and unorthodox. He is notable especially for his ingenious scenographic staircases, e.g., Palazzo Sanfelice, Palazzo Serra Cassano.

SANGALLO, Antonio da (Antonio Giamberti), the elder (1455–1534), was born in Florence. His only notable building is one of the great masterpieces of Renaissance architecture, S. Biagio, Montepulciano (c. 1519–26). It was inspired by BRAMANTE's plan for St Peter's, i.e., a Greek cross with central dome and four towers (only one of which was built) between the arms.

SANGALLO, Antonio da (Antonio Giamberti), the younger (1485–1546), who was born in Florence, was the most notable member of the Sangallo family: nephew of Antonio the elder and Giuliano. He became the leading High Renaissance architect in Rome for two decades after RAPHAEL's death. He began as an architectural draughtsman, employed first by BRAMANTE then by PERUZZI. In 1520 he became Raphael's assistant as architect at St Peter's, and was employed there to strengthen Bramante's work. His masterpiece is Palazzo Farnese, Rome (begun 1534, completed after 1546 by MICHELANGELO), the most monumental of Renaissance palaces. The façade is astylar and the walls are smooth except for string courses dividing the storeys and bold quoins, which combine to give a horizontal emphasis stressing the gravity of the composition. It is at once sober, elegant, and restful. Several other palaces have been attributed to him, notably Palazzo Sacchetti, Rome (begun 1542). In 1539 he became chief architect of

St Peter's, and supplied designs for the alteration of Bramante's plan (not executed). He designed the interior of the Capella Paolina in the Vatican (1540). For many years he was employed as a military engineer on the fortifications around Rome. On his death he was succeeded as architect of St Peter's by Michelangelo, whose dynamic style makes a striking contrast to Sangallo's suave, self-confident classicism.

SANGALLO, Giuliano da (Giuliano Giamberti, 1445–1516), military engineer and sculptor as well as architect, was born in Florence. The brother of Antonio da Sangallo the elder, he was one of the best followers of BRUNELLESCHI, and maintained the Early Renaissance style into the age of BRAMANTE and RAPHAEL. Most of his buildings are in and around Florence: Villa del Poggio a Caiano (1480–5, later altered internally); S. Maria delle Carceri, Prato (1485), the first Renaissance church on a Greek cross plan, with a marble-clad exterior and Brunelleschian interior; and Palazzo Gondi, Florence (1490–4), with a rusticated façade deriving from Palazzo Medici-Riccardi and a monumental staircase rising from the interior courtyard. He also worked in Rome, where he built S. Maria dell'Anima (1514) and provided a project for St Peter's (c. 1514).

SANMICHELI, Michele (c. 1484–1559), the leading Mannerist architect in Verona, was famous as a military engineer; most of his works have a rather fortress-like appearance, and the façade he designed for S. Maria in Organo, Verona (1547), might almost be mistaken for one of the fortified gateways to the city. He is often compared with PALLADIO, who was indebted to him and succeeded him as the leading architect in the Veneto, but there is a striking contrast between the massive muscularity of Sanmicheli's works and the far more intellectual and polished buildings of Palladio.

Born in Verona, the son of an architect, he went to Rome c. 1500. He supervised work on the Gothic façade of Orvieto Cathedral (1510–24), where he also designed the altar of the Magi (1515). In 1526 he was employed by the Pope on the fortifications of Parma and Piacenza, and in the following year he settled in Verona. He was much in demand as a military architect, fortifying Legnago (1529), in charge of the fortifications at Verona (from 1530) and Venice (from 1535), and also in Corfu and Crete. The buildings he designed in this capacity are among his best – boldly rusticated gateways and whole fortresses with robust Doric columns and a few strongly effective ornaments such as coats of arms and giant heads frowning out of keystones, e.g., Porta Nuova, Verona (1539–50), Forte di S. Andrea a Lido, Venice (1535–49), Porta S. Zeno, Verona (1542), and most forceful of all, the Porta Palio, Verona (1557).

His palaces begin in the tradition of BRAMANTE and RAPHAEL with Palazzo Pompei, Verona (c. 1529), but he soon developed a more individual style, making much play with strong contrasts of light and shade. Palazzo Canossa, Verona (c. 1530), has a very high rusticated base and simplified Serlian windows on the first floor; Palazzo Bevilacqua, Verona (c. 1530), is richer, with an elaborate pattern of windows, spiral columns, and a rather oppressive use of sculpture. Here he adopted a device which later became very popular, projecting the triglyphs of the order to form consoles for a balcony. In his later palaces he strove towards the elimination of the wall surface, and at Palazzo Grimani, Venice (begun 1556, later altered), he almost entirely filled the spaces between the pilasters and columns with windows. He was little employed for churches, but the Cappella Pellegrini which he added to S. Bernardino, Verona (c. 1528), and Madonna di

Campagna, Verona (1559), are of interest for their peculiar domes, rather squat, on high drums decorated with alternating groups of two blank arches and three windows.

SANSOVINO, Jacopo (1486–1570), who was primarily a sculptor, introduced the High Renaissance style of architecture to Venice. Born in Florence, the son of Antonio Tatti, he was trained under Andrea Sansovino, whose name he took. From 1505 he worked mainly in Rome as a sculptor and restorer of antique statues. In 1517 he quarrelled with MICHELANGELO, and became even more classical in style as a result. At the Sack of Rome (1527) he fled to Venice, intending to go to France, but he was commissioned to repair the main dome of S. Marco, appointed Protomagister of S. Marco in 1529, and then stayed on in Venice for the rest of his life. Friendship with Titian and Aretino introduced him into the Venetian 'establishment', and he soon became the leading architect, a position he maintained until the arrival of PALLADIO, who owed much to him.

His main buildings are all in Venice: the Library and Mint (1537–54) facing the Doge's Palace, and the nearby Loggietta (1537–40) at the base of the Campanile. They show a happier combination of architecture and figure sculpture than had previously been achieved in Venice. Palladio called the Library the richest building erected since classical times. Sansovino built several churches, notably S. Francesco della Vigna (1534, completed by Palladio) and the façade of S. Giuliano (1553–5). In Palazzo Corner on the Grand Canal he adapted a Roman-type palace to Venetian requirements (before 1561). On the mainland he built Villa Garzoni, Pontecasale (c. 1530), a somewhat severe structure surrounding a wide courtyard, where he came nearer to the feeling of an antique villa than any other C16 architect.

SANT'ELIA, Antonio (1888–1916), the architect of Italian Futurism, was killed in the war, too early to have had a chance to do any actual building. However, his drawings, chiefly of 1913–14, are a vision of the industrial and commercial metropolis of the future, with stepped-back skyscrapers, traffic lanes at different levels, factories with boldly curved fronts. The forms are influenced by the Vienna Sezession (see OLBRICH), but are also curiously similar to those of MENDELSOHN's sketches of the same years. The metropolitan content, however, is Futurist.

SANTINI, see AICHEL.

SARACENIC ARCHITECTURE, see ISLAMIC ARCHITECTURE.

SASH WINDOW. A window formed with sashes, i.e., sliding glazed frames running in vertical grooves; imported from Holland into England in the late C17.

SATELLITE TOWN. A self-contained town which is nevertheless dependent upon a larger centre for certain facilities, such as higher education.

SCAGLIOLA. Material composed of cement or plaster and marble chips or colouring matter to imitate marble; known in Antiquity but especially popular in the C17 and C18.

SCALLOP. An ornament carved or moulded in the form of a shell.

SCAMOZZI, Vincenzo (1552–1616), the most important of PALLADIO's immediate followers, was a conservative and rather pedantic formalist who maintained the principles of the C16 Mannerist style in the age of the Baroque. But he designed a handful of buildings of outstanding merit. Born in Vicenza, he was the son of a carpenter-cum-architect, from whom he received his training. Before 1576 he built his masterpiece, the Rocca Pisana at Lonigo, a villa perched on a hilltop and commanding spectacular views which the windows were designed to frame in an unprecedented manner. The villa is a simplified version of Palladio's Rotonda with an inset portico on the main façade and Venetian windows on the others. (Lord BURLINGTON took elements from both villas for Chiswick House.) His later houses, e.g., Villa Molin alla Mandria near Padua (1597), tended to be enlargements and elaborations of Palladian themes. From 1578 to 1580 he travelled in South Italy, visiting Naples and Rome, where he gathered material for his *Discorsi sopra le antichità di Roma* (1582). After Palladio's death he took over several of his unfinished works, notably S. Giorgio Maggiore, Venice. At the Teatro Olimpico, Vicenza, he added the elaborate permanent stage set (1585). In 1588 he designed a similar theatre at Sabbioneta. In 1582 he began the somewhat overweighted church of S. Gaetano, Padua. The same year he won the competition for the Procuratie Nuove in Piazza S. Marco, Venice, with a design based on Sansovino's Library – much elongated and heightened by a third storey. Also in Venice, in 1595, he began S. Nicola da Tolentino, a derivation from Palladio's Redentore. In 1599 he went to Prague, then across Germany to Paris, returning to Venice in 1600; four years later he visited Salzburg, where he made designs for the cathedral (not executed), a cross between the Redentore and S. Giorgio Maggiore. The fruits of these travels were incorporated in his *L'idea dell'architettura universale* (1615), the last and most academic of the theoretical works of the Renaissance and the first to mention medieval as well as classical and Renaissance buildings.

SCANDINAVIAN ARCHITECTURE. The most original Scandinavian contributions to medieval architecture are the wooden stave churches of Norway and the wooden bell frames of Sweden. The ornamental decoration of the stave churches is among the most fantastic and exciting of its time in Europe. Medieval stone architecture in Scandinavia is on the whole dependent on Germany (and her Lombard sources) as far as the Romanesque style goes, and on England and North Germany during the Gothic centuries. With the Renaissance the Netherlands became the principal source of inspiration: Kronborg and Frederiksborg in Denmark are the work of architects from Antwerp and Holland. Of equal standing and similar style is the Royal Exchange at Copenhagen with its twisted spire.

The finest buildings in the classical style of the mid and late C17 in Sweden (such as the Riddarhus at Stockholm) are dependent on the Holland of van CAMPEN and VINCKEBOONS, although the leading architect Simon LA VALLÉE was a Frenchman. His son Jean studied in Rome, and in the Oxenstjerna Palace at Stockholm (1650) introduced to the north the style of Roman *palazzi*, rather Mannerist than Baroque. The climax of the classical style in Scandinavia is the Royal Palace at Stockholm by the younger TESSIN (begun in the 1690s), again designed under Roman, but now BERNINI's, influence. For the C18 Denmark led, with the Amalienborg and the Frederick Church. The best native architect was Nikolai Eigtved. Both Denmark and Sweden have excellent buildings in the neoclassical and the Greek Revival styles. Desprez, working in Sweden, was one of the first to convey the message of PIRANESI to the north, and C. F. Hansen's Frue Kirke (1810 etc.) represents the French faith in internal colonnades without arches and in coffered tunnel vaults.

In the C20 Sweden and Denmark are among the most important Continental countries – Nyrop's Town Hall at Copenhagen and ØSTBERG's City Hall at Stockholm for the transition from historicism to the independent style of the new century; KLINT's Grundtvig Church at Copenhagen for Expressionism; the work of Kampmann, Kay Fisker, Arne JACOBSEN, and others for a refined C20 classicism;

and that of ASPLUND and many others in Sweden for the modern style at its best. Sweden is especially noted for its housing estates with point blocks placed well in landscape, and for bold urban compositions such as the centre of Vällingby near Stockholm and the present remodelling of the centre of Stockholm itself. Both Sweden and Denmark excel in interior design and furniture.

SCHÄDEL, Gottfried (d. 1752). A German working in St Petersburg, where his masterpiece was the vast, exuberantly Baroque palace for Prince Menshikov at Oranienbaum (1713–25) the first large western-style palace to be built in Russia. Its scale was immense, a central block with long curving wings which terminated in domed pavilions, built on an escarpment faced with decorative niches to give the appearance of two storeys below the ground floor.

SCHAROUN, Hans (b. 1893), presents us with the curious case of an architect who, because of his style, stood in the forefront when he was thirty, who through a shift in style among others fell into oblivion, and who, with a return to something approaching the style which had been his in his youth and which he had never felt compelled to change, found himself in the forefront once again at the age of sixty-five to seventy. Scharoun belonged among the Expressionists and fantasts of post-1918 Germany; like them he freely penned his dreams. In the later twenties he built some houses and flats, but major jobs were offered him only in the post-Second-World-War mood, in which sympathy with the twenties plays such an important part; then the *Wirtschaftswunder* made it possible to build what had remained on paper forty years earlier. His chief recent jobs are an estate at Charlottenburg-North, Berlin (1955–61); Romeo and Juliet, a twin scheme of flats at Stuttgart (1955–9); and the Berlin Philharmonie (1956–63).

SCHINKEL, Karl Friedrich (1781–1841), the greatest German architect of the C19, was Prussian and worked almost exclusively in Prussia. He was the son of an archdeacon, went to school in Berlin, and received his architectural training there too, under GILLY, in whose father's house he boarded, and at the newly founded Academy. He was powerfully influenced by the original and francophile style of Gilly. He stayed in Italy and in Paris in 1803–5, then worked as a painter of panoramas and dioramas, and a little later (chiefly c. 1810–15), did independent paintings too, in an elevated Romantic style (landscapes and Gothic cathedrals). This led on to theatrical work, and Schinkel designed for the stage from 1816 right into the thirties (forty-two plays, including *The Magic Flute*, *Undine*, *Käthchen von Heilbronn*). Meanwhile, however, he had begun to submit architectural designs, hoping to attract attention to himself. The first was for a mausoleum for the much beloved Prussian Queen Luise. This was eminently romantic in the Gothic style, with coloured glass in the windows and life-size white angels by the head of the sarcophagus. It was followed by church designs, e.g., a cathedral in the trees, centrally planned with a steep Gothic dome. In 1810 Schinkel had secured a job in the administration of Prussian buildings, with the help of Wilhelm von Humboldt. In 1815 he was made Geheimer Oberbaurat in the newly created Public Works Department, a high title for so young a man, and in 1830 he became the head of the department.

All his principal buildings were designed between 1816 and 1830. The earliest are pure Grecian, yet always serviceable, functionally planned, and with the motifs of the façade, in the spirit of Gilly, modified with originality to ensure that the stylistic apparatus does not interfere with the use of the building. The New Guard House came first (1816; Greek Doric portico), then the Theatre (1818–21), large, with a raised Ionic portico and excellent interiors, and after that the Old Museum (1823–30), with its completely unbroken row of slender Ionic columns along the façade, its Pantheon-like centre rotunda, taken obviously from Durand, and its staircase open to the portico and picturesquely introducing a degree of interpenetration of spaces not to be expected from outside. This is the first sign of hidden resources in Schinkel, making it impossible to label him a Grecian and leave it at that. Side by side with these major buildings, Schinkel designed the War Memorial on the Kreuzberg (1818), Gothic and of cast iron, Tegel, Humboldt's country house (1822–4) in a characteristic domestic Grecian, and the Werdersche Kirche (1821–31). The design for this last was submitted in a classical and a Gothic version, both vaulted; the Gothic version won, evidently inspired by the English type of Late Gothic Royal Chapels with their four angle turrets.

Schinkel was, indeed, keenly interested in England, and in 1826 travelled through the country, after staying for a while in Paris. It was not his first major journey since Italy: in 1816 he had been to the Rhine, where he developed an interest in the preservation of monuments, and in 1824 he went again to Italy. In England he was more interested in industrial developments than in architecture proper, the promotion of crafts and industry being part of his official responsibilities.

His principal late works show a remarkable change of style and widening of possibilities. They include unexecuted designs for an exchange or merchants' hall with warehouse (1827?) and for a library (1830s), both utilitarian without any period trimmings. Among executed works, the Nikolaikirche at Potsdam (1830–7) is classical, whereas the building for the Academy of Architecture is only

vestigially period (North Italian Quattrocento), but essentially also unenriched functional. A widening in another direction led to projects for centrally and longitudinally planned churches in arcuated styles, vaguely Early Christian or Italian Romanesque (the so-called *Rundbogenstil* of Lombardy; *see* GÄRTNER), while a broadening of yet another kind is represented by two small buildings in the park of Potsdam – Charlottenhof and the Roman Bath (1826 and 1833) – and the costly projects for a palace on the Acropolis (1834) and on the Crimea (1838), in all of which Grecian motifs are applied to picturesquely irregular compositions where architecture and nature collaborate.

SCHLÜTER, Andreas (c. 1660–1714), who was primarily a sculptor, ranks as an architect below his great contemporaries HILDEBRANDT and FISCHER VON ERLACH. He began in Poland, then in 1693 was summoned to Berlin by the Elector Friedrich III, who sent him to France and Italy for some months to study. The influence of BERNINI and LE PAUTRE was evident in his principal buildings (all in or near Berlin and all destroyed), especially in his masterpiece the Royal Palace (begun c. 1698) and in the Villa Kamecke (1711–12). The Royal Palace had true High Baroque weight and majesty. He was appointed Director of the Berlin Academy of Fine Arts in 1702 and became artistic dictator of Prussia. Technical faults in some of his buildings brought disgrace, and just before his death he settled in St Petersburg.

SCOTIA. A concave moulding which casts a strong shadow, as on the base of a column between the two TORUS mouldings. *See figures 66 and 74.*

SCOTT, Sir George Gilbert (1811–78) the son of a clergyman and himself an evangelical, regarded himself as an architect of the multitude, not of the chosen few, and his sturdy stand on the *juste milieu* secured him an

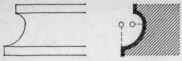

Fig. 74. Scotia

unparalleled multitude of buildings. He started with workhouses – a speciality of Sampson Kempthorne, the architect with whom he had worked – and he did them in partnership with W. B. Moffatt. The Royal Wanstead School at Wanstead, Essex, formerly an Orphan Asylum, is their first important work; it is Jacobean in style. But one year later they built St Giles, Camberwell, London, and here Scott found his feet. This is a Gothic church which was substantial, no longer papery as the earlier neo-Gothic churches had been, and which was, moreover, both knowledgeable and, with its properly developed chancel, ritualistically acceptable to the Cambridge Camden group. In the same year Scott began to restore Chesterfield church, and so started on his career as a busy, undaunted restorer. In the next year, 1844, he won the competition for St Nicholas at Hamburg with a competent German Gothic design which established him internationally. He restored more cathedrals and parish churches than can be remembered, was made surveyor of Westminster Abbey in 1849, and built – to name but a few – the grand Doncaster parish church (1854 onwards), the chapels of Exeter College, Oxford (1856), and St John's College, Cambridge (1863–9), and the parish church of Kensington, London (1869–72). His style is mixed Anglo-French High Gothic (late c13 to early c14).

He was also active as a secular architect. Examples are Kelham Hall, Nottinghamshire (1857 etc.), the St Pancras Station and Hotel in London (1865), the Albert Memorial (1864), and the group of houses in Broad Sanctuary, just west of Westminster Abbey (1854). Scott even wrote a persuasive book to prove that the Gothic style was as suited to secular as to clerical c19 tasks (*Remarks on Secular and Domestic Architecture*, 1858), and was deeply hurt when he found himself forced by Lord Palmerston to do the new Government offices in Whitehall in the Renaissance style (final design 1861). Scott was ambitious and fully convinced he was as good an architect as any; this comes out clearly in his *Personal and Professional Recollections* (1879). He was, in fact, a competent, careful architect, but he lacked genius. As a restorer he believed in careful preservation, but was ruthless in action. In spite of this he was quite a medieval scholar, as is demonstrated by his *Gleanings from Westminster Abbey* (1862).

His sons George Gilbert (1839–97) and John Oldrid (1842–1913) were both Gothicists too, competent and careful like their father, but they had in addition a sensitivity which belongs to the Late as against the High Victorian milieu. George Gilbert's *chef d'œuvre* was St Agnes, Kennington, London (1877), remarkably bare and grand; John Oldrid's is Newborough, Staffs (1901). The two together, first George then John, did the grand Catholic church of Norwich (1884–1910).

SCOTT, Sir Giles Gilbert (1880–1960), rose to sudden and very early fame with his design for Liverpool Cathedral, won in competition in 1904. It is a design that is still Gothicist in the c19 manner, but of an originality of plan and a verve of verticals which promised much. Scott's early ecclesiastical buildings, such as St Joseph, Lower Sheringham, Norfolk (1910–36), and the Charterhouse School Chapel (1922–7), are indeed both original and bold, and in addition much less dependent on a style from the past. Scott exploited a surprising variety of possibilities. The results included Battersea Power Station in London (1932–4), which became the pattern for post-war brick-built power stations all over England, and the new Waterloo Bridge (1939–45), with the fine sweep of its shallow arches. However, his official representational architecture lost the early tensions and turned commonplace: Cambridge University Library (1931–4), the new building for the Bodleian Library, Oxford (1936–46), Guildhall Building, London (1954–8).

SCREENS PASSAGE. The space at the service end of a medieval hall between the screen and the buttery, kitchen, and pantry entrances.

SCROLL. I. An ornament in the form of a scroll of paper partly rolled. 2. In classical architecture, the VOLUTE of an Ionic or Corinthian CAPITAL. 3. In Early English and Decorated Gothic architecture, a moulding in such a form. *See figure 75.*

Fig. 75. Scroll

SEDILIA. Seats for the clergy, generally three (for priest, deacon, and subdeacon), and of masonry, in the wall on the south side of the CHANCEL.

SEGMENT. Part of a circle smaller than a semicircle.

SELVA, Antonio (1751–1819), a leading neo-classical architect in Venice, trained under TEMANZA, then visited Rome, Paris, and London (1779–83). His early works are in a simplified neo-Palladian style, e.g., Teatro La Fenice, Venice (1788–92, burnt down but rebuilt to his design). But he developed a much stronger neo-classical manner later on, e.g., Duomo, Cologna Veneta (1806–17), with its vastly imposing octastyle Corinthian portico.

SEMPER, Gottfried (1803–79), the most important German architect of the Early and High Victorian decades, was born at Hamburg and studied at Göttingen, and then in Munich (under GÄRTNER). In 1826, after fighting a duel, he fled to Paris, where he worked under GAU and HITTORF. The years 1830–3 were spent in Italy and Greece, and after that journey Semper published a pamphlet on polychromy in Greek architecture, immediately influenced by Hittorf. In 1834 he was appointed to a chair at the Dresden Academy and there built his finest buildings. The Opera came first (1838–41). It was, in its original form, neo-Cinquecento, with subdued ornamentation and an exterior that expressed clearly its interior spaces. The semicircular front was inspired by Moller's theatre at Mainz (*see* GILLY). After that followed the synagogue, a mixture of Lombard, Byzantine, Moorish, and Romanesque elements (1839–40); the Quattrocento Villa Rose (1839); and the Cinquecento Oppenheim Palais (1845). Then came the Picture Gallery, closing with its large arcuated façade the Baroque Zwinger at the time left open to the north (1847–54), and the Albrechtsburg, a grand terraced Cinquecento villa above the river Elbe (1850–5), symmetrical, yet the German equivalent to, say, Osborne. After the revolution of 1848 Semper fled Germany and went first to Paris (1849–51) – an unsuccessful time, which made him contemplate emigration to America – and then to London (1851–5), where he did certain sections of the 1851 Exhibition and advised Prince Albert on the tasks for the museum which is now the Victoria and Albert.

Semper was, in fact, keenly interested in art applied to industry, and his *Der Stil* (1861–3, only two volumes published) is the most interesting application of materialist principles to craft and design, an attempt at proving the origin of ornament in certain techniques peculiar to the various materials used. In architecture Semper believed in the expression of the function of a building in its plan and exterior, including any decorative elements.

In 1855 Semper went to the Zürich Polytechnic and taught there till 1871. During that time he made designs for the Wagner National Theatre (1864–6) which considerably influenced the building as it was erected at Bayreuth (by O. Brückwald, 1841–1904; opened 1876). Semper's last years were spent in Vienna. His style then, as is clearly seen in the Dresden Theatre (redesigned 1871 after a fire), was more Baroque, less disciplined, and looser. This is also evident in the two large identical museum buildings for Vienna, forming a forum with the Neue Hofburg (1872 etc., and 1881 etc.), and in the Burgtheater (1873). These last buildings were executed by Karl von Hasenauer (1833–94), but the well-thought-out, clearly articulated plans are Semper's.

SENS, see WILLIAM OF SENS.

SERLIANA (or SERLIAN MOTIF). An archway or window with three openings, the central one arched and wider than the others: so called because it was first illustrated in SERLIO's *Architettura* (1537), though it probably derived from BRAMANTE. It was much used by PALLADIO, and became one of the hallmarks of PALLADIANISM, especially in C17–18 England. It is more commonly known as Venetian or Palladian. *See figure 76.*

SERLIO, Sebastiano (1475–1554), painter and architect, was more important as the author of *L'Architettura*, which appeared in six parts between 1537 and 1551 (augmented from his drawings 1575). This was the first book on architecture whose aim was practical rather than theoretical, and the first to codify the five ORDERS: it diffused the style of BRAMANTE and RAPHAEL throughout Europe, and provided builders with a vast repertory of motifs. Born and trained in

Fig. 76. Serliana

Bologna, he went to Rome *c.* 1514, and remained there until the sack of 1527 as a pupil of PERUZZI, who bequeathed him plans and drawings used extensively in his book. He then went to Venice until 1540, when he was called to France, and advised on building operations at Fontainebleau. Here he built a house for the Cardinal of Ferrara (destroyed), and the *château* at Ancy-le-Franc near Tonnerre (begun 1546). Neither building had much influence, but the fantastic designs, especially for rusticated portals, in the later parts of his books, which were published in France, were much imitated by French Mannerist architects.

SERVANDONI, Giovanni Niccolò (1695–1766), born in Florence and trained as a painter under Pannini, began as a stage designer in France in 1726, but soon turned to architecture. In 1732 he won the competition for the west façade of St Sulpice, Paris. Though not executed until 1737, and revised meanwhile, this is among the earliest manifestations of a reaction against the Rococo.

SEXPARTITE VAULT, see VAULT.

SGRAFFITO. Decoration on plaster of incised patterns, the top coat being cut through to show a differently coloured coat beneath.

SHAFT. The trunk of a column between the base and CAPITAL. *See figure 64.*

SHAFT-RING (or ANNULET). A motif of the C12 and C13 consisting of a ring round a SHAFT.

SHARAWADGI. Artful irregularity in garden design and, more recently, in town planning. The word, probably derived from the Japanese, was first used in 1685 to describe the irregularity of Chinese gardens: it was taken up again and popularized in mid-C18 England and, in connexion with town planning, some twenty years ago.

SHAW, Richard Norman (1831–1912), was a pupil of William Burn (1789–1870), a very successful, competent, and resourceful architect of country houses, and won the Academy Gold Medal in 1854, after having travelled in Italy, France, and Germany. He published a hundred of the travel sketches in 1858 and in the same year went as chief draughtsman to STREET, following WEBB in this job. He started in practice with a friend from Burn's office, Eden Nesfield (1835–88), but they mostly worked separately. Shaw began in the Gothic style, and did a number of churches, some of them remarkably powerful (Bingley, Yorkshire, 1864–8; Batchcott, Shropshire, 1891–2), and one at least partaking of his happily mixed, mature style (Bedford Park, Middlesex, 1880). But this style was not reached by Shaw and Nesfield at once. A few years intervened of highly picturesque, still somewhat boisterous country mansions, timber-framed as well as of stone (Leys Wood, Sussex, 1868; Cragside, Northumberland, 1870 etc.). At the same time, however, a change took place to a more intimate style, simpler details, and local materials (Glen Andred, Sussex, 1868). This both architects have entirely in common.

Shaw and Nesfield's mature style is much more subdued, and its period sources are mid-C17 brick houses under Dutch influence and the William and Mary style, rather than Gothic and Tudor. Decoration is more refined than was usual, and interior decoration was here and there left to MORRIS's firm. Which of the two architects really started this style is not certain. Nesfield is the more likely – see his Dutch C17 Lodge at Kew Gardens (1866) and his William-and-Mary-cum-Louis XIII Kinmel Park (*c.* 1866–8) – but Shaw made an international success of it. That some inspiration from Webb stands at the beginning is indubitable. The key buildings were New Zealand Chambers in the City of London (1872), Lowther Lodge, Kensington (1873, now Royal Geographical Society), Shaw's own house in Ellerdale Road, Hampstead (1875), and the exquisite Swan House, Chelsea Embankment (1876). At the same time Shaw designed Bedford Park, Turnham Green, Middlesex, as the earliest garden suburb ever. About 1890 (Bryanston, Dorset) Shaw turned away from the dainty elegance of this style towards a grand classicism with giant columns and Baroque details (Chesters, Northumberland, 1891; Piccadilly Hotel, 1905); this also was very influential.

SHELL. A thin, self-supporting membrane on the eggshell principle; used for roofing in timber or concrete.

SHEPPARD, Richard (b. 1910) The most interesting buildings by R. Sheppard, Robson & Partners to date are Churchill College, Cambridge (1959 etc.), with a number of small and medium-sized courts grouped loosely round the towering concrete-vaulted hall; hostels for Imperial College, London (1961–3); the School of Navigation of Southampton University (1959–61); Digby Hall, Leicester University (1958–62); and the West Midland Training College at Walsall (1960–3).

SHINGLE STYLE. The American term for the Domestic Revival of the 1870s and 1880s, influenced initially by Norman SHAW, but replacing his tile-hanging by shingle-hanging. The pioneer building is the Sherman House at Newport, Rhode Island, by H. H. RICHARDSON (1874). MCKIM, MEAD & WHITE also participated. The masterpiece is Richardson's Stoughton House at Cambridge, Massachusetts (1882). The shingle style is almost exclusively a style of the medium-sized private house, and its most interesting and most American feature, not implied in the name, is open internal planning.

SHINGLES. Wooden tiles for covering roofs and spires.

SHOULDERED ARCH, see ARCH.

SHUTE, John (d. 1563), the author of the first English architectural book *The First and Chief Groundes of Architecture* (1563), described himself as a painter and architect, and was a member of the household of the Duke of Northumberland who sent him to Italy about 1550. His book included illustrations of the five orders, derived mainly from SERLIO. It went into four editions before 1587 and must have been widely used.

SHUTTERING, see FORMWORK.

SILL. The lower horizontal part of a window-frame.

SILOE, Diego de (c. 1495–1563), who was a sculptor as well as an architect, was one of the main practitioners of the PLATERESQUE style. Born in Burgos, he studied in Italy (Florence and possibly Rome), where he acquired a Michelangelesque style of sculpture and picked up the vocabulary of Renaissance architecture. His finest work as both sculptor and architect is the Escalera Dorada in Burgos Cathedral (1519–23) – a very imposing interior staircase rising in five flights and derived from that designed by BRAMANTE to link the terraces of the Belvedere Court. To decorate it *putti*, portraits in roundels, winged angel heads, and other Renaissance motifs are used with a still Gothic profusion. In 1528 Siloe began his masterpiece,

Granada Cathedral, where his main innovation was a vast domed chancel very skilfully attached to the wide nave. Here he adopted a purer and more severe manner which was to have wide influence in Spain. His other buildings include the tower of S. Maria del Campo, near Burgos (1527); the Salvador Church, Ubeda (1536); Guadix Cathedral (1549); and S. Gabriel, Loja (1552–68), with its unusual trefoil *chevet*.

SIMA RECTA, see CYMA RECTA.

SIMA REVERSA, see CYMA REVERSA.

SIMÓN DE COLONIA (d. c. 1511). Son of Juan de Colonia (d. 1481), and father of Francisco de Colonia (d. 1542). Juan no doubt came from Cologne, and, indeed, the spires of Burgos Cathedral (1442–58) look German Late Gothic. Juan was also the designer of the Charterhouse of Miraflores outside Burgos (1441 etc.). Simon, sculptor as well as architect, followed his father at Burgos Cathedral and Miraflores and designed, in a typically Spanish wild Late Gothic, the Chapel of the Constable of the cathedral (1486 etc.) and the façade of S. Pablo at Valladolid (1486–99). He became master mason of Seville Cathedral in 1497. Francisco, who probably completed the façade of S. Pablo, is responsible (with Juan de Vallejo) for the crossing tower of Burgos Cathedral (1540 etc.), still essentially Gothic, though Francisco had done the Puerta de la Pellejería of the cathedral in the new Early Renaissance in 1516. Francisco was made joint master mason with JUAN DE ÁLAVA at Plasencia Cathedral in 1513, but they quarrelled over this job and also over Álava's work at Salamanca Cathedral. Álava commented on Francisco's *'poco saber'*.

SINAN, Mi'mar (1489–1578 or 1588), the greatest Turkish architect, was supposedly of Greek origin. He worked for Suleiman I 'The Magnificent' throughout the Ottoman Empire, from Budapest to Damascus, and, according to himself, built no less than 334 mosques, schools, hospitals, public baths, bridges, palaces, etc. His mosques developed from Haghia Sophia, the most famous being the enormous Suleimaniyeh in Istanbul (1550–6), though he himself considered his masterpiece to be the Selimiye at Edirne (Adrianople) (1570–4).

SITTE, Camillo (1843–1903), Austrian town-planner and architect, was director of the Trades' School of Salzburg (1875–93), and then of Vienna (1893 onwards). His fame rests entirely on his book *Der Städtebau* (1889), which is a brilliant essay in visual urban planning. Sitte, with the help of a large number of diagrammatic plans, analyses open spaces in towns and the many ways in which irregularities of plan can cause attractive effects. His subject is really 'townscape', in the sense in which this term is now used by the *Architectural Review* and such writers as Gordon Cullen.

SKELETON CONSTRUCTION. A method of construction consisting of a framework (*see* FRAMED BUILDING) and an outer covering which takes no load (*see* CLADDING). The skeleton may be visible from the outside.

SKEWBACK. That portion of the ABUTMENT which supports an arch.

SKIDMORE, OWINGS & MERRILL (Louis Skidmore, 1897–1962; N. A. Owings, b. 1903; and J. O. Merrill, b. 1896). One of the largest and at the same time best architectural firms in the United States. They have branches in New York, Chicago, and other centres, each with its own head of design. Gordon Bunshaft (b. 1909), a partner in 1945, is an especially distinguished designer. Outstanding among the works of the firm are the following: Lever House, New York (completed 1952), which started the international vogue for curtain-walled skyscrapers rising on a podium of only a few storeys, and which has, moreover,

a garden-court in the middle of the podium; the Hilton Hotel at Istanbul (begun 1952); the United States Air Force Academy at Colorado Springs (begun 1955). Other important buildings are the Manufacturers' Trust Bank in New York (1952–4), memorably low in a city of high buildings and (although a bank and in need of security) largely glazed to the outside, and the Connecticut General Life Insurance at Hartford (1953–7), beautifully landscaped and detailed. Skidmores' style is developed from that of MIES VAN DER ROHE and, until recently, rarely departed from its crispness and precision.

SKYSCRAPER. A multi-storey building of considerable height. The term originated in the United States in the 1880s. By 1890 the Pulitzer Building had reached 309 ft or 26 storeys. To go much beyond this was impossible with traditional building materials, and further development was based on the introduction of metal framing. This took place at Chicago in 1883 (*see* JENNEY). The highest skyscraper before the First World War was C. Gilbert's Woolworth building in New York (792 ft); the highest to date is the Empire State Building of 1930–2 (1,250 ft).

SLATEHANGING. A wall covering of overlapping rows of slates on a timber substructure.

SLEEPER WALL. An underground wall either supporting SLEEPERS, or built between two PIERS, two walls, or a pier and a wall, to prevent them from shifting. The foundation walls of an ARCADE between nave and aisle would thus be sleeper walls.

SLEEPERS. In a building, strong horizontal beams on which the JOISTS rest. The term can apply to: *a.* beams laid lengthwise on the walls under the ground floor, supporting the floor joists; *b.* in buildings of more than one storey, the beams between the principal posts, marking the divisions and carrying the joists and any other similar cross-beams. With a span of more than 15 ft or so, transverse sleepers are inserted to carry longitudinal joists. The modern term comes from the medieval *dormant*, so called because lesser timbers 'slept' on them.

SLYPE. A covered way or passage, especially in a cathedral or monastic church, leading East from the cloisters between transept and chapterhouse.

SMIRKE, Sir Robert (1780–1867), the leading Greek Revival architect in England, nevertheless lacked the genius of his almost exact contemporary in Germany, SCHINKEL, by whom he may have been influenced. The son of a painter and Academician, he was articled to SOANE, but quarrelled after a few months. From 1801 to 1805 he travelled in Italy, Sicily, and Greece, sketched most of the ancient buildings in the Morea, and on his return to London published the first and only volume of his projected *Specimens of Continental Architecture* (1806). His first buildings were medieval in style – Lowther Castle (1806–11) and Eastnor Castle (c. 1810–15). He made his name with Covent Garden Theatre (1808, destroyed), the first Greek Doric building in London and as such very influential. It showed with what simple means gravity and grandeur might be achieved. His cool businesslike efficiency quickly brought him fame and fortune, and in 1813 he reached the head of his profession when he joined Soane and NASH as Architect to the Board of Works. His masterpieces came in the next decade, first the British Museum (1823–47), then the General Post Office (1824–9, demolished), both immense in scale and massively Grecian in style. Though less uncompromising and less impressive than Schinkel's Altes Museum in Berlin (1825) the British Museum with its tremendous Ionic colonnade has a noble dignity and illustrates his admirable directness and scholarly detailing

at their best. Knighted in 1832, he retired in 1845.

SMITHSON, Peter and Alison (b. 1923 and 1928). Their school at Hunstanton in Norfolk (1954) was one of the most controversial buildings of the time; it is not informal but a symmetrical group, and in its details is inspired by MIES VAN DER ROHE. The Smithsons then turned in the direction of BRUTALISM, but their biggest and most mature building, for the *Economist* in London (1962–4), has none of the quirks of that trend. It is a convincingly grouped scheme of various heights, with a façade to St James's Street that succeeds in establishing a *modus vivendi* with the C18 clubs around, and with two high blocks of different heights behind.

SMYTHSON, Robert (c. 1536–1614), the only Elizabethan architect of note, perfected the spectacular if rather outlandish country-house style developed by the courtiers and magnates of the period. First heard of at Longleat, where he worked as principal freemason (1568–75), he built his masterpiece, Wollaton Hall, during the next decade (1580–8). This was a revolutionary building – a single pile with corner towers and a central hall, planned symmetrically on both axes. The plan probably derives from SERLIO and the whimsical Flemish carved ornamentation of banded shafts, strapwork, etc., from de VRIES, but the fantastic and romantic sham-castle silhouette is his own invention and wholly English. He settled near Wollaton, acquiring property there and the style of a 'gentleman'. But he almost certainly had a hand in the design of two later houses of note, Worksop Manor (c. 1585, now destroyed) and Hardwick Hall (1590–7). His son John (d. 1634) designed Bolsover Castle (1612 etc.), perhaps the most romantic of all the sham castles.

SOANE, Sir John (1753–1837). The most original English architect after VAN-

BRUGH. His extremely personal style is superficially neo-classical but, in fact, romantic or 'picturesque' in its complicated and unexpected spatial interplay. Intense, severe, and sometimes rather affectedly odd, his buildings reflect his tricky character. He was always slightly uncertain of himself and, despite his genius, never achieved complete confidence and authority even in his own style. The son of a Berkshire builder, he trained under DANCE and HOLLAND, then studied for three years in Italy, where he probably knew PIRANESI; but French influence, especially that of Peyre and LEDOUX, was more profound. He returned to London in 1780, but his career only really began with his appointment as Surveyor to the Bank of England in 1788. His work at the Bank, now destroyed, was among the most advanced in Europe. The Stock Office (begun 1792) and Rotunda (begun 1796) must have seemed shockingly austere, with their shallow domes and general emphasis on utility and structural simplicity, not to mention his reduction of classical ornamentation to rudimentary grooved strips and diagrammatic mouldings. The romantic or picturesque element in his work is felt increasingly after 1800, notably in the Dulwich College Art Gallery (1811–14), a 'primitivist' construction in brick with each element curiously detached by some slight break or recession, and, above all, in his own house, No. 13 Lincoln's Inn Fields, London (1812–13), now the Sir John Soane Museum. This is highly eccentric and personal to the point of perversity, especially inside, with its congested, claustrophobic planning, complicated floor-levels, ingenious top-lighting, hundreds of mirrors to suggest receding planes and blurr divisions, and hanging, Gothic-inspired arches to detach ceilings from walls. The exterior perfectly illustrates his linear stylization and emphasis on planes

rather than masses. His last buildings of note are the astylar utilitarian stables at Chelsea Hospital (1814–17), St Peter's, Walworth (1822), and Pell Well (1822–8) a small villa-type house with curious features reminiscent of Vanbrugh. He was made Professor of Architecture at the Royal Academy in 1806 and knighted in 1831.

SOCLE. A base or pedestal.

SOFFIT. The underside of any architectural element, e.g. an INTRADOS.

SOFFIT CUSPS. Cusps springing from the flat soffit (*see* INTRADOS) of an arched head, and not from its chamfered sides or edges.

SOLAR. An upper living-room in a medieval house; from the Latin *solarium* (a sunny spot or a sun-roof).

SOLARI, Guiniforte (1429–81), a Milanese 'last-ditch' Gothic conservative, completed FILARETE's Renaissance Ospedale Maggiore in the Gothic style, built the simplified Gothic nave of S. Maria delle Grazie, Milan (1465–90, completed by BRAMANTE), and worked on the Gothic Milan Cathedral.

SOLARI, Santino (1576–1646), one of the first Italian architects to work extensively in Germany and Austria, came of a large family of artists from Como. His main work is Salzburg Cathedral (1614–28), an entirely Italian basilican church with dome and with twin towers flanking the west façade. For the Bishop of Salzburg he built the Italianate Lustschloss at Hellbrunn, outside Salzburg (1613–19). He also designed (*c.* 1620) the solemn little shrine of the black-faced Virgin at Einsiedeln, Switzerland, later surrounded by MOOSBRUGGER's fantastic Baroque abbey church.

SOLARIUM. A sun terrace or LOGGIA.

SOMMARUGA, Giuseppe (1867–1917), a native of Milan, was a pupil of the Brera Academy and of Boito and Beltrami, but turned to ART NOUVEAU and became, side by side with Raimondo d'Aronco (1857–1932;

buildings for the Turin Exhibition, 1902), its most important representative in Italy. His principal works are the Palazzo Castiglioni on the Corso Venezia (1901) and the Hotel Tre Croci at Campo dei Fiori, near Varese (1909–12).

SOPRAPORTA. A painting above the door of a room, usually framed in harmony with the doorcase to form a decorative unit.

SOUFFLOT, Jacques Germain (1713–80), the greatest French neo-classical architect, was the son of a provincial lawyer against whose wishes he went off to Rome to study architecture in 1731. He stayed seven years, settling on his return in Lyon, where he was commissioned to build the enormous Hôtel-Dieu (1741 etc.). This made his reputation, and in 1749 he was chosen by Mme de Pompadour to accompany her brother, M. de Marigny, to Italy, where he was to spend two years preparing himself for his appointment as Surintendant des Bâtiments. The tour was very successful and may be regarded as marking the beginning of neo-classicism in France, of which the great masterpiece was to be Soufflot's Ste Geneviève (called the Panthéon since the Revolution) in Paris (begun 1757). This was a revolutionary building for France and was hailed by the leading neo-classical critic and theorist, LAUGIER, as 'the first example of perfect architecture'. It perfectly expresses a new, more serious, not to say solemn attitude towards Antiquity, and combines Roman regularity and monumentality with a structural lightness derived from Gothic architecture. Soufflot himself said (1762) that one should combine the Greek orders with the lightness one admired in Gothic buildings. He continued working on his masterpiece to the end of his life, but did not live to see it finished. His other buildings are of much less interest, e.g., École de Droit, Paris (1771–83) and various follies in the park of the Château de Menars (1767

etc.) including a rotunda, nymphaeum, and orangery, all in an elegant but rather dry neo-classical style.

SOUNDING BOARD, see PULPIT.

SPACE-FRAME. A three-dimensional framework for enclosing spaces, in which all members are interconnected and act as a single entity, resisting loads applied in any direction. Systems can be designed to cover very large spaces, uninterrupted by support from the ground, and the surface covering can be integrated to play its part in the structural whole. Some types have the appearance of egg-boxes (pyramidal in their elements), others are based on hexagonal or other geometric figures. The chief exponents to date are Z. Makowski (*space-grid*) Le Ricolais, Konrad Wachsmann, and Buckminster FULLER, whose dome, designed for the Union Tank Car Co., Baton Rouge, U.S.A. (1958), has a diameter of 384 ft. *See figure 77.*

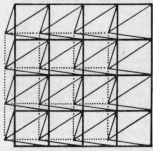

Fig. 77. Space-frame

SPANDREL. The triangular space between the side of an arch, the horizontal drawn from the level of its apex, and the vertical of its springing; also applied to the surface between two arches in an arcade.

SPANISH ARCHITECTURE. After the Roman aqueducts, etc., the first noteworthy monuments in Spain are a few relics of the Visigothic age, notably S. Juan de Baños (661). They are followed by splendid examples of ISLAMIC ARCHITECTURE, especially the Mosque of Cordova (786 etc., with its most ornate parts dating from *c.* 970). By that time the Christian north of Spain had already produced a series of eminently interesting small buildings with tunnel vaults, centralizing spaces, and very original details (Sta Cristina de Lena, S. Miguel de Liño). One of them, now a church, was originally a royal hall (Sta Maria de Naranco). The date of this series is the mid C9. S. Miguel de Escalada (*c.* 900) is an example of a mixture of Christian and Arabic elements called the MOZARABIC style. The term MUDÉJAR refers to Christian architecture in a purely Moslem style, and this remained characteristic of secular architecture in Spain nearly to the end of the Middle Ages. No wonder, considering the glories and luxurious comforts of the Alhambra of Granada which – in the one remaining Moslem part of the peninsula – was built as late as the C14.

Meanwhile, however, the ROMANESQUE style had started in the early C11 in Catalonia in a version similar to that of Lombardy. The French Romanesque of the great pilgrimage churches has an outstanding representative in the far north-west corner of Spain in the celebrated church of Santiago de Compostela (begun *c.* 1075 and completed with the splendidly sculptured Pórtico de la Gloria in 1188). Other Romanesque churches are at León, Ávila, and Lugo. In sculpture the Spanish churches at first were ahead of the French, who have nothing to compare with the C10 capitals of S. Pedro de Nave and the early C11 capitals of Jaca. At that time (1030 etc.) the architecture of Ripoll may well have been just as progressive, but it is too ruthlessly restored to be accepted as evidence now.

The GOTHIC style arrived, as in most other countries, with the Cistercians. The most French cathedrals of the C13 are those of Burgos (1221 etc.), Toledo (1226 etc.), and León,

but the most original version of the Spanish Gothic is Catalan (Barcelona Cathedral, 1298 etc.; Sta María del Mar, Barcelona, 1329 etc.; Palma Cathedral, Majorca), with very wide and high naves and very high aisles or with aisles replaced by chapels between internal buttresses (Sta Catalina, Barcelona, 1223 etc.; Sta María del Pino, Barcelona, *c.* 1320 etc.). The Late Gothic style was much influenced by Germany and the Netherlands, as is shown by such works as the towers of Burgos Cathedral by Hans of Cologne (begun 1442). Late Gothic vaults with their lierne rib patterns also have German origins. Spatially, however, Spain was entirely Spanish: the vast rectangles of her cathedrals hark back to the mosques of Islam, but their height and the height of the aisles are her own. Seville Cathedral was begun in 1402 and is 430 ft long and 250 ft wide, with a nave 130 ft high and aisles 85 ft high. Spain continued to embark on new cathedrals on this scale right up to the time of the Reformation. Salamanca was started in 1512, Segovia in 1525. In Spain those were the years of greatest wealth, resulting in the many funerary monuments and the excessively lavish decoration of such buildings as the Constable's Chapel at Burgos Cathedral (1482 etc.) and S. Juan de los Reyes, Toledo (1476 etc.), or of such façades as those of S. Pablo (1486 etc.) and S. Gregorio (*c.* 1492) at Valladolid. No square inch must remain without its complicated and lacy carving. The spirit of Islam re-asserted itself in this, and the desire to over-decorate surfaces was carried on with Renaissance details in the C16 (PLATERESQUE style) and with Baroque details in the C18 (CHURRIGUERESQUE style).

The Italian Renaissance had actually reached Spain early, and such monuments as the courtyard of the castle of La Calahorra (1509–12) or the staircase of the Hospital of Toledo (1504 etc.) are pure and perfectly at ease. But almost at once the crowding of motifs started again, and the façade of the University of Salamanca (c. 1515 etc.) is no more than a furnishing of the Late Gothic façade with new motifs. Soon, however, the pure Italian High Renaissance also entered Spain. The first and for a while the only example is Charles V's unfinished palace on the Alhambra (1526), with its circular courtyard and its motifs reminiscent of RAPHAEL and GIULIO ROMANO. The severest and vastest palace in the Italian style is Philip II's Escorial (1563 etc.), but such austerity remained rare, and Spain came once again into her own when, in the late C17, she developed that style of excessive Baroque surface decoration which culminated in such buildings as the façade of Santiago de Compostela (1738 etc.), the sacristy of the Charterhouse of Granada (1727 etc.), the Transparente in Toledo Cathedral (1721–32), the portal of the Hospital of S. Ferdinand in Madrid (1722) and that of the Dos Aguas Palace at Valencia (1740–4). Greater sobriety in an Italian and French sense characterizes the Royal Palace in Madrid, by the Italian SACCHETTI (1738 etc.), the Royal Palace of La Granja, partly by the Italian JUVARRA (1719 etc.), and the Royal Palace of Aranjuez, by the Italian Bonavia (1748 etc.). Among the Spanish academics Ventura RODRÍGUEZ was the most conspicuous figure; his giant portico for Pamplona Cathedral was built in 1783. Of 1787 is the even more neo-classical design for the Prado in Madrid by Juan de VILLANUEVA.

To the C19 and C20 Spain has not made any essential contributions except for the fabulous work of GAUDÍ at Barcelona which is the international climax of ART NOUVEAU in architecture.

SPENCE, Sir Basil (b. 1907), before the war designed mostly large country houses in Scotland; after the war he made his name in England as well by exhibition work (Sea and Ships, Festival of Britain, 1951). In 1951 he won the competition for Coventry Cathedral, and the building was consecrated in 1962. It is outstanding in the use made of the steeple of the old Perpendicular cathedral as its one vertical accent; in the use of the shell of the old nave and chancel as a landscaped atrium; in the saw-tooth side walls treated so that only those sides have windows which face towards the altar; and in the ample opportunities given to artists and craftsmen (Graham Sutherland, John Piper, Geoffrey Clarke). Since 1954 Sir Basil Spence and his firm have done much university work (Edinburgh, Southampton, Nottingham, Liverpool, and most recently and spectacularly the University of Sussex).

SPERE-TRUSS. A wooden arch with PIERS - the latter attached with trusses to the side walls - which stood, at least at wall-plate height, at the kitchen end of a medieval timber-framed hall, marking the division between the hall proper and the SCREENS PASSAGE; so-called from the screen or *spere* which separated the hall from the kitchen.

SPIRE. A tall pyramidal, polygonal, or conical structure rising from a tower, turret, or roof (usually of a church) and terminating in a point. It can be of stone, or of timber covered with SHINGLES, or lead. A *broach* spire is usually octagonal in plan, placed on a square tower and rising without an intermediate parapet. Each of the four angles of the tower not covered by the base of the spire is filled with an inclined mass of masonry or broach built into the oblique sides of the spire, carried up to a point, and covering a SQUINCH. A broach spire is thus the interpenetration of a lower-pitch pyramid with a much steeper octagon. A *needle* spire is a thin spire rising from the centre of a tower roof, well inside a parapet protecting a pathway upon which scaffolding could be erected for repairs. *See figure 78.*

springer. See also SKEWBACK *and figure 4.*

SPUR. An ornament, usually of foliage, on the corner of a square plinth sur-

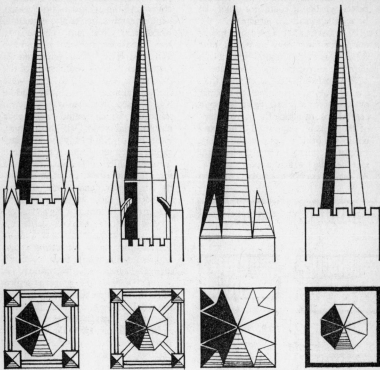

Octagonal spire over tower with pinnacles;

2. Spire and octagon over tower with flying buttresses;

3. Broach spire;

4. Needle spire

Fig. 78. Spire

SPIRELET, *see* FLÈCHE.

SPLAY. A sloping, chamfered surface cut into the walls. The term usually refers to the widening of doorways, windows, or other wall-openings by slanting the sides. *See also* REVEAL.

SPRINGING LINE. The level at which an arch springs from its supports. The bottom stone of the arch resting on the IMPOST each side can thus be called a

mounted by a circular PIER; also called a *griffe*.

SPUR STONE. A stone projecting from the angle of a corner or arch to prevent damage by passing traffic: it is usually circular in section.

SQUINCH. An arch or system of concentrically wider and gradually projecting arches, placed diagonally at the internal angles of towers to fit a polygonal or round superstructure on to a square plan. *See figure 38.*

SQUINT. An obliquely cut opening in a wall or through a PIER to allow a view of the main altar of a church from places whence it could not otherwise be seen; also called a *hagioscope*.

STAIR, STAIRCASE. There are special names for the various parts of a stair: the *tread* is the horizontal surface of a step; the *riser* is the vertical surface; a *winder* is a tread wider at one end than the other. A *newel staircase* is a circular or winding staircase with a solid central post in which the narrow ends of the steps are supported. The *newel* is also the principal post at the end of a flight of stairs; it carries the *handrails* and the *strings* which support the steps. A *dog-leg staircase* consists of two

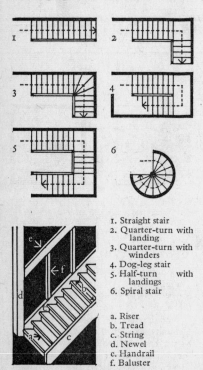

1. Straight stair
2. Quarter-turn with landing
3. Quarter-turn with winders
4. Dog-leg stair
5. Half-turn with landings
6. Spiral stair

a. Riser
b. Tread
c. String
d. Newel
e. Handrail
f. Baluster

Fig. 79. Stair

flights at right angles, with a half landing. *See figure 79.*

Staircases seem to have existed as long as monumental architecture: a staircase of *c.* 6000 B.C. has been discovered in the excavations of Jericho. Monumental staircases also existed at Knossos in Crete and Persepolis in Iran. The Greeks and the Romans were not apparently much interested in making an architectural feature of the staircase, and medieval staircases were also utilitarian as a rule. In the Middle Ages the accepted form was the newel staircase, which could assume a monumental scale (Vis du Louvre, Paris, late C14), but only did so to any extent after 1500 (Blois). The standard form of the Italian Renaissance is two flights, the upper at an angle of 180° to the lower, and both running up between solid walls. However, a few architects, notably FRANCESCO DI GIORGIO and LEONARDO DA VINCI, worked out on paper a number of other, more interesting types, and these seem to have been translated into reality in the C16, mostly in Spain. There is the staircase which starts in one flight and returns in two, the whole rising in one well; the staircase which starts in one and turns at right angles into two (BRAMANTE's Belvedere Court in the Vatican; Escalera Dorada, Burgos); and, the most frequent type, the staircase which runs up in three flights at right angles round an open well, i.e., a squared spiral stair with intermediate landings. But Bramante in the Vatican still built a normal spiral stair, though also with an open well, and BERNINI (Palazzo Barberini) made this oval, a characteristically Baroque turn. PALLADIO invented the flying staircase (Academy, Venice), a spiral staircase without any support other than the bonding of the steps into the outer wall.

The Baroque is the great age of monumental and inventive staircases. The finest of all are in Germany (Würzburg, Brühl, and especially

Bruchsal, all by NEUMANN), but there are excellent ones also in France (MANSART at Blois) and in Italy (Naples).

In C20 architecture the staircase has assumed a new significance as the element in a building which is most expressive of spatial flow. The earliest staircase in a glass cage is GROPIUS's at Alfeld (1910). Since then much has been made of flying staircases, staircases without risers, and similar effects.

STALACTITE WORK. Ceiling ornament in ISLAMIC ARCHITECTURE formed by corbelled SQUINCHES made of several layers of brick scalloped out to resemble natural stalactites.

STALL. A carved seat of wood or stone in a row of similar seats; if hinged, often carved on the underside (see MISERICORD).

STANCHION. A vertical supporting member, nowadays mainly of steel.

STARLING. A pointed projection on the PIER of a bridge to break the force of the water. See CUTWATER.

STAROV, Ivan Yegorovich (1743–1808), the first Russian-born architect to work successfully in the West European manner, was born in Moscow and trained at the St Petersburg Academy of Fine Arts. He then went to Paris, where he was trained under de Wailly (1762–8). His works are neo-classical and rather solid, e.g., church and columned rotunda belfry at Nikolskoe (1774–6), Cathedral of the Trinity, Leningrad (1776). His masterpiece is the vast Tauride Palace, Leningrad (1783–8), built for Potemkin and very rich in columns inside and out.

STAVE CHURCH. A timber-framed and timber-walled church; the walls are of upright planks with corner-post columns. The term is applied exclusively to Scandinavian churches built from the early or mid C11 onwards. Later stave churches usually have inner rows of posts or piers, sometimes an external covered arcade, and roofs

arranged in tiers. A third system was also used from c. 1200, incorporating a central column from the floor to the roof.

STEEPLE. The tower and spire or lantern of a church taken together.

STETHAIMER, Hans (d. 1432), worked at Landshut in Bavaria. He came from Burghausen, is usually called Hans von Burghausen and may not have been called Stethaimer. He began St Martin's, the chief parish church of Landshut, in 1387. On his funerary monument other works of his are mentioned: they include the chancel of the Franciscan Church at Salzburg (begun 1408). He was one of the best of the German Late Gothic architects, believed in the 'hall church', in brick as a material, where he could use it, and in a minimum of decoration. At Salzburg the most fascinating motif is that of the long slender piers of the chancel placed axially, due east, so that the eye faces not an interstice but a pier with the light from the east playing round it. Stethaimer's monument may indicate that he was also concerned with sculpture. His source is the style of the PARLER family.

STIFF-LEAF. A late C12 and early C13 type of sculptured foliage, found chiefly on CAPITALS and BOSSES, a development from the CROCKETS of crocket capitals; almost entirely confined to Britain. See figure 24.

STILE LIBERTY. The Italian term for ART NOUVEAU.

STILTED ARCH, see ARCH.

STIRLING & GOWAN (James Stirling and James Gowan, b. 1926 and 1924). Their small housing estate at Ham, near London (1958), established their sympathy with the trend influenced by LE CORBUSIER and often called BRUTALISM. Their Department of Engineering, Leicester University (1959–63), is their most complete statement to date.

STOA. In Greek architecture, a detached colonnade.

STOEP. The Dutch term for veranda.

STOP-CHAMFER. An ornamental termination to a CHAMFER, common in the Early English period and very much favoured by Victorian architects, bringing the edge of the pared-off stone or beam back to a right angle; also called a *broach-stop*. See figure 80.

Fig. 80. Stop-chamfer

STOPS. Projecting stones at the ends of HOOD-MOULDS, STRING COURSES, etc., against which the mouldings finish; often carved. See also LABEL-STOP.

STOREY (or STORY). The space between any two floors or between the floor and roof of a building. In England the ground-level storey is usually called the ground floor, in America the first floor, in France the *rez-de-chaussée*.

STOUP. A vessel to contain holy water, placed near the entrance of a church; usually in the form of a shallow dish set against a wall or pier or in a niche.

STRADDLE STONES. Mushroom-shaped stones used as bases to support timber-built granaries or hay barns, especially in Sussex.

STRAINER ARCH, *see* ARCH.

STRAPWORK. Decoration originating in the Netherlands *c.* 1540, also common in Elizabethan England, consisting of interlaced bands and forms similar to fretwork or cut leather; generally used in ceilings, screens, and funerary monuments. *See figure 81.*

STREET, George Edmund (1824–81), a pupil of George Gilbert SCOTT, was in practice in 1849, after having already designed some churches in Cornwall. In 1850–1 he travelled in

Fig. 81. Strapwork

France and Germany, in 1853 in North Italy (a book on the marble and brick buildings of North Italy, 1855), in 1854 in Germany again, in 1861–3 three times in Spain (an important book on Spanish Gothic architecture, 1865). In 1852 Street started a practice at Oxford, and among his first assistants were WEBB and MORRIS. The first important building is the Cuddesden Theological College. Street was a High Church man much appreciated by the Cambridge Camden group (*see* BUTTERFIELD), a tremendous worker, a fertile draughtsman who liked to design all details himself. His first large church is St Peter, Bournemouth (1853 etc.).

The practice was moved to London in 1855, and there Street's most characteristic early church is St James the Less, off Vauxhall Bridge Road (1860–1), a very strong design encouraged no doubt by Butterfield but not in imitation of him, and inspired by RUSKIN. The Gothic is Continental rather than English. Among Street's most notable churches are Oakengates, Shropshire (1855); Boyne Hill, Berkshire (1859); St Philip and St James, Oxford (1860–2); All Saints, Clifton, Bristol (1863–8); St John, Torquay (1861–71); St Mary Magdalen, Paddington, London (1868–78); and Holmbury St Mary, built at his own expense (1879). Street is always unconventional and inventive, yet hardly ever as aggressive as Butterfield. His principal secular work is the Law Courts, won in competition in 1866. It is a high-minded essay in C13 Gothic, yet picturesque in grouping. The Great Hall inside is particularly impressive.

STRESSED-SKIN CONSTRUCTION. A form of construction in which the outer skin acts with the frame members to contribute to the flexural strength of the unit as a whole.

STRETCHER, *see* BRICKWORK.

STRICKLAND, William (1788–1854), a pupil of LATROBE in Philadelphia, rose to fame with the Bank of the United States, Philadelphia, now the Custom House. This had first been designed by Latrobe, but was then built to a modified design by Strickland (1818–24). It is Grecian in style, whereas Strickland's earlier Masonic Temple (1810) had been Gothic. His finest building is the Philadelphia Merchants' Exchange (1834 etc.), with its elegant corner motif crowned by a copy of the Lysicrates Monument. He also built the United States Mint, Washington (1829–33), in a style similar to MILLS's, and the United States Naval Asylum (1827) with an Ionic portico and tiers of long balconies left and right. Strickland was a very versatile man: in his early days he painted and did stage design, and he was also throughout his later life engaged in major engineering enterprises (canals, railways, the Delaware Breakwater).

STRING COURSE. A continuous projecting horizontal band set in the surface of a wall and usually moulded.

STRUT, *see* ROOF.

STUART, James 'Athenian' (1713–88), a minor architect, is nevertheless important in the history of GREEK REVIVAL architecture for his temple at Hagley (1758), the earliest Doric Revival building in Europe. He and Revett went to Greece in 1751–5 and in 1762 published the *Antiquities of Athens* (2nd vol. 1789), which had little immediate influence except on interior decoration. Indolence and unreliability lost him many commissions, and he built very little. The Triumphal Arch, Tower of the Winds, and Lysicrates Monument in the park at Shugborough are his best surviving works. They date from between 1764 and 1770. His chapel at Greenwich Hospital (1779–88) seems to have been designed largely by his assistant William Newton.

STUART ARCHITECTURE. For most of the reign of James I see ELIZABETHAN AND JACOBEAN ARCHITECTURE. The Stuart style in architecture starts with Inigo JONES's Queen's House at Greenwich and Banqueting House in Whitehall. Jones's style was continued by John WEBB, Sir Roger PRATT, and Hugh MAY. Another contributing factor was the domestic architecture of Holland, which influenced England first in a semiclassical form with Dutch gables. The Jones style was too pure and exacting to find favour immediately outside the most cultured circles. The universal acceptance of classical architecture came only with the time of WREN, but in domestic building the so-called Wren type of house – quite plain, with a middle pediment, a pedimented doorway, and a hipped roof – is not a creation of Wren. Stuart churches are a rarity. They also become more frequent only at the time of Wren and are largely the result of the Fire of London. They are of a wide variety of plans, longitudinal or central or a synthesis of the two, and also of a wide variety of elevational features, especially in the steeples.

STUCCO. Plasterwork.

STUDS. Upright timbers in timber-framed houses. *See figure 83.*

STUPA. A Buddhist sepulchral monument, usually domed or beehive-shaped.

STYLOBATE. The substructure on which a colonnade stands; more correctly, the top step of the structure forming the CREPIDOMA.

SUGER, Abbot (1081–1151), was not an architect; neither does he seem to have been responsible, even as an amateur, for any architectural work. But as he was abbot of St Denis, outside Paris, when the abbey church was partly rebuilt (*c.* 1135–44), and as this was the building where the Gothic style was to all intents and purposes invented, or where it finally evolved out of the scattered elements already existing in many places, his name must be recorded here. He wrote two books on the abbey in which the new building is commented on, but nowhere refers to the designer or indeed explicitly to the innovations incorporated in the building.

SULLIVAN, Louis Henry (1856–1924), who was of mixed Irish, Swiss, and German descent, was born at Boston, studied architecture briefly at the Massachusetts Institute of Technology, and moved to Chicago in 1873. He worked there under JENNEY, then, after a year in Paris in VAUDREMER's *atelier*, returned to Chicago. In 1879 he joined the office of Dankmar Adler, and the firm became Adler & Sullivan in 1881. Their first major building, and no doubt the most spectacular in Chicago up to that time, was the Auditorium (1886–90), which was strongly influenced by RICHARDSON. The auditorium itself is capable of seating more than 4,000. Sullivan's interior decoration is exceedingly interesting, of a feathery vegetable character, derived perhaps from the Renaissance but at the same time pointing forward into the licence of ART NOUVEAU. His two most familiar skyscrapers, the Wainwright Building, St Louis (1890), and the Guaranty Building, Buffalo (1894), have not the exclusively functional directness of HOLABIRD & ROCHE's Marquette Building of 1894, but they do express externally the skeleton structure and the cellular interior arrangements. However, Sullivan, though pleading in his *Kindergarten Chats* (1901) for a temporary embargo on all decoration, was himself as fascinated by ornament as by functional expression, and this appears even in the entrance motifs of his major building, the Carson, Pirie & Scott Store (1899–1904), which is most characteristic of the 'Chicago School'. For the Chicago Exhibition of 1893 Sullivan designed the Transportation Building, with its impressively sheer giant entrance arch. He recognized the setback which the classicism otherwise prevailing at the exhibition would mean to the immediate future of American architecture.

Adler died in 1900, and after that time Sullivan's work grew less until it dried up almost entirely. He was a difficult man, uncompromising and erratic, but his brilliance is undeniable – see the passages which his pupil WRIGHT has devoted to his *Lieber Meister*.

SUMERIAN ARCHITECTURE, *see* ASSYRIAN AND SUMERIAN ARCHITECTURE.

SWAG, *see* FESTOON.

SWAN-NECK. An OGEE-shaped member, e.g., the curve in a staircase handrail where it rises to join the newel post.

SWEDISH ARCHITECTURE, *see* SCANDINAVIAN ARCHITECTURE.

SWISS ARCHITECTURE. The position of Switzerland between Germany, France, and Italy and the trilingual character of the republic have moulded its architecture from its beginnings to the present day. Churches such as Chur and Münster are Carolingian in the German manner, the C11 Romainmôtier and the C12 minster of Schaffhausen are German, and the later C12 cathedral of Basel is Alsatian, i.e., mixed German and Burgundian, though Lombardy also played its part. With the Gothic style Switzerland first turned more resolutely to the West. The cathedrals of Geneva and Lausanne are closely related to the styles of Burgundy and Champagne. Later, the South German hall churches with their intricate vaults became the pattern (Minster, Berne; St Leonard, Basel).

There are plenty of medieval castles in Switzerland dominating the many routes through the mountains. The country is also rich in town houses, and

Fribourg and Berne are models of medieval hill-towns. The Italian Renaissance was naturally most widely accepted in the Ticino, which culturally belongs to Lombardy (façade of cathedral, Lugano, 1517), but in Northern Switzerland the beginnings are only a little later. The earliest Renaissance house in Lucerne is of 1534. The Ritter Palace (1556) has an arcaded courtyard of entirely Italian type. Altogether the Swiss Renaissance is less gross and exuberant than that of Southern Germany; during the Baroque on the other hand the best buildings in Switzerland are closely connected with Germany, the abbeys of Einsiedeln and St Gall. Neo-classicism naturally looked to Paris, as witness the portico façade of the cathedral, Geneva (1752–6), and the excellent town hall of Neuchâtel (1782–90). The most important contribution of Switzerland to the architecture of the C20 is the concrete bridges of MAILLART (1905 etc.). Switzerland also led in applying the International Style to churches.

SYSTYLE. With an arrangement of columns spaced two diameters apart. *See also* ARAEOSTYLE; DIASTYLE; EUSTYLE; PYCNOSTYLE.

T

TABERNACLE. 1. An ornamented recess or receptacle to contain the Holy Sacrament or relics. 2. A free-standing canopy.

TABLINUM. In Roman architecture, a room with one side open to the ATRIUM or central courtyard.

TAENIA, *see* TENIA.

TALMAN, William (1650–1720), WREN's most distinguished contemporary, was the leading country-house architect until eclipsed by VANBRUGH. Little is known about him personally, though he seems to have been difficult and quarrelsome. His country houses are by far the largest and most lavish of their period in England, and display a mixed French and Italian Baroque character. They were very influential, e.g., in the use of giant pilasters with architrave and frieze to frame a façade, the cornice alone continuing across. Thoresby (1683–5, destroyed), the east front of Chatsworth (1687–96), Dyrham Park (1698–1700), and the new front at Drayton (*c.* 1701) were his main works, all country houses. He succeeded Hugh MAY as Comptroller of the Office of Works in 1689, serving under Wren, whose design for Hampton Court he probably revised and altered in execution.

TAMBOUR. 1. The core of a Corinthian or Composite CAPITAL. 2. The circular wall carrying a DOME or CUPOLA (*see* DRUM).

TANGE, Kenzo (b. 1913), studied at Tokyo University 1935–8 and 1942–5, then joined the office of Kunio Maekawa. Maekawa (b. 1905) and Junzo Sakakura (b. 1904) were the pioneers in Japan of the international post-war style sparked off by LE CORBUSIER's Unité and Chandigarh. Maekawa was in Le Corbusier's office in 1928–30,

and then worked with Antonin Raymond (b. 1890), who was European by birth, had been for a long time at Taliesin in the Frank Lloyd WRIGHT circle, and transferred the new international style to Japan. Sakakura had worked in Le Corbusier's office from 1929 to 1937. The most striking characteristic of Tange's buildings is also that of the other two: excessively heavy members of exposed concrete composed with a robustness bordering on the brutal (the style is sometimes called BRUTALISM). Tange's principal buildings are the Memorial Hall at Hiroshima (1950); the Tokyo City Hall (1956); the offices of the Prefecture of Kagawa at Takamatsu (1958); the Dentsu Building at Osaka (1960); and the Hotel at Atami (1961).

TARSIA, *see* INTARSIA.

TAS-DE-CHARGE. The lowest courses of a vault or arch, laid horizontally and bonded into the wall.

TAUT, Bruno (1880–1938) a pupil of Theodor Fischer in Munich, settled in Berlin in 1908. He was professor at the College of Technology, Berlin, in 1931, and at Ankara 1936; between these posts he visited Russia in 1932 and Japan in 1933. Taut was first noticed for his highly original glass pavilion at the Werkbund Exhibition of 1914 in Cologne (*see* GROPIUS, van de VELDE), a polygonal building with walls of thick glass panels, a metal staircase inside, and a glass dome, the elements set in lozenge framing (a SPACE-FRAME). In the years of the wildest Expressionism in Germany, Taut wrote his frantic *Die Stadtkrone* (1919) and designed fantastic buildings for imprecisely formulated purposes.

TAYLOR, Sir Robert (1714–88), son of a mason-contractor, trained as a sculptor under Cheere and visited Rome *c.* 1743. Though sufficiently successful to be commissioned by Parliament to design and carve the monument to Captain Cornewall in Westminster Abbey (1744), he soon abandoned sculpture for architecture and by assiduity and businesslike methods quickly built up a large practice. He and PAINE were said to have 'nearly divided the practice of the profession between them' during the mid-century. He was conservative and uninspired but highly competent, and worthily carried on the neo-Palladian tradition of BURLINGTON and KENT. Most of his work has been destroyed, notably that in the Bank of England which included his last and by far his most original work, the Reduced Annuities Office, a top-lit hall with circular clerestory carried on segmental arches. It anticipated SOANE. Asgill House, Richmond (1758–67), and Stone Building, Lincoln's Inn, London (begun 1775), are the best of his surviving buildings. He was knighted when sheriff of London, 1782–3, and left the bulk of his large fortune to found the Taylorian Institute in Oxford for the teaching of modern languages.

TEBAM. A dais or rostrum for the reader in a synagogue. Adjoining it to the east is the Chief Rabbi's seat.

TELAMONES, *see* ATLANTES.

TELFORD, Thomas (1757–1834), son of a Scottish shepherd, trained as a mason, worked in Edinburgh, then in London, and by 1784 had been made supervisor of works on Portsmouth Dockyard. In 1788 he became surveyor to the county of Shropshire. He built several churches in the county, notably Bridgnorth (1792), and several bridges, notably the brilliant Buildwas Bridge (1795–8), which was of iron (the Coalbrookdale Bridge had been built in iron in 1777) and had a 130 ft span. In 1793 work started on the Ellesmere Canal, and Telford was put in charge.

He built the Chirk Aqueduct at Ceiriog, 700 ft long and 70 ft high (1796 etc.), and the Pont Cysylltan Aqueduct, 1000 ft long and 120 ft high (1795 etc.). In 1800 he suggested the rebuilding of London Bridge with a single span of 600 ft. Telford was responsible for other canals (Caledonian, 1804 etc.; Göta, 1808 etc.), for the St Katherine's Docks (1825; *see* HARDWICK), for fen drainage, for roads, and for further bridges, including the beautiful Dean Bridge, Edinburgh, of stone (1831), the Menai Straits Suspension Bridge, of iron, with a 530 ft span (1819 etc.), and the Conway Suspension Bridge, also of iron (1826).

TEMANZA, Tommaso (1705–89). The most sensitive of Venetian neo-Palladians. His masterpiece is the little church of the Maddalena, Venice (*c.* 1760), with its interior freely derived from PALLADIO's chapel at Maser. He wrote *Le vite dei più celebri architetti e scultori veneziani* (1778).

TEMPLATE. The block of stone set at the top of a brick or rubble wall to carry the weight of the JOISTS or roof-trusses; also called a *pad stone*.

TENIA. The small moulding or fillet along the top of the ARCHITRAVE in the Doric ORDER.

TERM. A pedestal tapering towards the base and usually supporting a bust; also a pedestal merging at the top into a sculptured human, animal, or mythical figure. *See figure 82.*

TERRACOTTA. Fired but unglazed clay, used mainly for wall covering and ornamentation as it can be fired in moulds.

TERRAZZO. A flooring finish of marble chips mixed with cement mortar and laid *in situ*; the surface is then ground and polished.

TESSERAE. The small cubes of glass, stone, or marble used in MOSAIC.

TESSELATED. A cement floor or wall covering in which TESSERAE are embedded.

TESSIN, Nicodemus, the elder (1615–

Fig. 82. Term

81), a leading Baroque architect in Sweden, was born at Stralsund and began by working under Simon LA VALLÉE. In 1651-2 he made a tour of Europe and in 1661 was appointed city architect of Stockholm. His main work is Drottningholm Palace (begun 1662), built in an individual Baroque style derived from Holland, France, and Italy. His other works include Kalmar Cathedral (1660), Götenborg Town Hall (1670), and numerous small houses in Stockholm. His son Nicodemus the younger (1654–1728) succeeded him as the leading Swedish architect. Trained under his father, he travelled in England, France, and Italy (1673–80), and completed his father's work at Drottningholm. His main building is the vast royal palace in Stockholm (begun 1697), where he adopted a Baroque style reminiscent of, and probably influenced by, BERNINI's Louvre project.

TESTER, see PULPIT.

TETRASTYLE. Of a PORTICO with four frontal columns.

THATCH. A roof covering of straw or reeds, Norfolk reeds being the best in England.

THERMAE. In Roman architecture public baths, usually of great size and splendour and containing libraries and other amenities as well as every provision for bathing. Their remains in Rome were closely studied by architects from PALLADIO onwards and had great influence on planning.

THERMAL WINDOW. A semicircular window divided into three lights by two vertical mullions, also known as a Diocletian window because of its use in the Thermae of Diocletian, Rome. Its use was revived in the C16 especially by PALLADIO and is a feature of PALLADIANISM.

THOLUS. The dome of a circular building or the building itself, e.g., a domed Mycenaean tomb.

THOMSON, Alexander (1817–75), lived and worked at Glasgow, and was in practice from about 1847. He was known as 'Greek' Thomson, and rightly so, for to be a convinced Grecian was a very remarkable thing for a man belonging to the generation of PUGIN, SCOTT, and RUSKIN. The formative influence on his style was SCHINKEL rather than English Grecians. This comes out most clearly in such monumental terraces as Moray Place (1859), where the purity of proportion and the scarcity of enrichment suggest a date some thirty years earlier. His churches, on the other hand, though essentially Grecian, are far from pure: they exhibit an admixture of the Egyptian, even the Hindu, as well as a boldness in the use of iron, which combine to produce results of fearsome originality. The three churches – all United Presbyterian – are the Caledonian Road Church (1856), the Vincent Street Church (1859), and the Queen's Park Church (1867). All three are among the most forceful churches of their date anywhere in Europe. Equally interesting are Thomson's warehouses, especially the Egyptian Halls.

THORPE, John (c. 1563–1655), an unimportant clerk in the Office of Works and later a successful land surveyor, was not, as is sometimes thought, the architect of Longleat, Kirby, Wollaton, Audley End, and other great Elizabethan and Jacobean houses. Plans and a few elevations of these and many other Elizabethan buildings are in a volume of drawings by him in the Sir John Soane Museum, London.

TIE-BEAM, see ROOF.

TIERCERON, see VAULT.

TILEHANGING. A wall covering of overlapping rows of tiles on a timber structure.

TIMBER-FRAMING. A method of construction where walls are built of timber framework with the spaces filled in by plaster or brickwork. Sometimes the timber is covered with plaster or boarding laid horizontally (see WEATHERBOARDING). See figure 83.

TOLEDO, Juan Bautista de (d. 1567), philosopher and mathematician as well as architect, spent many years in Italy and for some time before 1559 was architect to the Spanish Viceroy in Naples. In 1562 he was appointed architect of the Escorial, drew up the entire ground plan, but built only the two-storeyed Court of the Evangelists, modelled on SANGALLO's Palazzo Farnese, Rome, and the vast severe south façade.

TOMB-CHEST. A chest-shaped stone coffin, the most usual medieval form of funerary monument. See also ALTAR-TOMB.

TOMÉ, Narciso (active 1715–42), began as a sculptor with his father and brothers on the façade of Valladolid University (1715). His famous Transparente in Toledo Cathedral (1721–32) is the most stupefying of all Baroque extravaganzas in spatial illusionism. It goes farther than anything invented by

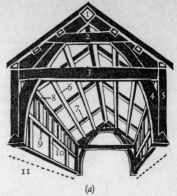

(a)

Key:
1. Ridge piece
2. Collar-beam
3. Tie-beam
4. Arched brace
5. Post
6. Purlins
7. Rafters
8. Wall plate
9. Bressumer
10. Studs
11. Line of ground wall

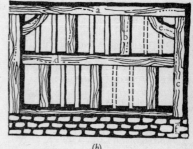

(b)

Key:
a. Wall plate
b. Stud
c. Post
d. Bressumer
e. Bracing
f. Ground wall

Fig. 83. Timber-framing

Italian Baroque architects and is exceptional even for Spain.

TORRALVA, Diogo de (1500–66), the leading Portuguese Renaissance architect, was the son-in-law of ARRUDA but abandoned his rich Manueline style for one much simpler, sterner, and more Italianate. His main work is the cloister of the Cristo Monastery, Tomar (1557), with the SERLIAN MOTIF used as an open arcade on the upper floor. He designed the apse for the Jeronimite Church at Belem (1540–51). Several other buildings have been attributed to him, notably the octagonal church of the Dominican Nuns at Elvas (1543–57).

TORUS. A large convex moulding of semicircular profile, e.g., at the base of a column. *See also* ASTRAGAL *and figure 66.*

TOUCH. A soft black marble quarried near Tournai, used chiefly for monuments.

TOURELLE. A turret CORBELLED out from the wall.

TOWN, Ithiel, *see* DAVIS.

TRABEATED. The adjective describing a building constructed on the post-and-lintel principle, as in Greek architecture, in contrast to an ARCUATED building.

TRACERY. The ornamental intersecting work in the upper part of a window, screen, or panel, or used decoratively in blank arches and vaults. The earliest use of the term so far traced is in Sir Christopher WREN, the medieval word being *form-pieces* or *forms*.

In windows of more than one light in Early Gothic churches the SPANDREL above the lights is often pierced by a circle, a quatrefoil, or some such simple form. This is known as *plate tracery*. Later, and first at Reims (1211 etc.), the circle is no longer pierced through a solid spandrel; instead the two lights are separated by a moulded MULLION and the mouldings of this are continued at the head forming bars of circular, quatrefoil, etc., forms and leaving the rest of the spandrels open. This is called *bar tracery*, and throughout the later Middle Ages it was one of the principal decorative elements of churches. The patterns made by the bars were first the simple geometrical forms already indicated (*geometrical tracery*), later fantastical forms including double curves (*flowing tracery*), and later still – at least in England – plain, vertical, arched panels repeated more or less

exactly (*panel tracery*). In Germany, France, and Spain forms similar to the English flowing tracery became the rule in the late Middle Ages. With the end of the Middle Ages tracery generally disappeared.

Bar tracery, introduced at Reims and brought to England *c.* 1240, consists of intersecting ribwork made up of slender shafts continuing the lines of the mullions up to a decorative mesh in the window-head.

Flowing tracery is made up of compound or OGEE curves, with an uninterrupted flow from curve to curve; also called *curvilinear* or *undulating tracery*. It was used from the beginning of the C14 in England, and throughout the C15 in France, where it rapidly became fully developed and FLAMBOYANT, with no survival of the geometrical elements of the early flowing tracery of England.

Geometrical tracery is characteristic of *c.* 1220–1300 and consists chiefly of circles or foiled circles.

In *intersecting tracery* each mullion of a window branches into curved bars which are continuous with the mullions. The outer arch of the window being of two equal curves (*see* ARCH), all sub-divisions of the window-head produced by these tracery bars following the curves of the outer arch must of necessity be equilateral also. The bars and the arch are all drawn from the same centre with a different radius. Such a window can be of two, or usually more, lights, with the result that every two, three, or four lights together form a pointed arch. Additional enrichment, e.g., circles, CUSPING, is always of a secondary character. The form is typical of *c.* 1300.

Kentish tracery is foiled tracery in a circle with barbs between the foils.

Panel tracery is PERPENDICULAR tracery formed of upright, straight-sided panels above the lights of a window, also called *rectilinear*.

Plate tracery is a late C12 and early C13 form where decoratively shaped openings are cut through the solid stone infilling in a window-head.

Reticulated tracery, a form used much in the early to mid C14, is made up entirely of circles drawn at top and bottom into OGEE shapes resulting in a net-like appearance.

In *Y-tracery* a mullion branches into two forming a Y shape; typical of *c.* 1300.

See figure 84.

TRACHELION. The neck of a Greek Doric column, between the SHAFT-RING and HYPOTRACHELION.

TRANSENNA. An openwork screen or lattice, usually of marble, in an Early Christian church.

TRANSEPT. The transverse arms of a cross-shaped church, usually between NAVE and CHANCEL, but also occasionally at the west end of the nave as well, and also doubled, with the eastern arms farther east than the junction of nave and chancel. The latter form is usual in English Gothic cathedrals.

TRANSITIONAL ARCHITECTURE. A term usually referring to the period of transition from the ROMANESQUE to the GOTHIC, or in Britain from the NORMAN to the EARLY ENGLISH style. Sometimes details of the later styles are used on the general forms of the earlier.

TRANSOM. A horizontal bar of stone or wood across the opening of a window or across a panel.

TRANSVERSE ARCH, *see* VAULT.

TREAD, *see* STAIR.

TREFOIL, *see* FOIL.

TREZZINI, Domenico (Andrei Petrovich Trezini, 1670–1734), the first of the Western European architects employed by Peter the Great of Russia, was of Italo-Swiss origin. He is first recorded in 1700 working on the palace of Frederick IV in Copenhagen. In 1703 he was invited to become architect of the new city of St Petersburg. He was employed mainly to design small wooden houses, also the Summer Palace (1711–14) in a pre-

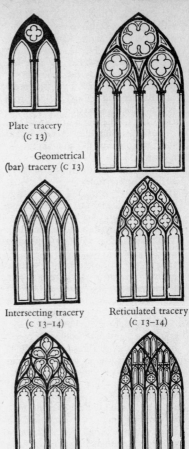

Plate tracery
(C 13)

Geometrical
(bar) tracery (C 13)

Intersecting tracery
(C 13–14)

Reticulated tracery
(C 13–14)

Curvilinear of flowing tracery (C 14)

Late C 14 tracery

Panel tracery (C 15)
Fig. 84. Tracery

dominantly Dutch style and the rather gawky Dutch Baroque Cathedral of St Peter and St Paul, St Petersburg (1714–25). His main work was the terrace of twelve pavilion-like buildings to house the government ministries, each with a colossal order of pilasters and a high hipped roof (1722–32, later altered).

TRIBUNE. 1. The APSE of a BASILICA or basilican church. 2. A raised platform or rostrum. 3. The GALLERY in a church.

TRICLINIUM. The dining-room in an ancient Roman house.

TRIFORIUM. An arcaded wall-passage facing on to the NAVE, at a level above the arcade and below the CLERE-STORY windows (if there are any). The term is often wrongly applied to a tribune or GALLERY.

TRIGLYPHS. Blocks with vertical grooves separating the METOPES in a Doric FRIEZE. *See figure 64.*

TRILITHON. A prehistoric monument consisting of a horizontal stone resting on two upright ones, as at Stonehenge.

TRIM. The framing or edging of openings and other features on a façade or indoors. It is usually of a colour and material (wood, stucco, or stone) different from that of the adjacent wall surface.

TROPHY. A sculptured group of arms or armour used as a memorial to victory, sometimes with floreated motifs intermingled to form a FESTOON.

TRUMEAU. The stone MULLION supporting the TYMPANUM of a doorway.

TRUSS. A number of timbers framed together to bridge a space or form a

BRACKET, to be self-supporting, and to carry other timbers. The trusses of a roof are usually named after the particular feature in their construction, e.g., king-post, queen-post, etc. *See* ROOF.

TUFA. The commonest Roman building stone, formed from volcanic dust; it is porous and grey.

TURKISH ARCHITECTURE. In the Seljuq period (C11–13) religious architecture was derived from Persia, though stone was employed instead of brick. With the advent of the Ottomans (*c.* 1400) and their capture of Constantinople in 1453 the BYZANTINE style was adopted with modifications. As in other countries under Islamic rule, the Moslems began by adapting existing buildings: thus Haghia Sophia and other Christian churches were converted into mosques. The influence of Byzantium persisted in later buildings, e.g., the Suleimaniyeh, Istanbul, by SINAN (1550–6), and the Ahmediyeh or Mosque of Ahmed I, Istanbul (1608–14). A new type of minaret was developed – a very tall and slender circular tower capped by an attenuated cone like a candle-snuffer. Glazed tiles were much used for decoration. Domestic buildings, of which the KIOSK is the most typical, were constructed mainly of wood and are notable for the elaborate carved wood MUSHRABEYEH lattices.

TURRET. A very small and slender tower.

TUSCAN ORDER, *see* ORDER.

TYMPANUM. The area between the LINTEL of a doorway and the arch above it.

U

UNDERCROFT. A vaulted room, sometimes underground, below an upper room such as a church or chapel.

UNITED STATES ARCHITECTURE. The incunabula of New England's domestic architecture, dating from the C17, are of no more than strictly local interest, first Dutch in inspiration, then English. A monumental scale was only rarely achieved (William and Mary College, Williamsburg, 1695, much restored as is the whole of Williamsburg). Churches are entirely Georgian in the C18, often influenced in their spires by GIBBS. Houses are equally Georgian, in the country as well as the towns. But in both houses and churches timber plays a prominent part alongside, or instead of, brick. Among the best churches are Christ Church, Philadelphia (1727 and 1754); Christ Church, Cambridge (1761); St Michael, Charleston (1761); and the Baptist Church at Providence (1775). The finest Early Georgian house is Westover, Virginia (1726). From the mid C18 notable examples are Mount Airy, Virginia, Mount Pleasant, Philadelphia, and Whitehall, Maryland, with its giant Corinthian portico. Later porticos tend to have attenuated columns (Homewood, Baltimore). As town *emsembles* Salem and Nantucket (Mass.) and Charleston (South Carolina) may be singled out. The United States has still quite a few C18 public buildings: Old State House, Boston (1710); Independence Hall, Philadelphia (1732); Faneuil Hall, Boston (1742); and so to the Capitol in its original form (1792) and the Boston State House by BULLFINCH (1793–1800). The earliest university buildings are also Georgian: at Harvard (1720, 1764 etc.); at Yale (1750–2); and then Thomas

JEFFERSON'S University of Virginia at Charlottesville (1817–26), the first American campus, i.e., with buildings composed round a spacious lawn. JEFFERSON'S own house, Monticello, is of 1770–1809.

The Greek Revival starts with LATROBE'S Doric Bank of Pennsylvania of 1798. From 1803 he did much in a Grecian taste inside the Capitol in Washington. His finest work, comparable with that of SOANE in elegance and originality, is Baltimore Cathedral (begun 1805). But for this building he also submitted a Gothic design; a country house of his (Sedgeley, Philadelphia) was Gothic too. However, except in church design, Gothic made slow progress, and the most thoroughly Grecian years are the 1820s and 1830s, with the big government buildings in Washington by MILLS and several state capitols by TOWN & DAVIS. Davis experimented in many styles, including the Egyptian and the Old-English cottage. The most prominent Gothic churches are RENWICK'S Grace Church, New York (1846), and UPJOHN'S Trinity Church, New York, of the same years. Henry Austin deserves a special mention; if ever there was rogue architecture, his New Haven railway station (1848–9) is it. Its style cannot be derived from any clear direction.

Already in the second quarter of the century certain American specialities began to appear. One is hotels, especially of the size and type that became standard in Europe later (Tremont House, Boston, by Isaiah Rogers, 1828–9); another is such technical equipment as bathrooms and lifts.

The United States moved from a marginal to a central position with the work of H. H. RICHARDSON, both in the field of the massive uncompromising commercial building for which his style was a French-inspired Romanesque (Marshall Field Wholesale Warehouse, Chicago, 1885–7) and in the field of the informal, comfortable, moderately dimensioned private house (Sherman House, Newport, 1874–6). Even more independent are some of the houses designed in their early years by McKim, Mead & White (see MCKIM), notably one at Bristol, Rhode Island (1887). Otherwise that firm is principally remembered for their Italian Renaissance Revival (Villard Houses, New York, 1885; Boston Public Library, 1887), Colonial Revival, and also Palladian Revival, the latter on a grand scale (Pennsylvania Station, New York, 1906–10).

Meanwhile, however, Chicago had established a style of commercial architecture all her own and vigorously pointing forward into the C20 (Chicago School). It started from the introduction of the principle of steel framing (see SKYSCRAPER) about 1884 and reached its climax in such buildings as the Tacoma (1887–9) by HOLABIRD & ROCHE, the Marquette (1894) by BURNHAM & ROOT, and, most personal, the Wainwright at St Louis (1890) by SULLIVAN. With Sullivan's Carson, Pirie & Scott Store, Chicago (1899 etc.), a totally unhistoricist style of unrelieved verticals and horizontals was reached, though Sullivan was perhaps at his most original in his feathery, decidedly ART NOUVEAU ornament.

Sullivan's principal pupil was Frank Lloyd WRIGHT, whose work, chiefly in the domestic field, bridges the whole territory from c. 1890 to nearly 1960. But his brilliant style of sweeping horizontals and of intercommunication between spaces inside a house and between inside and outside spaces found little recognition in his own country. In fact, the C20 style on a major scale had to be imported from Europe: the pioneer building was the Philadelphia Savings Fund Building by Howe & Lescaze (1930–2) – a relatively late date in European terms – and the spectacular development of C20 architecture in the United States belongs entirely to the years after the Second World War. The flowering was fostered by such distinguished immigrants as GROPIUS, MIES VAN DER ROHE, NEUTRA, and BREUER. The first stage belongs to the rational, cubic, crisp so-called INTERNATIONAL MODERN and culminates in Mies van der Rohe's houses and blocks of flats of c. 1950 onwards and most of the work of SKIDMORE, OWINGS & MERRILL. The second stage is that of the neo-sculptural, anti-rational, highly expressive style current in many countries while this dictionary is being produced. The United States is richer than any other part of the world in such buildings, from a love of novelty as well as from a prosperity that encourages display. Trends within this trend cannot here be separated: they run from the powerful concrete curves of Eero SAARINEN to the dainty eclecticism of Edward Stone (b. 1902; Huntingdon Hartford Museum, New York, 1962–4), and include such mercurial and controversial figures as Philip JOHNSON, Minoru Yamasaki (b. 1912, St Louis Airport), and Paul RUDOLPH. See also FULLER and KAHN.

UNWIN, Sir Raymond (1863–1940). The leading English town-planner of his day and the man who – in partnership from 1896 to 1914 with Barry Parker (1867–1941) – translated into reality the garden city scheme conceived by Ebenezer HOWARD. The 'First Garden City', as the company for its realization was actually called, was Letchworth in Hertfordshire (begun 1903). However, while the growth of Letchworth did not progress as rapidly or as smoothly as had been anticipated, two garden suburbs did extremely well, the Hampstead

Garden Suburb outside London (begun 1907), and Wythenshawe outside Manchester (begun 1927). The Hampstead Garden Suburb in particular must be regarded as the *beau idéal* of the garden city principles of domestic and public planning, with its formal centre – the two churches and the institute designed by LUTYENS – its pattern of straight main and curving minor vehicular roads and its occasional pedestrian paths, its trees carefully preserved and its architectural style controlled in no more than the most general terms of a free neo-Tudor. Unwin also showed his sense of subtle visual planning effects in his *Town Planning in Practice*, first published in 1909, and a textbook to this day.

UPJOHN, Richard (1802–78), was born at Shaftesbury, where he was later in business as a cabinet-maker. He emigrated to America in 1829 and opened a practice as an architect at Boston in 1834. His speciality was Gothic churches: the first came in 1837, and the principal ones are Trinity Church, New York (1841–6), an effort in a rich Anglo-Gothic, and Trinity Chapel, W. 25th Street (1853), also Anglo-Gothic. He built in other styles as well (Trinity Building, New York, 1852, is Italianate). Upjohn was the first president of the American Institute of Architects.

URBAN RENEWAL. The replanning of existing towns or centres to bring them up to date and to improve amenities and traffic circulation.

V

VACCARINI, Giovan Battista (1702–68), was born in Palermo. He studied under Carlo FONTANA in Rome and settled in Catania (1730), where his exuberant Sicilian Rococo style is seen in the façade of the cathedral (begun 1730), Palazzo Municipale (1732), Collegio Cutelli (1754), and S. Agata (begun 1735).

VALADIER, Giuseppe (1762–1839), archaeologist, town planner, and a prolific though rather reactionary architect. His main buildings are neo-Palladian rather than neo-classical, e.g., interior of Spoleto Cathedral (1784), interior of Urbino Cathedral (1789), and façade of S. Rocco, Rome (1833), though the boldly simple S. Pantaleo, Rome (1806), is more in tune with his times. His masterpiece is the reorganization of Piazza del Popolo, Rome, for which he published a design in 1794 and which he began in 1813.

VANBRUGH, Sir John (1664–1726), soldier, adventurer, playwright, and herald, was also the outstanding English Baroque architect. His father was a Flemish refugee who became a rich sugar-baker and married the daughter of Sir Dudley Carleton. He was brought up as a gentleman and commissioned in the Earl of Huntingdon's regiment in 1686. In 1690 he was arrested in Calais for spying and imprisoned for two years, part of the time in the Bastille. After his release he took London by storm with his witty and improper comedies *The Relapse* and *The Provok'd Wife*. Then he switched his talents to architecture – 'without thought or lecture', said Swift – having been invited by the Earl of Carlisle to try his hand at designing Castle Howard (1699). Lord Carlisle also had him appointed Comptroller at the Office of Works

(1702), and thus he became, without any training or qualifications, WREN's principal colleague. But he turned out to be an architect of genius. The Tories later deprived him of his Comptrollership, but he was reinstated after the death of Queen Anne and knighted (1714). Witty and convivial, a friend of Tonson and Congreve and a member of the Kit Cat Club, he lived on terms of easy familiarity with the great men who became his clients.

His style derives from Wren at his grandest – e.g., Greenwich Hospital – and probably owes much to HAWKSMOOR, his assistant from 1699 onwards. But every building he designed is stamped with his own unique personality – expansive, virile, and ostentatious, more Flemish than English and often rather coarse and theatrical. Castle Howard (1699–1726) is an amazing trial of strength by a young undisciplined genius. His great opportunity came in 1705 at Blenheim Palace, the nation's gift to Marlborough in honour of his victories. Here he had almost unlimited funds at his disposal and the whole megalomaniac conception suited his temperament perfectly. He was always at his best on the largest possible scale, and his genius for the dramatic and heroic, for bold groupings of masses and for picturesque recessions and projections and varied skylines had full play.

His style reached sudden maturity at Blenheim – indeed, English Baroque architecture culminates there – and it changed little afterwards. The best of his surviving houses are Kimbolton (1707–9), King's Weston (1711–14), Seaton Delaval (c. 1720–8), Lumley Castle (entrance front and interior alterations, c. 1722), and Grimsthorpe (north range only, c. 1723–4). He said he wanted his architecture to be 'masculine' and to have 'something of the Castle Air', and nowhere does his peculiar version of the Baroque come closer to the massiveness of a medieval fortress than at Seaton Delaval. Sombre and cyclopean, this extraordinary house is unlike any other building in England or anywhere else. His strong sense of the picturesque led him to further and more explicit medievalisms elsewhere, notably at his own house at Greenwich (after 1717), which is castellated and has a fortified-looking round tower. He seems here to have foreshadowed the romantic spirit of later Gothic revivals.

VANVITELLI, Luigi (1700–73), was born in Naples, the son of the painter Gaspar van Wittel, studied painting under his father in Rome, and emerged as an architect only in the 1730s. He worked at Pesaro, Macerata, Perugia, Loreto, Siena, Ancona, and Rome (monastery of S. Agostino and remodelling of S. Maria degli Angeli) before he was summoned to Naples by Carlo III in 1751 to build the enormous 1,200-room palace at Caserta. This is the last great Italian Baroque building. Its immense internal vistas, ceremonial staircase, and central octagonal vestibule rival the most extravagant stage-set in scenographic fantasy, though the exterior already veers towards neo-classical restraint. Almost equally impressive are his Chiesa dell' Annunziata (1761–82), Piazza Dante (1757–63), and twenty-five mile long Acquedotto Carolino (1752–64).

VARDY, John (d. 1765). Friend and close associate of KENT, whose designs for the Horse Guards, London, he carried out (with W. Robinson, 1750–8). His most important surviving work is Spencer House, London (1750–65), an excellent example of PALLADIANISM freely interpreted.

VASARI, Giorgio (1511–74). A painter and author of the famous *Vite de' più eccellenti architetti, pittori e scultori italiani* (1550, revised 1568), which by its eulogistic account of MICHELANGELO exerted an important influence on architectural taste. As an architect he had a hand, with VIGNOLA and della PORTA, in designing the Villa di Papa Giulio, Rome (1552). His only important independent work is the Uffizi, Florence (begun 1560), with a long narrow courtyard stretching down towards the river and closed by a range with two superimposed Serlian arcades – an adaptation of Michelangelo's Laurentian Library to external architecture.

VÁZQUEZ, Lorenzo, to whom the earliest works of the Renaissance in Spain are now attributed, was master mason to Cardinal Mendoza, and for the Cardinal the Colegio de Santa Cruz at Valladolid was begun in 1487, with its Quattrocento frontispiece medallion. The next buildings in order of date were also commissioned by members of the Mendoza family: the palace at Cogolludo (probably 1492–5), with windows still floridly Late Gothic; the palace at Guadalajara (before 1507); and the castle of La Calahorra (1509–12). In the latter case, however, it is known that Michele Carlone of Genoa was called in to take charge. For other early major Renaissance designs in Spain see EGAS.

VAUDREMER, J. Auguste E. (1829–1914), after a training under the sober utilitarian architects Blouet and Gilbert, started with his large Santé Prison, Paris (1862 etc.), in the same spirit. However, in 1864 he was commissioned to build the church of St Pierre de Montrouge in Paris, and here his very sobriety and directness made him choose the Romanesque rather than the Gothic style. The building must have impressed H. H. RICHARDSON. Romanesque also, but internally with much grander stone vaults is Notre Dame, rue d'Auteuil, Paris (1876 etc.). The much larger and more famous Sacré Cœur on Montmartre is by Paul Abadie (1812–84) and was started in 1876. It is inspired by St Front at Périgueux, which Abadie disastrously restored.

VAULT. An arched ceiling or roof of stone or brick, sometimes imitated in wood or plaster.

Barrel vault, see tunnel vault.

Cloister vault, see domical vault.

Cross vault, see groin vault.

Domical vault. A dome rising direct on a square or polygonal BAY, the curved surfaces separated by GROINS. In America called a cloister vault. See figure 38.

A fan vault consists of solid concave-sided semi-cones, meeting or nearly meeting at the apex of the vault. The areas between are flat and, if the cones meet, form concave-sided lozenges. The cones and centres are decorated with panelling so as to give the appearance of a highly decorated rib vault. See figure 85.

A groin vault is produced by the intersection at right angles of two tunnel vaults of identical shape. See figure 85.

Lierne. A tertiary rib, that is, one which does not spring either from one of the main springers or from the central BOSS. See figure 85.

For Net vault see definition under RIETH.

In a quadripartite vault one bay is divided into four quarters or CELLS.

A rib vault is a framework of diagonal arched ribs carrying the cells which cover in the spaces between them. See figure 85.

Ridge-rib. The rib along the longitudinal or transverse ridge of a vault, at an angle of approximately 45° to the main diagonal ribs. See figure 85.

In a sexpartite vault one bay of quadripartite vaulting is divided transversely into two parts so that each bay has six compartments.

Tierceron. A secondary rib, which springs from one of the main springers, or the central boss, and

leads to a place on the ridge-rib. See figure 85.

A transverse arch separates one bay of a vault from the next. It can be either plain in section or moulded.

Tunnel vault (also called barrel vault and wagon vault). The simplest form of vault, consisting of a continuous vault of semicircular or pointed sections, unbroken in its length by cross

Key:
a. Tunnel vault   c. Rib vault
b. Groin vault   d. Fan vault

1. Transverse rib;   5. Tiercerons;
2. Diagonal rib;   6. Liernes;
3. Transverse ridge-rib; 7. Boss
4. Longitudinal ridge-rib;

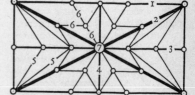

Fig. 85. Vault

vaults. BUTTRESSING is needed to ground the thrust, which is dispersed all along the wall beneath. Tunnel vaults can be subdivided into bays by transverse arches. *See figure 85.*

Wagon vault, see tunnel vault.

VAUX, Calvert, *see* DOWNING.

VELDE, Henri van de (1863–1957), who was born at Antwerp of a well-to-do family, was first a painter influenced aesthetically by the Neo-Impressionists (Pointillists), socially by the ideals which at the time also inspired van Gogh. About 1890, under the impact of RUSKIN and MORRIS, he turned from painting to design and in 1892 produced the first works that are entirely his own and at the same time are entirely representative of ART NOUVEAU, the anti-historical movement just then emerging. They are works of typography and book decoration, with long flexible curves, and an appliqué panel called *The Angels Watch*. Their stylistic source seems to be the Gauguin of Pont Aven and his circle, especially Émile Bernard.

In 1895 van de Velde designed a house and furnishings at Uccle near Brussels for his own young family. It was his first achievement in architecture and interior design, and both now became his principal concerns. He was commissioned to design interiors for Bing's newly established shop L'Art Nouveau in Paris (1895) and then showed most of this work at an exhibition in Dresden (1897). In both centres its impact was great, but whereas reactions were largely hostile in France, they were enthusiastic in Germany, and so van de Velde decided to leave Brussels and settle in Berlin. In the next year he did much furnishing work for the wealthy and the refined, including the shop of the imperial barber (Haby, 1901). In 1901 he was called to Weimar as a consultant on the coordination of crafts, trades, and good design. He furnished the Nietzsche-Archive there (1903), and rebuilt the Art School and the School of Arts

and Crafts (1904, 1907), of which latter he became director. He also did the interior of the Folkwang Museum at Hagen (1901–2) and the Abbe Monument at Jena (1908).

His style is characterized by the long daring curves of Art Nouveau, endowed by him with a peculiar resilience, and in architecture also by the use of the curve rather than the angle – e.g., for roofs. For the Werkbund Exhibition at Cologne in 1914 (*see* GROPIUS; TAUT) he did the theatre, also with curved corners and a curved roof.

Being Belgian he left his job in Germany during the war, lived through restless years of émigré life and only in 1925 settled down again, now back in Brussels. However, the years of his great successes and his European significance were over. His late style is less personal, close to that of the School of Amsterdam (*see* OUD): its finest example is the Kröller-Müller Museum at Otterlo in Holland, beautifully coordinated with the heath scenery around (1937–54).

VENETIAN WINDOW, *see* SERLIANA.

VERANDA. An open gallery or balcony with a roof supported by light, usually metal, supports.

VERMICULATION. Decoration of masonry blocks with irregular shallow channels like worm tracks. *See figure 72.*

VERTUE, Robert (d. 1506), and William (d. 1527), were brothers and both masons. Robert, the elder, appears at Westminster Abbey from 1475. About 1501 both brothers were master masons for Bath Abbey, begun at that time by Bishop King. This grandly Perpendicular building has a fan vault which, so they told the bishop, would be such that 'there shall be none so goodly neither in England nor in France'; and as at that moment neither the vault of King's College Chapel, Cambridge, nor that of Henry VII Chapel in Westminster Abbey, or that of St George's Chapel,

Windsor, existed (though the latter was building), the claim was just. The Vertues' precise connexion with these three works cannot be proved, but as they were jointly the King's Master Masons, with Robert Janyns and John Lebons (*see* REDMAN), it is likely that a connexion existed. William, in any case, signed a contract with another (John Aylmer) to vault the chancel at Windsor, and visited King's College Chapel once in 1507, once (with Redman) in 1509, and once (with WASTELL) in 1512, if not more often.

In 1516 Vertue appeared at Eton (with Redman), where he made a design (the design?) for Lupton's Tower. From 1515 he was joint King's Mason with Redman. In 1526 he probably designed the fan-vaulted cloister chapel in the Palace of Westminster.

VESICA. An upright almond shape; found chiefly in medieval art to enclose a figure of Christ enthroned.

VIADUCT. A long series of arches carrying a road or railway.

VICENTE DE OLIVEIRA, Mateus (1710–86), the leading Portuguese Rococo architect, began under LUDOVICE but forsook his grandiose manner for one more delicate and intimate. His masterpiece is the Palace of Queluz (1747–52, interior destroyed), where a large building is disguised behind an exquisitely frivolous façade swagged with garlands of carved flowers. He also designed the very large Estrêla Church in Lisbon (1778).

VIGNOLA, Jacopo Barozzi (1507–73), the leading architect in Rome after the death of MICHELANGELO, was born at Vignola, near Modena, and studied painting and architecture at Bologna. In 1530 he settled in Rome. His first important work was the completion of Palazzo Farnese, Caprarola (1550), begun on a pentagonal plan by PERUZZI: he designed the rather stern façades, the very elegant circular courtyard in the centre, and probably the garden. He seems to have played the leading part in designing the Villa di Papa Giulio, Rome (1550–5) in collaboration with della PORTA and VASARI. It is a masterpiece of Mannerist architecture and garden design, with much play with vistas from one courtyard to another, hemicycles echoing each other, a curious rhythmical use of the orders, and very shallow relief decorations applied to the surfaces.

In 1564 he took over the building of Palazzo Farnese in Piacenza. He may also have designed the Villa Lante, Bagnaia (begun 1566), with its wonderful hillside water gardens. In about 1550 he built the little Tempietto di S. Andrea, Rome, for Pope Julius III, using for the first time in church architecture an oval plan which he was to repeat on a larger scale in his design for S. Anna dei Palafrenieri, Rome (begun 1573), and which was to be used extensively by Baroque architects. His most influential building was the Gesù, Rome (begun 1568); it has probably had a wider influence than any church built in the last 400 years. The plan, which owes something to ALBERTI'S S. Andrea, Mantua, combines the central scheme of the Renaissance with the longitudinal scheme of the Middle Ages. The aisles are replaced by a series of chapels opening off the nave, and various devices – e.g., lighting and the placing of the nave pilasters – direct attention to the high altar. (The interior was redecorated in High Baroque style in 1668–73.)

Vignola was architect to St Peter's (1567–73) and continued Michelangelo's work there faithfully. In 1562 he published *Regole delli cinque ordini*, a simple modular interpretation of the architectural orders which, on account of its straight-forward approach, enjoyed immense popularity.

VILLA. In Roman architecture, the landowner's residence or farmstead on his country estate; in Renaissance architecture, a country house; in C19 England, a detached house 'for opulent persons', usually on the outskirts of a town; in modern architecture, a small detached house.

VILLANUEVA, Juan de (1739–1811), the leading Spanish neo-classical architect, was the son of a sculptor under whom he trained. He began in the CHURRIGUERESQUE tradition, then became a draughtsman to SACCHETTI in Madrid and adopted an Italianate Baroque style. He was sent by the Royal Academy to Rome (1759–65), and on his return his brother Diego (1715–74) published his *Colección de papeles críticos sobre la arquitectura* (1766), the first neo-classical attack on the Churrigueresque and Rococo to appear in Spain. Rather tentatively he began to put these ideas into practice in the Palafox Chapel in Burgo de Osma Cathedral (1770), Casita de Arriba at the Escorial (1773), and Casita del Príncipe at El Pardo (1784). His outstanding work is the Prado Museum, Madrid, designed (1787) as a museum of natural history but later adapted to house the royal collection of pictures. With its sturdy Tuscan portico in the centre and its boldly articulated wings with Ionic colonnades at first-floor level, it is an effective and undoctrinaire essay in neo-classicism.

VILLARD DE HONNECOURT, a French architect who was active around 1225–35 in the north-west of France, was probably master mason of Cambrai Cathedral, which no longer exists. Villard is known to us by the book of drawings with short texts which he compiled for the learners in his lodge, the masons' workshop and office. The book is in the Bibliothèque Nationale in Paris and contains plans of buildings (both copied and invented), elevational details, figure sculpture, figures drawn *al vif*, foliage ornament, a lectern, a stall end, a *perpetuum mobile*, and in addition many small technical drawings, more of an

engineering kind, which were added to the book by two successors of Villard. From the text and the examples illustrated it is certain that Villard knew Reims, Laon, Chartres, Lausanne, and that he travelled as far as Hungary. The sculptural style of his figures connects him with work of about 1230 at Reims. Villard's book gives us the clearest insight we can obtain into the work of a distinguished master mason and the atmosphere of a lodge.

VINCKEBOONS, Philip Davidsz (1607–1678), the leading Amsterdam architect of his day and very prolific, modified the traditional domestic style by symmetrical planning, by introducing rectangular gables in place of curvilinear or stepped gables, and by articulating façades with superimposed or giant orders. In his later houses – e.g., Neuremburg House, Amsterdam (1665) – the order is reduced to plain strips. His brother Justus built the imposing Trippenhuis, Amsterdam (*c.* 1660).

VIOLLET-LE-DUC, Eugène-Emanuel (1814–79), was born into a wealthy, cultured, and progressive family. His opposition to the 'establishment' began early: he helped to build barricades in 1830 and refused to go to the École des Beaux Arts for his training. In 1836–7 he was in Italy studying buildings with industry and intelligence. His future was determined by his meeting with Prosper Mérimée (1803–70), author of *Carmen* and Inspector in the newly founded Commission des Monuments Historiques. Viollet-le-Duc, inspired by Victor Hugo's enthusiasm on the one hand and by Arcisse de Caumont's scholarship on the other, now turned resolutely to the French Middle Ages and soon established himself both as a scholar and as a restorer. His first job was Vézelay (1840). He then did the Sainte Chapelle in Paris with Duban, and Notre Dame with Lassus. The number of his restorations is legion.

As a scholar he developed new and highly influential ideas on the Gothic style, which to him is socially the outcome of a lay civilization succeeding the sinister religious domination of the earlier Middle Ages. The Gothic style to Viollet-le-Duc is also a style of rational construction based on the system of rib vault, flying buttress, and buttress. The ribs are a skeleton, like a C19 iron skeleton; the webs or cells are no more than light infilling. All thrusts are conducted from the ribs to the flying buttresses and buttresses, and thin walls can be replaced by large openings. These ideas were laid down and made universal property by Viollet-le-Duc's *Dictionnaire raisonné de l' architecture française* (published 1854–68). A comparison between Gothic skeleton and C19 iron skeleton building was drawn, or rather implied, in Viollet-le-Duc's *Entretiens* (2 vols., published 1863 and 1872), and especially in the second of them. Here Viollet-le-Duc appears as a passionate defender of his own age, of engineering, and of new materials and techniques, especially iron for supports, for framework, and indeed for ribs. The plates to the three parts of the *Entretiens* are extremely original, but aesthetically none too attractive. As an architect Viollet-le-Duc had in fact little merit. Time and again one is struck by the discrepancy between the consistency and daring of his thought and the looseness and commonplace detailing of his original buildings, e.g., Saint-Denys-de-l'Estrée, St Denis (1864–7).

VITRUVIAN SCROLL, *see* RUNNING DOG.

VITRUVIUS POLLIO, Marcus (active 46–30 B.C.), a Roman architect and theorist of slight importance in his own time but of enormous influence from the Early Renaissance onwards, served under Julius Caesar in the AfricanWar (46 B.C.), built the basilica at Fano (destroyed), and in old age composed a treatise on architecture in ten books *De architectura*, written in a somewhat obscure style and dedicated to Augustus. This is the only complete treatise on architecture to survive from Antiquity. Several manuscript copies were known and used in the Middle Ages. In 1414 Poggio Bracciolini drew attention to a copy at St Gall, and the treatise soon came to be regarded as a vade-mecum for all progressive architects. Both ALBERTI and FRANCESCO DI GIORGIO derived much from it for their writings and buildings. The first printed text was published in Rome *c.* 1486 and the first illustrated edition by Fra GIOCONDO in 1511; an Italian translation was prepared under RAPHAEL's direction *c.* 1520, and another translation was printed in 1521 with an extensive commentary by Cesare Cesariano and numerous illustrations. A vast number of subsequent editions and translations in nearly all European languages appeared. The obscurity of the text, which made a strong appeal to the Renaissance intellect, enabled architects to interpret its gnomic statements in a variety of ways.

VITTONE, Bernardo (1704/5–1770), a little-known architect of real if rather freakish genius, worked exclusively in Piedmont where he was born. He studied in Rome and edited GUARINI's posthumous *Architettura civile* (1737). His secular buildings are dull; not so his numerous churches, mostly small and scattered in remote villages, in which the unlikely fusion of Guarini and JUVARRA had surprising and original results in a gay Rococo vein. Of his structural inventions the pendentive-squinch (e.g. S. Maria di Piazza, Turin, 1751–4) and fantastic three-vaulted dome are the most successful. His churches at Vallinotto (1738–9), Brà (1742), and Chieri (1740–4) show his structural ingenuity at its prettiest. Later churches – Borgo d'Ale, Rivarola Canavese, Grignasco – are larger, less frivolous, but suavely calm and sinuous. He had several followers and disciples in Piedmont, but no influence whatever farther afield.

VOLUTE. A spiral scroll on an Ionic CAPITAL; smaller versions appear on Composite and Corinthian capitals. *See figure 64.*

VORONIKHIN, Andrei Nikiforovich (1760–1814), one of the leading figures in the neo-classical transformation of St Petersburg, was born a serf on the estates of Count Stroganov, who sent him to study in Moscow, then on a European tour (1784–90), and finally employed him to design the state apartments in his palace. His main works are in Leningrad, e.g., Cathedral of the Virgin of Kazan (1801–11), the most Catholic and Roman church in Russia, and the Academy of Mines (1806–11) with a dodecastyle Paestum portico.

VOUSSOIRS. The wedge-shaped stones used in arch construction. *See figure 4.*

VOYSEY, Charles F. Annesley (1857–1941), worked first under Seddon, then with Devey, and set up in practice in 1882. He was at once as interested in design as in architecture, under the general influence of MORRIS and of MACKMURDO in particular. The earliest designs for wallpapers and textiles are of 1883 and are indeed very reminiscent of Mackmurdo. His first commissions for houses date from 1888–9, and from then until the First World War he built a large number of country houses and hardly anything else. They are never extremely large, never grand, never representational; instead they are placed in intimate relation to nature – perhaps an old tree preserved in the courtyard – and developed informally. They spread with ease and, having lowish comfortable rooms, are often on the cosy side. The exteriors are usually rendered with pebbledash and have horizontal windows. They are no longer period imitations at all – in fact, more independent of the past than most architects ventured to be before 1900 – but they never lack the admission of a sympathy for the rural Tudor and Stuart traditions. Voysey designed the furniture and all the details, such as fireplaces, metalwork, etc., himself, and the furniture is again inspired by Mackmurdo's (and in its turn inspired MACKINTOSH's). It is reasonable, friendly, and in the decoration not without a sweet sentimentality; the same is true of textiles and wallpapers.

Among his houses which had a tremendous influence at home (right down to the caricatures produced between the wars by speculative builders) and abroad, the following may be listed: Perrycroft, Colwall, 1893; Annesley Lodge, Hampstead, London, 1895; Merlshanger (Grey Friars), Hog's Back, 1896; Norney, Shackleford, 1897; Broadleys and Moor Crag, both Gill Head, Windermere, 1898; The Orchard, Chorley Wood, 1899. After the war Voysey was rarely called upon to do any architectural work.

VRIES, Hans Vredeman de (1527– *c.* 1604), began as a painter, settled in Antwerp, and published fantastic ornamental pattern-books – *Architectura* (1565), *Compertimenta* (1566) – which had enormous influence on architecture all over northern Europe including England (e.g., SMYTHSON's Wollaton). His style represents the Flemish and Dutch contribution to MANNERISM and expresses the northern feeling for flat pattern in strapwork or carved decoration of interlaced bands and forms similar to fretwork or cut leather.

VYSE. A spiral staircase or a staircase winding round a central column.

W

WAGNER, Otto (1841–1918), became professor at the Academy in Vienna in 1894, and delivered an inaugural address pleading for a new approach to architecture, for independence of the past, and for rationalism ('Nothing that is not practical can be beautiful'). Before that time he had himself designed in the neo-Renaissance style. His most familiar achievement is some stations for the Vienna Stadtbahn (1894–7), ART NOUVEAU with much exposed iron, though more restrained than Hector GUIMARD's contemporary ones for the Paris Métro. But his most amazingly modern and C20-looking job was the Post Office Savings Bank, Vienna (1904–6), the exterior faced with marble slabs held in place by aluminium bolts and the interior featuring a glass barrel vault realized with a clarity and economy hardly matched by anyone else at so early a date. Wagner had a decisive influence on the best younger architects of Vienna (see HOFFMANN. LOOS, OLBRICH). His most monumental building, also closer to the style of the Sezession, is the church of the Steinhof Asylum, outside Vienna, with its powerful dome (1906).

WAGON ROOF, see ROOF.

WAGON VAULT, see VAULT.

WAINSCOT. The timber lining to walls. The term is also applied to the wooden panelling of PEWS.

WALL PLATE, see ROOF.

WALL RIB, see FORMERET.

WALTER, Thomas U. (1804–87), was of German descent, and was born in Philadelphia where his father was a mason. He studied under STRICKLAND and started on his own in 1830. As early as 1833 he was commissioned to design Girard College, an ambi-tious, wholly peripteral (and thus functionally dubious) white marble building. In 1851 he began the completion of the Capitol in Washington: he added the wings, and the dominant dome on a cast-iron framing is his. He also completed MILLS's Treasury. Like nearly all the leading American architects, Walter was also capable of major engineering works – see a breakwater he built in Venezuela (1843–5).

WARD. The courtyard of a castle; also called a *bailey*.

WARE, Isaac (d. 1766). A protégé of Lord BURLINGTON and a strict Palladian. His buildings are competent but uninspired, e.g., Chesterfield House, London (1749, destroyed), and Wrotham Park (*c.* 1754). However, his *Complete Body of Architecture* (1756) was very influential and became a standard text-book.

WASTELL, John (d. *c.* 1515), lived at Bury St Edmunds and, though evidently highly appreciated, was not in the King's Works. He had probably started under and with Simon CLERK, and followed him both at the abbey of Bury and at King's College Chapel, Cambridge, where he appears from 1486 and was master mason throughout the years when the glorious fan vault was built and the chapel completed. The vault can therefore with some probability be considered his design, though the King's Masons, William VERTUE and Henry REDMAN, visited the building in 1507, 1509, and 1512. Wastell was also Cardinal Morton's mason and then the master mason of Canterbury Cathedral, where he was presumably the designer for Bell Harry, the crossing tower of the cathedral (built 1494–7). Other buildings have been attributed to him on stylistic grounds.

WATERHOUSE, Alfred (1830–1905), started in practice at Manchester in 1856 and moved to London in 1865. In Manchester he won the competitions for the Assize Courts (1859) and Town Hall (1869–77), both excellently planned and externally in a free, picturesque Gothic which yet does not depart too far from symmetry. Soon after, his style hardened and assumed that odd character of sharp forms and harsh imperishable materials (terracotta, best red brick) which one connects with him. He remained a planner of great clarity and resourcefulness and used ironwork freely for structural purposes. But he was a historicist all the same, happiest in a rigid matter-of-fact Gothic, but also going in for a kind of Romanesque (Natural History Museum, London, 1868 etc.) and for French Renaissance (Caius College, Cambridge, 1868 etc.). Of his many buildings the following may be mentioned: some very interestingly planned Congregational churches (Lyndhurst Road, Hampstead, 1883; King's Weigh House Chapel, 1889–91); the headquarters of the Prudential Assurance in Holborn (1876 etc.); the City and Guilds Institute in Kensington (1881); St Paul's School (1881 etc.); the National Liberal Club (1884); and a number of country mansions (Hutton Hall, Yorkshire, 1865; enlargement of Eaton Hall, Cheshire, 1870 etc.; Iwerne Minster, Dorset, 1877).

WATER-LEAF. A leaf shape used in later C12 CAPITALS. The water-leaf is broad, unribbed, and tapering, curving out towards the angle of the ABACUS and turned in at the top. See figure 24.

WATER-TABLE, see OFF-SET.

WATTLE AND DAUB. A method of wall construction consisting of branches or thin lathes (wattles) roughly plastered over with mud or clay (daub), sometimes used as a filling between the vertical members of TIMBER-FRAMED houses.

WAVE MOULDING. A compound moulding formed by a convex curve between two concave curves; typical of the DECORATED STYLE.

WEATHERBOARDING. Overlapping horizontal boards covering a TIMBER-FRAMED wall; the boards are wedge-shaped in section, the upper edge being the thinner.

WEATHERING. A sloping horizontal surface on sills, tops of buttresses, etc., to throw off water. See OFF-SET.

WEB, see CELL.

WEBB, Sir Aston (1849–1930). Perhaps the most successful of the providers of large public buildings in suitable styles around 1900. His favourite style, especially earlier in his career, was a free François I. Later there are also buildings in the Imperial-Palladian of the years of Edward VII. Chief buildings: Law Courts, Birmingham (with Ingress Bell, 1886–91); Metropolitan Life Assurance, Moorgate (with Bell, 1890–3), one of his best; Victoria and Albert Museum (1891 etc.); Christ's Hospital, Horsham (with Bell, 1894–1904); Royal Naval College, Dartmouth (1899–1904); Royal College of Science (1900–6); University, Birmingham (1906–9), Byzantino-Italian; Imperial College, Kensington (1911); Admiralty Arch (1911); façade of Buckingham Palace (1913).

WEBB, John (1611–72). A pupil and nephew by marriage of Inigo JONES, whose right-hand man he appears to have been from the 1630s onwards, e.g., at Wilton. He acquired technical skill and scholarship from Jones, but lacked imagination and originality. His independent work dates from after his master's death and much of it has been destroyed. Lamport Hall (1654–7), the portico and some interiors at The Vyne (1654–57), and the King Charles Building at Greenwich Hospital (1662–9) are the best that survive.

WEBB, Philip (1831–1915), hardly ever designed anything but houses. Among the architects of the great English Domestic Revival, he and Norman SHAW stand supreme: Shaw much more favoured, more inventive, more voluble, more widely influential; Webb harder, more of a thinker, totally deficient in any architectural bedside manner, and perhaps more deeply influential, even on Shaw himself. Webb chose his clients and never agreed to having a stable of assistants. His style is strangely ruthless: from the first he mixed elements from the Gothic and the C18, not for the fun or devilry of it, but because one should use the most suitable motifs regardless of their original contexts. He also liked to expose materials and show the workings of parts of a building.

His first job was Red House (1859) for William MORRIS, whose closest friend he remained throughout. For Morris's firm he designed furniture of a rustic Stuart kind, and also table glass and metalwork. He also joined in the stained glass work. His principal town houses are No. 1 Palace Green (1868) and No. 19 Lincoln's Inn Fields (1868–9). Of his country houses Joldwyns, Surrey (1873), Smeaton Manor, Yorkshire (1878), and Conyhurst, Surrey (1885) come nearest to Shaw in character – gabled, cheerful, with weatherboarding, tilehanging, and white window trim. Standen (1891–4) is best preserved. Clouds (1876) is the largest and least easy to take, strong no doubt, but very astringent indeed, designed, as it were, in a take-it-or-leave-it mood. Webb's interiors from the later seventies onwards often have white panelling and exhibit a marked sympathy with the C18 vernacular. In 1901 he retired to a country cottage and ceased practising.

WEINBRENNER, Friedrich (1766–1826), was born at Karlsruhe and visited Berlin (1790) and Rome (1792). His major achievement is the transformation of Karlsruhe into a neo-classical city, rather like a miniature version of Leningrad. The Marktplatz (1804–24), with balancing but not identical buildings and a pyramid in the centre, and the circular Rondellplatz (1805–13), with the Markgräfliches Palais are masterpieces of neo-classical town planning. He also built a handsome domed Catholic church (1808–17).

WELLS, Joseph Merrill, see McKIM.

WESTWORK. The west end of a Carolingian or Romanesque church, consisting of a low entrance hall and above it a room open to the nave and usually flanked or surrounded by aisles and upper galleries. The whole is crowned by one broad tower, and there are occasionally stair turrets as well. In the main upper room stood an altar as a rule.

WHEEL WINDOW, see ROSE WINDOW.

WHITE, Stanford (1853–1906), was of old New England stock and was brought up in a cultured house. He was a pupil of RICHARDSON and from 1879 a partner of McKIM and Mead. White was a rich *bon vivant*, a man who entertained sumptuously, and exuberant in other ways as well. He was a brilliant and effortless designer, his range stretching from magazine covers to a railway carriage, including Gordon Bennett's yacht, and houses more original than any by anyone anywhere at the time. The temerity of the Low House at Bristol, Rhode Island (1887, recently demolished), with its enormous spreading pitched roof, is almost beyond belief. For other buildings see McKIM. White was shot dead during a theatre rehearsal in 1906.

WILKINS, William (1778–1839), son of a Norwich architect, was educated at Caius College, Cambridge, where he was elected Fellow in 1802. He travelled in Greece, Asia Minor, and Italy (1801–4) and published *Antiquities of Magna Graecia* on his return. He pioneered the Greek Revival in England with his designs for Downing College, Cambridge (begun 1806),

Haileybury College (1806–9), and the temple-style country house Grange Park (1809) with its Theseum peristyle and other rather pedantically Athenian references. In fact, he was rather priggish and doctrinaire, and his rival SMIRKE had little difficulty in overtaking his lead in the movement. But Downing College is important historically as the first of all university campuses – separate buildings round a park-like expanse of lawn – preceding JEFFERSON's Charlottesville. His other university buildings in Cambridge were neo-Gothic, e.g., New Court, Trinity (1821–3), and the screen and hall-range at King's (1824–8). He had greater opportunities in London to develop his neo-Greek style but muffed them – University College (1827–8), St George's Hospital (1828–9), and finally the National Gallery (1834–8), which ruined his reputation. Only the main block of University College is his, and though the portico itself is very imposing he seems to have been unable to unite it satisfactorily with the rest of the composition. This inability to subordinate the parts to the whole resulted at the National Gallery in a patchy façade unworthy of its important site.

WILLIAM OF RAMSEY (d. 1349). A member of a family of masons who worked in Norwich and London from about 1300 onwards, William appears first in 1325 as a mason working on St Stephen's Chapel in the Palace of Westminster (see MICHAEL OF CANTERBURY). In 1332 he became master mason of the new work at St Paul's Cathedral, which meant the chapterhouse and its cloister. In 1336 he was appointed Master Mason to the King's Castles south of Trent, which included the Palace of Westminster and St Stephen's Chapel. William was also commissioned in 1337 to give his *sanum consilium* on Lichfield Cathedral. In the early thirties he may have been master mason to Norwich Cathedral also: the cloister there was taken over by one William of Ramsey from John of Ramsey, probably his father, who was already master mason to the cathedral in 1304. William was evidently an important man, and what we know from an old illustration and surviving fragments of the chapterhouse of St Paul's indicates that the creation of the Perpendicular style was due to him, or at least that he made a style out of elements evolved in London and especially at St Stephen's Chapel in the decade preceding 1330.

WILLIAM OF SENS (d. *c.* 1180). Designer and master mason of the chancel of Canterbury Cathedral, rebuilt after a fire had destroyed it in 1174. He was a Frenchman (or else his successor would not have been known as William the Englishman) and came from Sens Cathedral, which was begun *c.* 1140 and which contained features repeated at Canterbury (also in the Englishman's work, no doubt on the strength of drawings left in the lodge by William of Sens). He was, however, also familiar with more recent French work, notably Notre Dame in Paris (begun 1163), St Rémi at Reims, Soissons, and buildings in the north-west such as Valenciennes. William, as the true master mason of the Gothic Age (*see also* VILLARD DE HONNECOURT), was familiar with wood as well as stone and with devices to load stone on to ships. He had been chosen at Canterbury from a number of English and French masons assembled for consultation on action to be taken after the fire.

WILLIAM OF WYNFORD (d. *c.* 1405–10), was made master mason of Wells Cathedral in 1365, after having worked at Windsor Castle, where William of Wykeham was then clerk of the works. Wynford remained in the royal service and in 1372 received a pension for life. He also remained William of Wykeham's protégé, and worked for him at Winchester College and from 1394 at Winchester Cathedral, where he probably designed the new nave and west front. New College, Oxford, has also been attributed to him. He was obviously a much appreciated man; he dined with William of Wykeham, at the high table of Winchester College, and at the prior's table at the cathedral, and received a furred robe once a year from the cathedral. On several occasions he appeared, no doubt for consultations, together with YEVELE.

WIND-BRACE, see ROOF.

WINDE, William (d. 1722), was born in Holland, the son of a Royalist exile. He took up architecture in middle age about 1680, and became, with PRATT and MAY, a leader of the Anglo-Dutch school. His Buckingham House, London (1705, destroyed), with its unpedimented attic storey, fore-buildings, and quadrant colonnades, was very influential. None of his buildings survives.

WINDER, see STAIR.

WOOD, John, the elder (1704–54), a competent exponent of PALLADIAN-ISM (e.g., Prior Park near Bath, 1735–48), revolutionized town planning with his scheme for Bath (1727 etc.), unfortunately only partly executed. He began with Queen Square (1729–36), treating the north side as a palace front with a rusticated ground floor and attached central pediment. (This had recently been attempted in Grosvenor Square, London, c. 1730, by Edward Shepheard, but only partially realized.) Entirely original was the Circus (1754 etc.), a circular space with three streets radiating out of it; the elevations have superimposed orders so that it looks like the Colosseum turned outside in. He intended to follow the Circus with a Forum, of which North and South Parades are fragments, and an enormous Gymnasium (unexecuted), and thus make Bath once more into a Roman city. He died soon after placing the first stone of the Circus, but his work was carried on by his son John Wood the younger (1728–81), who took it a step further towards open planning with his Royal Crescent (1761–5), the first of its kind and an artistic conception of great originality and magnificence. It has been widely copied ever since. His other buildings – e.g., the Assembly Rooms (1769–71) and Hot Baths (1773–8) – are excellent late examples of Palladianism.

WOMERSLEY, J. L. (b. 1910). City Architect of Sheffield 1953–64 and a pioneer in England of large-scale housing in high and imaginatively interlocked ranges of flats (Parkhill Housing, 1955–60).

WREN, Sir Christopher (1632–1723). The greatest English architect. His father was Dean of Windsor and his uncle Bishop of Ely, both pillars of the High Church. He was educated at Westminster School and at fifteen became a demonstrator in anatomy at the College of Surgeons; then he went up to Oxford. Experimental science was just then coming to the fore, and he found himself in company with a group of brilliant young men who were later to found the Royal Society. He was entirely engrossed in scientific studies. Evelyn called him 'that miracle of a youth' and Newton thought him one of the best geometricians of the day. In 1657 he was made Professor of Astronomy in London, in 1661 in Oxford; but two years later his career took a different turn with his appointment to the commission for the restoration of St Paul's. After the Great Fire of London he was appointed one of the Surveyors under the Rebuilding Act (1667) and in 1669 became Surveyor General of the King's Work. Then he resigned his Oxford professorship and was knighted (1673). He was twice M.P. (1685–7 and 1701–2) and, despite his Tory connexions, survived the Whig revolution of 1688, but on the accession of George I in 1714 he lost his office. He was twice married, first to a daughter of Sir John Coghill, and secondly to a daughter of Lord Fitzwilliam of Lifford. He died aged ninety-one having, as he wrote, 'worn out (by God's Mercy) a long life in the Royal Service and having made some figure in the world'.

If Wren had died at thirty he would have been remembered only as a figure in the history of English science. His first buildings, the Sheldonian Theatre, Oxford (1663), and Pembroke College Chapel, Cambridge (1663), are the work of a brilliant amateur, though the trussed roof of the Sheldonian already displays his structural ingenuity. In 1665–6 he spent eight or nine months studying French architecture, mainly in Paris, and may well have visited Flanders and Holland as well. He met BERNINI in Paris, but learnt more from MANSART and LE VAU, whom he probably knew and whose works he certainly studied. French and Dutch architecture were to provide the main influences on his own style. The Fire of London in 1666 gave him his great opportunity. Though his utopian city plan was rejected, every facet of his empirical genius found scope for expression in the rebuilding of St Paul's and the fifty-one city churches. The latter especially revealed his freshness of mind, his bounding invention, and his adventurous empiricism. There were, of course, no precedents in England for classical churches except in the work of Inigo JONES. Wren's city churches were built between 1670 and 1686, nearly thirty being under construction in the peak year of 1677. Plans are extremely varied and often daringly original, e.g., St Stephen, Walbrook (1672–87), which foreshadows St Paul's, and St Peter's, Cornhill (1677–81), in which his two-storeyed gallery church with vaulted nave and aisles was first adumbrated. This type was later perfected at St Clement Danes (begun 1680) and St James's, Piccadilly (begun 1683).

But his originality and fertility of invention are best seen in the steeples, which range from the neo-Gothic of St Dunstan in the East to the Borrominesque fantasy of St Vedast and St Bride.

More scholarly and refined in detail than his sometimes rather hastily conceived and crudely executed city churches is his masterpiece, St Paul's Cathedral. Nothing like it had ever before been seen in England. It was a triumph of intellectual self-reliance, and the dome is one of the most majestic and reposeful in the world, purely classical in style. Baroque influences are evident elsewhere in the building, notably in the towers, the main façade, and such illusionist features as the sham-perspective window niches and the false upper storey in the side elevations to conceal the nave buttresses. The interior is ostensibly classical, but contains many Baroque gestures. It was begun in 1675, and Wren lived to see it finished in 1709.

His secular buildings range from the austere Doric barracks at Chelsea Hospital (1682–92) to the grandest and most Baroque of all his works, Greenwich Hospital (1694 etc.), where the Painted Hall (1698) is the finest room of its kind in England. Of his vast and elaborate additions and alterations to Whitehall Palace, Winchester Palace, and Hampton Court only a fragment of the latter survives (and this was probably revised and altered by his assistant William TALMAN). Like nearly all his work, these great schemes were carried out for the Office of Works. Of his few independent commissions the best are Trinity College Library, Cambridge (1676–84), and Tom Tower, Christ Church, Oxford (1681–2). Apart from Marlborough House, London (1709–10, now much altered), no town or country house can be certainly attributed to him, though his name has been optimistically given to many. HAWKSMOOR was his only pupil of note, but he had a wide and profound influence through his long reign at the Office of Works.

WRIGHT, Frank Lloyd (1869–1959). The greatest American architect to date. His *œuvre* ranges over more than sixty years and is never repetitive, routine, or derivative. He first worked with SULLIVAN, whom he never ceased to admire, and was responsible for much of his master's domestic work. The first type of building he developed as an independent architect is what he called the prairie house – low, spreading, with rooms running into each other, terraces merging with the gardens, and roofs far projecting. Houses of this type are located in the outer suburbs of Chicago (Oak Park, Riverside, etc.). The development was extremely consistent, ending up with designs more daringly novel than any other architect's in the same field. The series was heralded by houses before 1900 and was complete by about 1905; its climax is the Robie house (1908). Concurrently he had done one church, Unity Temple, Oak Park (1905–6), and one office building, Larkin Building, Buffalo (1904) – both with the same stylistic elements and the same freshness of approach as the private houses. The Larkin Building might well be called the most original office building of its date anywhere.

Some bigger jobs came along about the time of the First World War: Midway Gardens, Chicago (1913), a lavish and short-lived entertainment establishment, and the still surviving Imperial Hotel at Tokyo (1916–20). He was aided here by Antonin Raymond, who then settled in Japan (*see* TANGE). Both these buildings were very heavily decorated, and the elements of this decoration, polygonal and sharp-angled forms, are entirely Wright's, favoured by him from the very beginning, but less in evidence in the prairie houses, at least externally. The houses of the twenties introduced a new technique which allowed Wright to use surface decoration on the outside as well: precast concrete blocks.

In fact, from then onwards, Wright went more and more his own way, and it is very rare for his work to run parallel to international developments and conventions. One exception is Falling Water, Bear Run, Pennsylvania (1937–9), which is closer to the so-called International Modern of Europe (and by then of America) than anything else Wright designed. His own work which, about 1914–17, influenced GROPIUS as well as the Dutch De Stijl Group (*see* OUD) is not represented in Europe at all, as his harmless little Memorial Hostel for Venice was prevented from being executed. In his autobiography Wright tells of many such calamities, but as a writer he was biased and monotonously convinced that he was always right and blameless. This attitude seems to have distinguished his Taliesin community in Wisconsin from the fraternity ideals of RUSKIN: it was more of a master-and-disciples than a guild relationship. Wright built at Taliesin three times (1911, 1914, and 1925 etc.), and then added a Taliesin Winter Camp in Arizona (1927 etc.), eminently fantastical and very exciting.

World-wide recognition came late to Wright, and only in his last twenty years or so, that is from the time when he was nearly seventy, did large commissions come his way fairly evenly. The first was the Johnson Wax Factory at Racine, Wisconsin (1936–9). Here he built an office block with walls of brick and glass tubes, and an interior with reinforced concrete mushroom columns (*see* MAILLART). The laboratory tower was added in 1949. The chapel of Florida Southern College dates from 1940, the Unitarian Church at Madison from 1947, the design for the Guggenheim Museum in New York from 1942 (completed 1960), and the office skyscraper at Bartlesville, Oklahoma, was completed in 1955. The museum, designed as a spiral ramp on a circular plan, is functionally indefensible but formally certainly startling. The skyscraper and the two ecclesiastical buildings display Wright's inborn passion for sharp angles more radically than any of his earlier buildings, and it is interesting to observe that the recent turn of architecture towards aggressive sharp angles (*see* BREUER, SAARINEN) has given this pre-1900 passion of Wright's a new topicality. He lived through three phases of free decorative play in international architecture: the Arts and Crafts, Expressionism, and the most recent anti-rationalism.

WYATT, James (1747–1813), the most successful architect of his day, rivalled the ADAM brothers and even overshadowed CHAMBERS, whom he succeeded as Surveyor-General in 1796. But his brilliance was superficial, and his reputation now rests mainly on his neo-Gothic extravaganzas, though the best of these have been destroyed. The son of a Staffordshire timber-merchant and builder, he went to Venice for six years in 1762, studying there under the painter-architect Visentini. He leapt to fame on his return to London with the Pantheon in Regent Street (1770, now destroyed), an astonishing neo-classical version of Haghia Sophia in Constantinople. He was inundated with commissions from then onwards, despite his outrageously bad manners to clients and his general unreliability. His classical houses, very smooth and elegant, include Heaton House (1772), Heveningham (1788–99), Castle Coole in Northern Ireland (1790–7), and

Dodington (1798–1808), the latter very solemn and severe, owing much to the Greek Revival. His neo-Gothic work ranges from the exquisite miniature Lee Priory (1782, destroyed, but one room survives in the Victoria and Albert Museum) to the fabulous Fonthill Abbey (1796–1807, destroyed) for William Beckford and the almost equally extravagant Ashridge (1806–13). His numerous and ruthless restorations and 'improvements' to Gothic buildings include work at Salisbury, Durham, and Hereford Cathedrals, and earned him the name of 'Wyatt the Destroyer'.

WYATT, Thomas Henry (1807–80), and his brother Sir Matthew Digby (1820–77), are not related to James WYATT. Thomas Henry's *chef-d'œuvre* is Wilton Church, Wiltshire (1842–3), in an Early–Christian–Italian–Romanesque manner; it is perhaps the finest example of that style of the 1840s, rarer in England than in Germany. He also designed many Gothic churches (for a time in partnership with Raphael Brandon). Sir Matthew Digby belonged to the circle of Henry Cole and Owen Jones, who were responsible for much of the work on the Exhibition of 1851; Wyatt himself was Secretary of the Executive Committee. He was a poor architect (see the architectural parts of Paddington Station, 1854–5), but an extremely intelligent and far-seeing architectural journalist, a believer in the new materials of his century and the possibilities of machine production.

WYNFORD, *see* WILLIAM OF WYNFORD.

X

XYSTUS. An AMBULATORY. In Greek architecture, a long portico used for athletic contests; in Roman architecture, a long covered or open walk bordered by colonnades or trees.

Y

YEVELE, Henry (d. 1400), was admitted a citizen of London in 1353, became mason to the Black Prince about 1357, to the King (for Westminster, the Tower, and other palaces and castles) from 1360, and to Westminster Abbey from 1388 at the latest. It is probable that he had designed the nave of the abbey (as begun *c.* 1375), and the nave of Canterbury Cathedral, built in the 1390s, has also been attributed to him. He designed Westminster Hall in 1394. He was a wealthy man with property in many places, and he engaged in business both in connexion with and apart from his duties as the King's Master Mason.

YORKE, F. R. S. (1906–62), one of the pioneers in England of the INTERNATIONAL MODERN style of the twenties and thirties, started with a number of white cubic private houses in 1934. He was in partnership with Marcel BREUER 1935–7, and later the name of the firm became Yorke, Rosenberg & Mardall; it has been responsible for flats, housing, hospitals, schools (e.g., Stevenage, 1947–9) and for Gatwick Airport (1957 etc.).

YORKSHIRE LIGHTS. In a mullioned window, a pair of lights, one fixed and the other sliding horizontally.

Z

ZAKHAROV, Adrian Dmitrievich (1761–1811), the leading Russian neoclassicist and perhaps the greatest Russian architect, was trained at the St Petersburg Academy of Arts, then in Paris under CHALGRIN (1782–6), and travelled in Italy. His masterpiece is the Admiralty, Leningrad (1806–15), vast, bold, and solid, with a façade a quarter of a mile long, a huge columned tower supporting a needle-like spire over the central gate, and dodecastyle Tuscan porticos at the ends. To give expression to such an immense frontage without breaking its unity was a major achievement. But the side façades are still more successful, the nearest approach to BOULLÉE's architecture of geometrical shapes on a grand scale: each is in the form of a cubic pavilion capped by a low cylindrical drum, pierced by a vast semi-circular portal, and flanked by colonnades.

ZIGGURAT (or ZIKKURAT). An Assyrian or Babylonian temple-tower in the form of a truncated pyramid built in diminishing stages, each stage being reached by ramps. *See figure 86.*

ZIMBALO, Giuseppe (active 1659–86). The chief exponent of the wildly exuberant and rather coarse Baroque style developed at Lecce, e.g., Prefettura (1659–95), Cathedral (1659–82), S. Agostino (1663), and Chiesa del Rosario (1691). His pupil Giuseppe Cino carried his style on into the C18.

ZIMMERMANN, Dominikus (1685–1766), one of the greatest South German Rococo architects, but a craftsman before he was an architect, retained to the last his peasant vitality, spontaneity, and unquestioning piety. Perhaps it is significant that his masterpiece, Die Wies, was built neither for a great prince nor for the abbot of a

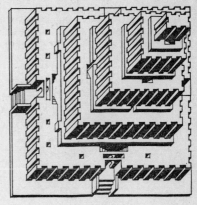

Fig. 86. Ziggurat

rich monastery but for a simple rustic community. Born at Wessobrunn, he began there as a stucco worker, then settled at Füssen (1798), and finally at Landsberg (1716), where he eventually became mayor. He continued to work as a stuccoist after becoming an architect and frequently collaborated with his brother Johann Baptist (1680–1758), who was a painter. His earliest building is the convent church at Mödigen (1716–18), but his mature style first becomes apparent in the pilgrimage church of Steinhausen (1727–35), which is also the first wholly Rococo church in Bavaria. It broke away decisively from its Baroque predecessors, the mystical indirect lighting and rich velvety colour of ASAM giving place to flat even lighting and a predominantly white colour scheme – bright, brittle, and porcellaneous. The colours used are all symbolical, as are the motifs in both painted and carved decoration. At the Frauenkirche, Günzburg (1736–41), he adopted an oblong plan, and at Die Wies (1746–

57) he combined an oval with an oblong, using the former for the nave with its wide ambulatory (necessary for a pilgrimage church), and the latter for the rather long chancel, which is treated with an intensified, predominantly pink colour scheme. Here stucco work, white-painted wooden statues, and frescoes combine with architecture to delight and instruct the pilgrim, be he never so humble or so sophisticated. In more ways than one it is the meeting-place of the courtly Rococo style and an ancient tradition of craftsmanship which stretches back to the Middle Ages.

ZOOPHORUS. A frieze with animal reliefs, as on the Theseum in Athens.

ZUCCALLI, Enrico (c. 1642–1724), the most important member of a family of Italian Baroque architects working mainly in South Germany and Austria, succeeded BARELLI in 1667 as architect of the Theatine church of St Cajetan, Munich, designing the dome, the façade, and the twin towers capped with scroll motifs probably derived from LONGHENA. Outside Munich he began the vast Baroque palace of Schleissheim (1701, completed by EFFNER). He also designed the abbey church of Ettal (1710–26, partly burnt and rebuilt 1744). His kinsman Gaspare (active 1685) built two Italianate churches at Salzburg: St Erhard (1685–9) and St Cajetan (1685–1700).

MORE ABOUT PENGUINS

Penguinews, which appears every month, contains details of all the new books issued by Penguins as they are published. From time to time it is supplemented by *Penguins in Print*, which is a complete list of all books published by Penguins which are in print. (There are well over three thousand of these.)

A specimen copy of *Penguinews* will be sent to you free on request, and you can become a subscriber for the price of the postage – 4s. for a year's issues (including the complete lists). Just write to Dept EP, Penguin Books Ltd, Harmondsworth, Middlesex, enclosing a cheque or postal order, and your name will be added to the mailing list.

Some other books published by Penguins are described on the following pages.

Note: *Penguinews* and *Penguins in Print*
are not available in the U.S.A. or Canada

AN INTRODUCTION TO MODERN ARCHITECTURE

J. M. Richards

'It has never been more important for the ordinary man to pick out what is bogus in modern architecture, and Mr Richards is a master at explaining architecture in simple language' – *The Times Literary Supplement*

An Introduction to Modern Architecture, which has been newly revised and brought up to date, sets out to explain what 'modern' architecture is all about. With the help of gravure illustrations, as well as line drawings, it explains how modern buildings come to look as they do, discussing the technical practices and the changing needs and ideals on which modern architects' work is based. Also, believing that architecture can only be explained as part of a continuous growth, he shows modern architecture against the background out of which it grew, giving an outline history of the struggle to produce a sane architecture which has been going on throughout the past hundred years.

AN OUTLINE OF EUROPEAN ARCHITECTURE

Nikolaus Pevsner

This seventh revised edition of Nikolaus Pevsner's classic history is presented in an entirely new and attractive style. The format has been enlarged and the illustrations appear next to the passages to which they refer. Their numbers have swelled to nearly 300, including drawings, plans, and photographs. The final chapter of the Penguin Jubilee edition (published in 1960 and still available) has been incorporated, carrying the story from 1914 to the present day, and there are substantial additions on the sixteenth to eighteenth centuries in France as well as many minor revisions. The book tells the story of architecture by concentrating on outstanding buildings, and reads exceedingly well in its concentration and its combination of warmth and scholarship.

Also available by the same author

PIONEERS OF MODERN DESIGN

THE PELICAN HISTORY OF ART

Edited by Nikolaus Pevsner

This series, which makes one of the most important contributions to the history of art in this century, is a comprehensive history of world art and architecture. The twenty-four volumes so far completed (fifty are planned) have been accepted by scholars all over the world as the most up-to-date and authoritative books on the periods they cover. Each volume in the series is cloth-bound, measures $10\frac{1}{4}$ by 7 inches, has 300 or more pages of text, and between 250 and 350 illustrations. When completed, the fifty volumes will cover every aspect and phase of world art.

'There can be no praise too high for ... this great series, for there is an outstanding need for such a corpus of volumes which will provide up-to-date and authoritative accounts of the different themes. A student will find these volumes exactly the guide with which to embark on a new subject or period' – *The Times Literary Supplement*

VICTORIAN ARCHITECTURE

Robert Furneaux Jordan

We are still in the Victorian age – the iron train sheds, the smoke-blackened monuments of the North, the shades of Gothic in churches, palaces, and suburban streets, the grim terraces of mining towns ... these form a backdrop to our world. In Victorian architecture are expressed the triumphs, contradictions, and failures of Victorian society. This book encourages us to understand what, as we look around, we cannot ignore.

NEO-CLASSICISM

Hugh Honour

David's martyr icons of the French Revolution, Ledoux's symbolic architecture of pure geometry, Canova's idealized erotic marbles – in such Neo-classical masterpieces the culminating phase of the Enlightenment found artistic expression. Neo-classicism was no mere antique revival. If it began with the elegant sophistication of Adam and Gabriel, it ended in the ruthless simplifications of Flaxman's rudimentary linear technique. This primitivism consciously evoked a Spartan world of simple, uncomplicated passions and blunt, uncompromising truths. And these virile and ennobling ideals inspired *avant-garde* painters, sculptors and architects as far apart as Jefferson in Virginia and Zakharov in Leningrad.

Also available in the Style and Civilization series

PRE-CLASSICAL
GOTHIC
EARLY RENAISSANCE

INIGO JONES

John Summerson

Inigo Jones was the first English classical architect, famous in his own time (he was nine years junior to Shakespeare) and the post-humous sponsor of the Palladianism of the eighteenth century.

In this revolutionary book Sir John Summerson clears away a mass of legend in order to direct attention to the essential Inigo, basing a new assessment of his genius on the evidence of buildings and designs of undoubted authenticity. While the Queen's House at Greenwich and the famous Whitehall Banqueting House receive due acknowledgement, such long-lost works as the Covent Garden *piazza* and the transformation of old St Paul's are shown, after rigorous examination of the records, to be even more eloquent of their architect's philosophy. Inigo Jones emerges as a unique figure in the Europe of his time and an architect of fundamental importance.

PALLADIO

James S. Ackerman

Palladio is the most imitated architect in history. His buildings have been copied all over the Western world – from Leningrad to Philadelphia – and his ideas on proportion are still current nearly four hundred years after his death. In this, the first full account of his career to be published in English, Professor James Ackerman investigates the reasons for his enormous and enduring success. He presents him in his historical setting as the contemporary of Titian, Tintoretto, and Veronese, but is constantly alert to his relevance for us today.

THE ARCHITECT AND SOCIETY

The aim of this series, specially written for Penguin Books, is to present the great architects of the world in their social and cultural environments.